Imadoki!
Nowadays

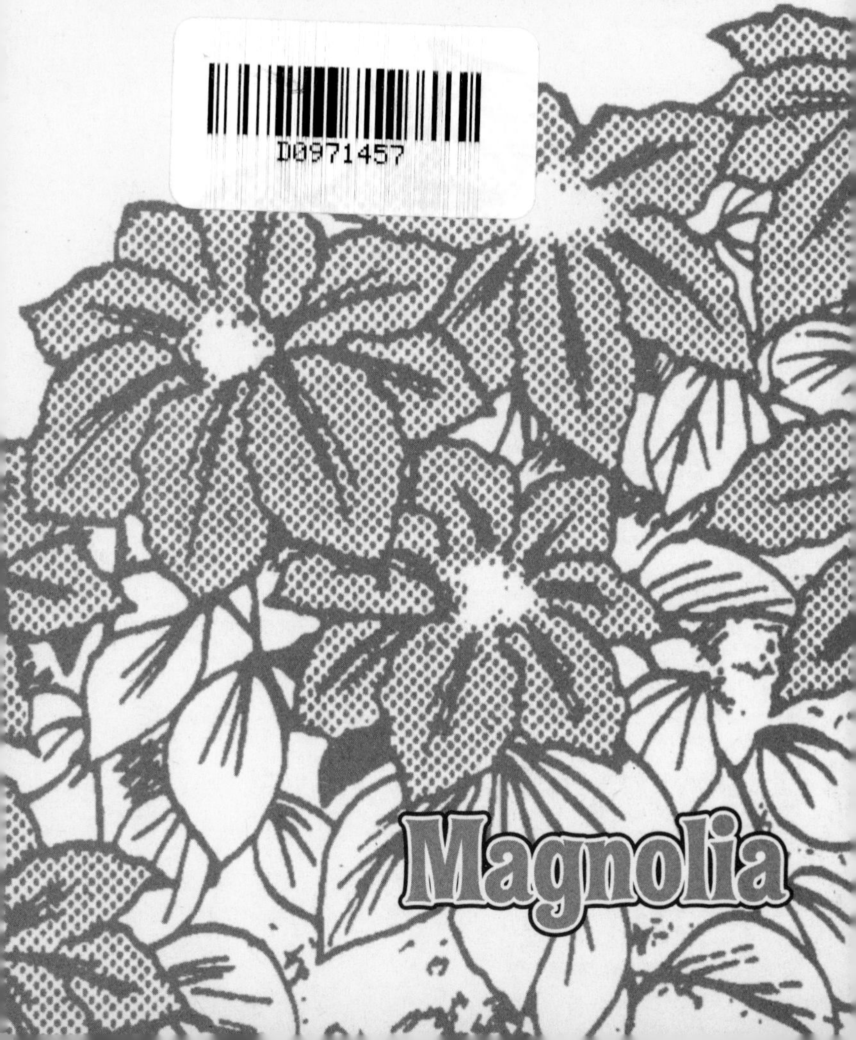

Magnolia

Imadoki!
Nowadays
Vol. 2
Magnolia

STORY AND ART BY Yuu Watase

English Adaptation/Lance Caselman
Translation/JN Productions
Lettering & Touch-Up Art/Walden Wong
Cover Design/Carolina Ugalde
Graphics & Layout/Nozomi Akashi
Editor/Megan Bates

Editor in Chief, Books/Alvin Lu
Editor in Chief, Magazines/Marc Weidenbaum
VP of Publishing Licensing/Rika Inouye
VP of Sales/Gonzalo Ferreyra
Sr. VP of Marketing/Liza Coppola
Publisher/Hyoe Narita

Printed in the U.S.A.

Published by VIZ Media, LLC
P.O. Box 77010 • San Francisco, CA 94107

Shôjo Edition
10 9 8 7 6 5
First printing, August 2004
Fifth printing, October 2007

www.viz.com

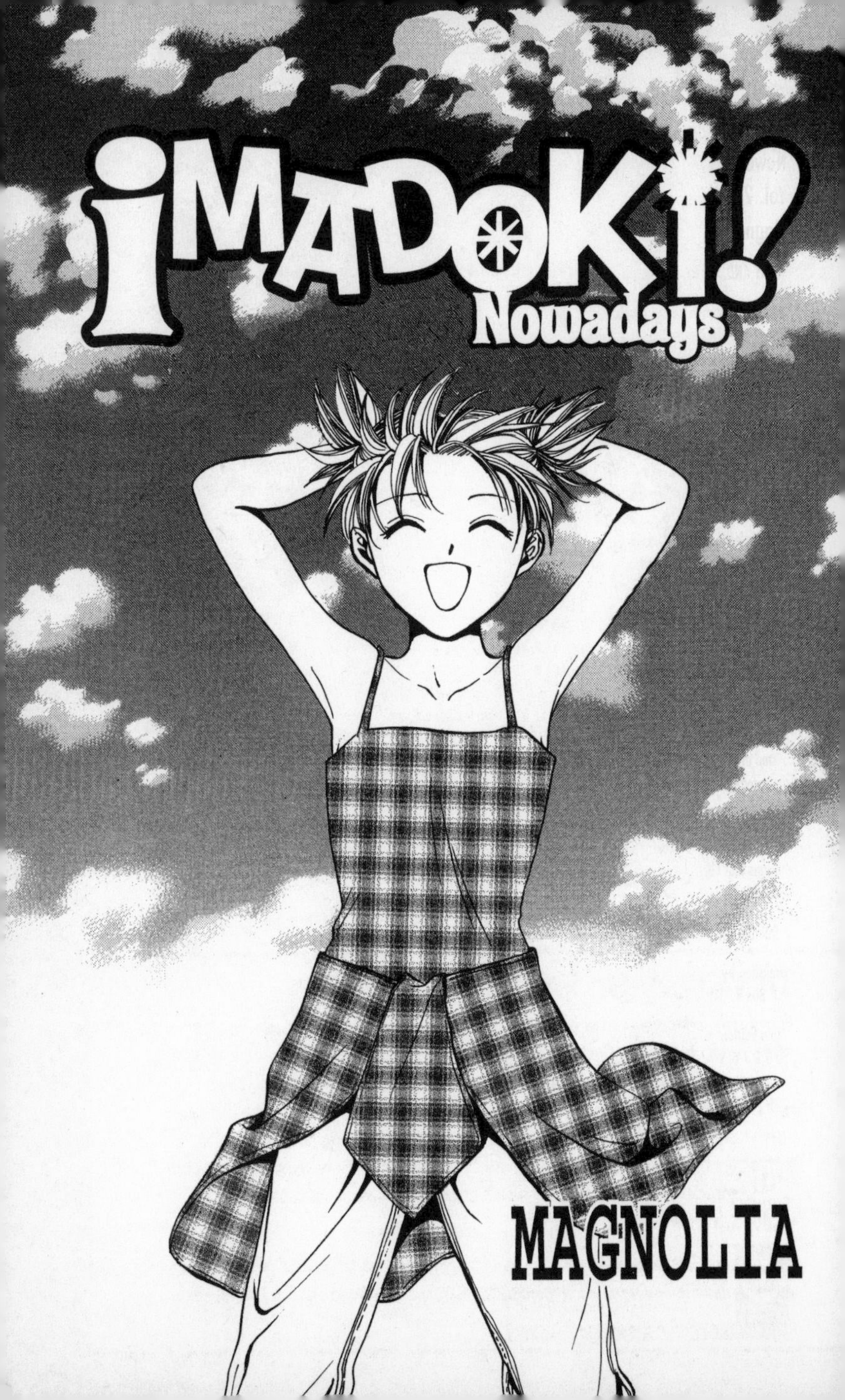

¡MADOKI!
Nowadays
MAGNOLIA

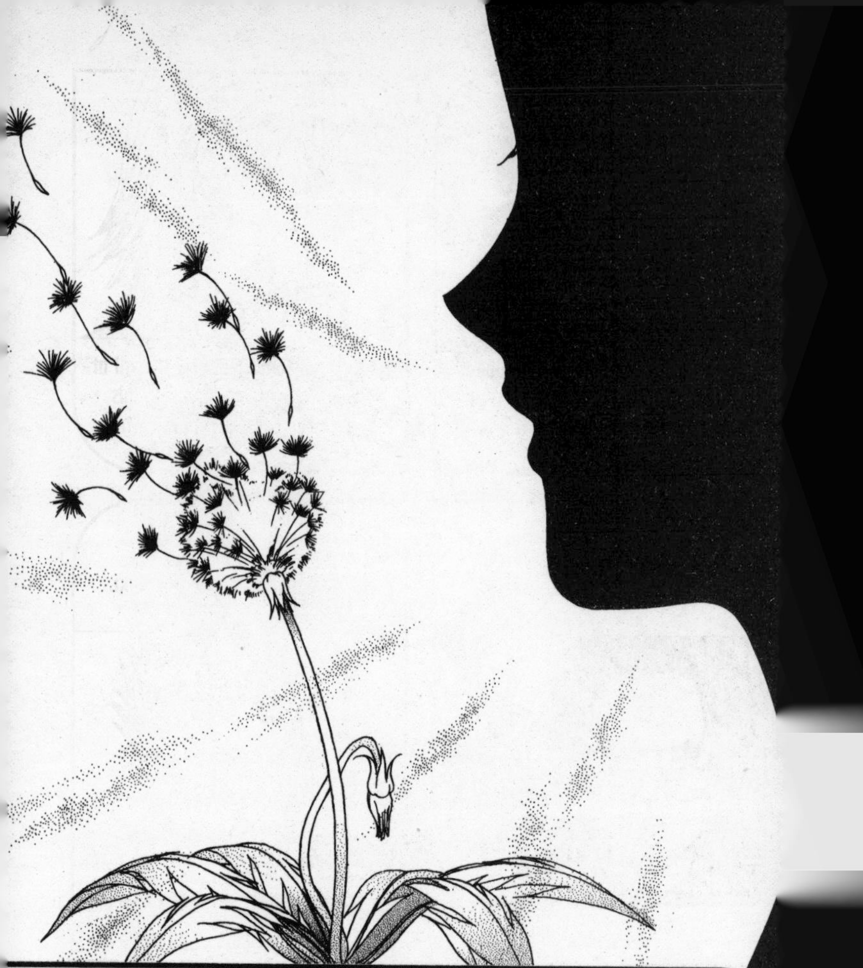

The Story So Far:

Tanpopo, whose name means "dandelion," is a new student at the elite Meio School. The country girl from rural Hokkaido is hopelessly out of place among the school's snobbish students who have nick named her "Weed." Her only defense is her natural resilience. Tanpopo meets the handsome but aloof Koki Kugyo, son of the school's founder, and "discovers" his secret: unbeknownst to the other students, Koki plants and tends a few real flowers in violation of Meio's policy.

Intrigued, Tanpopo tries to get closer, only to be rebuffed by Koki, who doesn't believe in friendship. But when Tanpopo is harassed

♥ Tanpopo Yamazaki, new student at Meio High School. Attending this elite school is a dream come true for her.

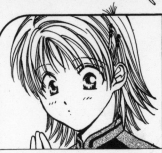

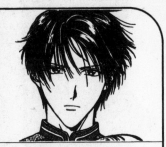

♥ Koki Kugyo, the popular scion of the Kugyo family.

♥ Aoi Kyogoku, computer geek, class mate of Tanpopo and Koki.

♥ Tsukiko Saionji, wealthy vixen. Aspires to be Mrs. Koki Kugyo.

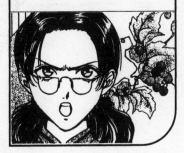

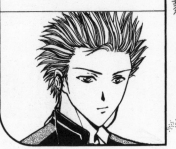

for replacing all the school's artificial flowers with real ones, he stands up for her. Koki and Tanpopo's budding relationship does not go unnoticed, especially by Tsukiko, who pretends to be Tanpopo's friend. But Tsukiko dreams of marrying Koki, the heir to a vast family fortune. After secretly sabotaging Tanpopo, Tsukiko admits her feelings—and intentions—toward Koki.

Despite it all, Tanpopo, Koki and Tsukiko continue to work together on the Planting Committee. But lurking in the shadows is a stranger who despises all three for his own reasons.

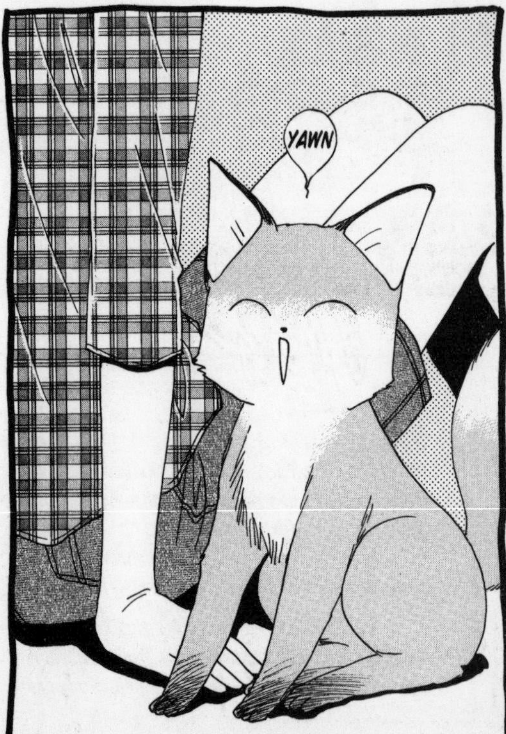
YAWN

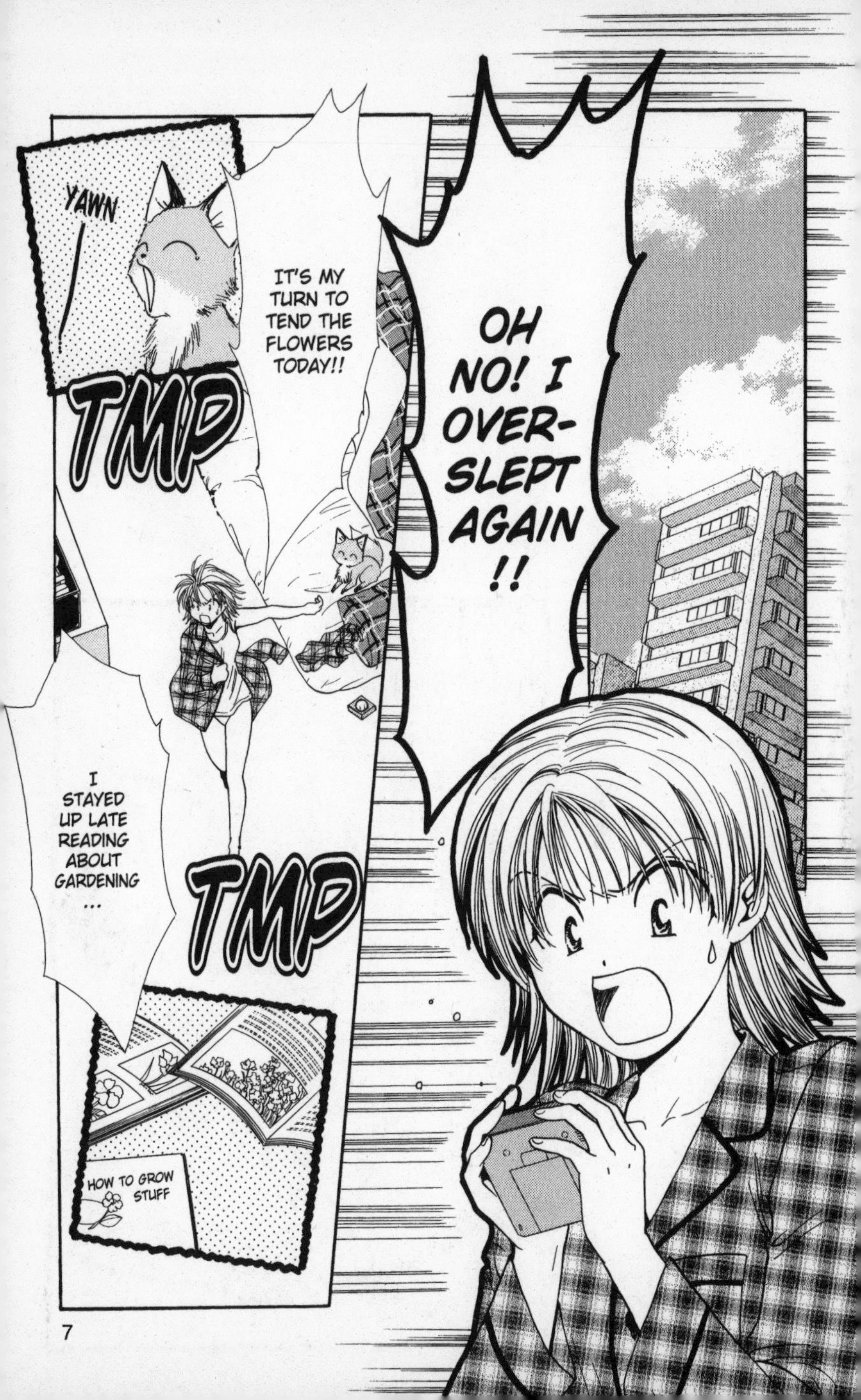
OH NO! I OVER-SLEPT AGAIN!!
YAWN
IT'S MY TURN TO TEND THE FLOWERS TODAY!!
TMP
TMP
I STAYED UP LATE READING ABOUT GARDENING ...
HOW TO GROW STUFF

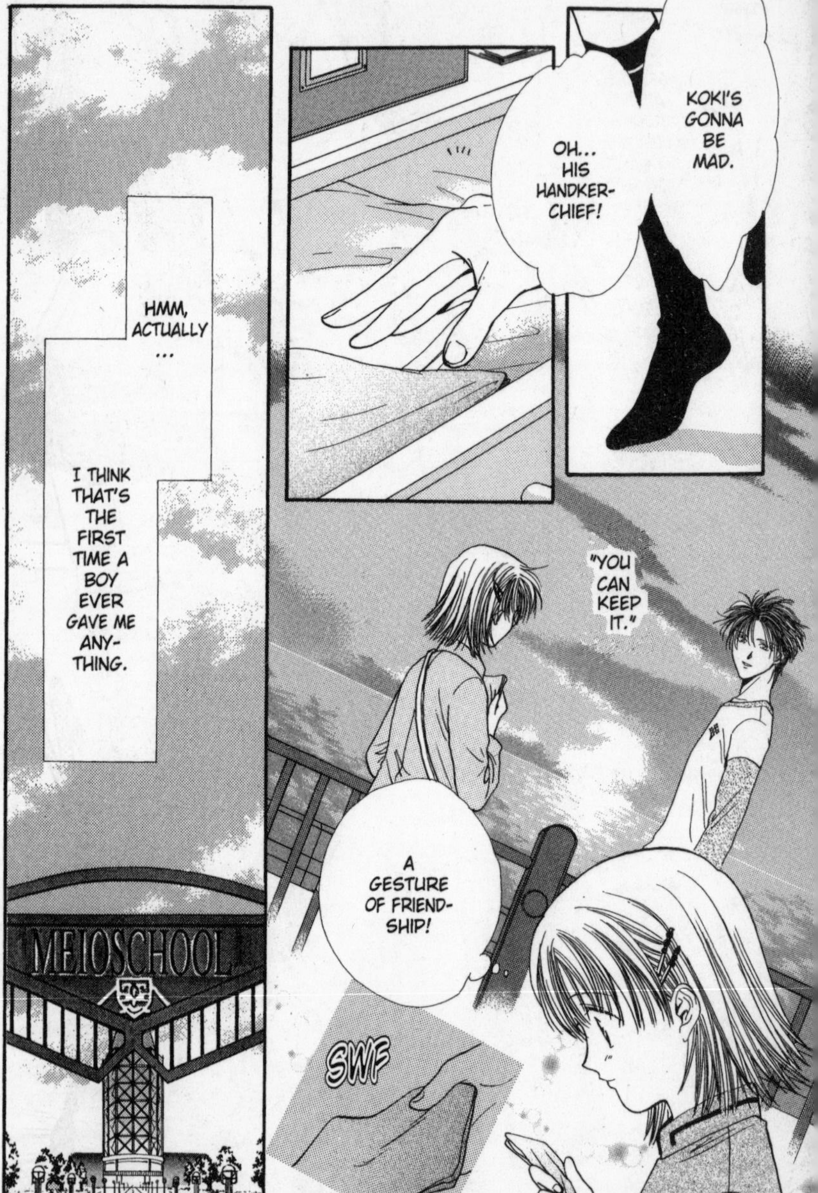

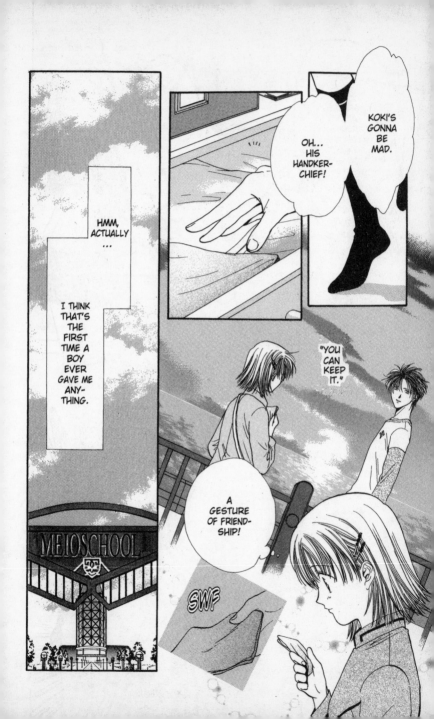

KOKI'S GONNA BE MAD.
OH... HIS HANDKER-CHIEF!
"YOU CAN KEEP IT."
A GESTURE OF FRIEND-SHIP!
SWF
HMM, ACTUALLY ...
I THINK THAT'S THE FIRST TIME A BOY EVER GAVE ME ANY-THING.
MEIOSCHOOL

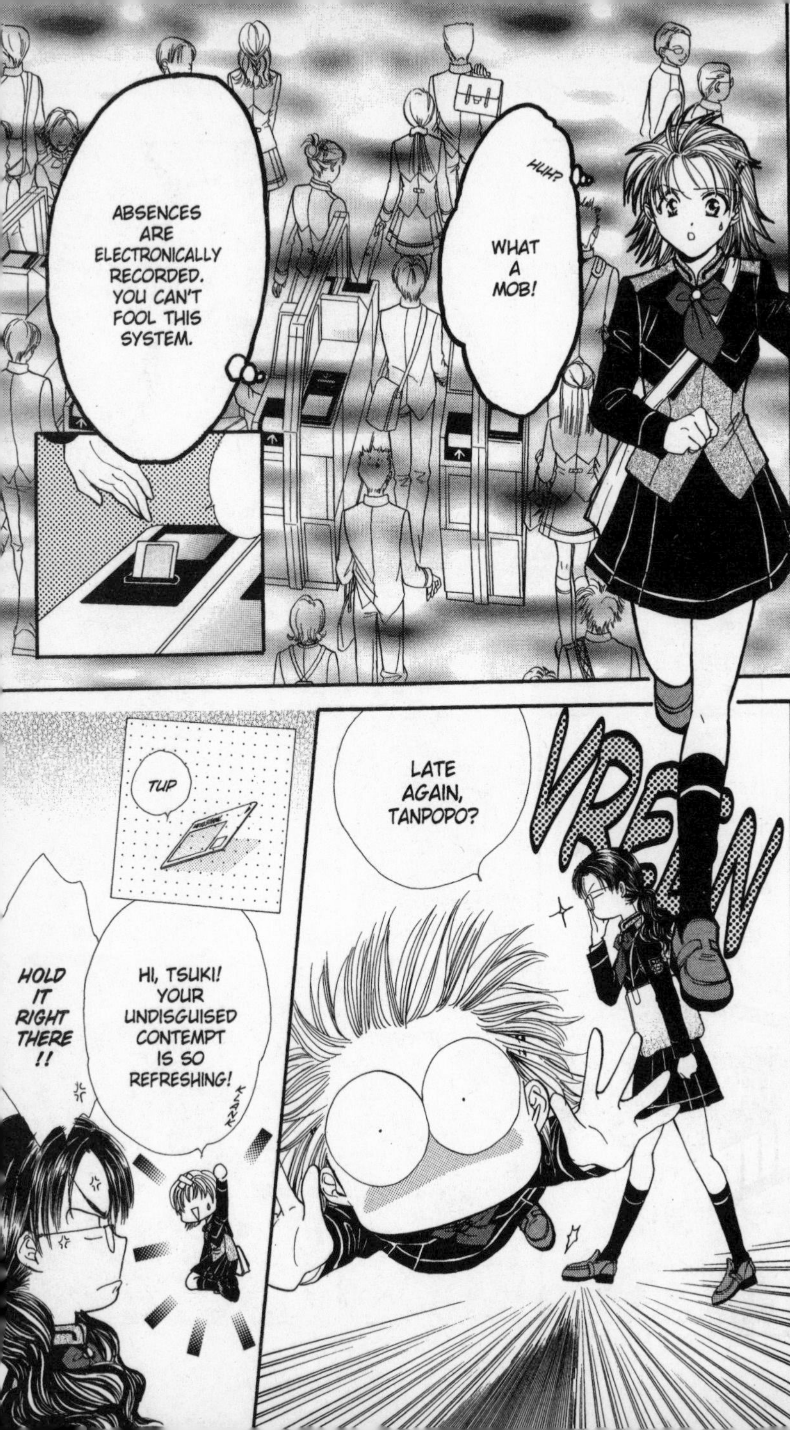
HUH?
WHAT A MOB!
ABSENCES ARE ELECTRONICALLY RECORDED. YOU CAN'T FOOL THIS SYSTEM.
VREEN
LATE AGAIN, TANPOPO?
TUP
HI, TSUKI! YOUR UNDISGUISED CONTEMPT IS SO REFRESHING!
KLANK
HOLD IT RIGHT THERE !!

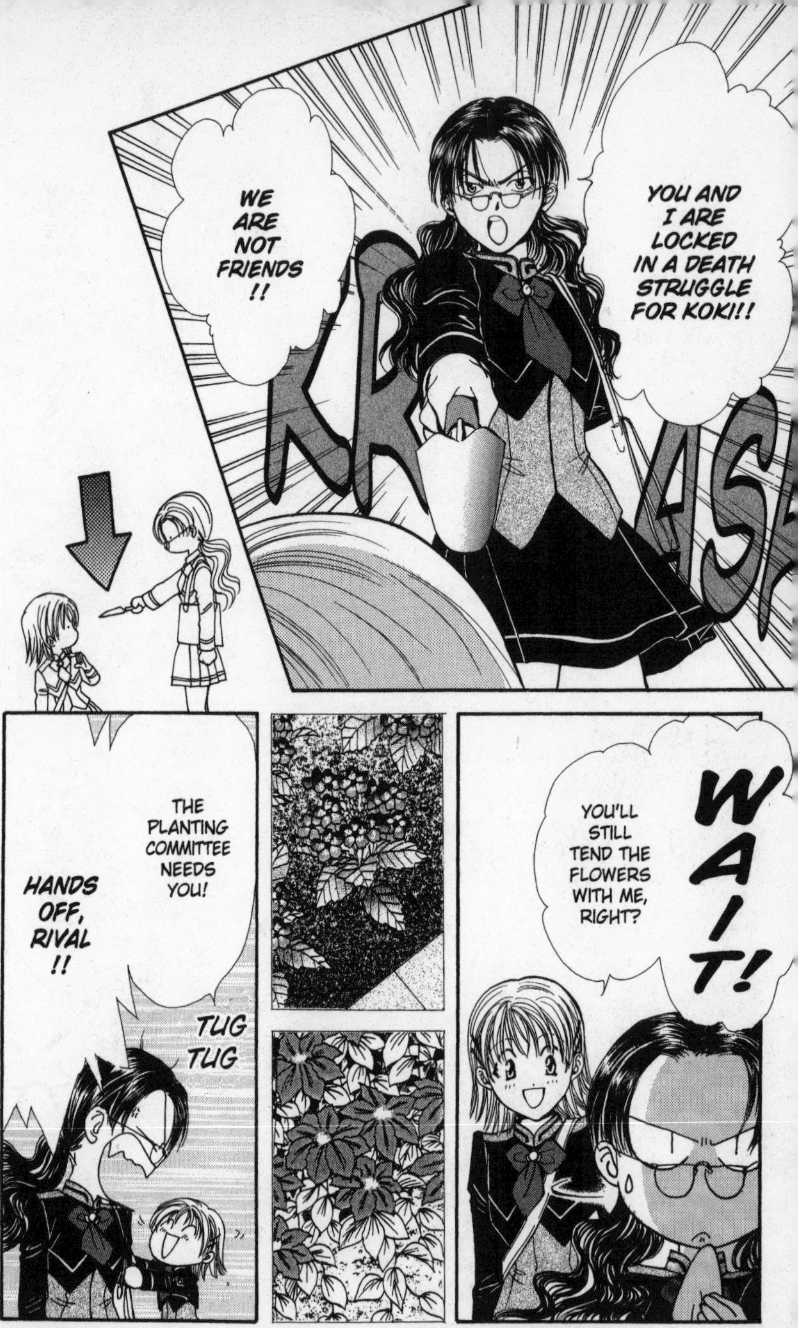
YOU AND I ARE LOCKED IN A DEATH STRUGGLE FOR KOKI!!
WE ARE NOT FRIENDS !!
WAIT!
YOU'LL STILL TEND THE FLOWERS WITH ME, RIGHT?
THE PLANTING COMMITTEE NEEDS YOU!
HANDS OFF, RIVAL !!
TUG TUG

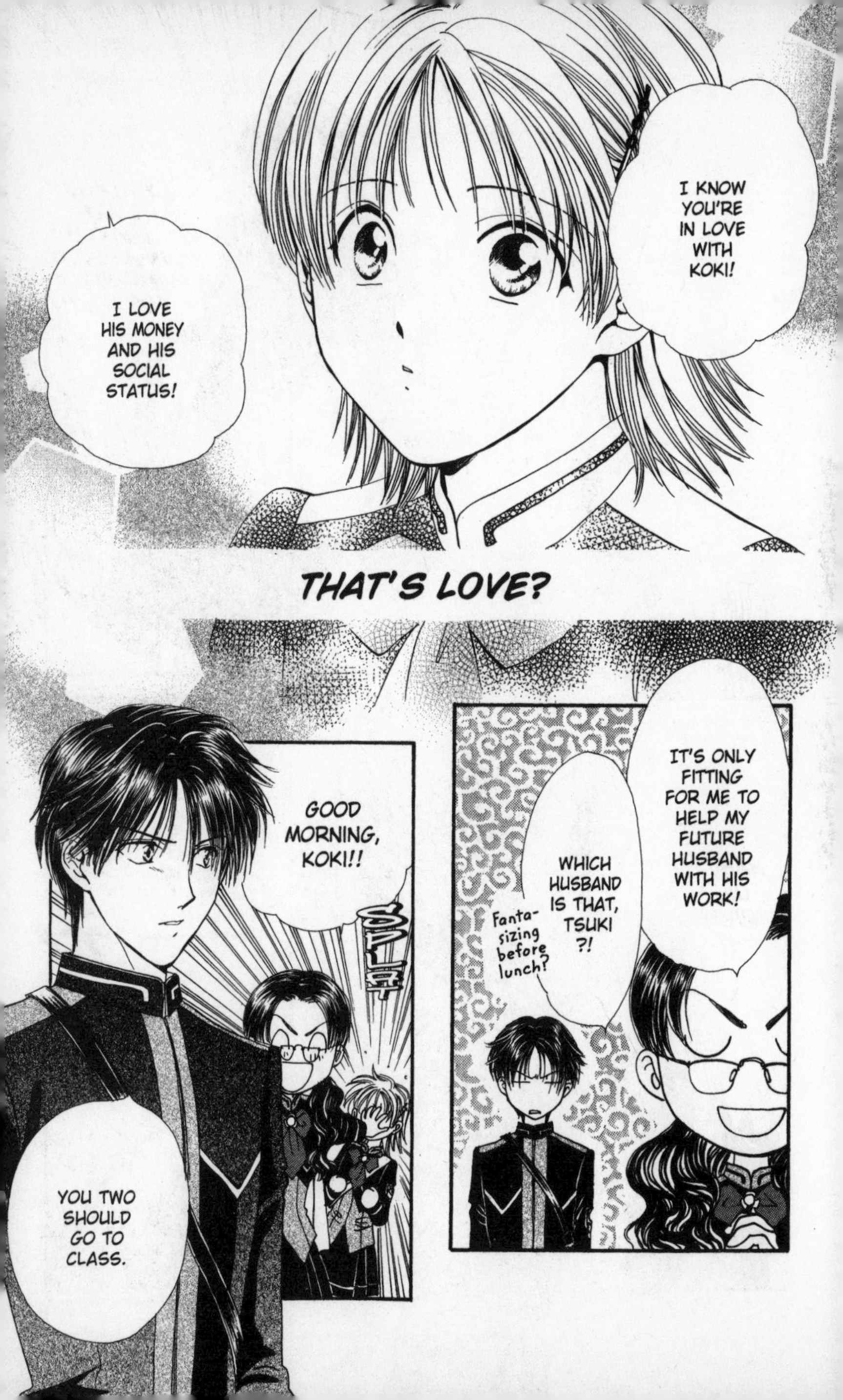
I KNOW YOU'RE IN LOVE WITH KOKI!
I LOVE HIS MONEY AND HIS SOCIAL STATUS!
THAT'S LOVE?
IT'S ONLY FITTING FOR ME TO HELP MY FUTURE HUSBAND WITH HIS WORK!
WHICH HUSBAND IS THAT, TSUKI ?!
Fanta-sizing before lunch?
GOOD MORNING, KOKI!!
SPLAT
YOU TWO SHOULD GO TO CLASS.

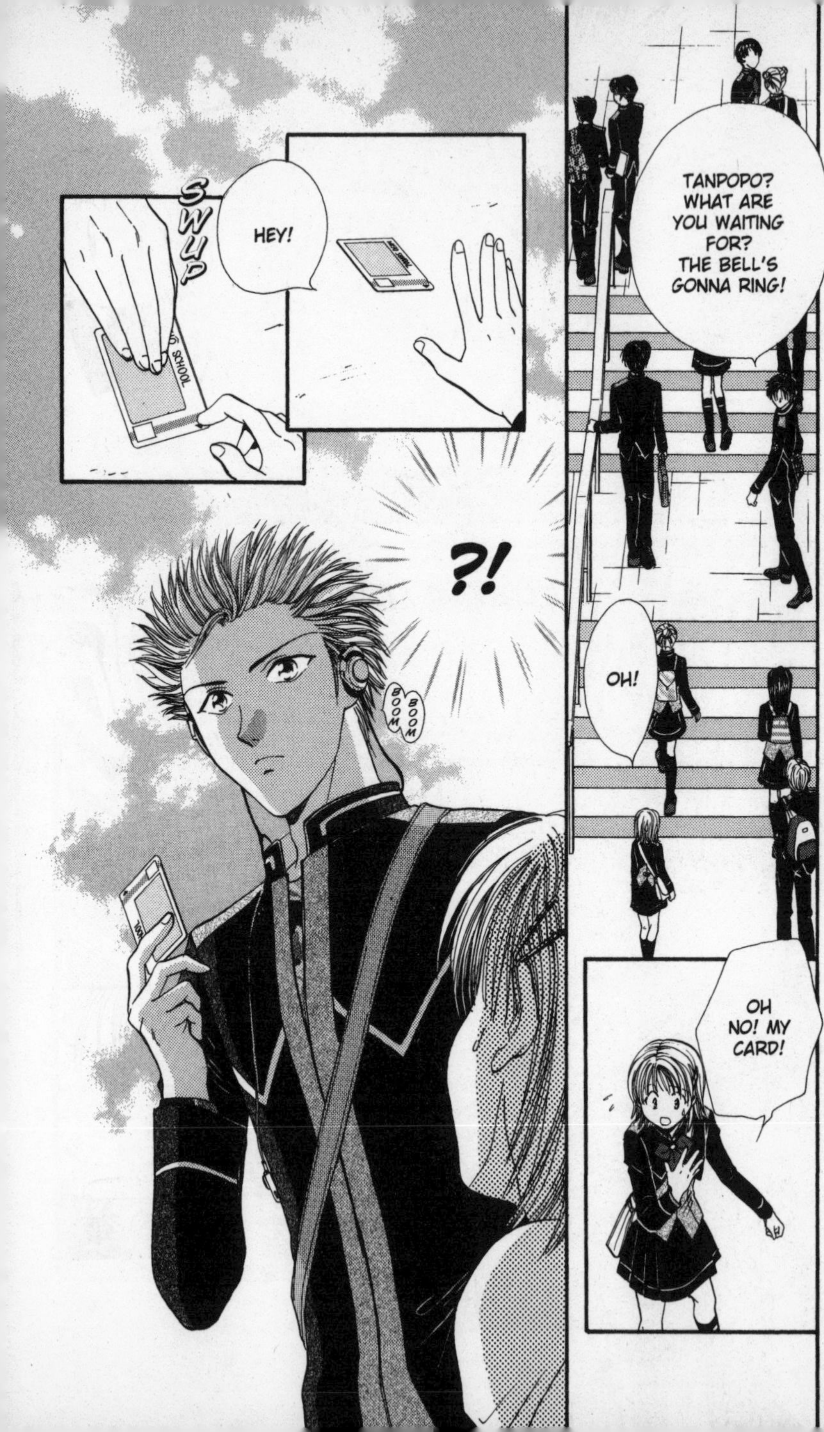
TANPOPO? WHAT ARE YOU WAITING FOR? THE BELL'S GONNA RING!
OH!
OH NO! MY CARD!
HEY!
SWUP
?!
BOOM BOOM

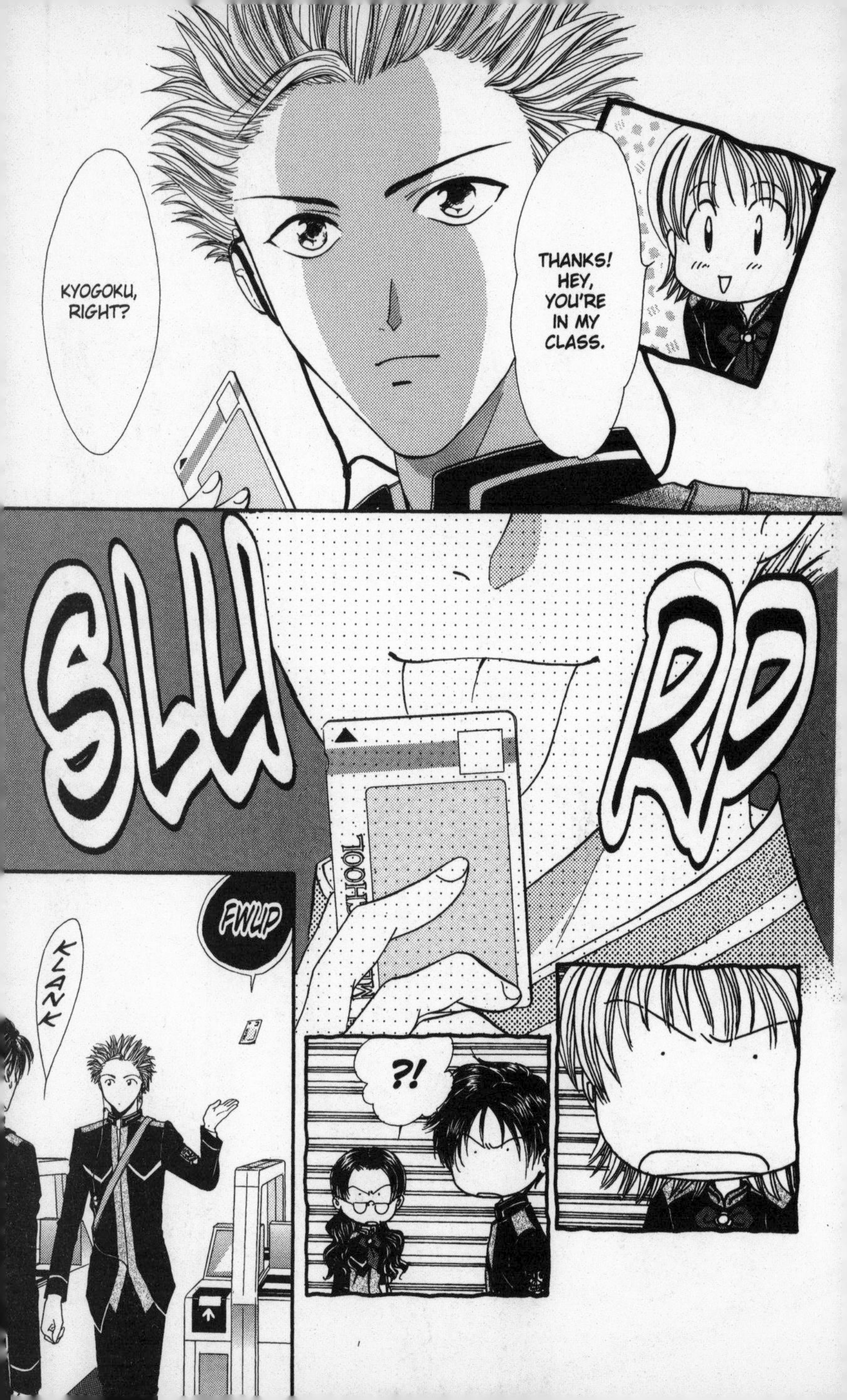
THANKS! HEY, YOU'RE IN MY CLASS.
KYOGOKU, RIGHT?
SLURP
?!
FWUP
KLANK

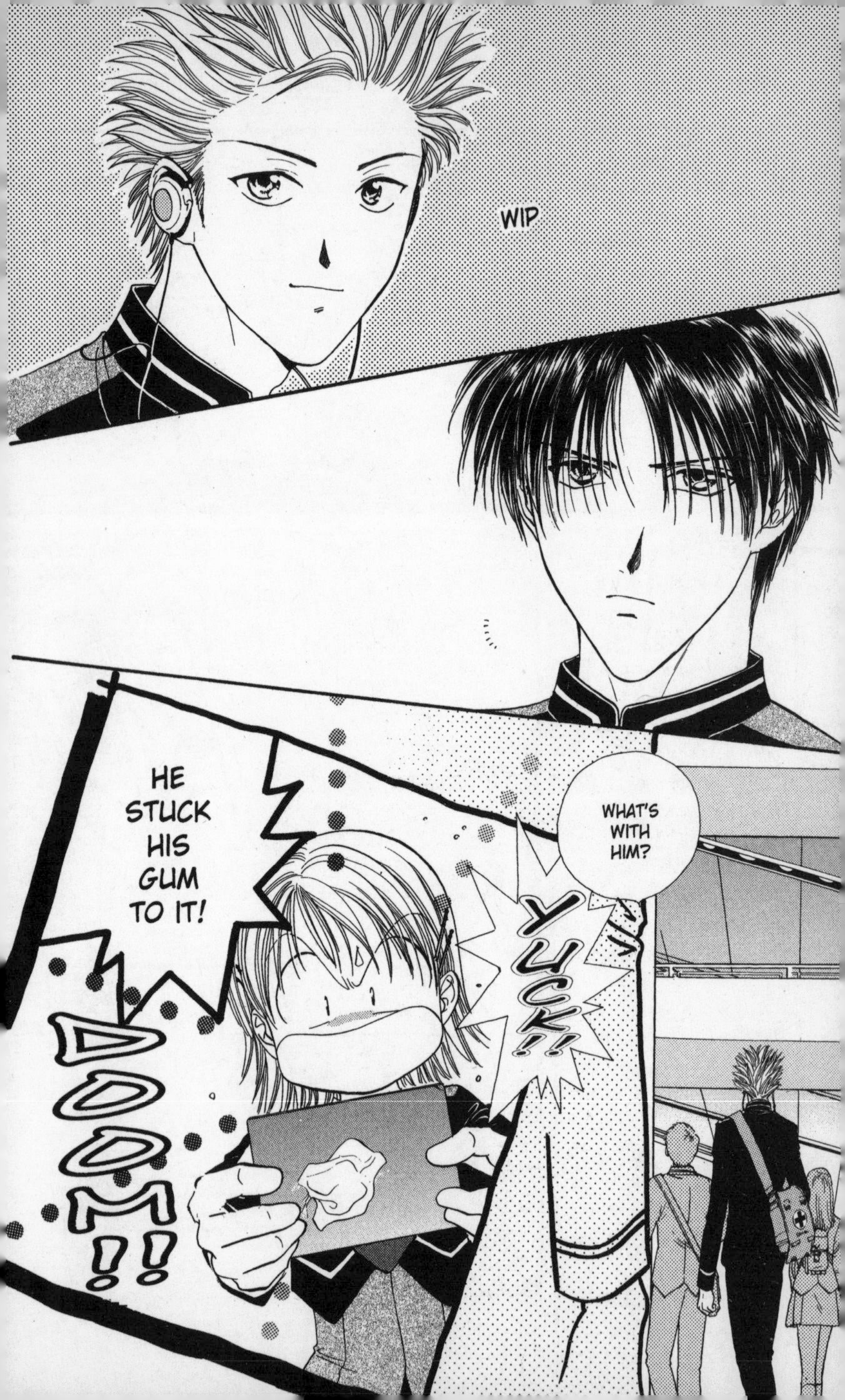
WIP
WHAT'S WITH HIM?
YUCK!!
HE STUCK HIS GUM TO IT!
DOOOM!!

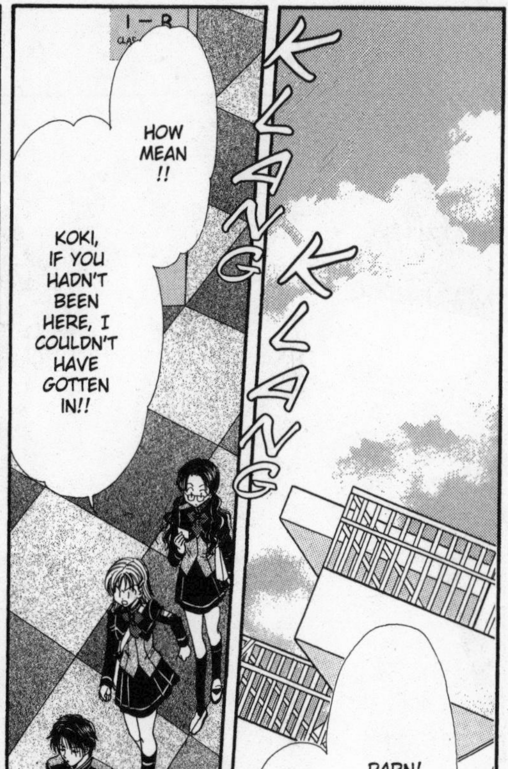
KLANG
KLANG
DARN! IT WON'T WORK!
IT'S BENT!
MEIO SCHO
1-B
HOW MEAN !!
KOKI, IF YOU HADN'T BEEN HERE, I COULDN'T HAVE GOTTEN IN!!
GO TO THE OFFICE AND GET A NEW CARD RIGHT AWAY.

Hello!! Welcome to Volume 2! I hope you're enjoying it!

Okay, first of all, the **Ayashi no Ceres** animation is safely completed. A big "thank you" to all our supporters!

Thanks to you, the broadcast (among non-scrambled broadcasts) got the highest ratings for anime. To those who saw it...my thanks. Don't forget about the video (rental) & DVD & CD (soundtrack 3 goes on sale 12/6/2001)!! The background music is great, I recommend all three! And the drama CD is a real bargain! And we have merchandise, so check it out. Okay, that's the end of my sales pitch. For now.

Imadoki! is a high school comic...but (!!) I've hardly ever read any myself!! I had zero interest in high school storylines for girl's comics. I did read **Seito Shokun!** long ago, but I don't remember it, so I can't say I've read much of this stuff. Despite that, I decided to take this one on. Anyway, I'm doing it now!

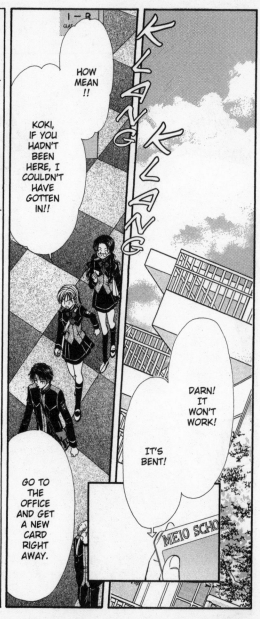

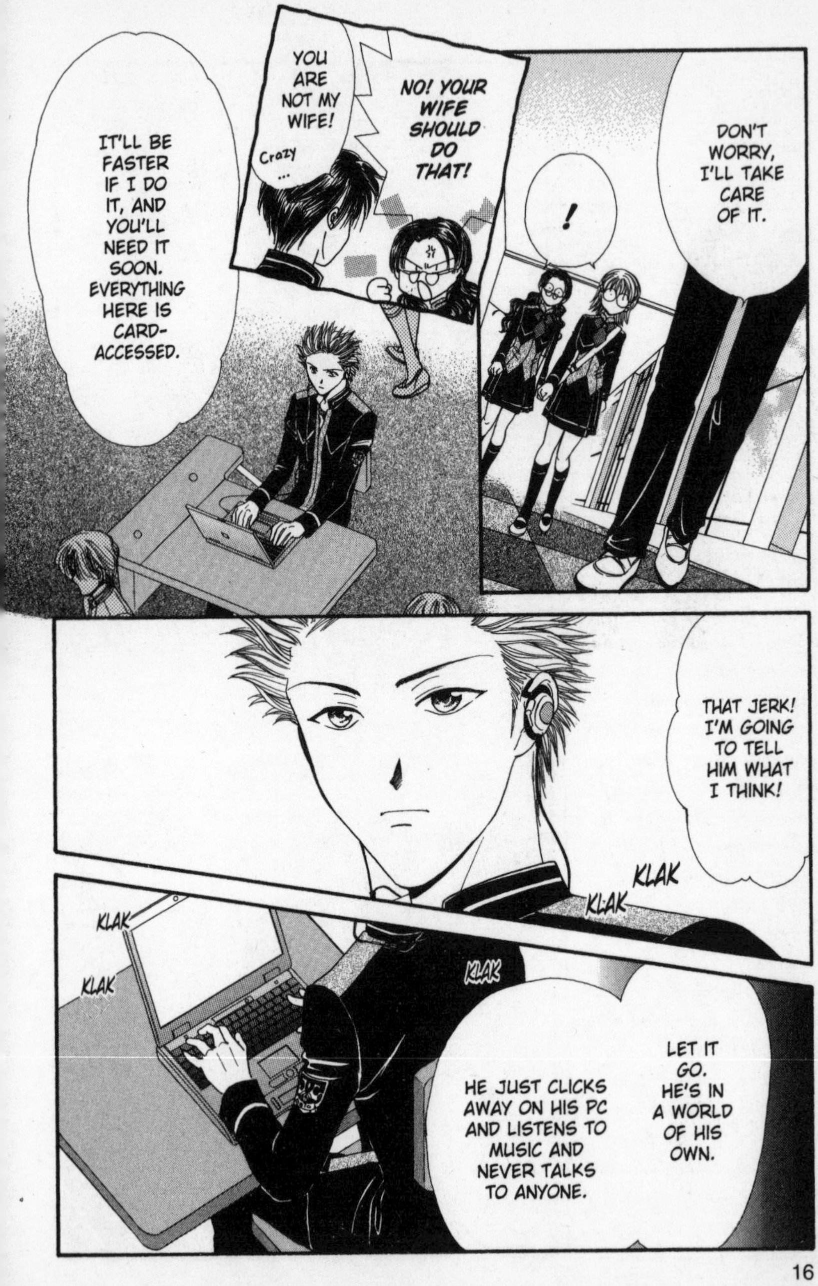
DON'T WORRY, I'LL TAKE CARE OF IT.
!
NO! YOUR WIFE SHOULD DO THAT!
YOU ARE NOT MY WIFE!
Crazy ...
IT'LL BE FASTER IF I DO IT, AND YOU'LL NEED IT SOON. EVERYTHING HERE IS CARD-ACCESSED.
THAT JERK! I'M GOING TO TELL HIM WHAT I THINK!
KLAK
KLAK
LET IT GO. HE'S IN A WORLD OF HIS OWN.
HE JUST CLICKS AWAY ON HIS PC AND LISTENS TO MUSIC AND NEVER TALKS TO ANYONE.
KLAK
KLAK
KLAK

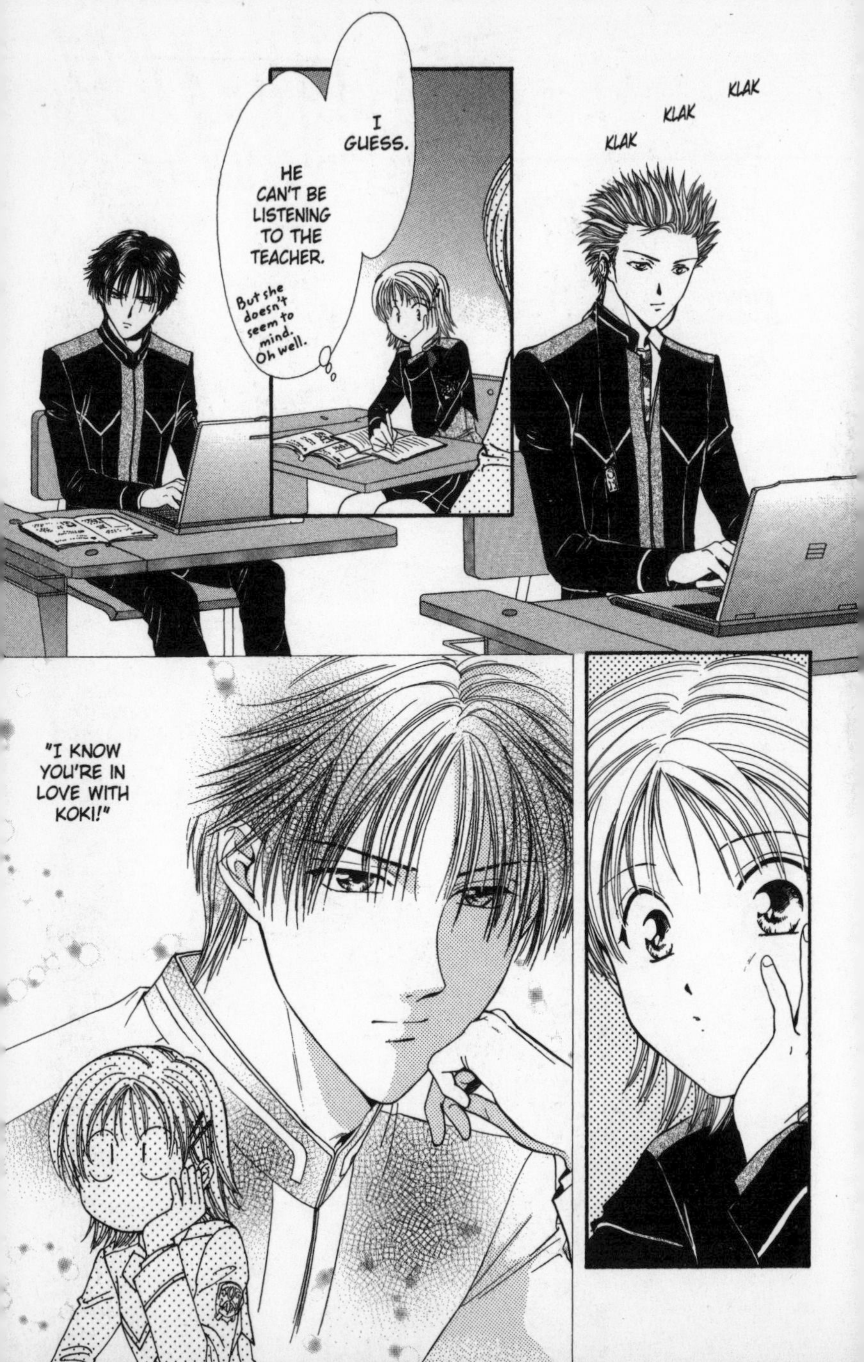
KLAK
KLAK
KLAK
I GUESS.
HE CAN'T BE LISTENING TO THE TEACHER.
But she doesn't seem to mind. Oh well.
"I KNOW YOU'RE IN LOVE WITH KOKI!"

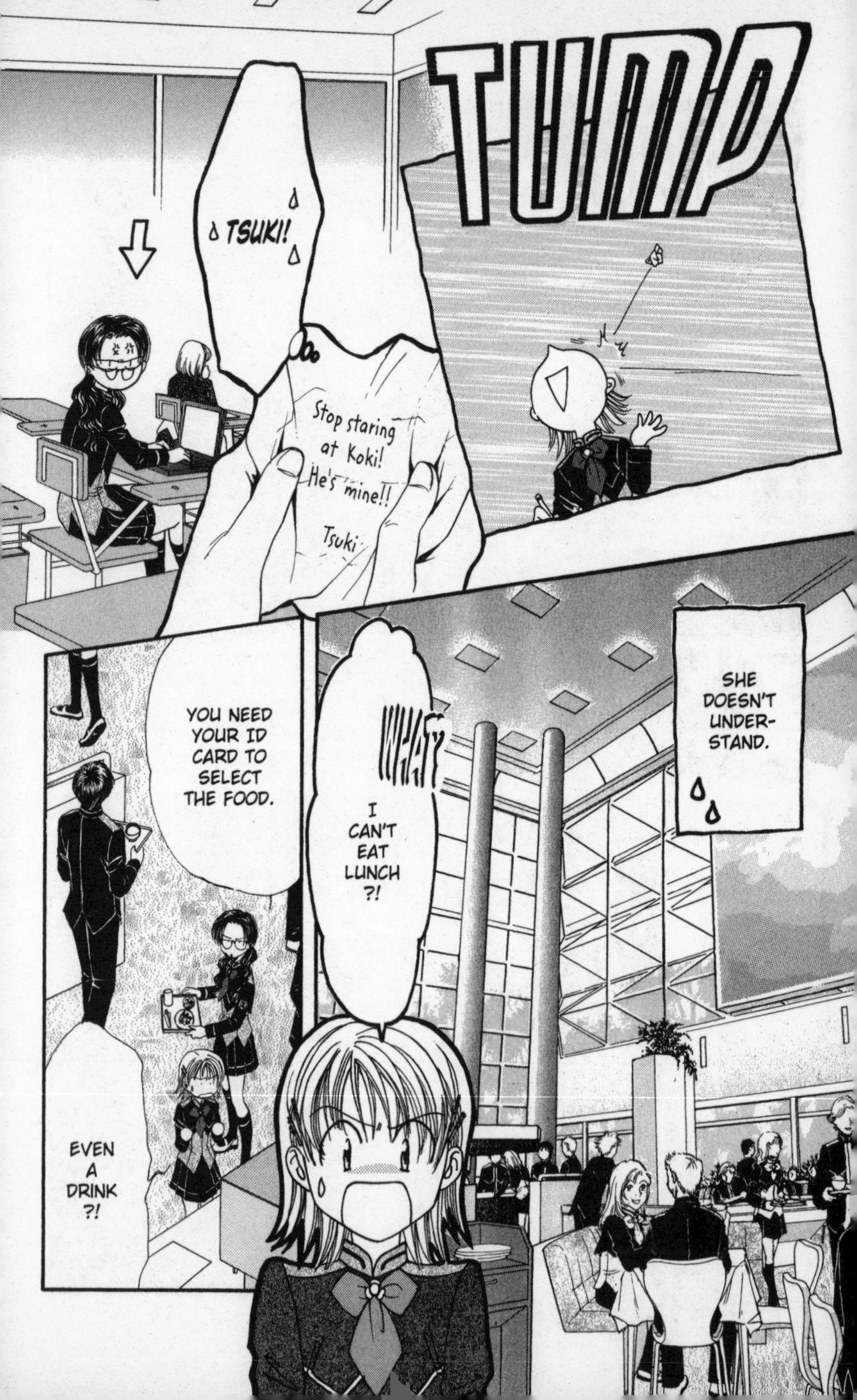
TUMP
TSUKI!
Stop staring at Koki! He's mine!! Tsuki
SHE DOESN'T UNDERSTAND.
WHAT?
I CAN'T EAT LUNCH ?!
YOU NEED YOUR ID CARD TO SELECT THE FOOD.
EVEN A DRINK ?!

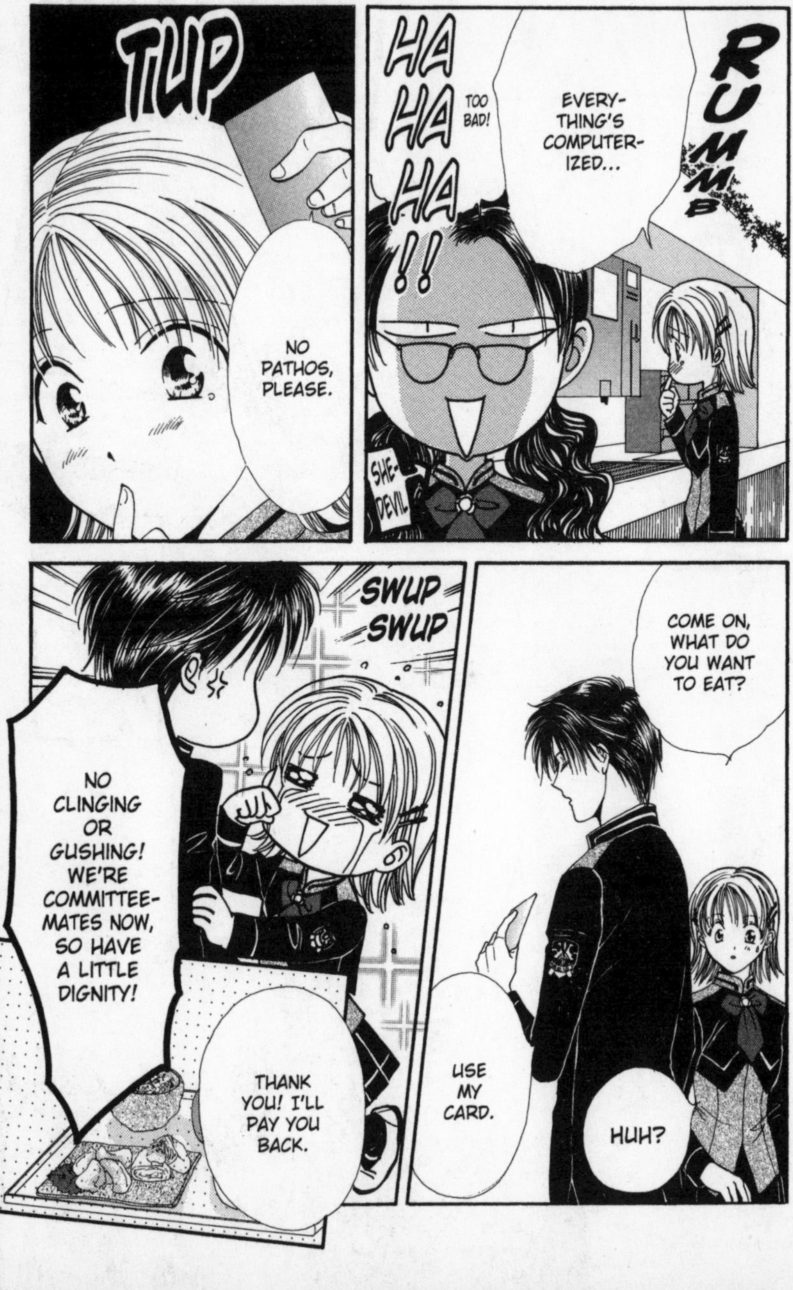
RUMMB
EVERYTHING'S COMPUTERIZED...
TOO BAD!
HA HA HA!!
SHE-DEVIL
TUP
NO PATHOS, PLEASE.
COME ON, WHAT DO YOU WANT TO EAT?
HUH?
USE MY CARD.
SWUP SWUP
NO CLINGING OR GUSHING! WE'RE COMMITTEE-MATES NOW, SO HAVE A LITTLE DIGNITY!
THANK YOU! I'LL PAY YOU BACK.

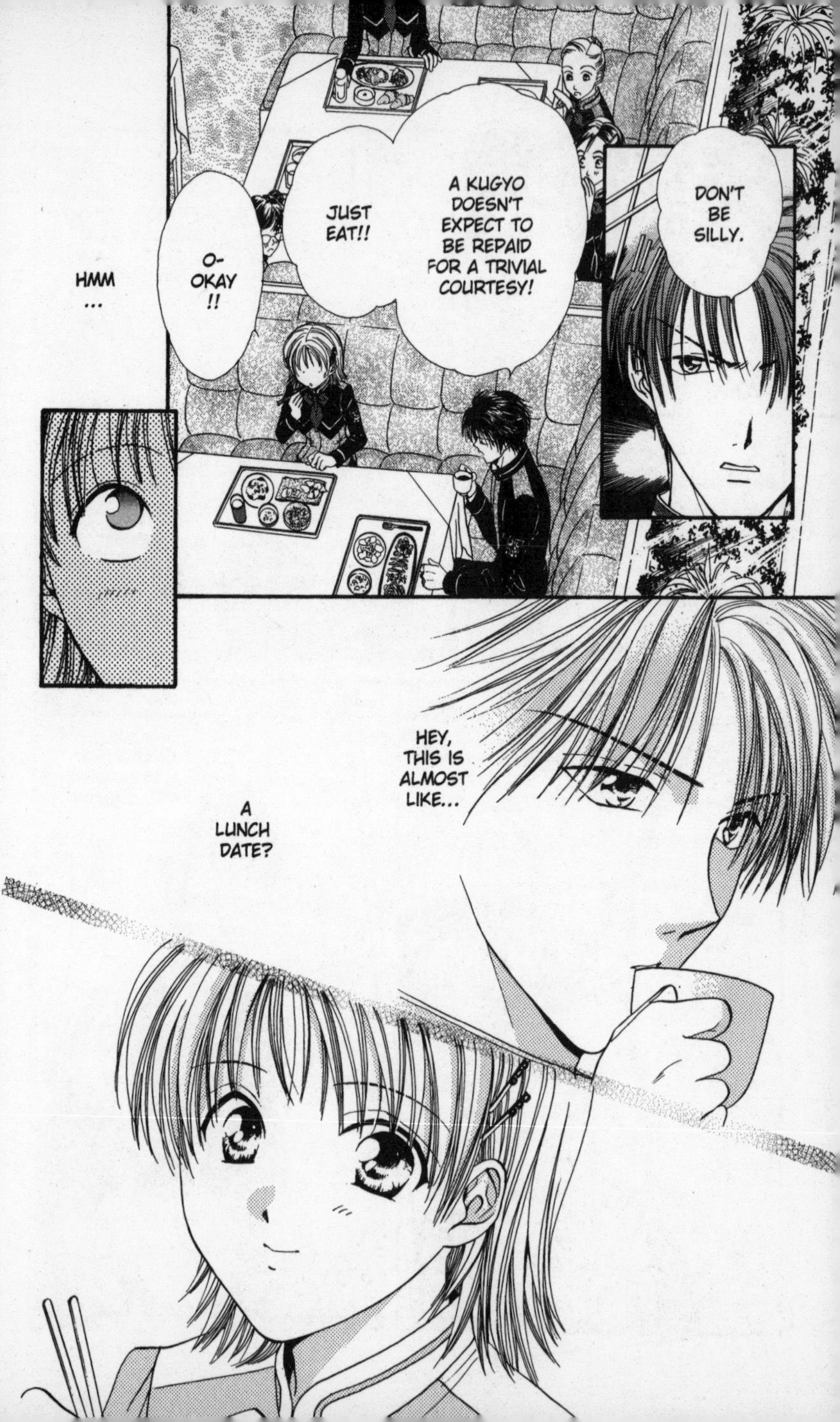
DON'T BE SILLY.
A KUGYO DOESN'T EXPECT TO BE REPAID FOR A TRIVIAL COURTESY!
JUST EAT!!
O-OKAY !!
HMM ...
HEY, THIS IS ALMOST LIKE...
A LUNCH DATE?

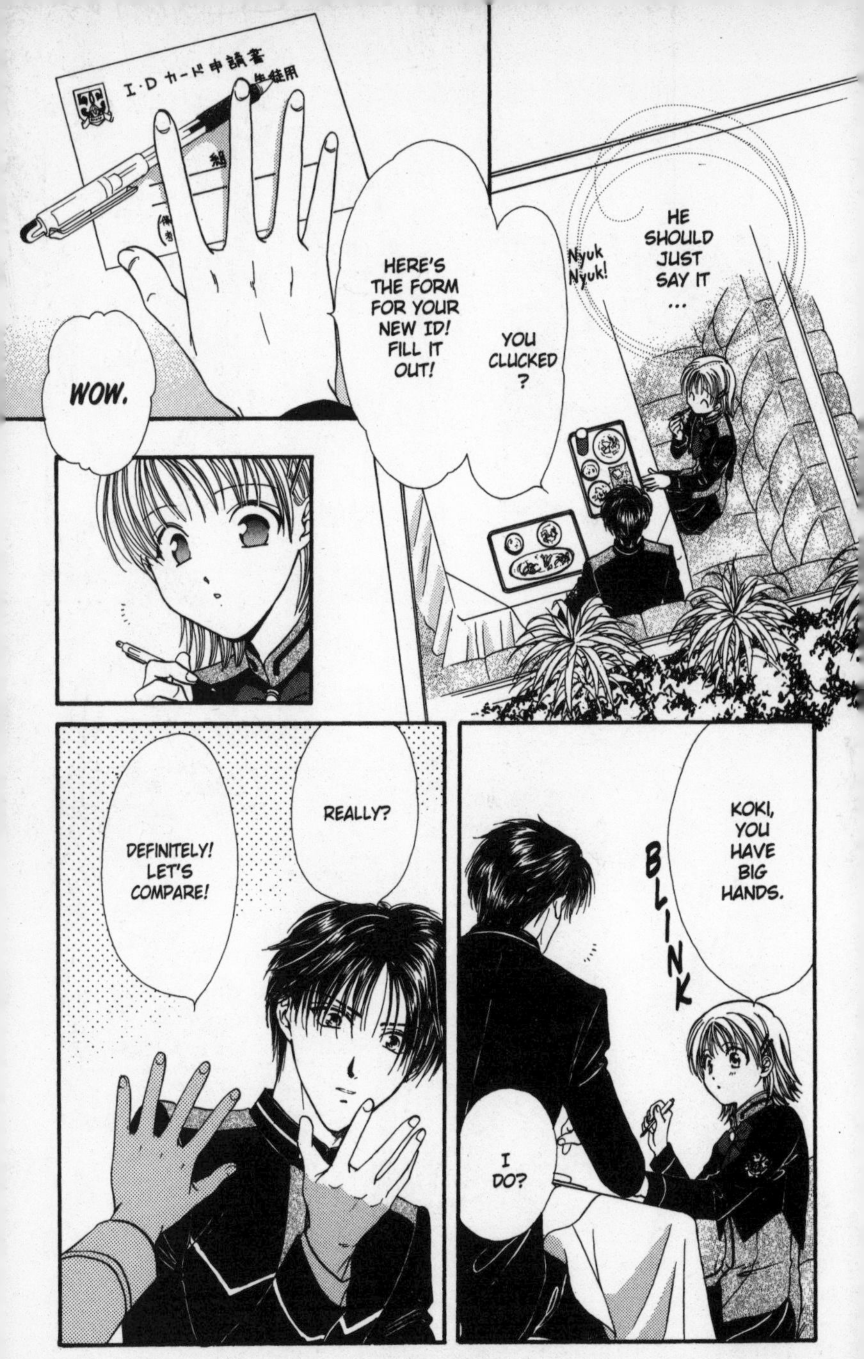
HE SHOULD JUST SAY IT ...
Nyuk Nyuk!
YOU CLUCKED?
HERE'S THE FORM FOR YOUR NEW ID! FILL IT OUT!
I・Dカード申請書
生徒用
WOW.
KOKI, YOU HAVE BIG HANDS.
BLINK
I DO?
REALLY?
DEFINITELY! LET'S COMPARE!

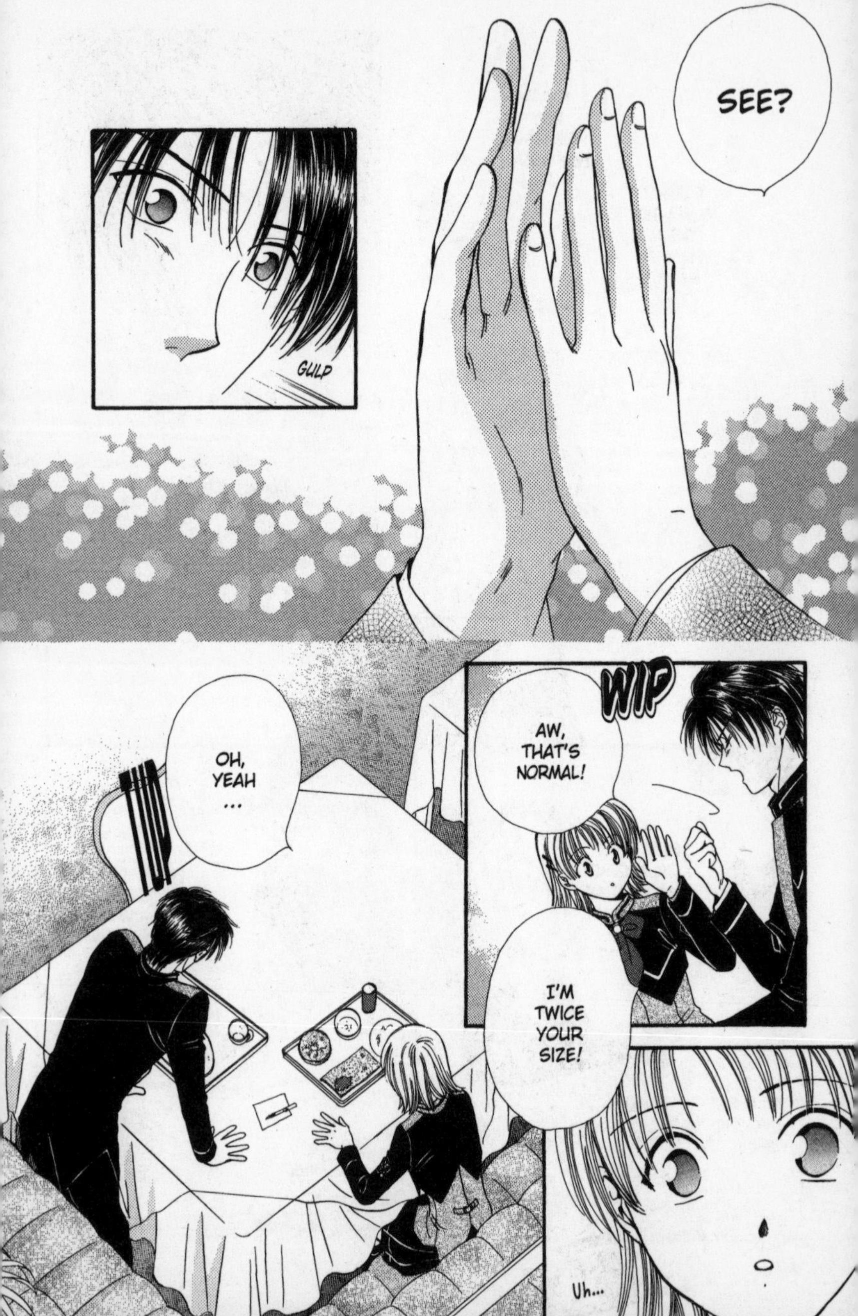
SEE?
GULP
WIP
AW, THAT'S NORMAL!
I'M TWICE YOUR SIZE!
Uh...
OH, YEAH ...

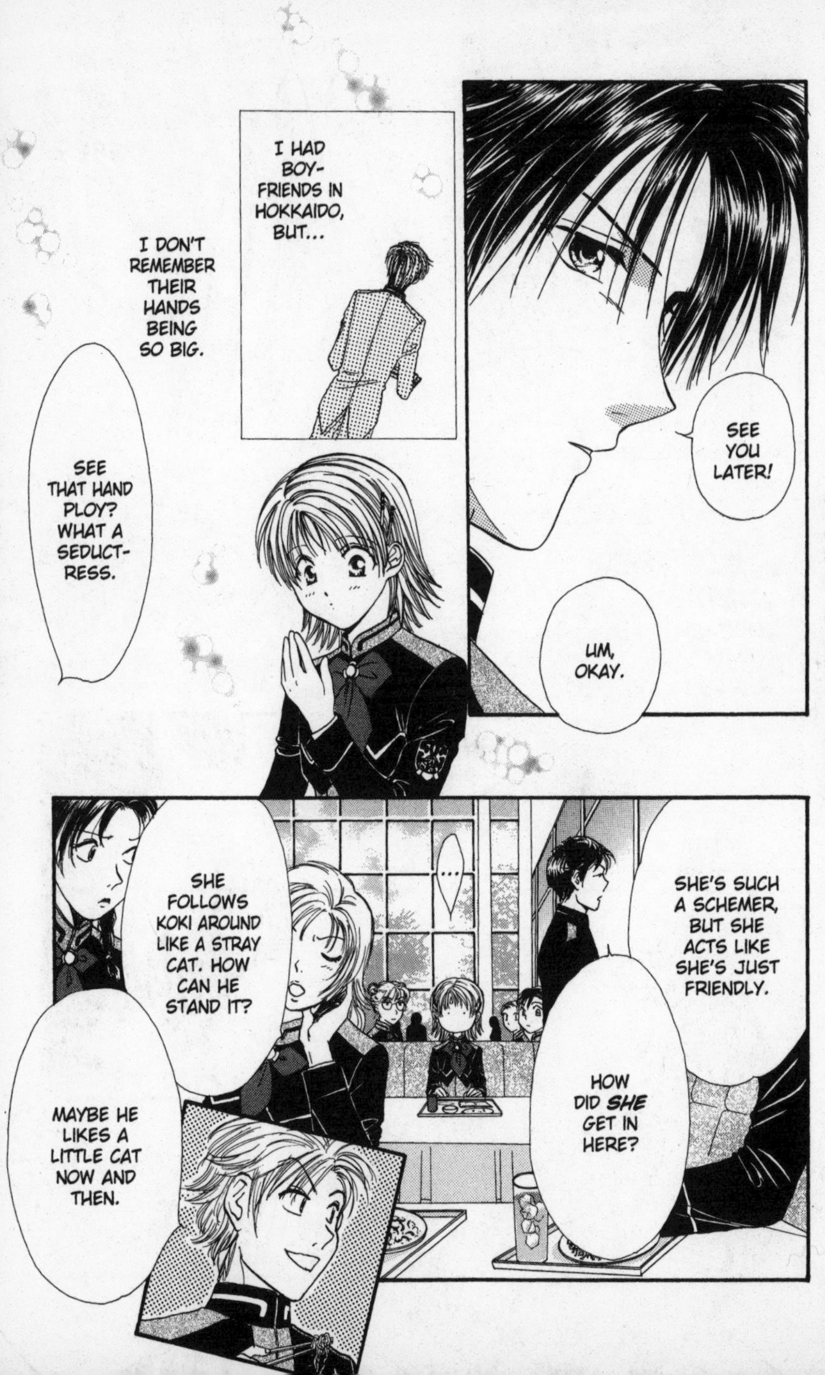
SEE YOU LATER!
UM, OKAY.
I HAD BOY-FRIENDS IN HOKKAIDO, BUT...
I DON'T REMEMBER THEIR HANDS BEING SO BIG.
SEE THAT HAND PLOY? WHAT A SEDUCT-RESS.
SHE'S SUCH A SCHEMER, BUT SHE ACTS LIKE SHE'S JUST FRIENDLY.
HOW DID *SHE* GET IN HERE?
...
SHE FOLLOWS KOKI AROUND LIKE A STRAY CAT. HOW CAN HE STAND IT?
MAYBE HE LIKES A LITTLE CAT NOW AND THEN.

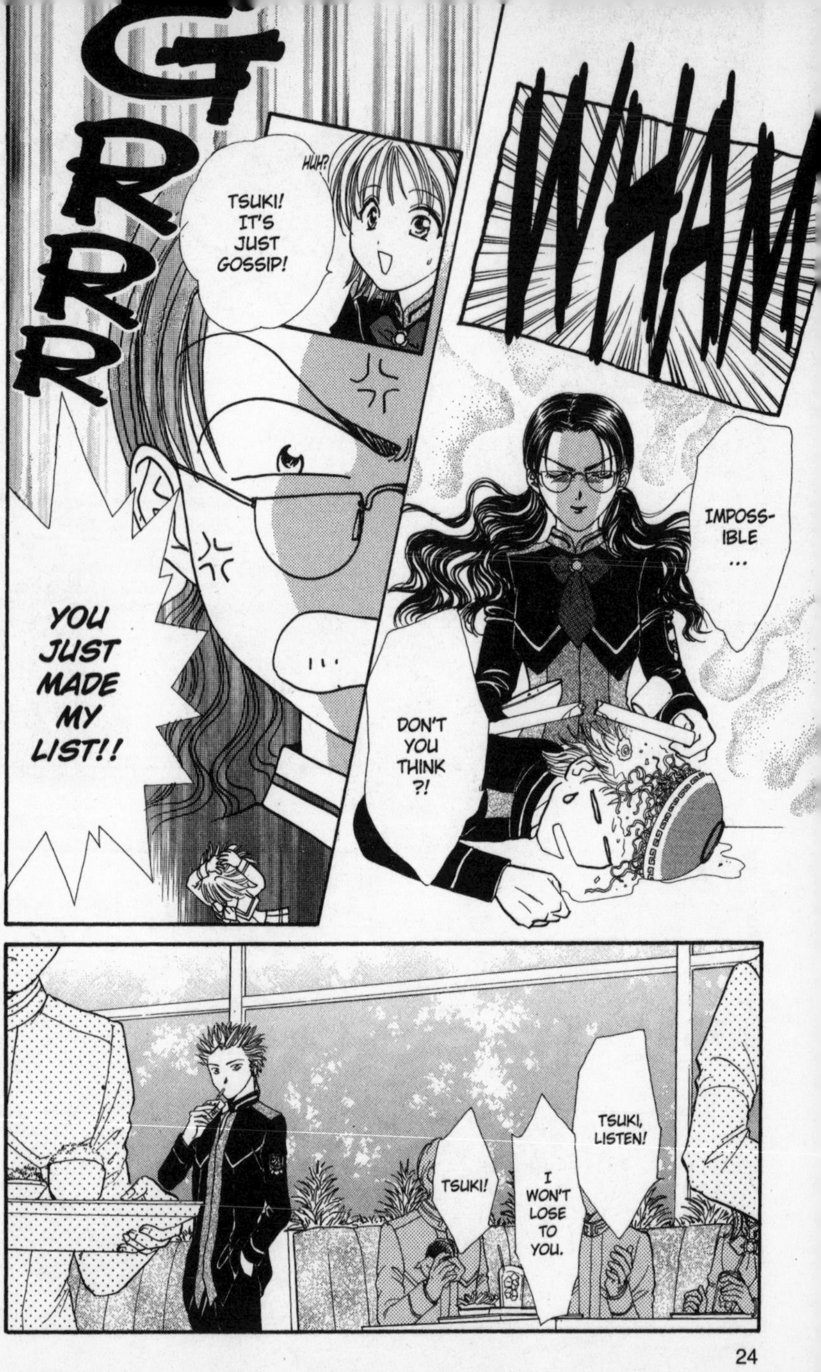
WHAM
IMPOSS-IBLE ...
DON'T YOU THINK ?!
GRRR
HUH?
TSUKI! IT'S JUST GOSSIP!
YOU JUST MADE MY LIST!!
TSUKI, LISTEN!
I WON'T LOSE TO YOU.
TSUKI!

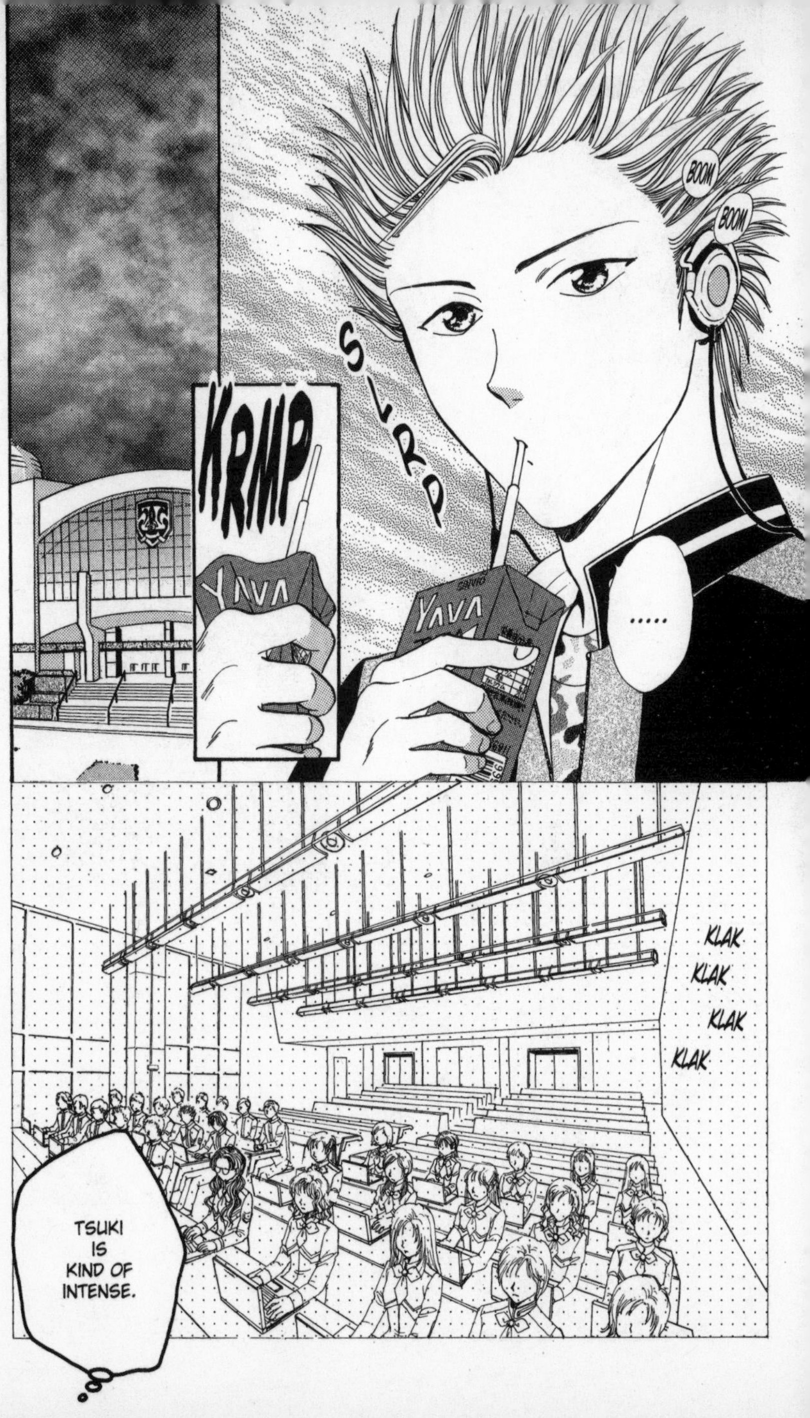
BOOM
BOOM
SLURP
YAVA
.....
KRMP
YAVA
KLAK
KLAK
KLAK
KLAK
TSUKI IS KIND OF INTENSE.

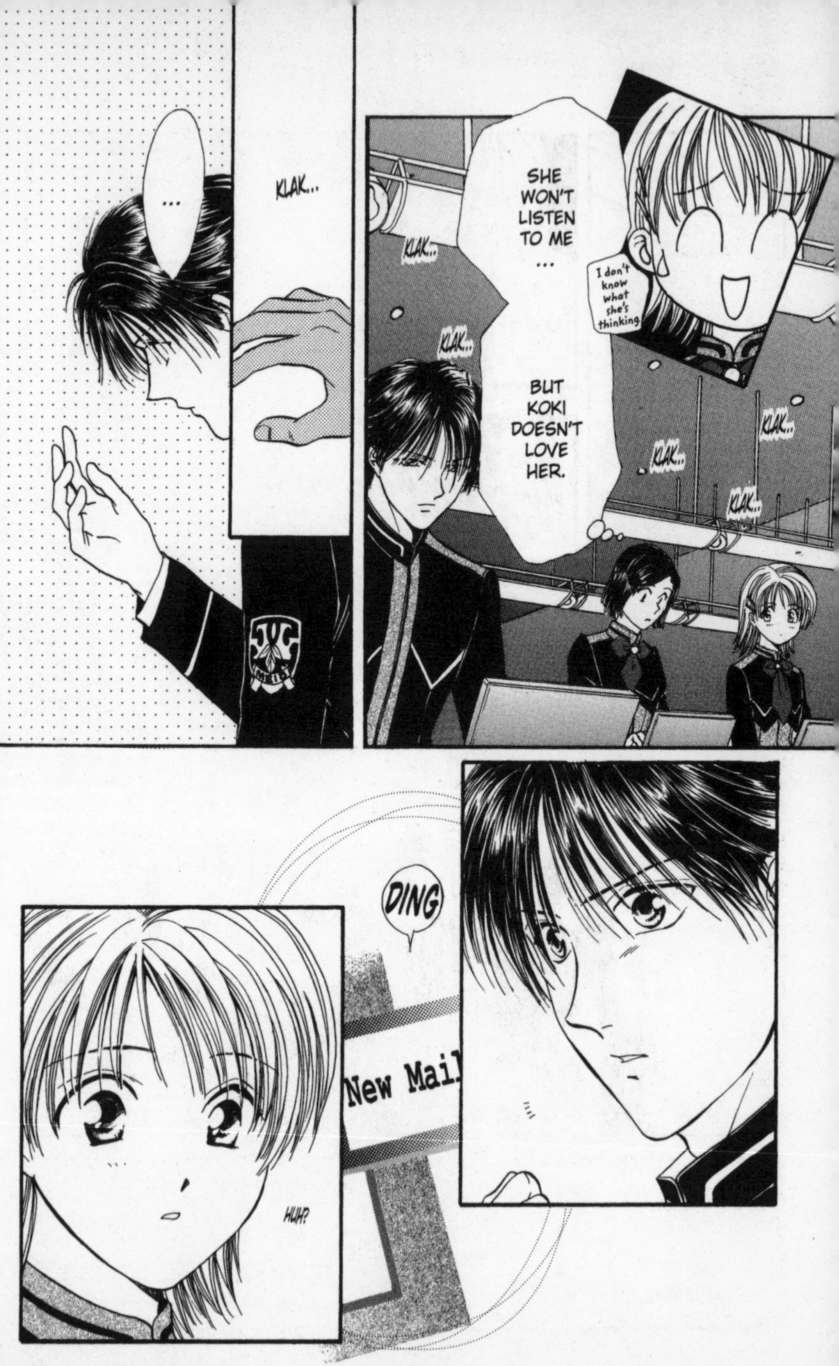
SHE WON'T LISTEN TO ME ...
I don't know what she's thinking.
BUT KOKI DOESN'T LOVE HER.
KLAK...
KLAK...
KLAK...
KLAK...
KLAK...
KLAK...
...
DING
New Mail
HUH?

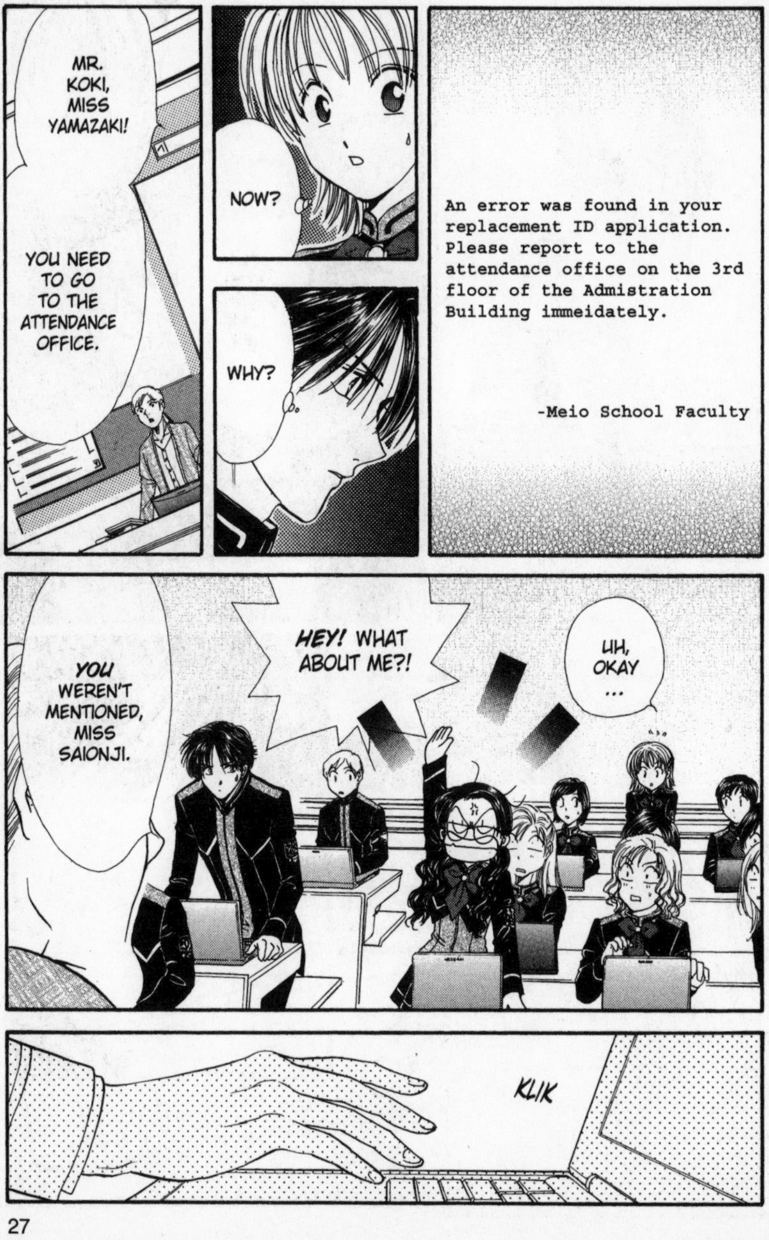
An error was found in your replacement ID application. Please report to the attendance office on the 3rd floor of the Admistration Building immeidately.
-Meio School Faculty
NOW?
WHY?
MR. KOKI, MISS YAMAZAKI!
YOU NEED TO GO TO THE ATTENDANCE OFFICE.
UH, OKAY ...
HEY! WHAT ABOUT ME?!
YOU WEREN'T MENTIONED, MISS SAIONJI.
KLIK

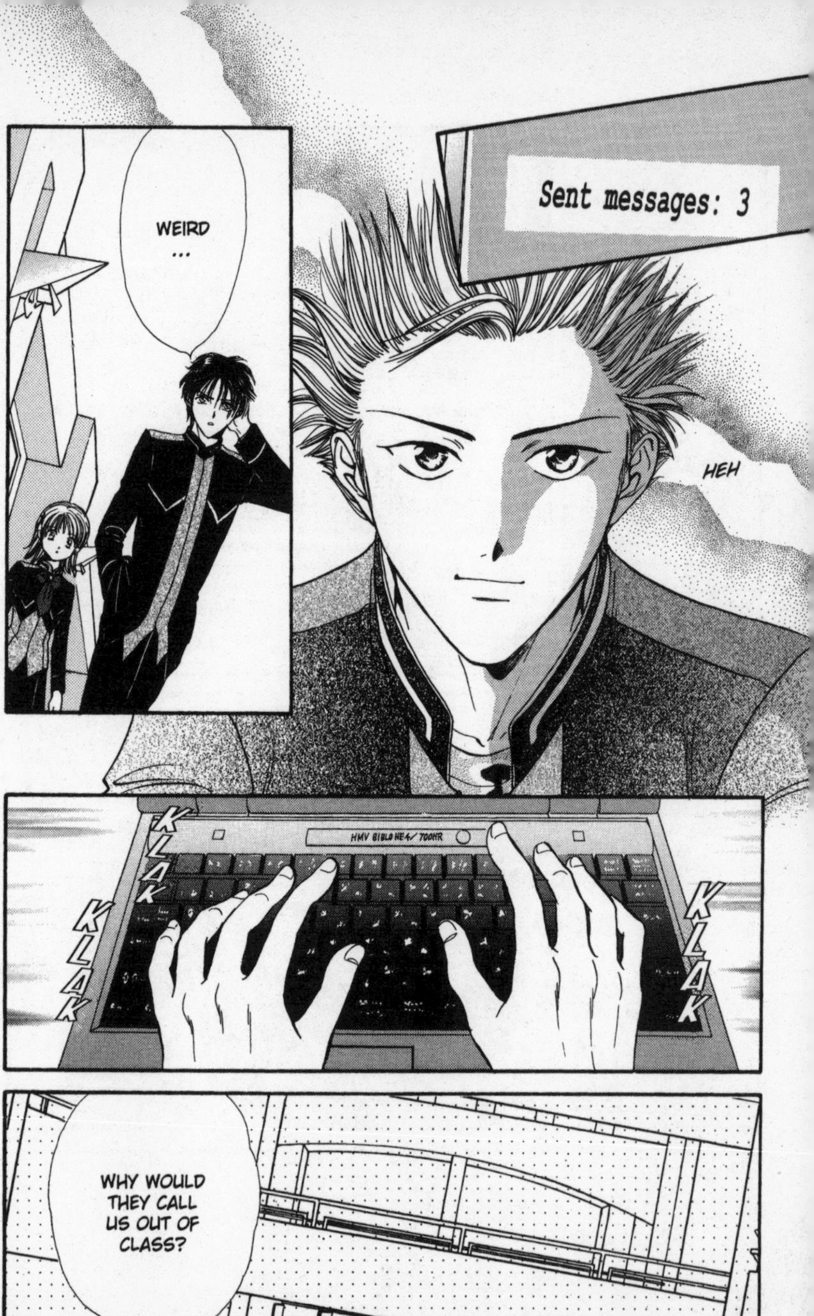
Sent messages: 3
HEH
WEIRD ...
KLAK
KLAK
KLAK
KLAK
WHY WOULD THEY CALL US OUT OF CLASS?

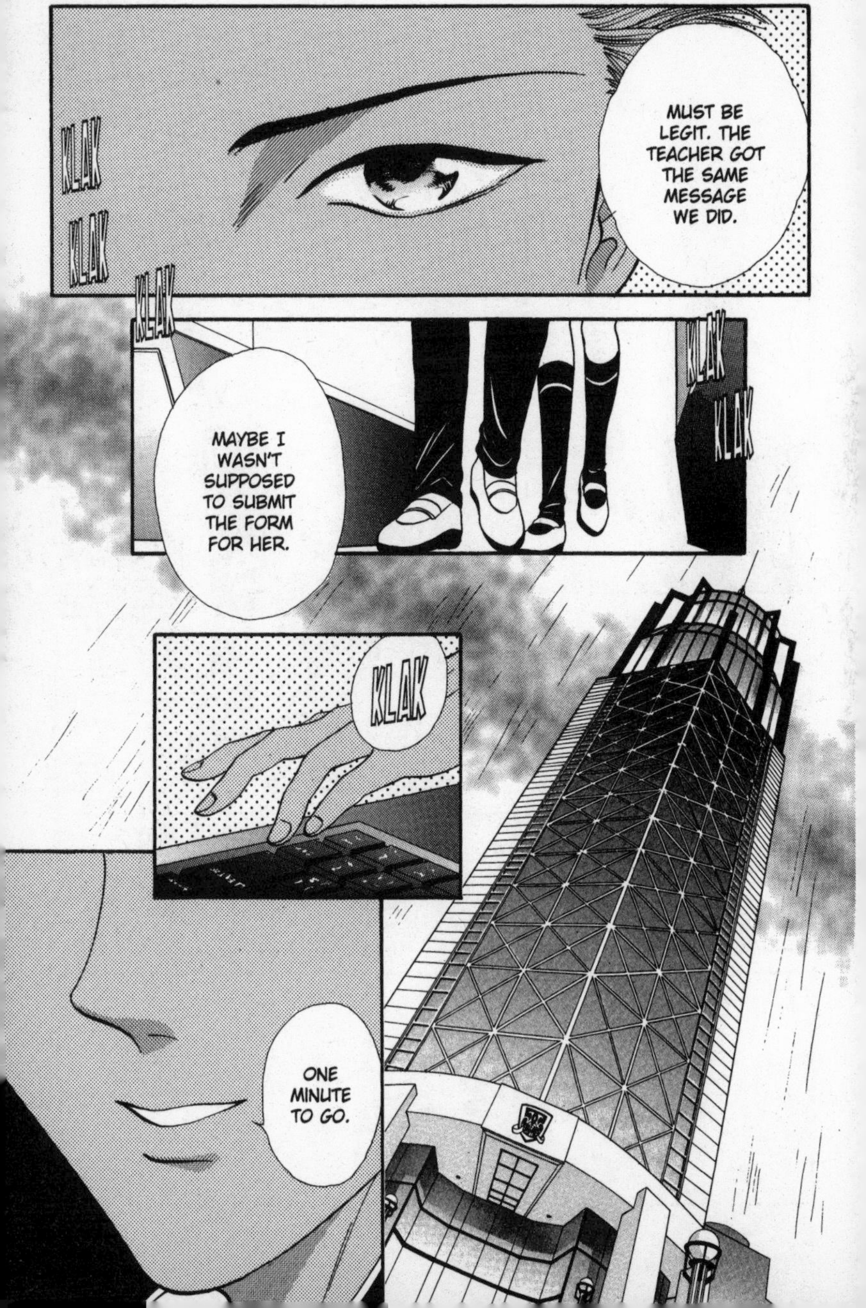
MUST BE LEGIT. THE TEACHER GOT THE SAME MESSAGE WE DID.
KLAK
KLAK
KLAK
KLAK
MAYBE I WASN'T SUPPOSED TO SUBMIT THE FORM FOR HER.
KLAK
KLAK
ONE MINUTE TO GO.

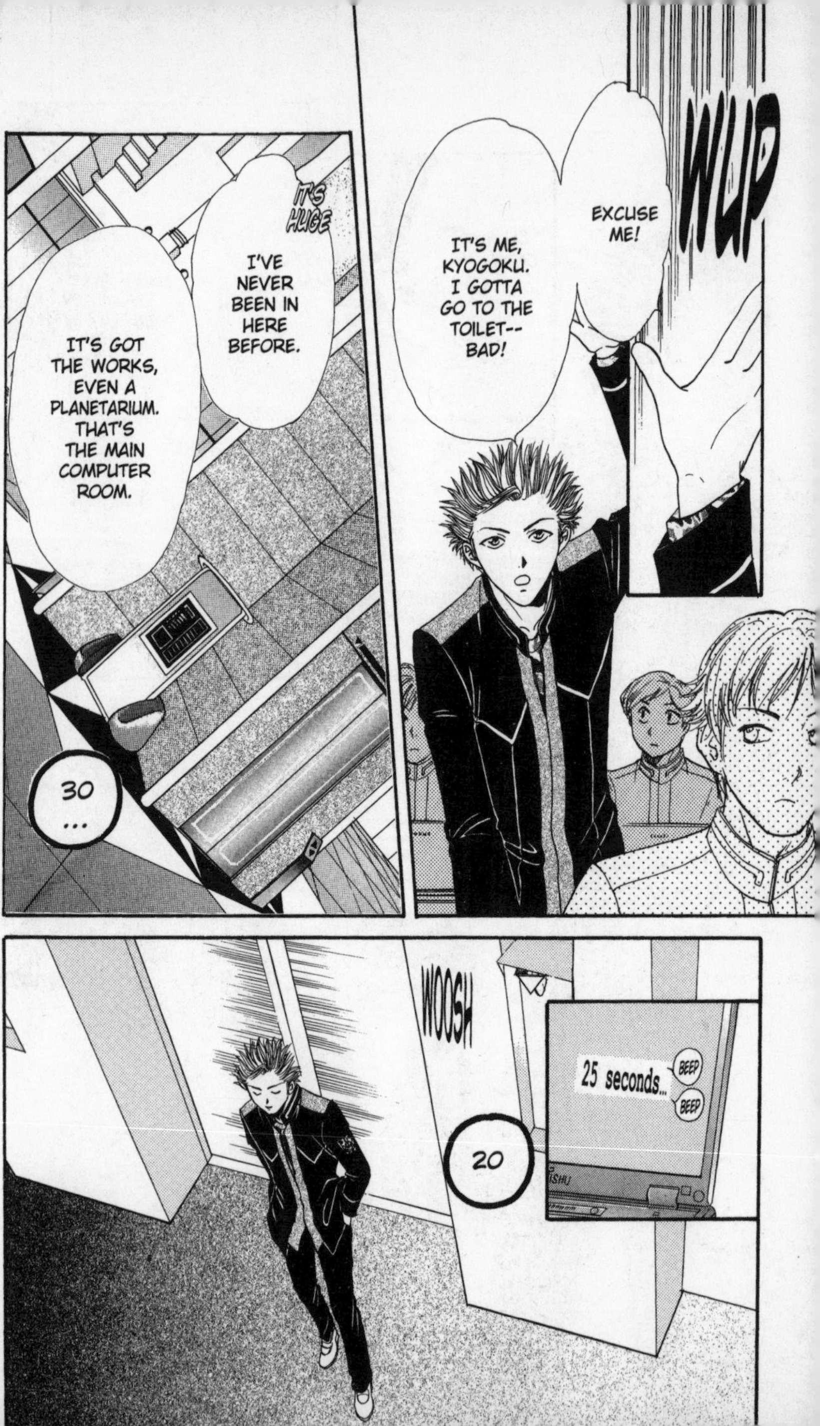
WUP
EXCUSE ME!
IT'S ME, KYOGOKU. I GOTTA GO TO THE TOILET--BAD!
IT'S HUGE
I'VE NEVER BEEN IN HERE BEFORE.
IT'S GOT THE WORKS, EVEN A PLANETARIUM. THAT'S THE MAIN COMPUTER ROOM.
30 ...
25 seconds...
BEEP
BEEP
WOOSH
20

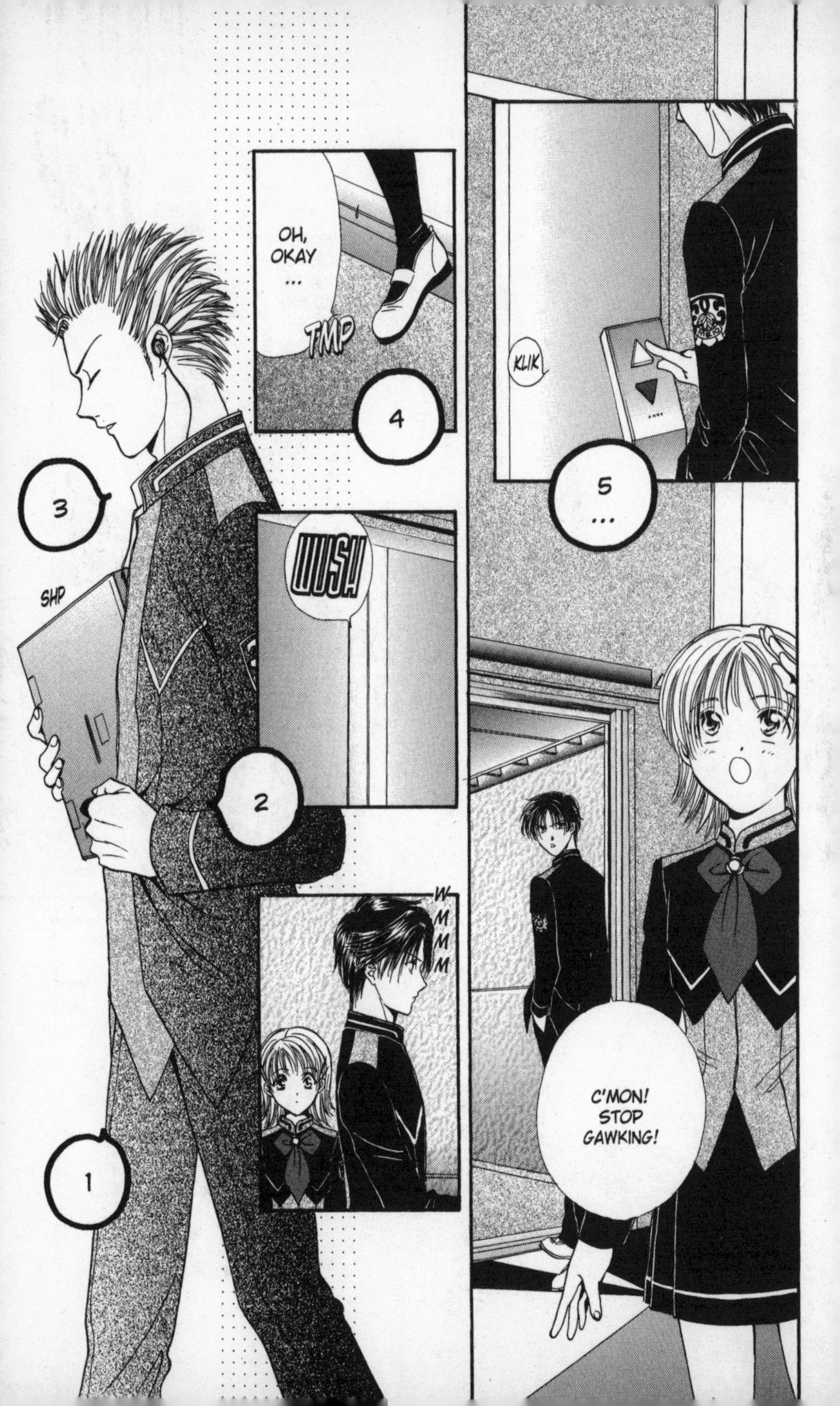
KLIK
5
...
C'MON! STOP GAWKING!
OH, OKAY ...
TMP
4
WUSH
2
W M M M M
3
SHP
1

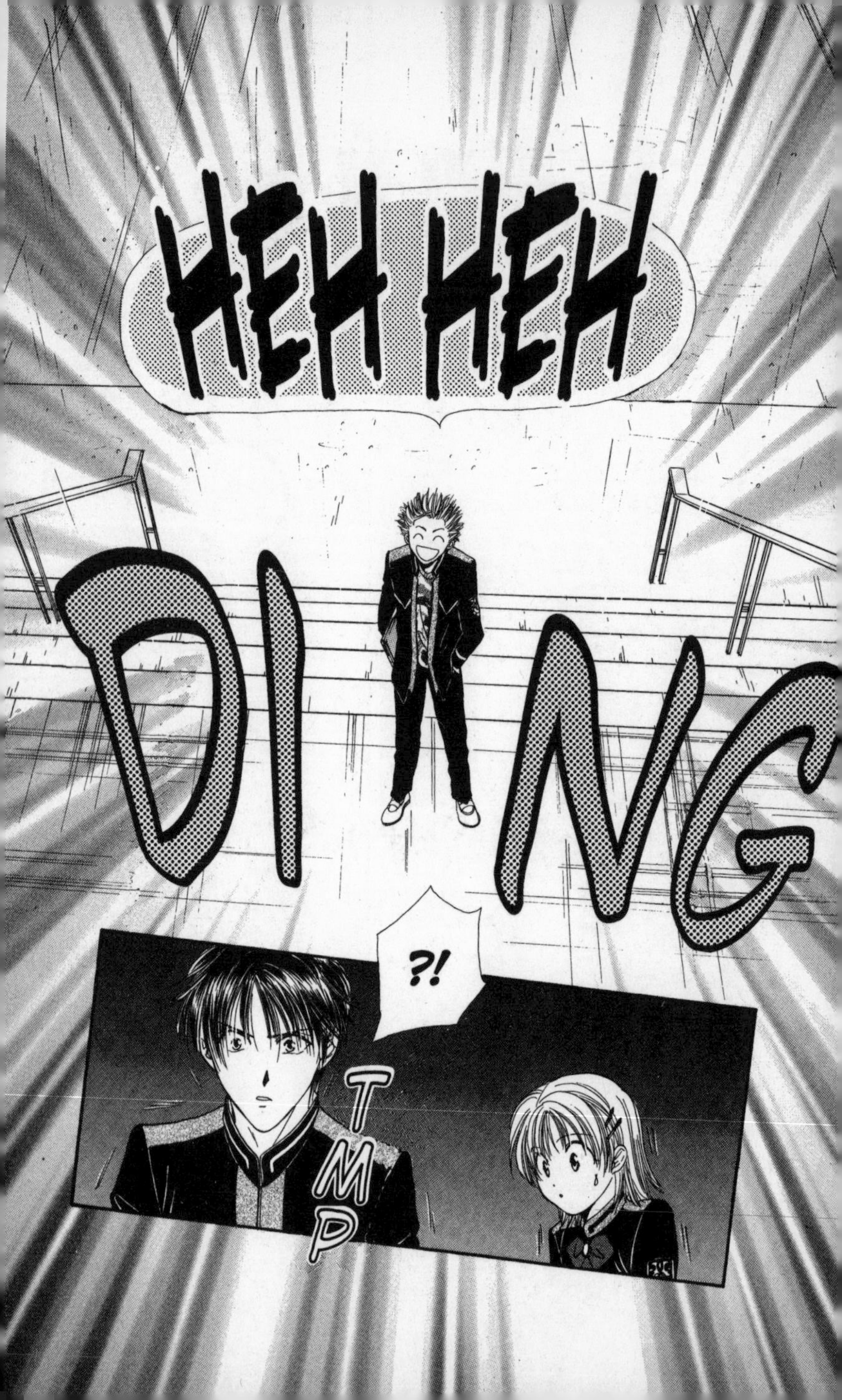
HEH HEH
DING
?!
TMP

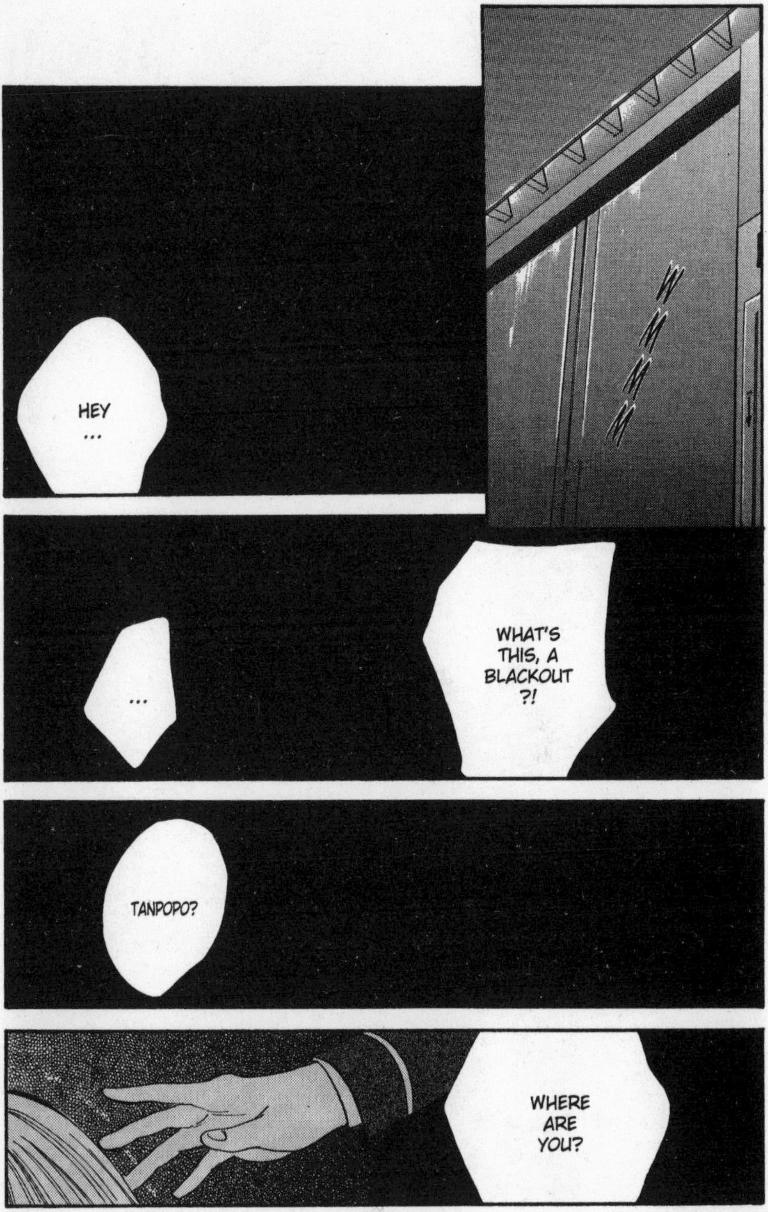
WMMM
HEY ...
WHAT'S THIS, A BLACKOUT ?!
...
TANPOPO?
WHERE ARE YOU?

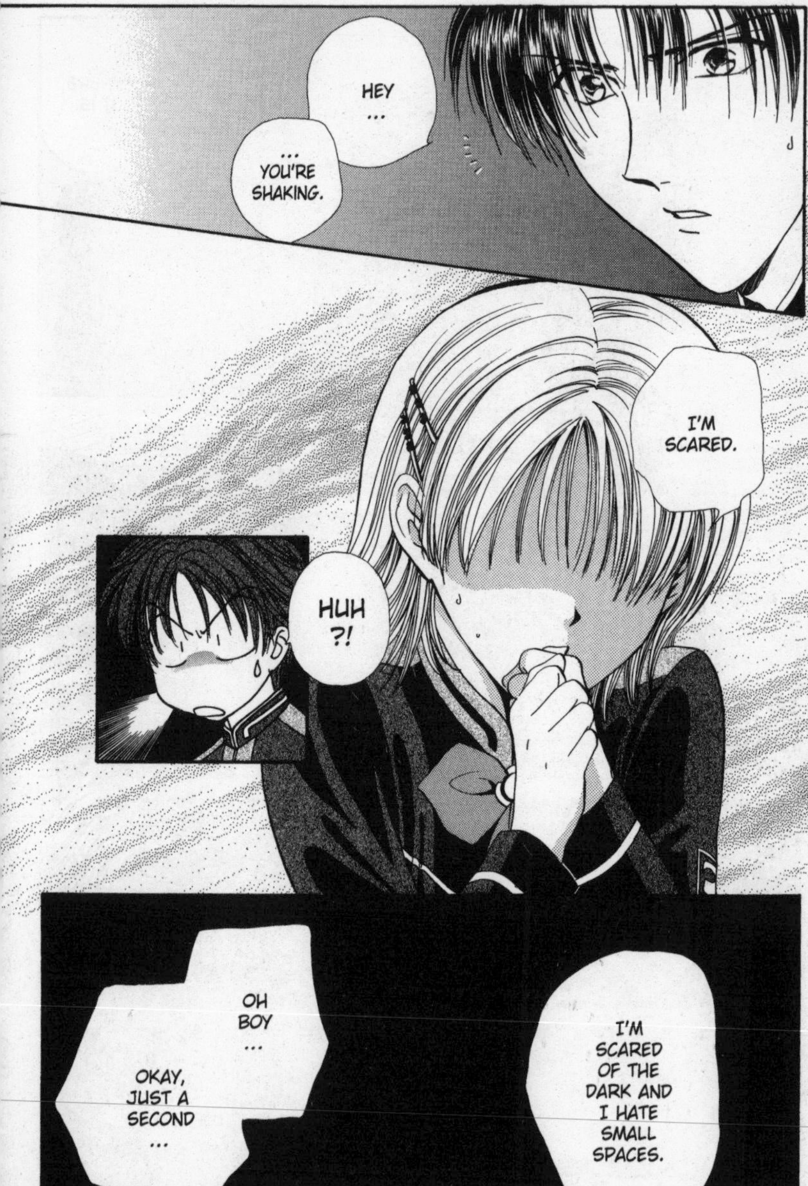
HEY ...
... YOU'RE SHAKING.
I'M SCARED.
HUH ?!
I'M SCARED OF THE DARK AND I HATE SMALL SPACES.
OH BOY ...
OKAY, JUST A SECOND ...

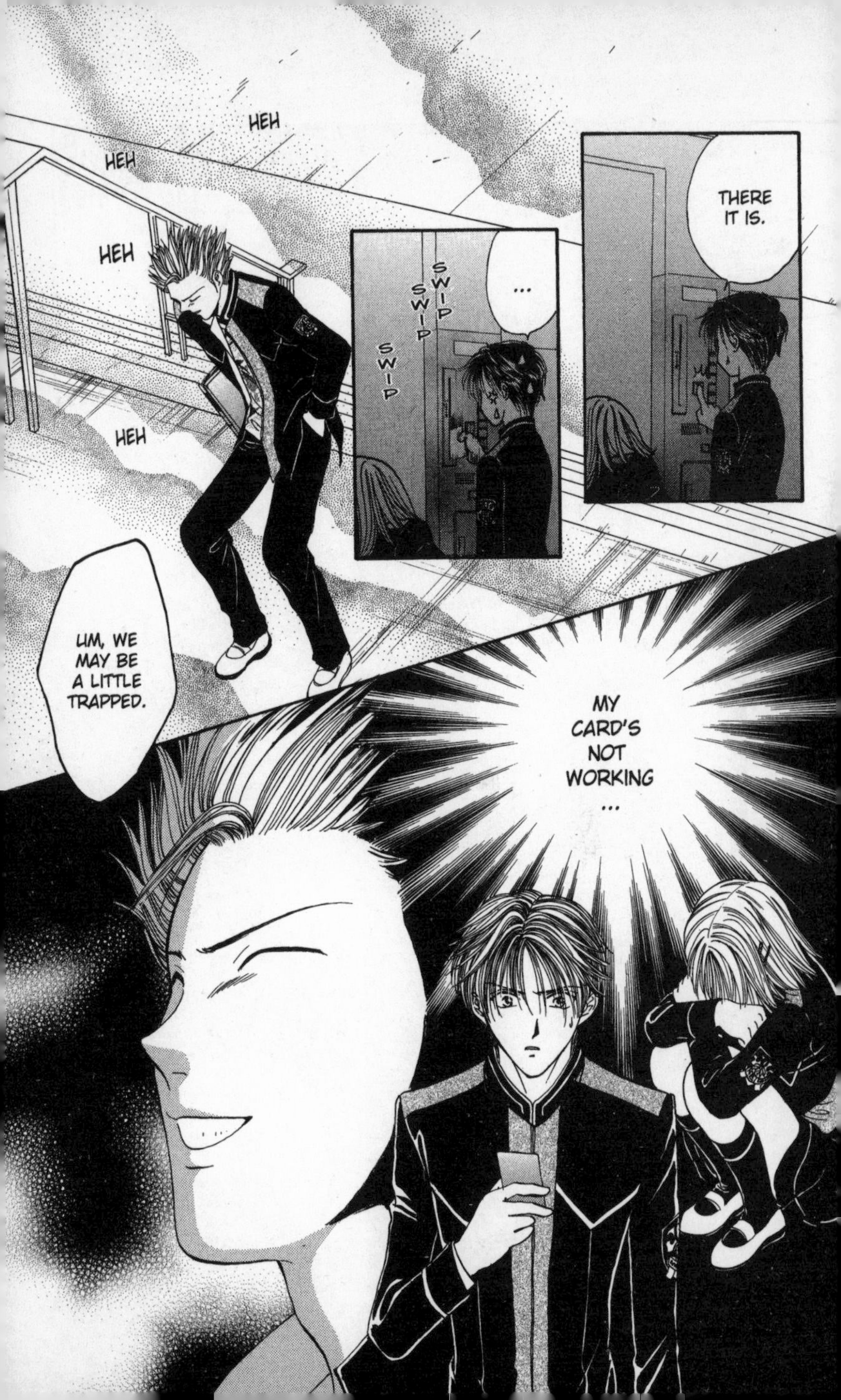
THERE IT IS.
SWIP SWIP
SWIP
...
MY CARD'S NOT WORKING ...
UM, WE MAY BE A LITTLE TRAPPED.
HEH
HEH
HEH
HEH

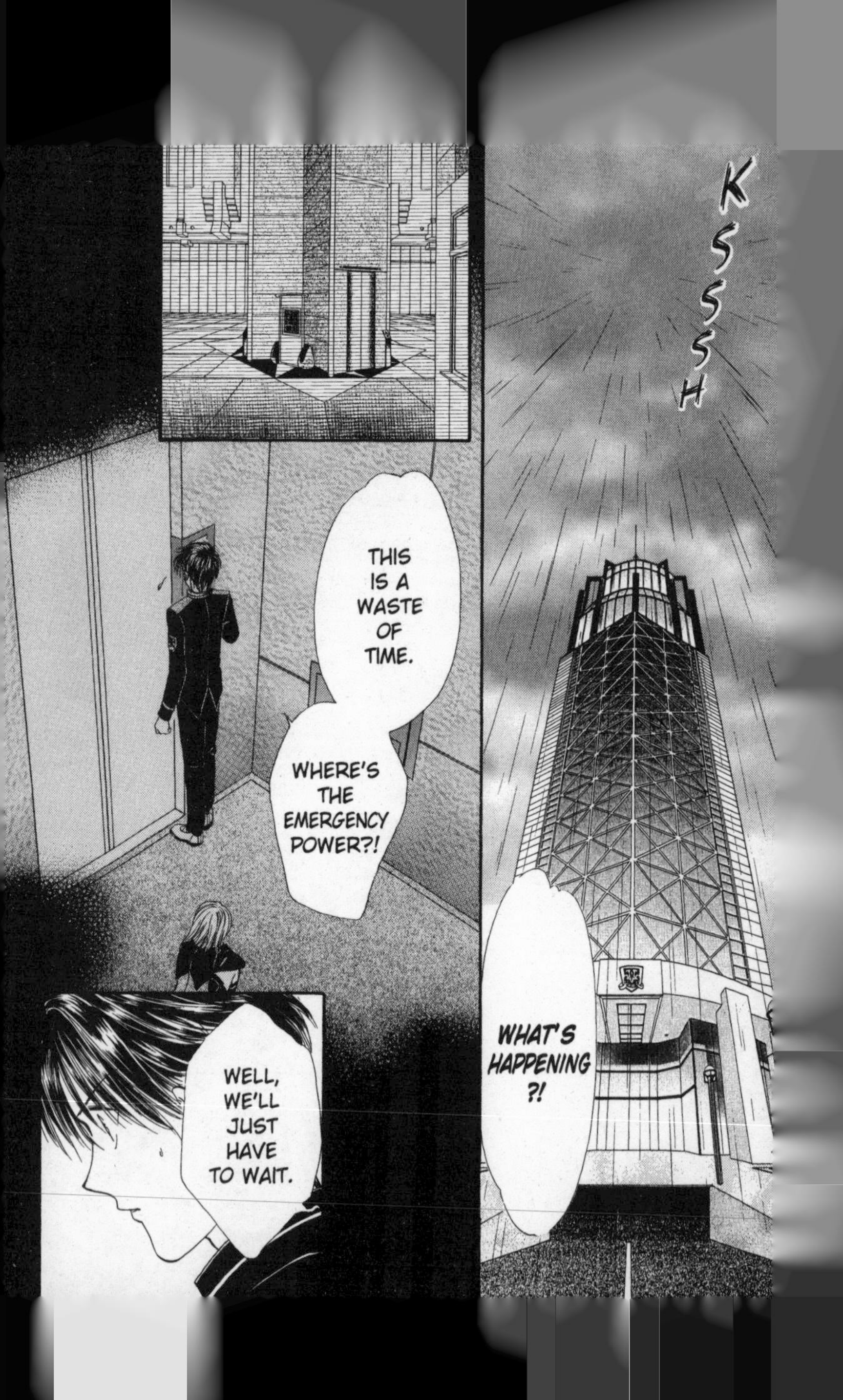
KSSSH
WHAT'S HAPPENING ?!
THIS IS A WASTE OF TIME.
WHERE'S THE EMERGENCY POWER?!
WELL, WE'LL JUST HAVE TO WAIT.

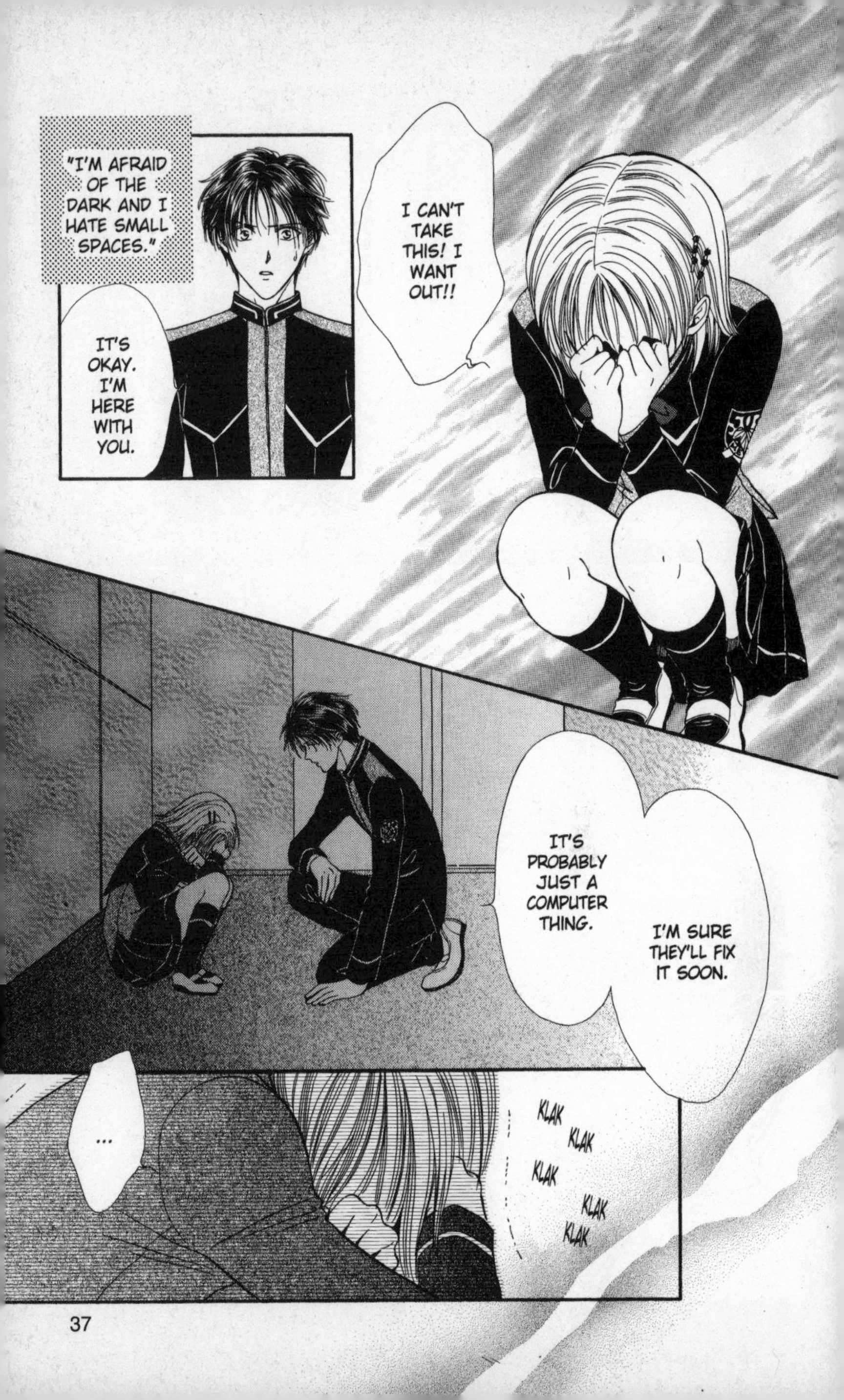
I CAN'T TAKE THIS! I WANT OUT!!
"I'M AFRAID OF THE DARK AND I HATE SMALL SPACES."
IT'S OKAY. I'M HERE WITH YOU.
IT'S PROBABLY JUST A COMPUTER THING.
I'M SURE THEY'LL FIX IT SOON.
KLAK KLAK KLAK KLAK KLAK
...

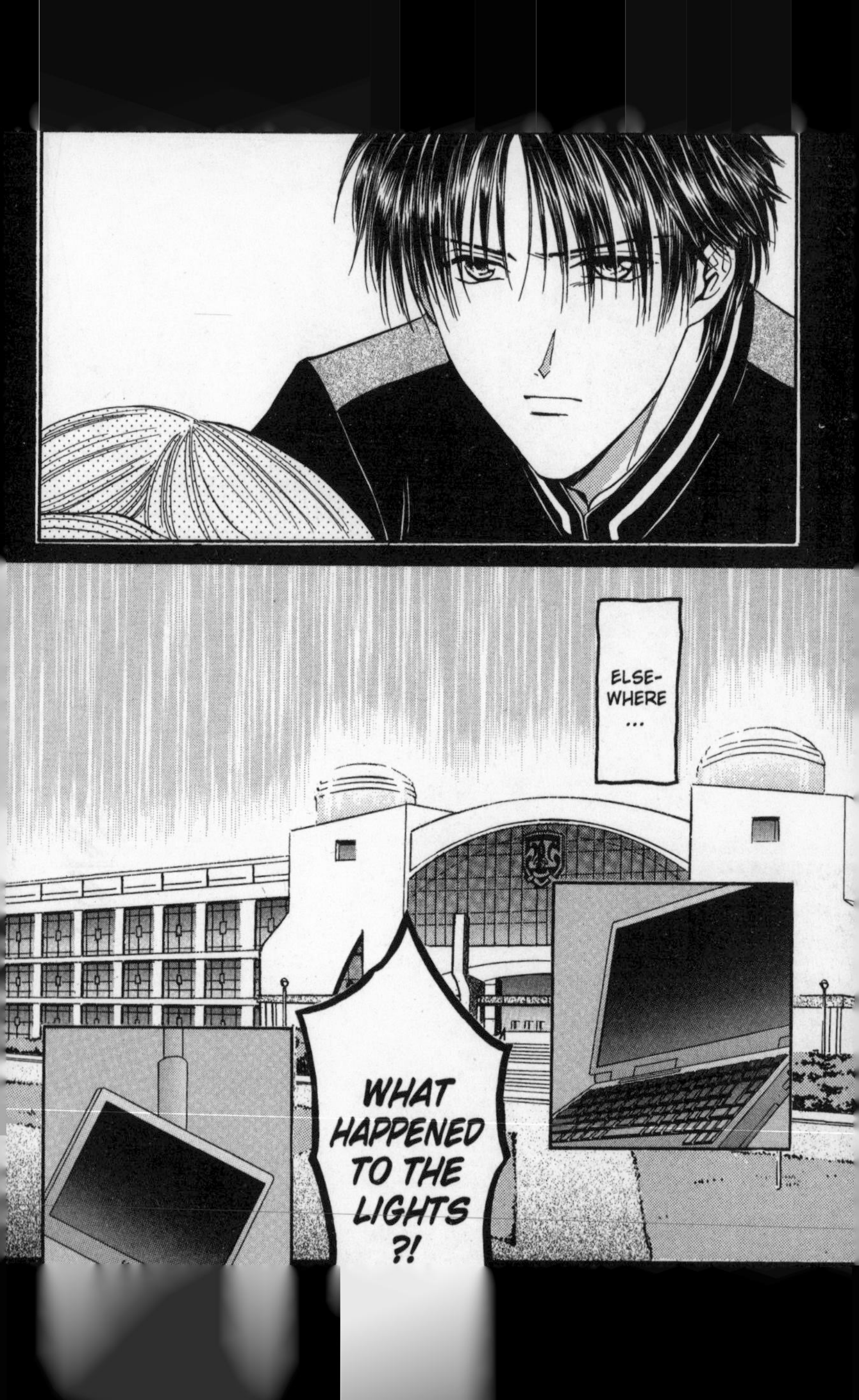
ELSE-WHERE ...
WHAT HAPPENED TO THE LIGHTS ?!

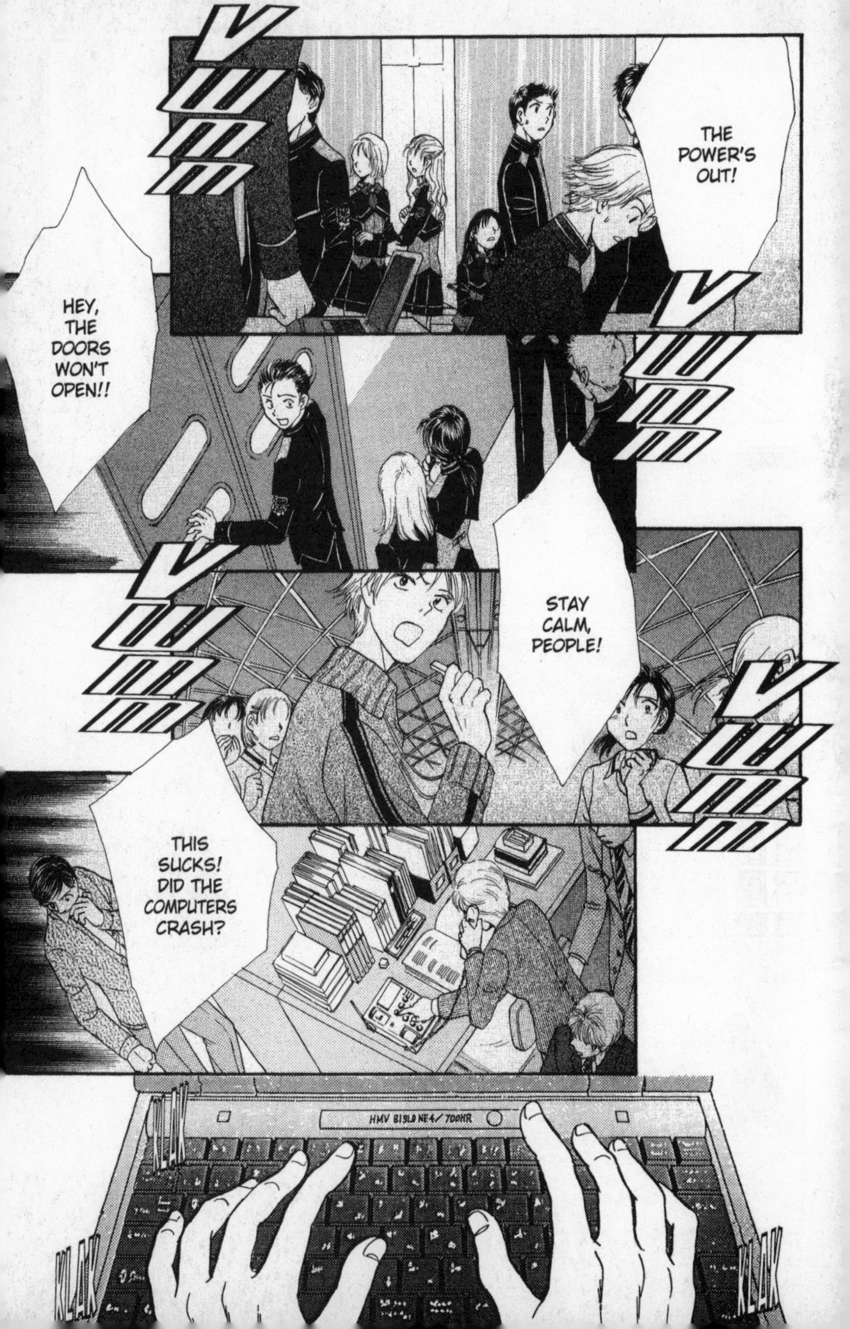
THE POWER'S OUT!
HEY, THE DOORS WON'T OPEN!!
STAY CALM, PEOPLE!
THIS SUCKS! DID THE COMPUTERS CRASH?
KLAK
KLAK
KLAK

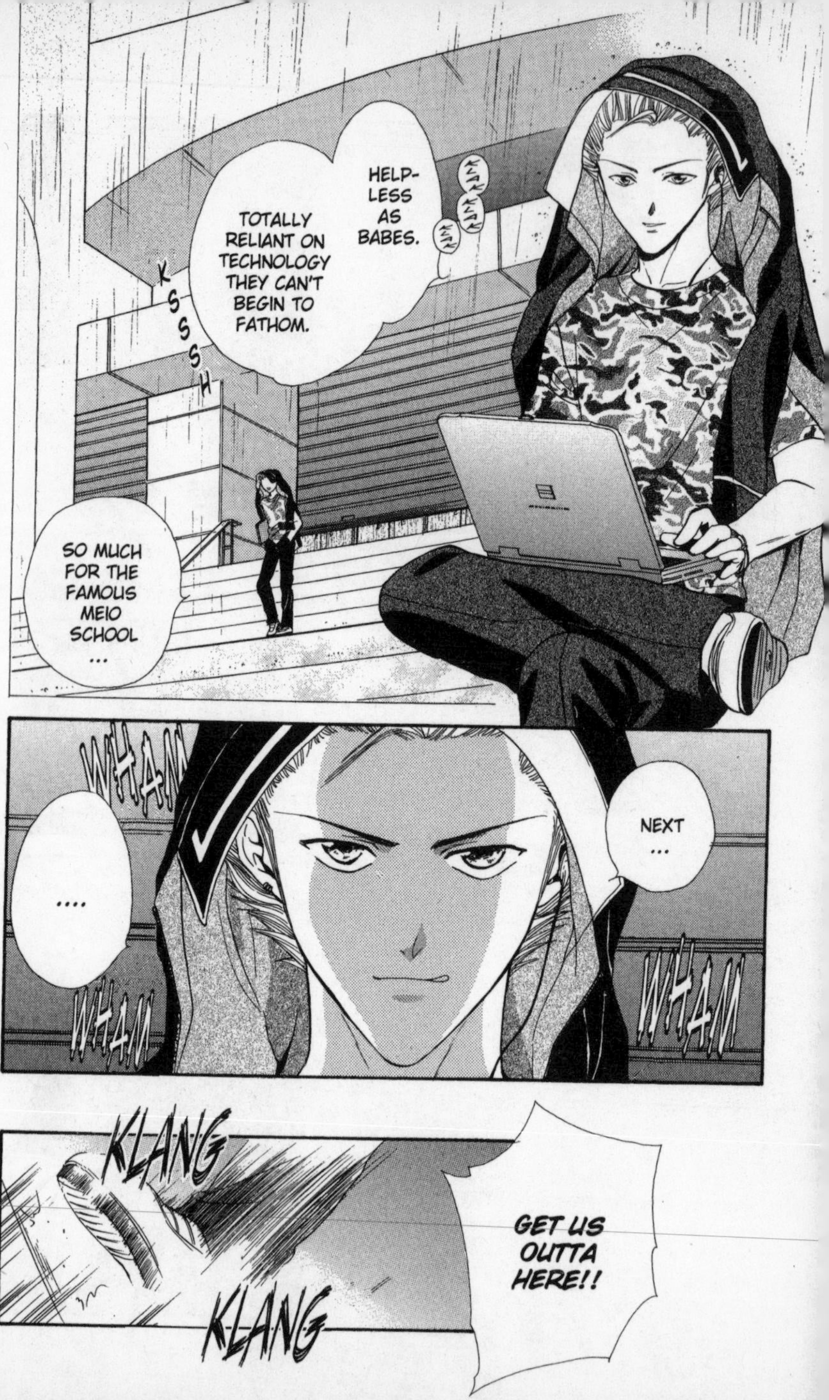
HELP-LESS AS BABES.
TOTALLY RELIANT ON TECHNOLOGY THEY CAN'T BEGIN TO FATHOM.
KSSSH
SO MUCH FOR THE FAMOUS MEIO SCHOOL ...
NEXT ...
WHAM
WHAM
....
WHAM
GET US OUTTA HERE!!
KLANG
KLANG

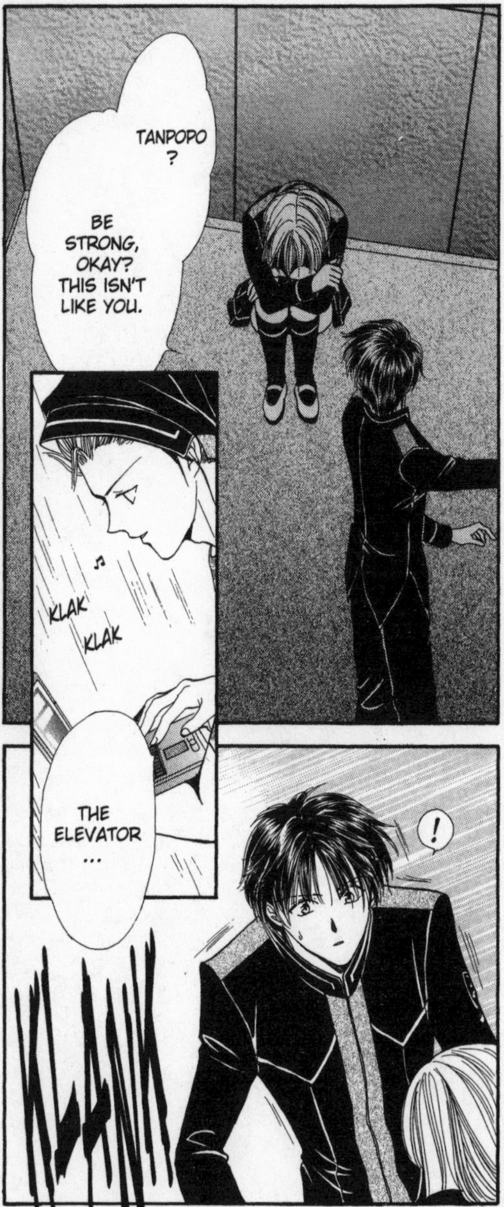
TANPOPO ?
BE STRONG, OKAY? THIS ISN'T LIKE YOU.
KLAK
KLAK
THE ELEVATOR ...
!
KLANK

I decided to put my previous work behind me. For this title, I'm taking a totally relaxed approach. But school days comics are sort of the basics of comics, right?

[small]Ooh... Writing with 0.8 pen is hard! [regular size] Well, it is for drawing, after all! The basics. I think most young up-and-coming comics artists want to do fantasy comics, but they must first clear the school days hurdle, or they're bound to fail. For me, I was going through puberty. It was challenging, but once I got the hang of it I even began to enjoy it toward the end. That's what I remember. But the school part wasn't the main theme.

Having been a comics artist for 10 years, I think it's important to get back to the basics. I really struggled with Tanpopo's name. I knew I wanted to name her after a flower, but couldn't find the right one. They either didn't sound right or a kanji was already part of another character's name. Tanpopo, dandelion, was the right flower for the character but I thought, "No one has that name." So I waffled until the last minute. Then the project leader simply said, "Why not?" to which I responded, "Well, it has impact." So I decided to go with it. Just like the Shichiseishi characters (smile) in **Fushigi Yuugi**, I had my doubts about the name, but after I got used to it, it felt just right.

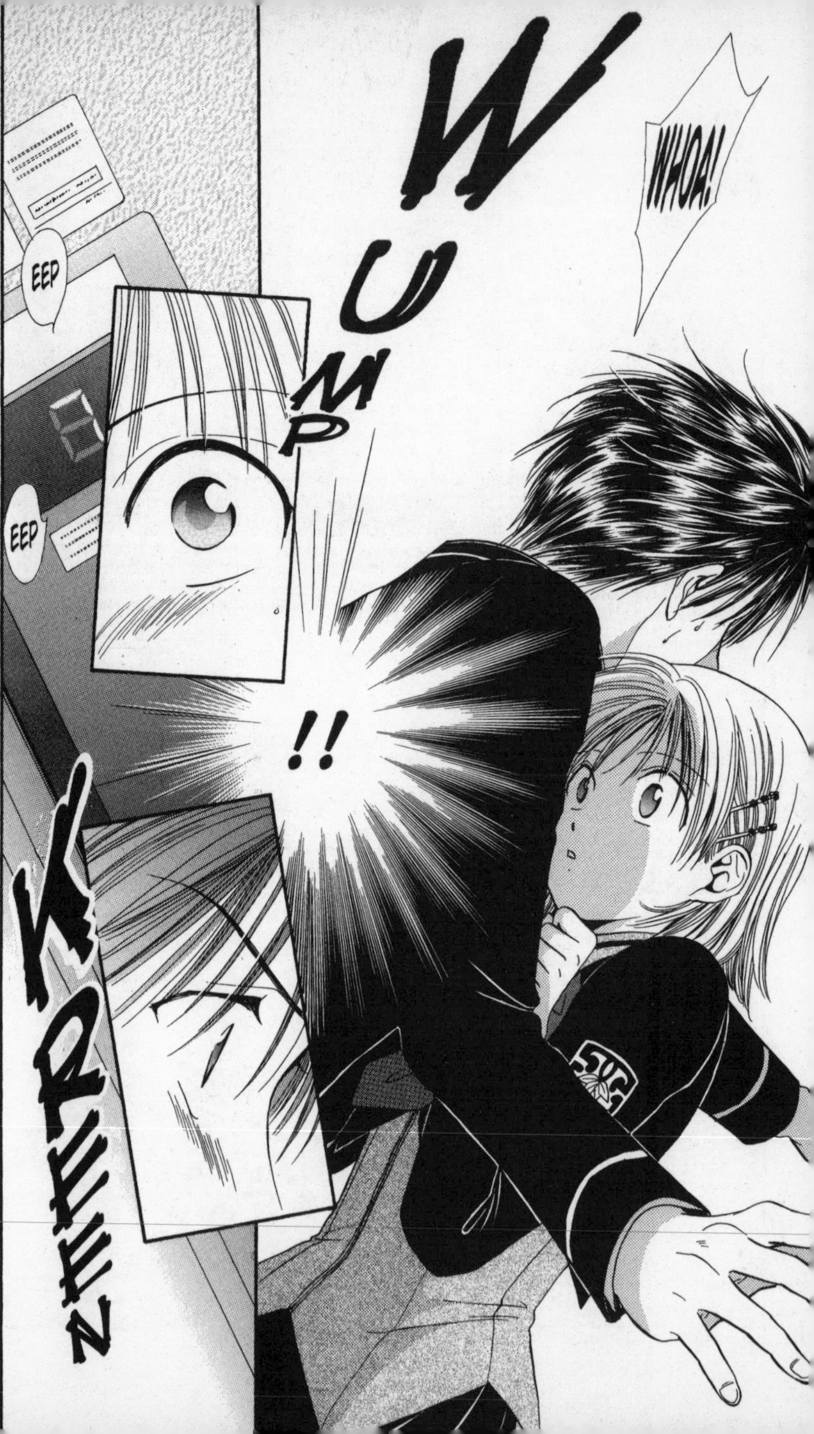
WHOA!
WUMP
EEP
EEP
!!
KREEN

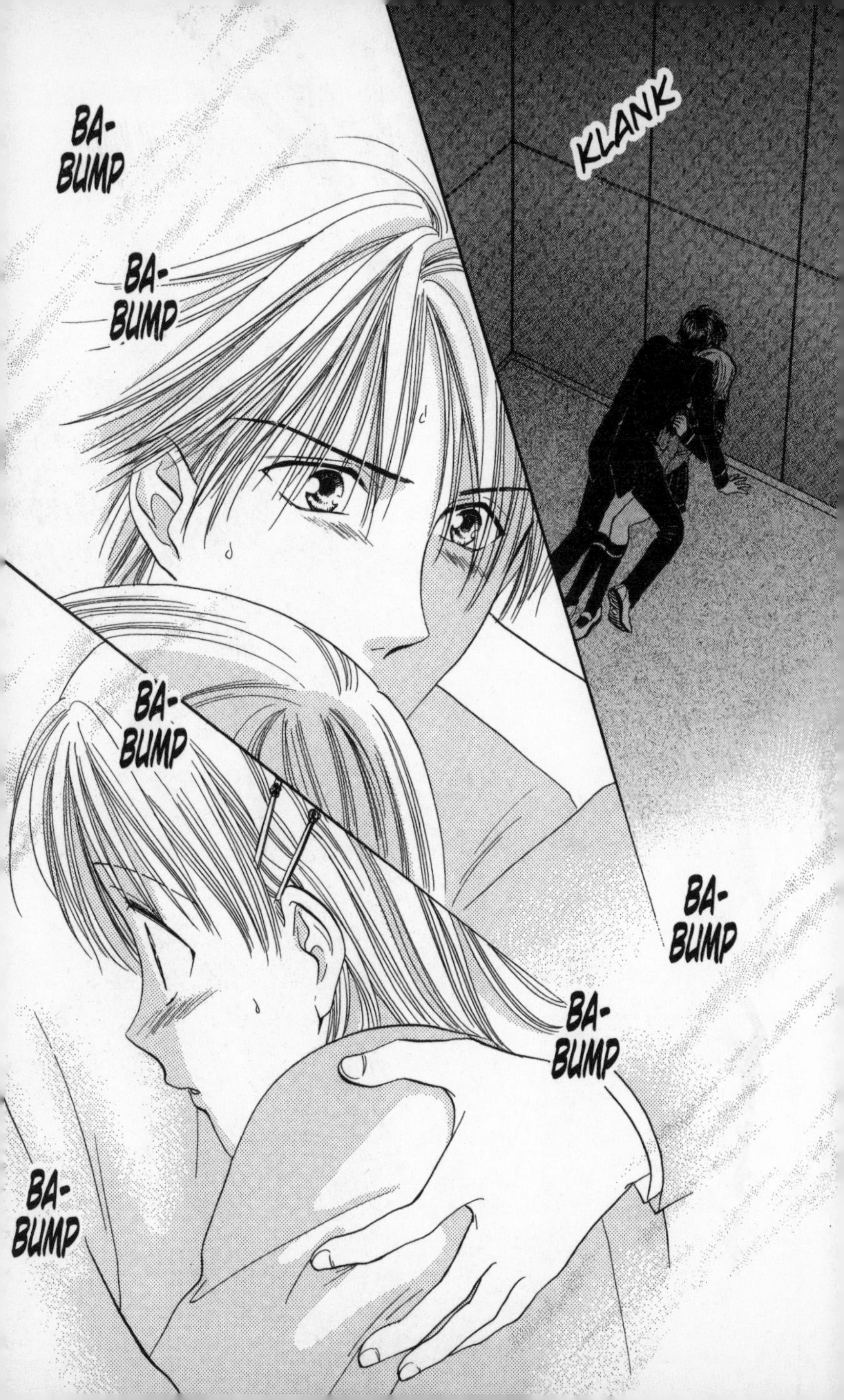
KLANK
BA-BUMP
BA-BUMP
BA-BUMP
BA-BUMP
BA-BUMP
BA-BUMP

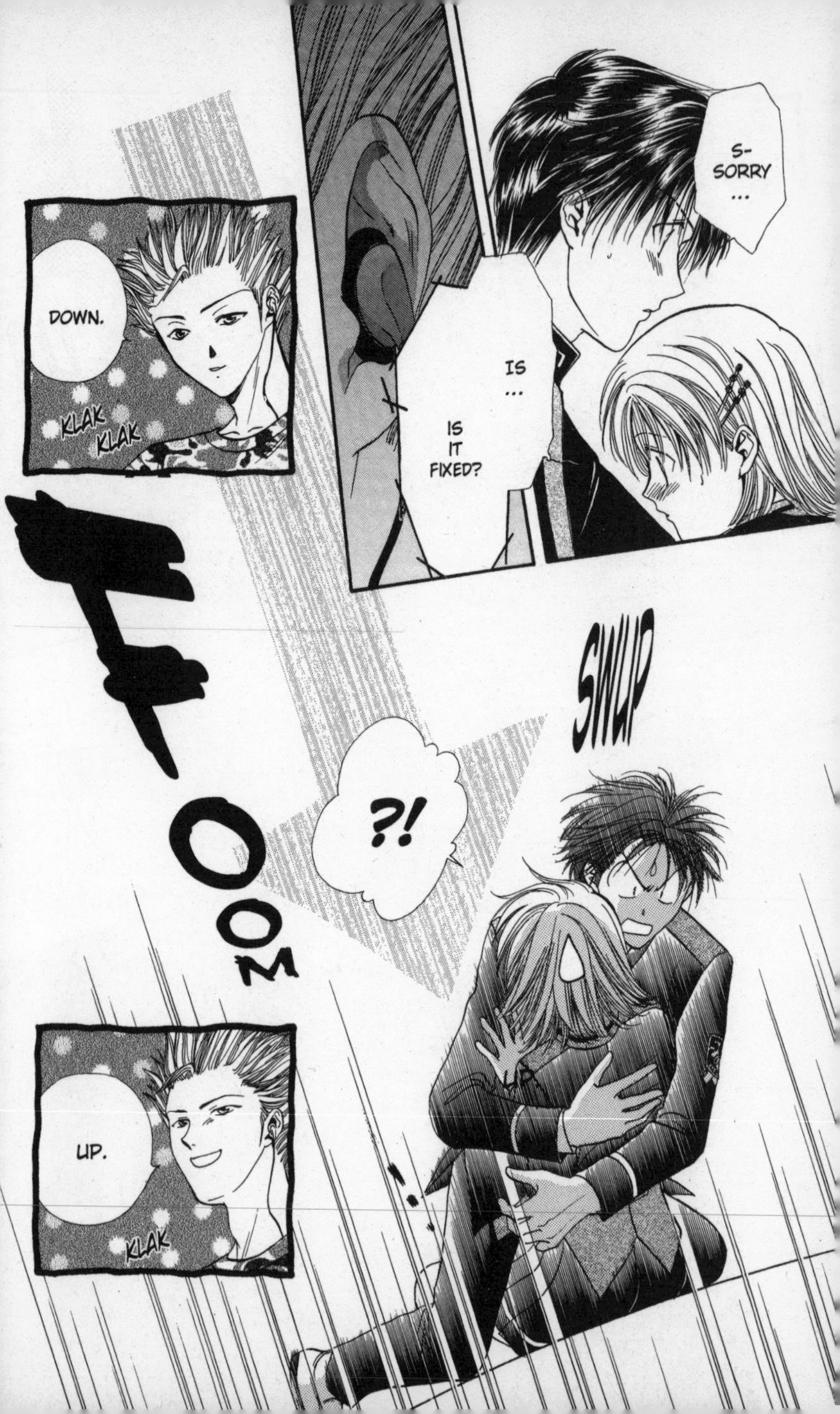

S-SORRY...
IS... IS IT FIXED?
DOWN.
KLAK KLAK
FOOM
SWUP
?!
UP.
KLAK

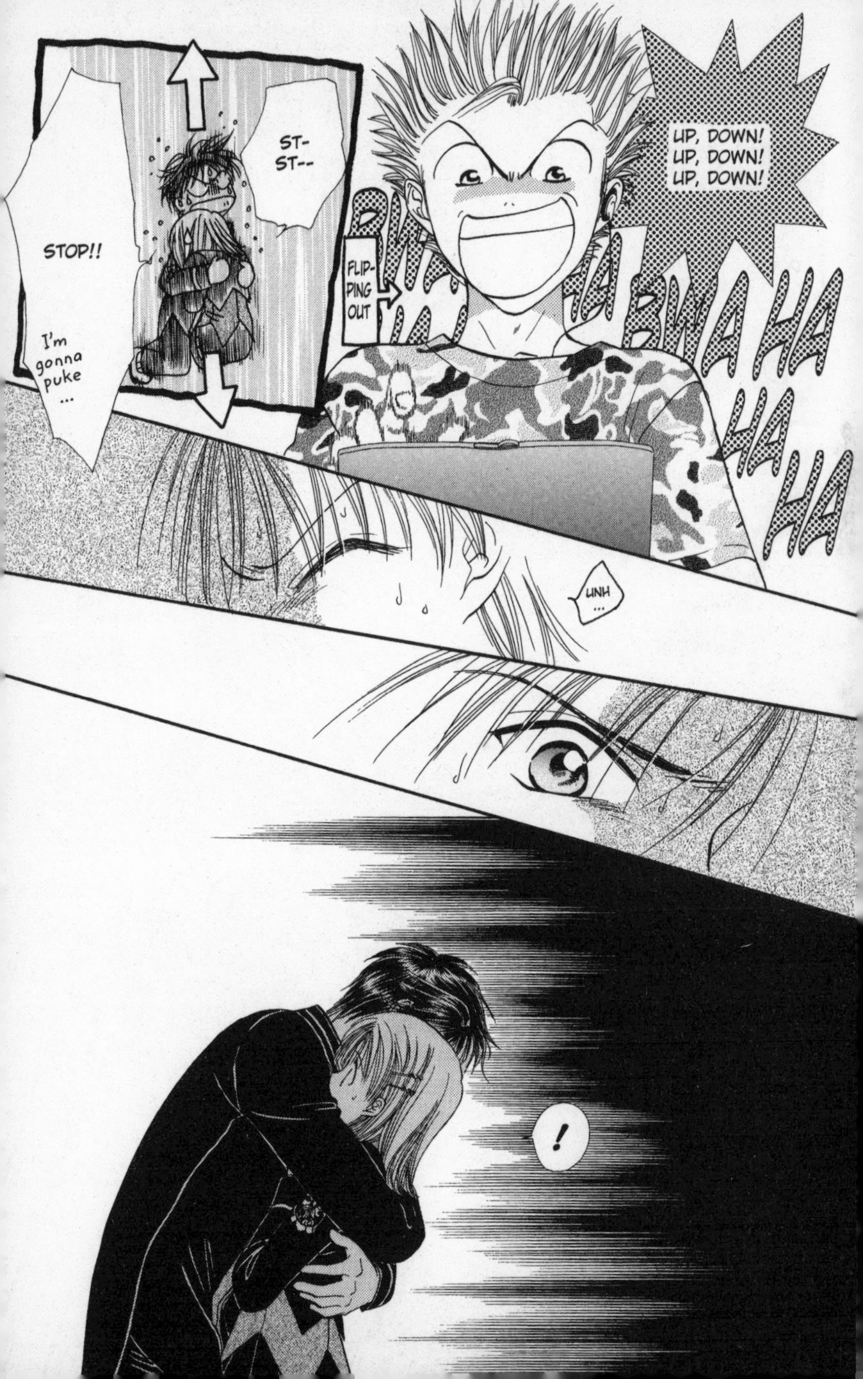
UP, DOWN!
UP, DOWN!
UP, DOWN!
BWA HA HA HA HA
FLIP-PING OUT
ST-
ST--
STOP!!
I'm gonna puke ...
UNH ...
!

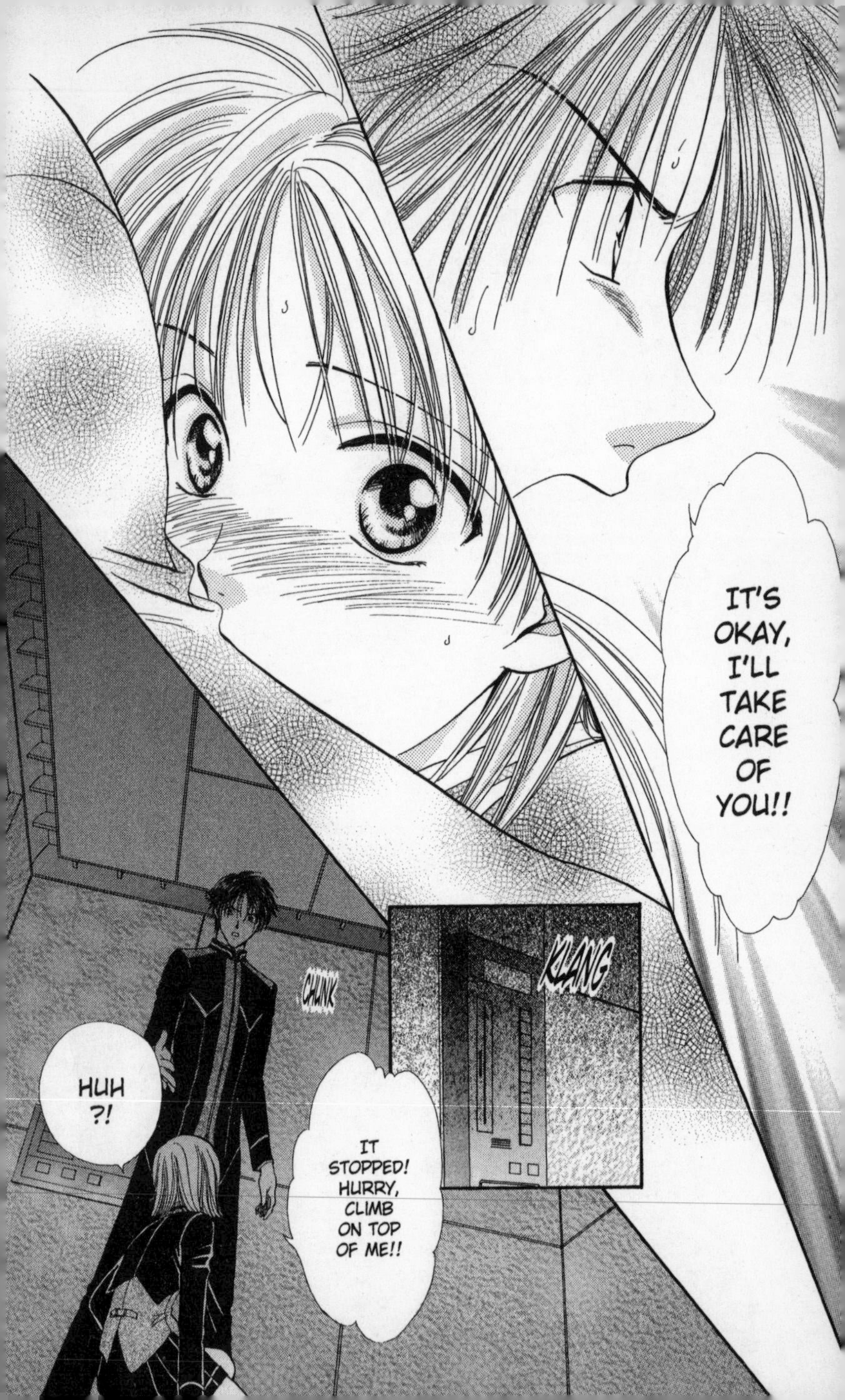
IT'S OKAY, I'LL TAKE CARE OF YOU!!
KLANG
CHUNK
IT STOPPED! HURRY, CLIMB ON TOP OF ME!!
HUH ?!

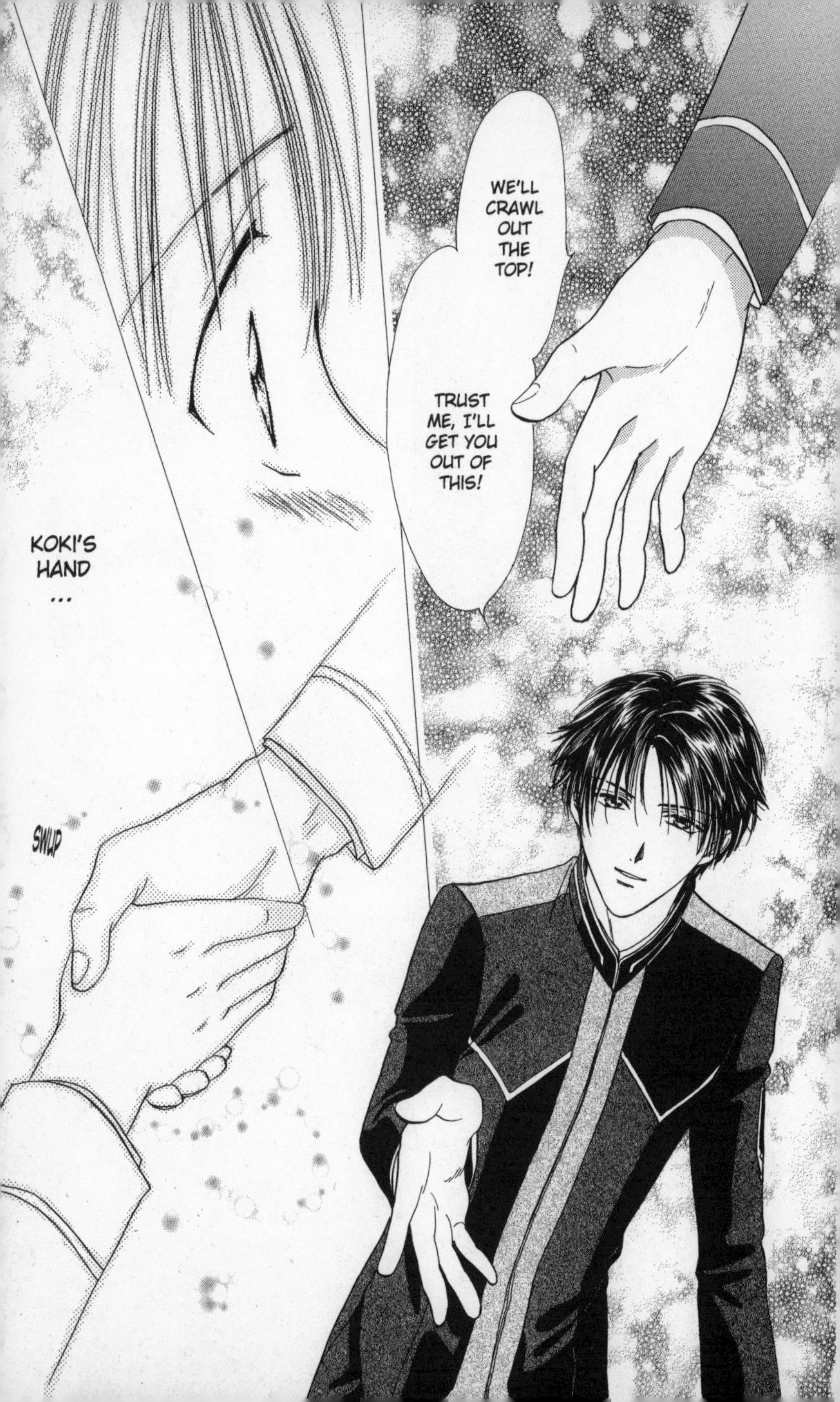
WE'LL CRAWL OUT THE TOP!
TRUST ME, I'LL GET YOU OUT OF THIS!
KOKI'S HAND ...
SWUP

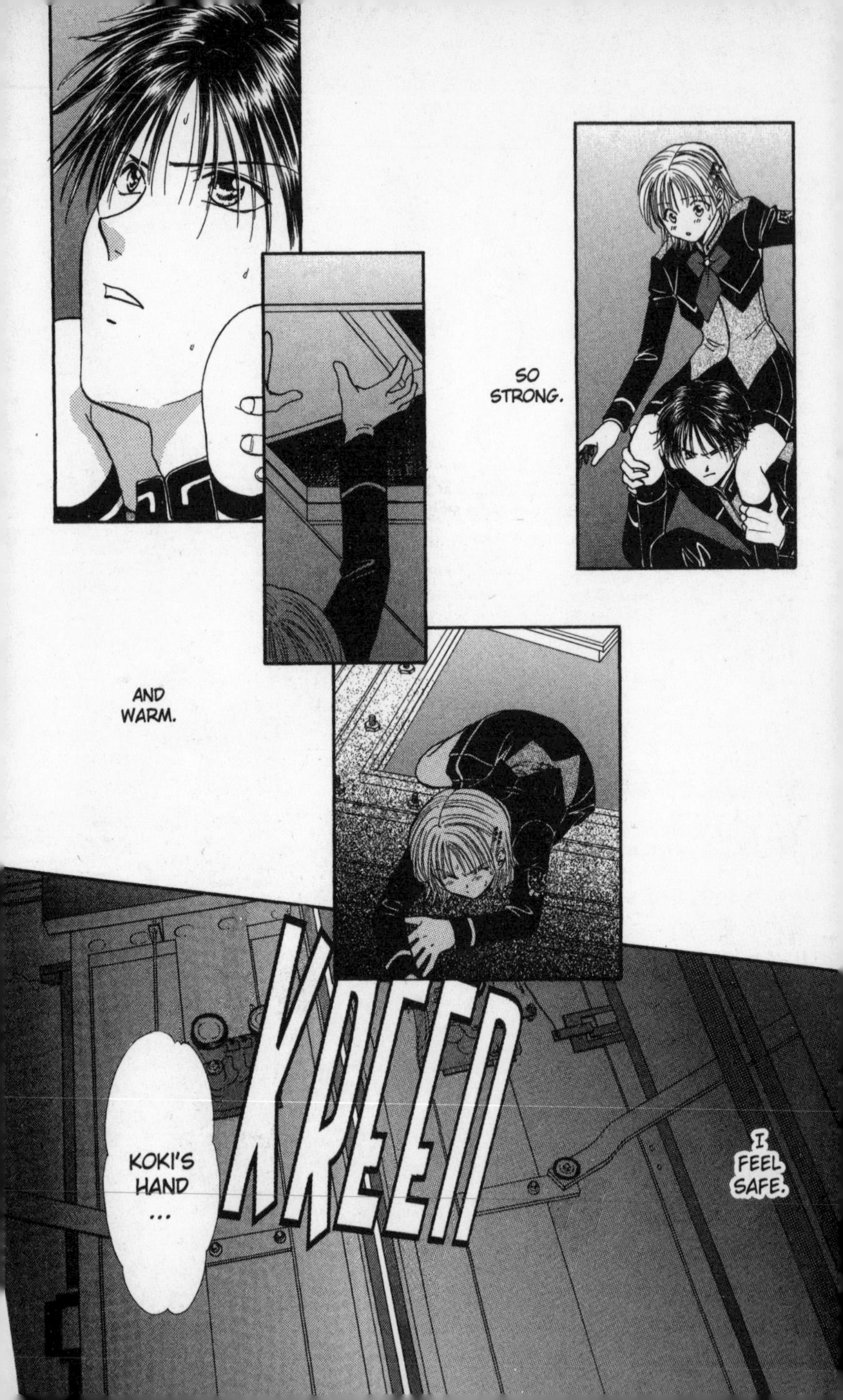
SO STRONG.
AND WARM.
I FEEL SAFE.
KREEN
KOKI'S HAND ...

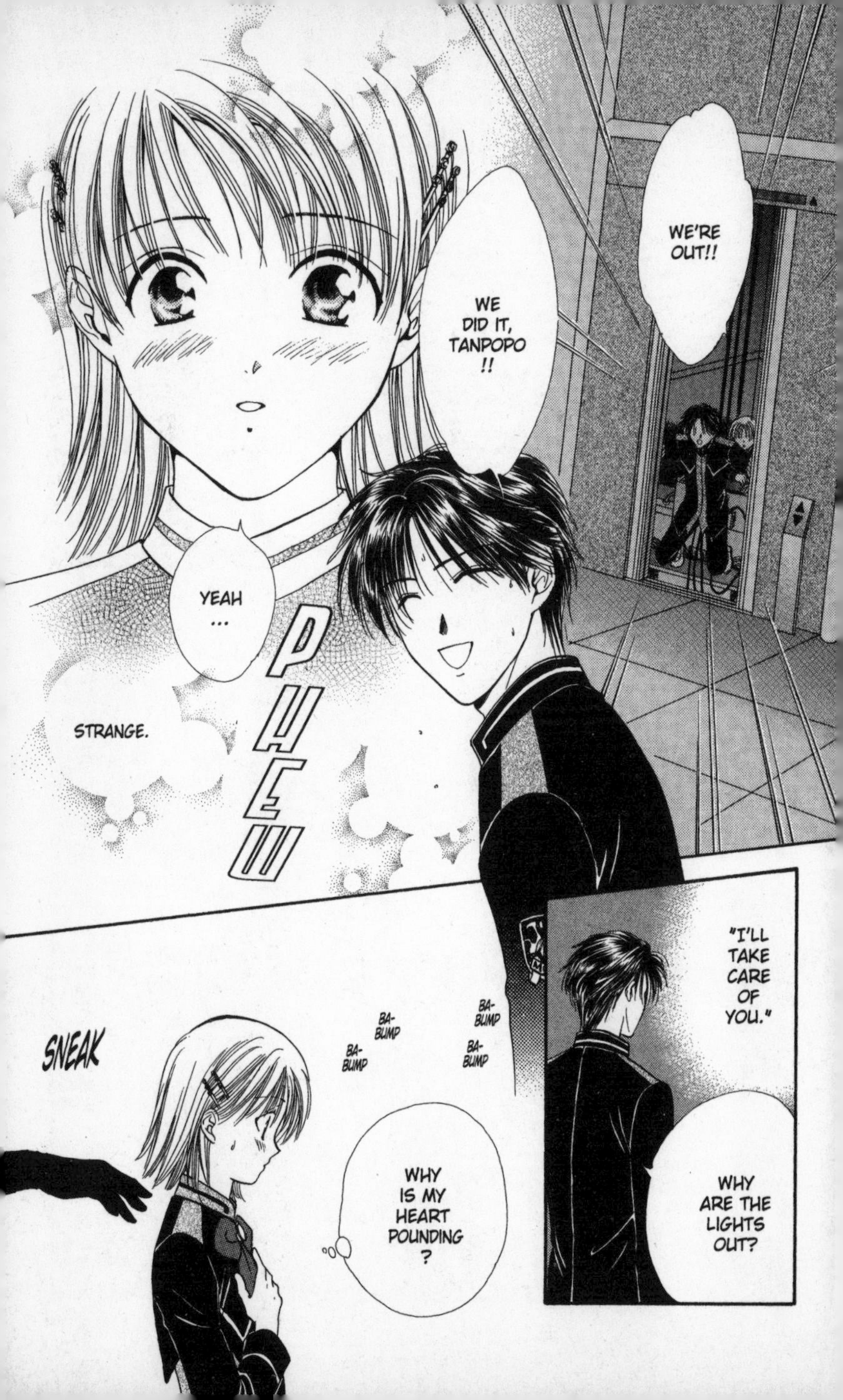
WE'RE OUT!!
WE DID IT, TANPOPO!!
YEAH...
PHEW
STRANGE.
"I'LL TAKE CARE OF YOU."
WHY ARE THE LIGHTS OUT?
BA-BUMP
BA-BUMP
BA-BUMP
BA-BUMP
WHY IS MY HEART POUNDING?
SNEAK

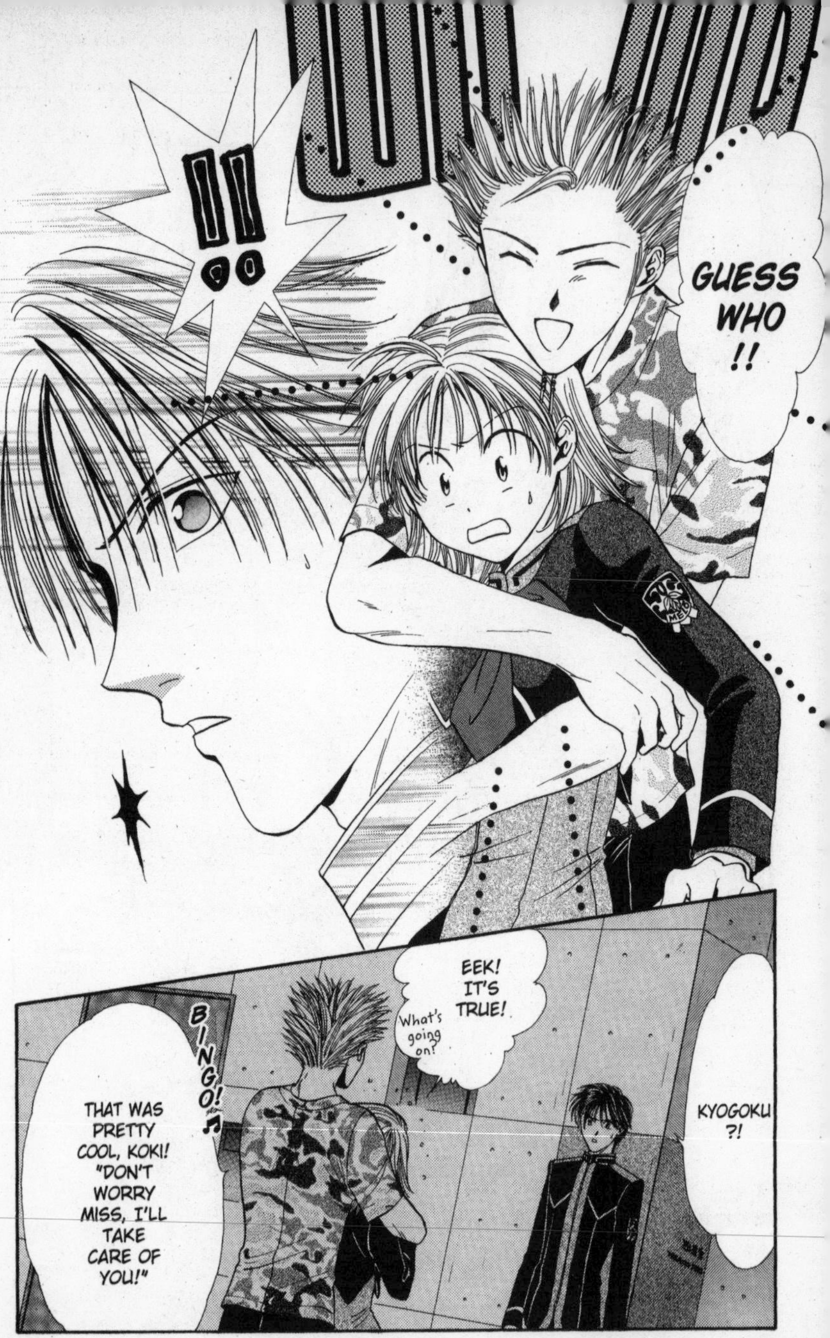
GUESS WHO !!
KYOGOKU ?!
EEK! IT'S TRUE!
What's going on?
BINGO! ♫
THAT WAS PRETTY COOL, KOKI! "DON'T WORRY MISS, I'LL TAKE CARE OF YOU!"

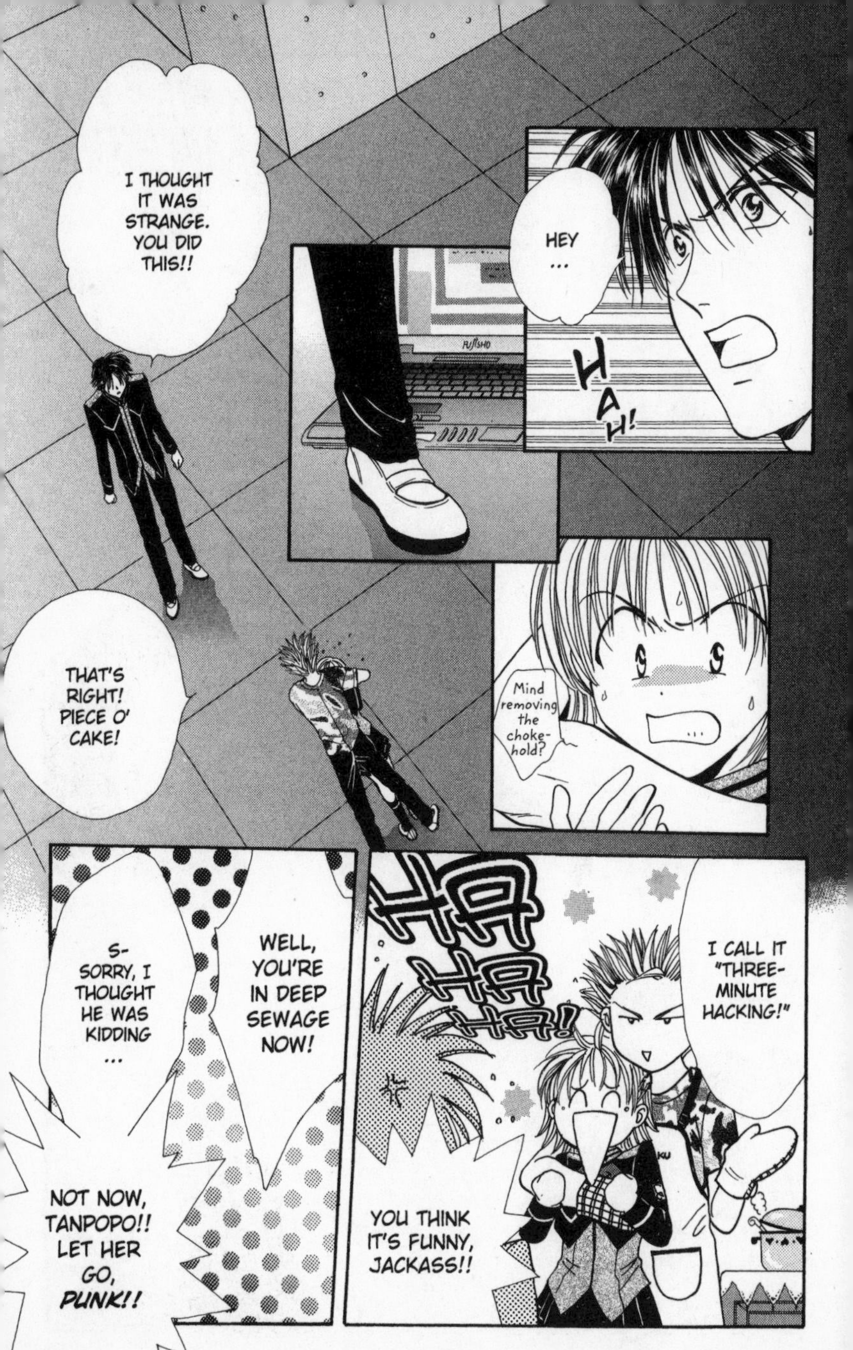
HEY ...
HAH!
I THOUGHT IT WAS STRANGE. YOU DID THIS!!
FUJISHO
Mind removing the choke-hold?
...
THAT'S RIGHT! PIECE O' CAKE!
I CALL IT "THREE-MINUTE HACKING!"
HA HA HA!
YOU THINK IT'S FUNNY, JACKASS!!
WELL, YOU'RE IN DEEP SEWAGE NOW!
S-SORRY, I THOUGHT HE WAS KIDDING ...
NOT NOW, TANPOPO!! LET HER GO, **PUNK!!**

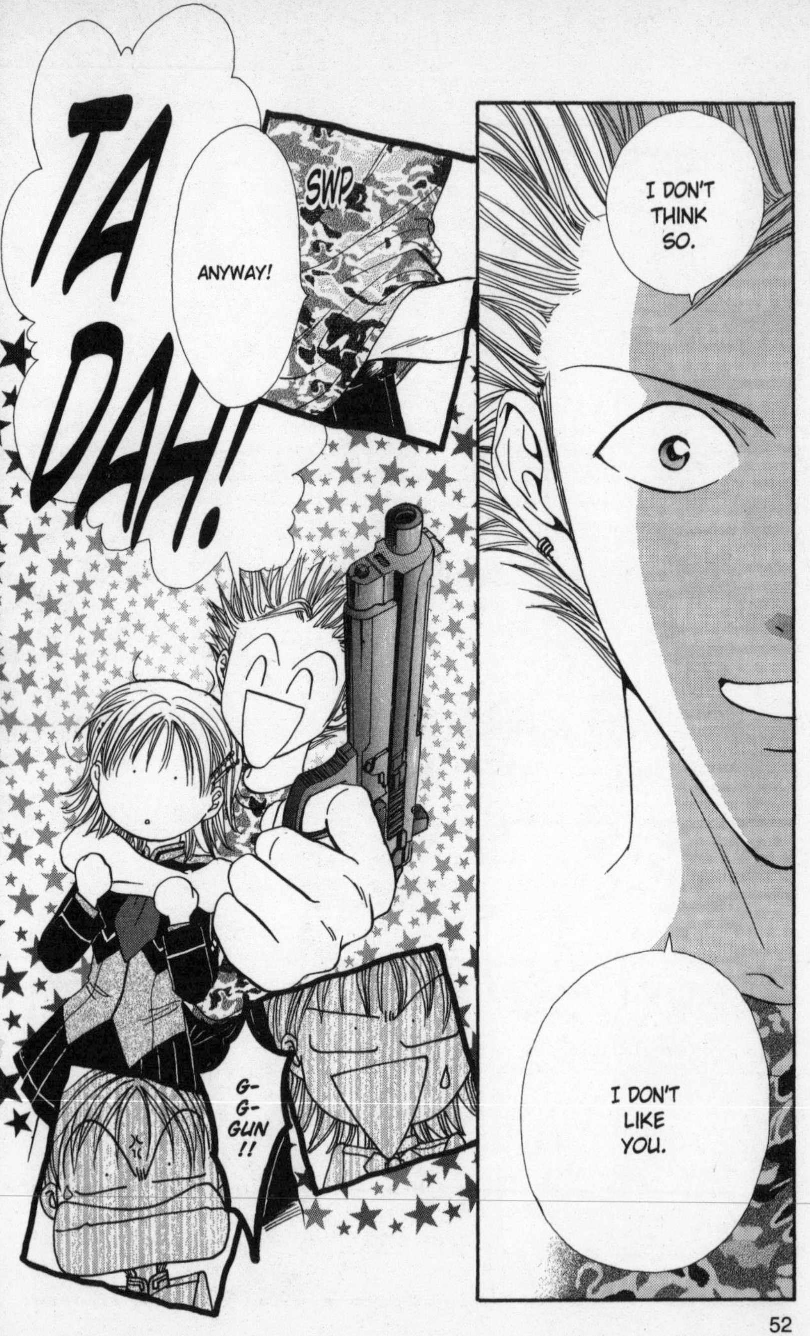
I DON'T THINK SO.
I DON'T LIKE YOU.
SWP
ANYWAY!
TA DAH!
G-G-GUN!!

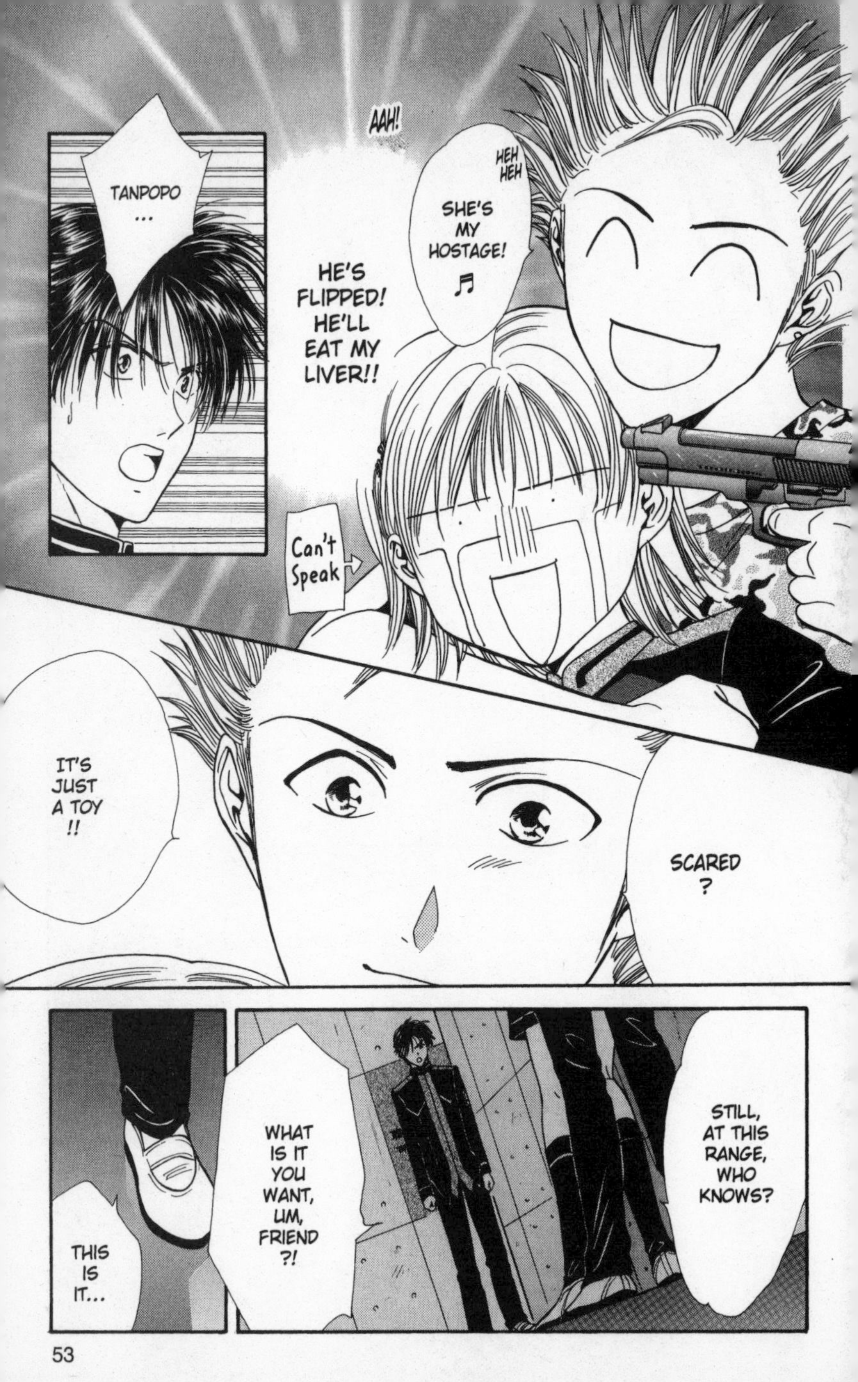
AAH!
HEH HEH
SHE'S MY HOSTAGE! ♬
HE'S FLIPPED! HE'LL EAT MY LIVER!!
Can't Speak
TANPOPO ...
SCARED ?
IT'S JUST A TOY !!
STILL, AT THIS RANGE, WHO KNOWS?
WHAT IS IT YOU WANT, UM, FRIEND ?!
THIS IS IT...

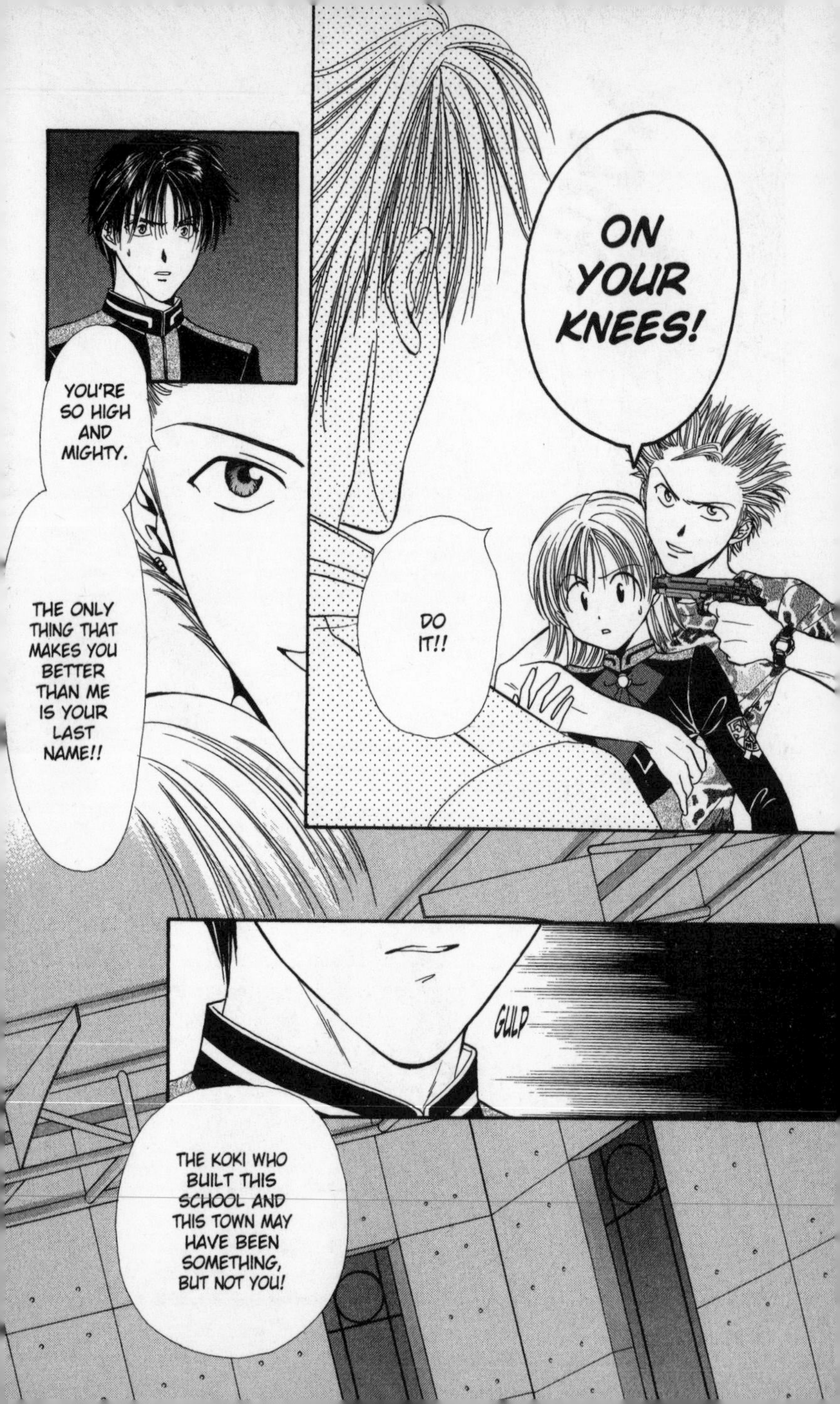

ON YOUR KNEES!
DO IT!!
YOU'RE SO HIGH AND MIGHTY.
THE ONLY THING THAT MAKES YOU BETTER THAN ME IS YOUR LAST NAME!!
GULP
THE KOKI WHO BUILT THIS SCHOOL AND THIS TOWN MAY HAVE BEEN SOMETHING, BUT NOT YOU!

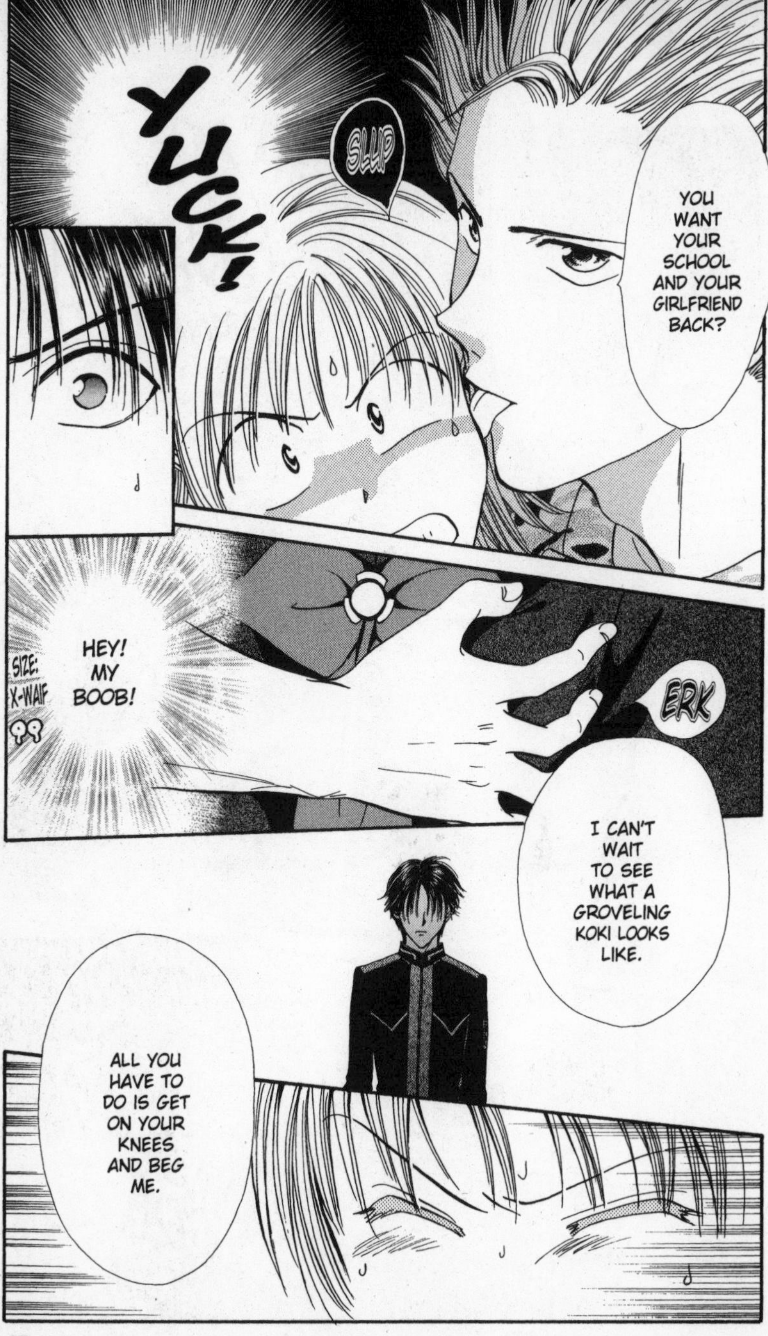
YOU WANT YOUR SCHOOL AND YOUR GIRLFRIEND BACK?
SLUP
YUCK!
ERK
HEY! MY BOOB!
SIZE: X-WAIF
I CAN'T WAIT TO SEE WHAT A GROVELING KOKI LOOKS LIKE.
ALL YOU HAVE TO DO IS GET ON YOUR KNEES AND BEG ME.

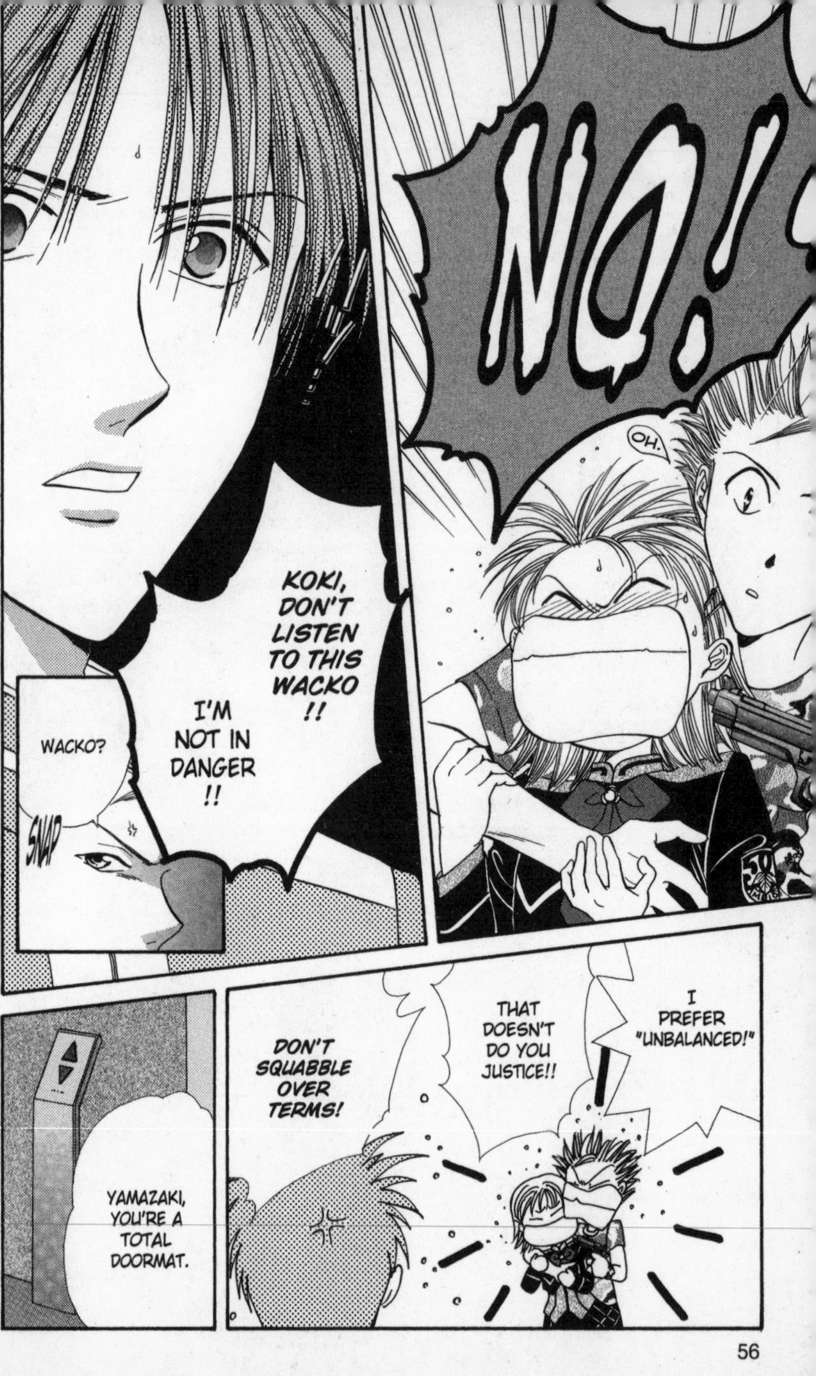
NO!!
OH.
KOKI, DON'T LISTEN TO THIS WACKO!!
I'M NOT IN DANGER!!
WACKO?
SNAP
I PREFER "UNBALANCED!"
THAT DOESN'T DO YOU JUSTICE!!
DON'T SQUABBLE OVER TERMS!
YAMAZAKI, YOU'RE A TOTAL DOORMAT.

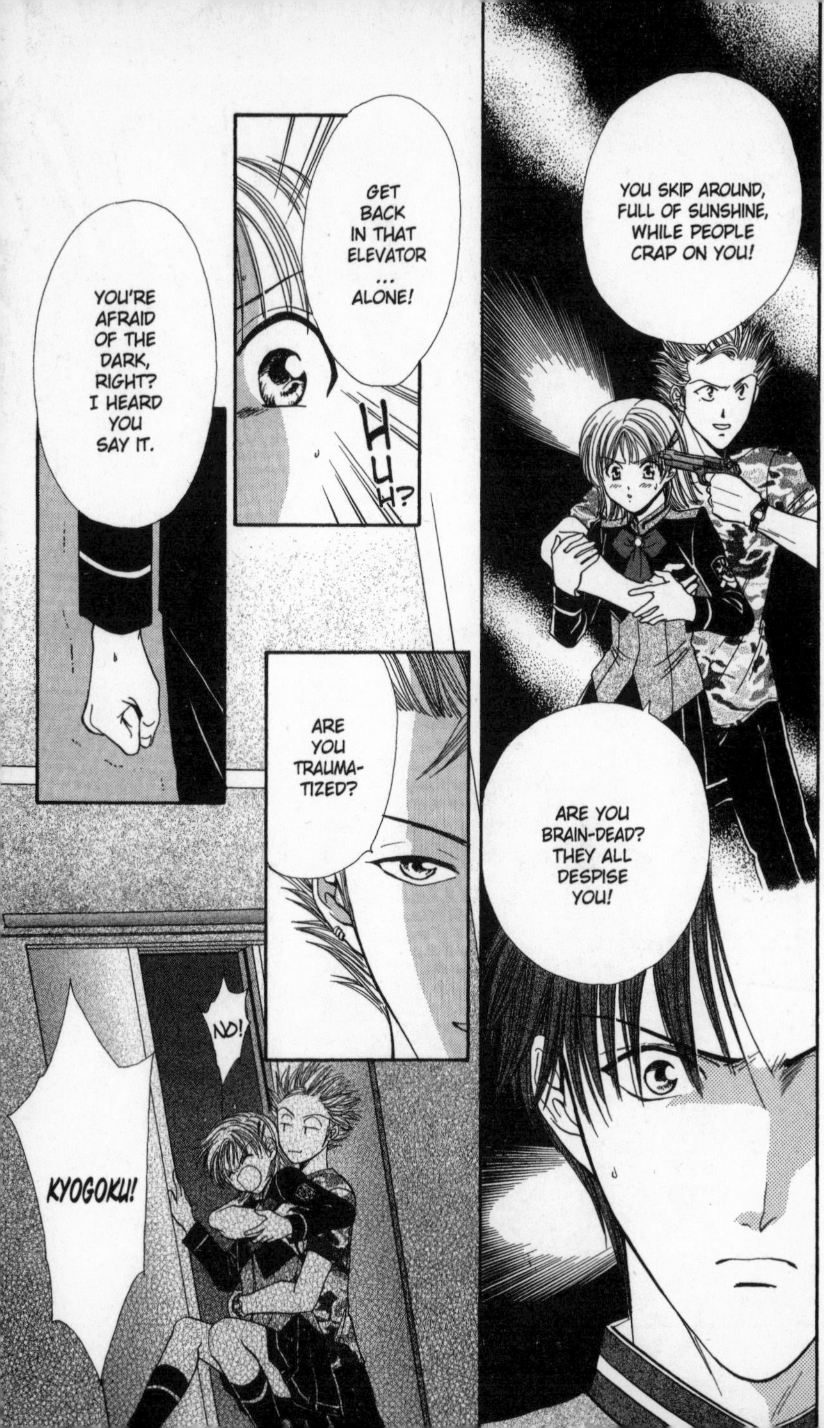
YOU SKIP AROUND, FULL OF SUNSHINE, WHILE PEOPLE CRAP ON YOU!
ARE YOU BRAIN-DEAD? THEY ALL DESPISE YOU!
GET BACK IN THAT ELEVATOR ... ALONE!
HUH?
YOU'RE AFRAID OF THE DARK, RIGHT? I HEARD YOU SAY IT.
ARE YOU TRAUMA-TIZED?
NO!
KYOGOKU!

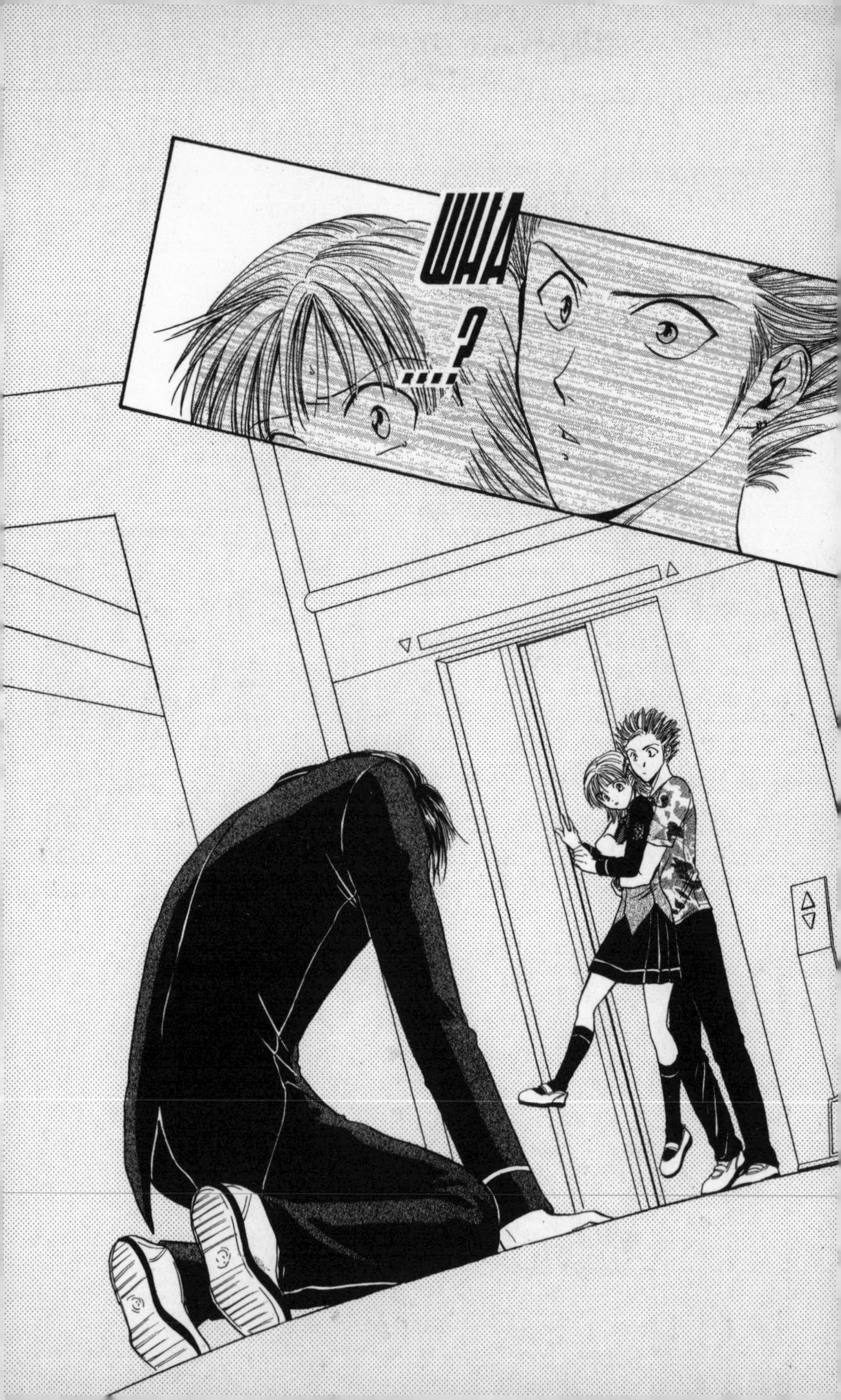
WHA
...?

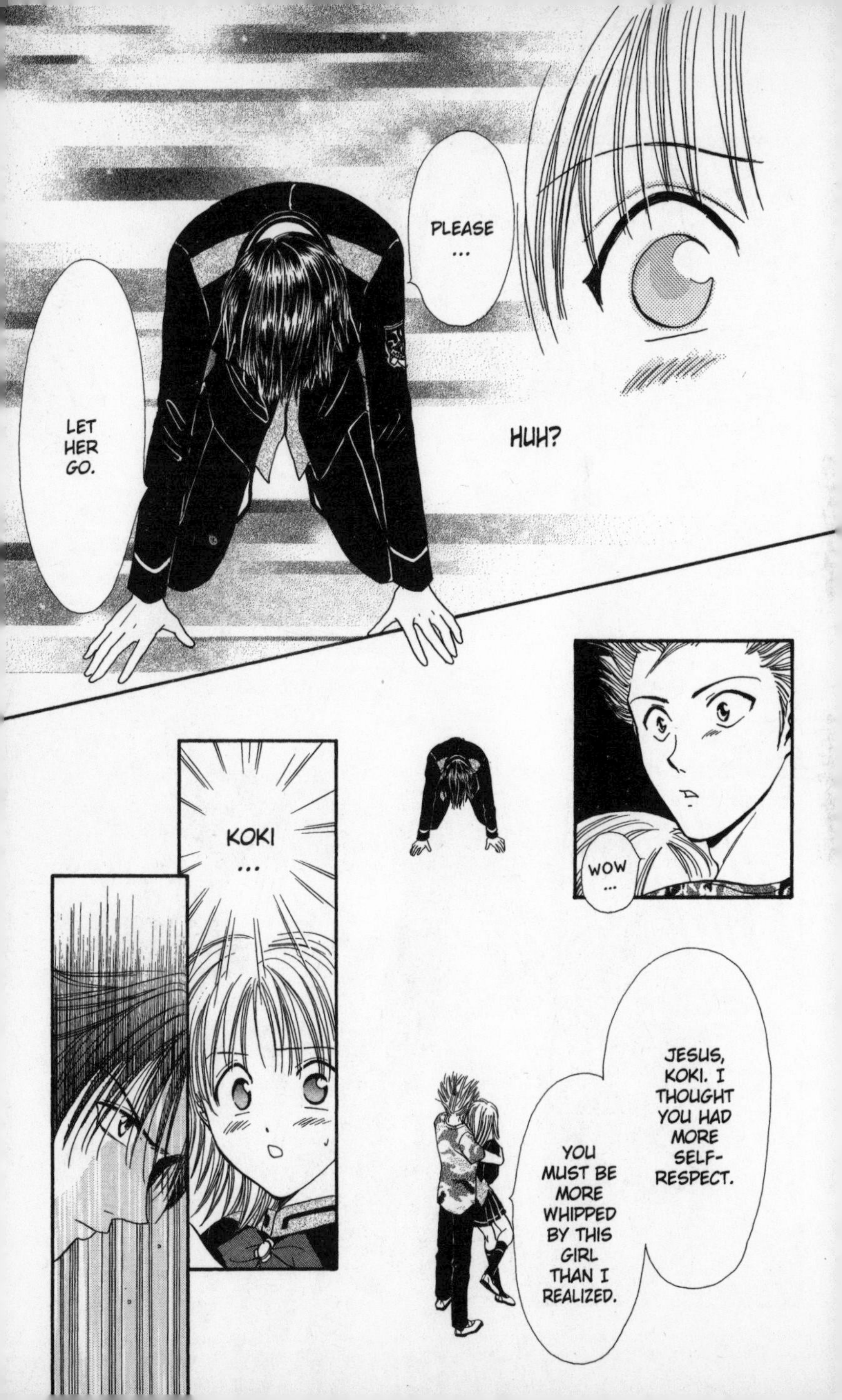
PLEASE ...
HUH?
LET HER GO.
WOW ...
KOKI ...
JESUS, KOKI. I THOUGHT YOU HAD MORE SELF-RESPECT.
YOU MUST BE MORE WHIPPED BY THIS GIRL THAN I REALIZED.

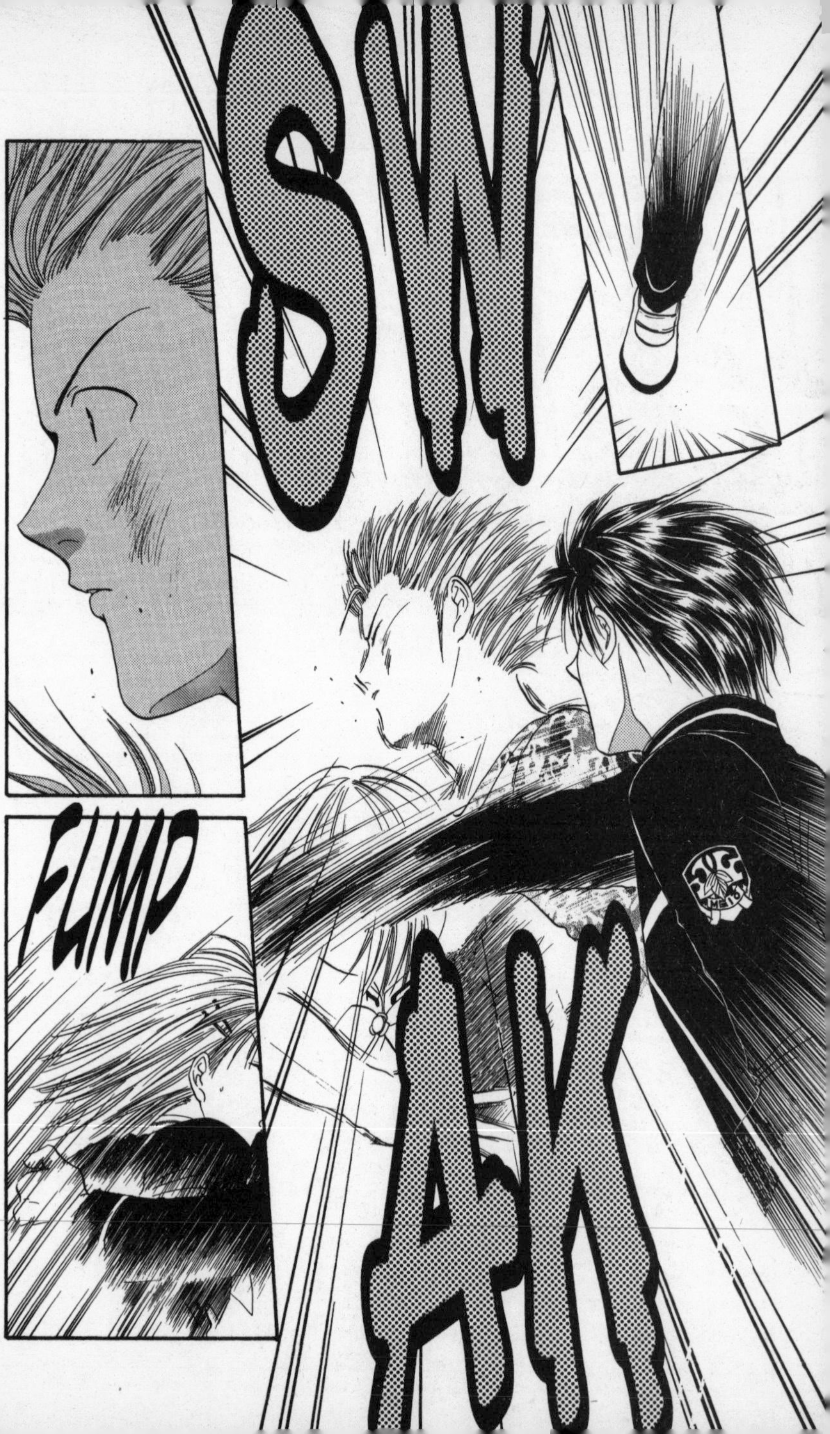
SW
ACK
FLUMP

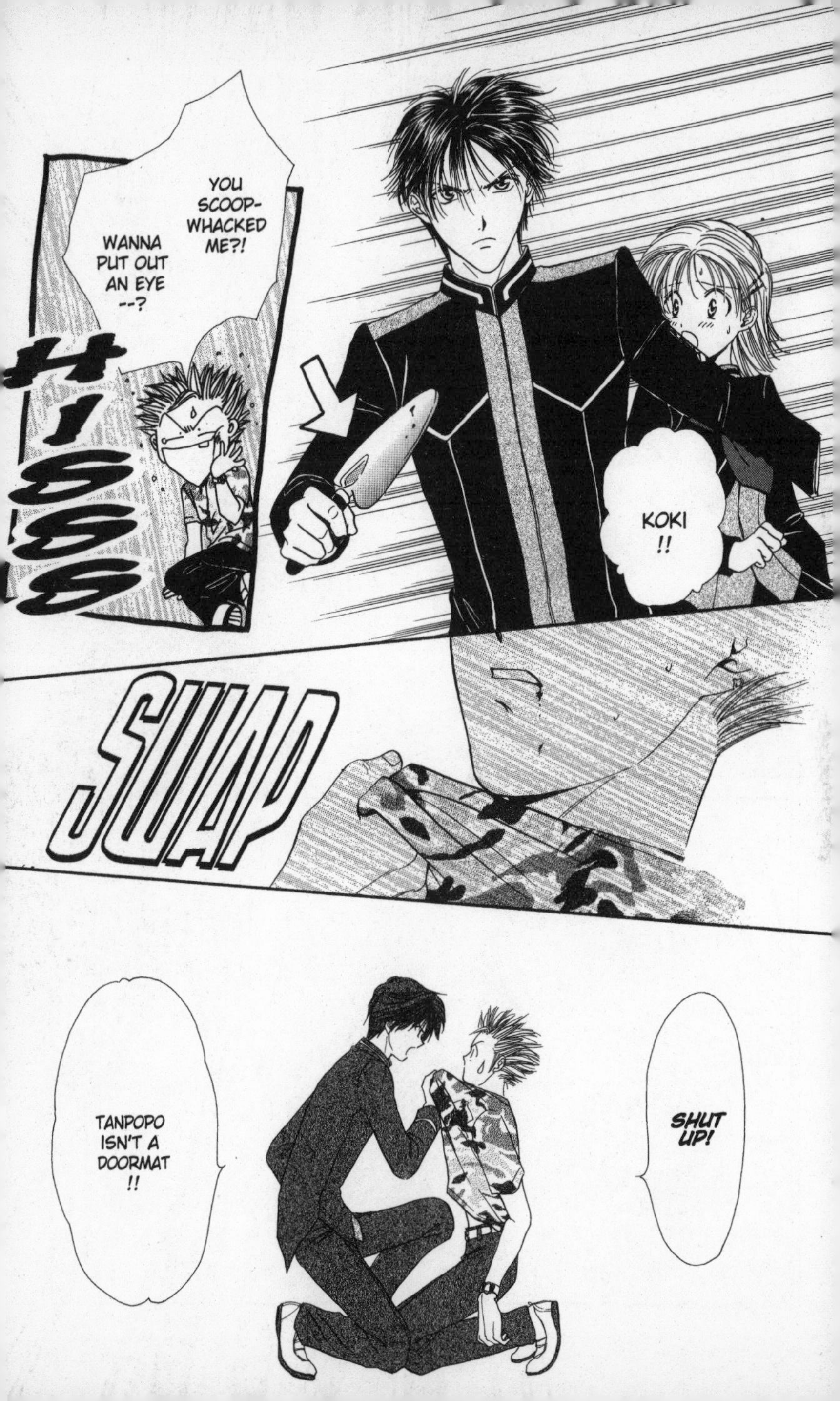
KOKI !!
YOU SCOOP-WHACKED ME?!
WANNA PUT OUT AN EYE --?
HISSSS
SWAP
SHUT UP!
TANPOPO ISN'T A DOORMAT !!

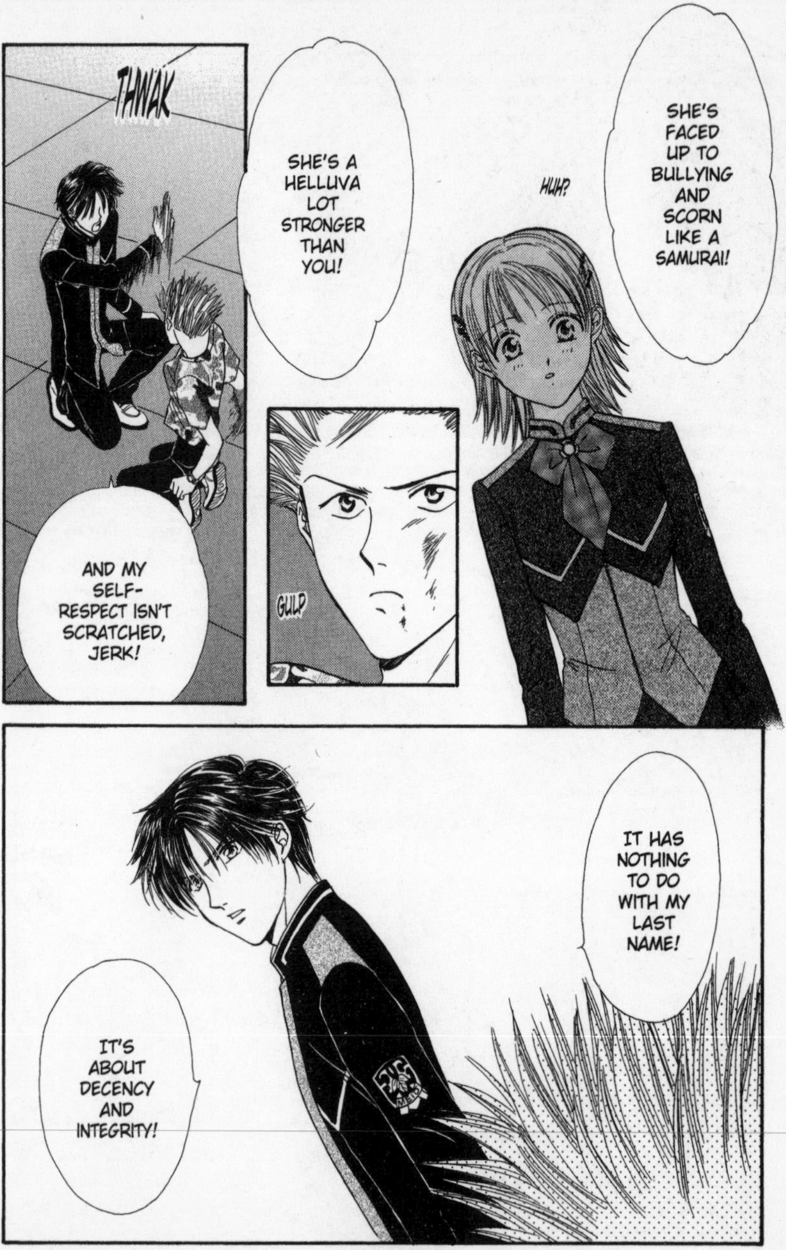
SHE'S FACED UP TO BULLYING AND SCORN LIKE A SAMURAI!
HUH?
SHE'S A HELLUVA LOT STRONGER THAN YOU!
GULP
THWAK
AND MY SELF-RESPECT ISN'T SCRATCHED, JERK!
IT HAS NOTHING TO DO WITH MY LAST NAME!
IT'S ABOUT DECENCY AND INTEGRITY!

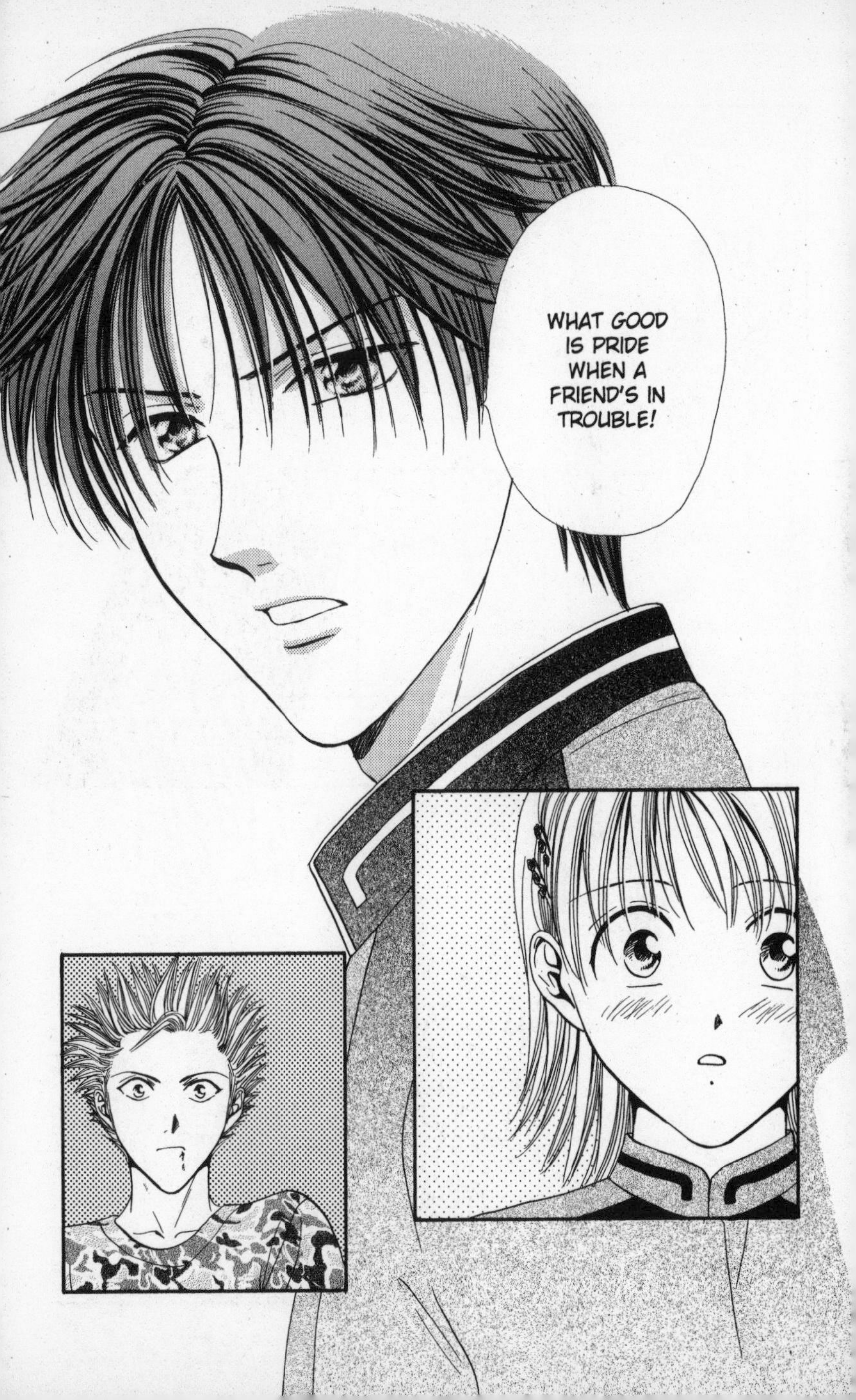
WHAT GOOD IS PRIDE WHEN A FRIEND'S IN TROUBLE!

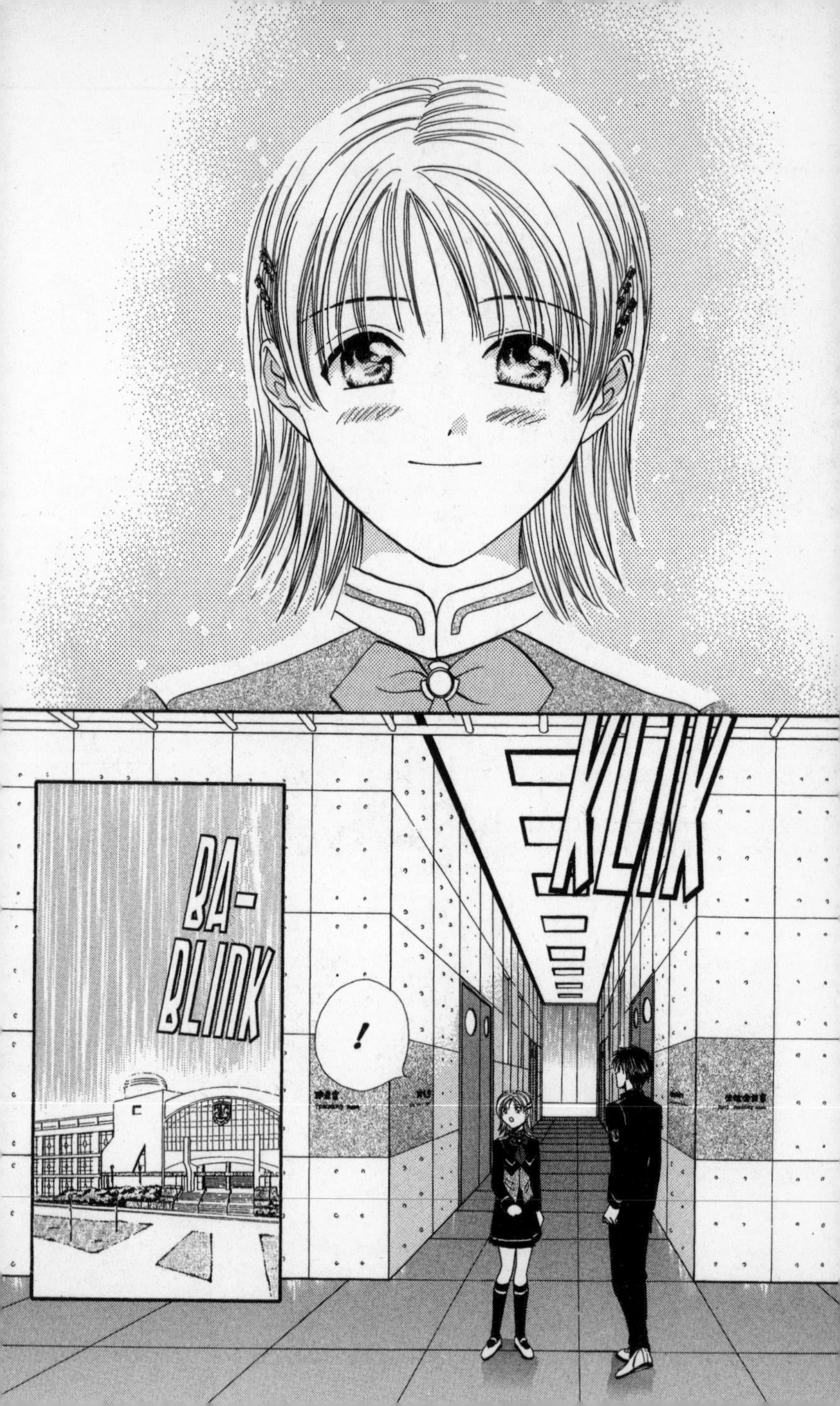
KLIK
!
BA-BLINK

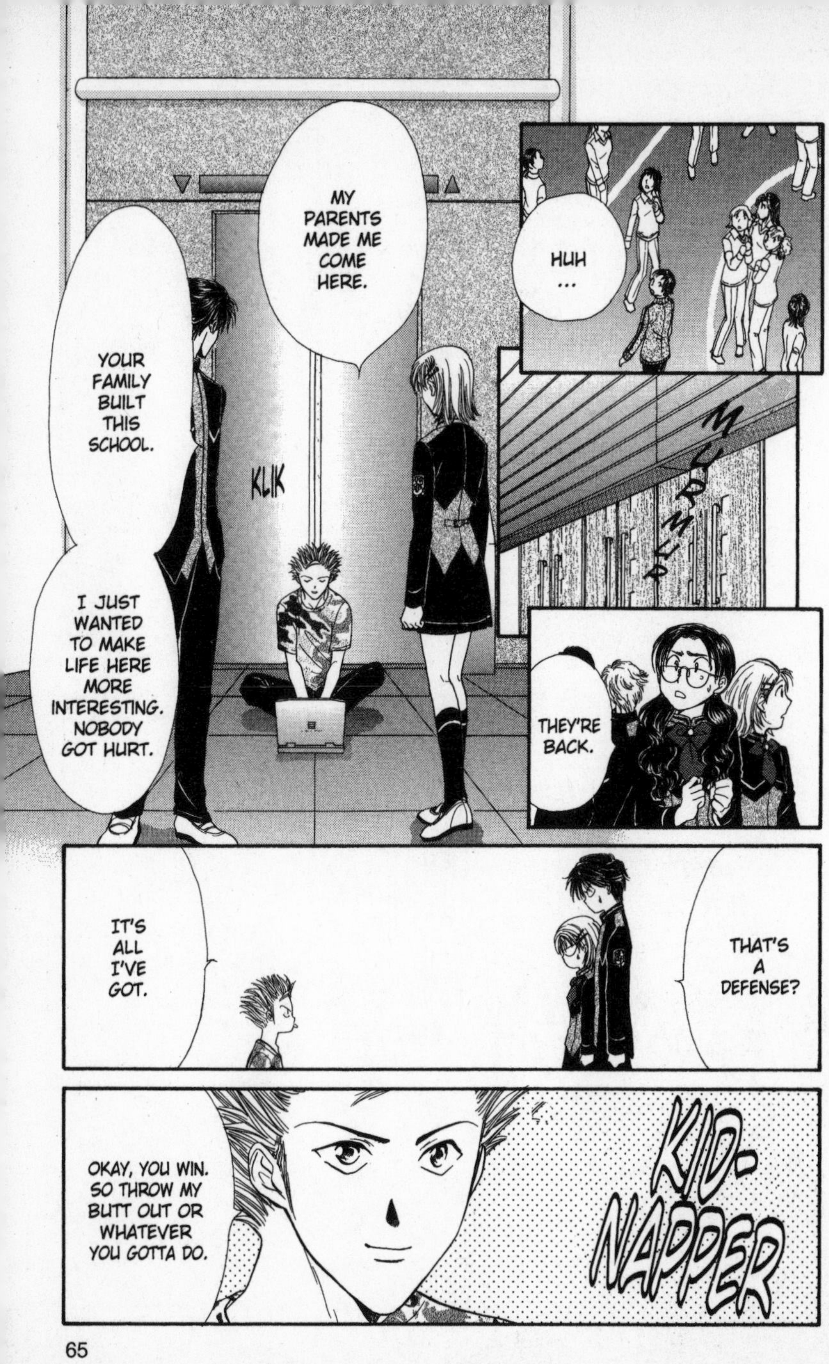
HUH ...
MURMUR MURMUR
THEY'RE BACK.
MY PARENTS MADE ME COME HERE.
KLIK
YOUR FAMILY BUILT THIS SCHOOL.
I JUST WANTED TO MAKE LIFE HERE MORE INTERESTING. NOBODY GOT HURT.
THAT'S A DEFENSE?
IT'S ALL I'VE GOT.
KID-NAPPER
OKAY, YOU WIN. SO THROW MY BUTT OUT OR WHATEVER YOU GOTTA DO.

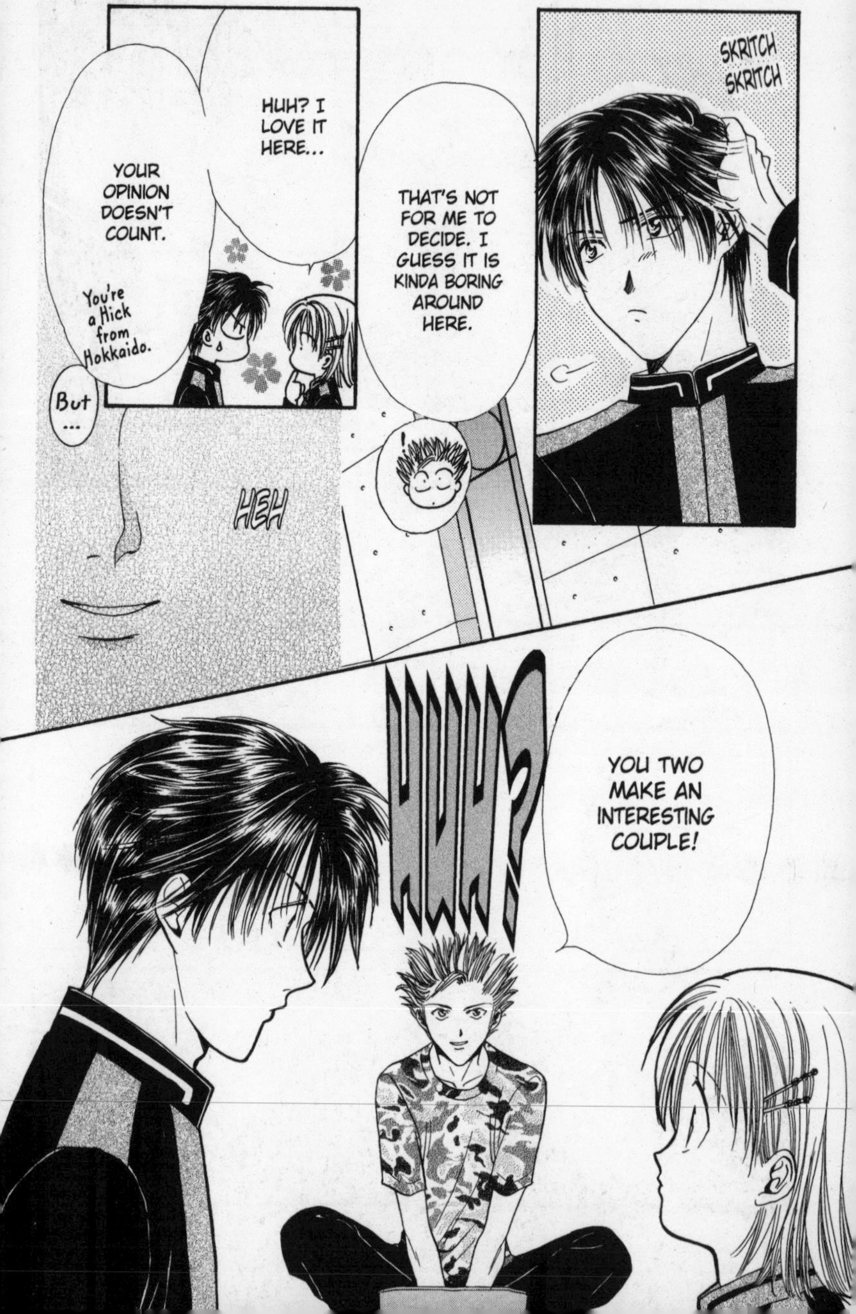
SKRITCH
SKRITCH
THAT'S NOT FOR ME TO DECIDE. I GUESS IT IS KINDA BORING AROUND HERE.
HUH? I LOVE IT HERE...
YOUR OPINION DOESN'T COUNT.
You're a Hick from Hokkaido.
But ...
HEH
YOU TWO MAKE AN INTERESTING COUPLE!
HUH?!

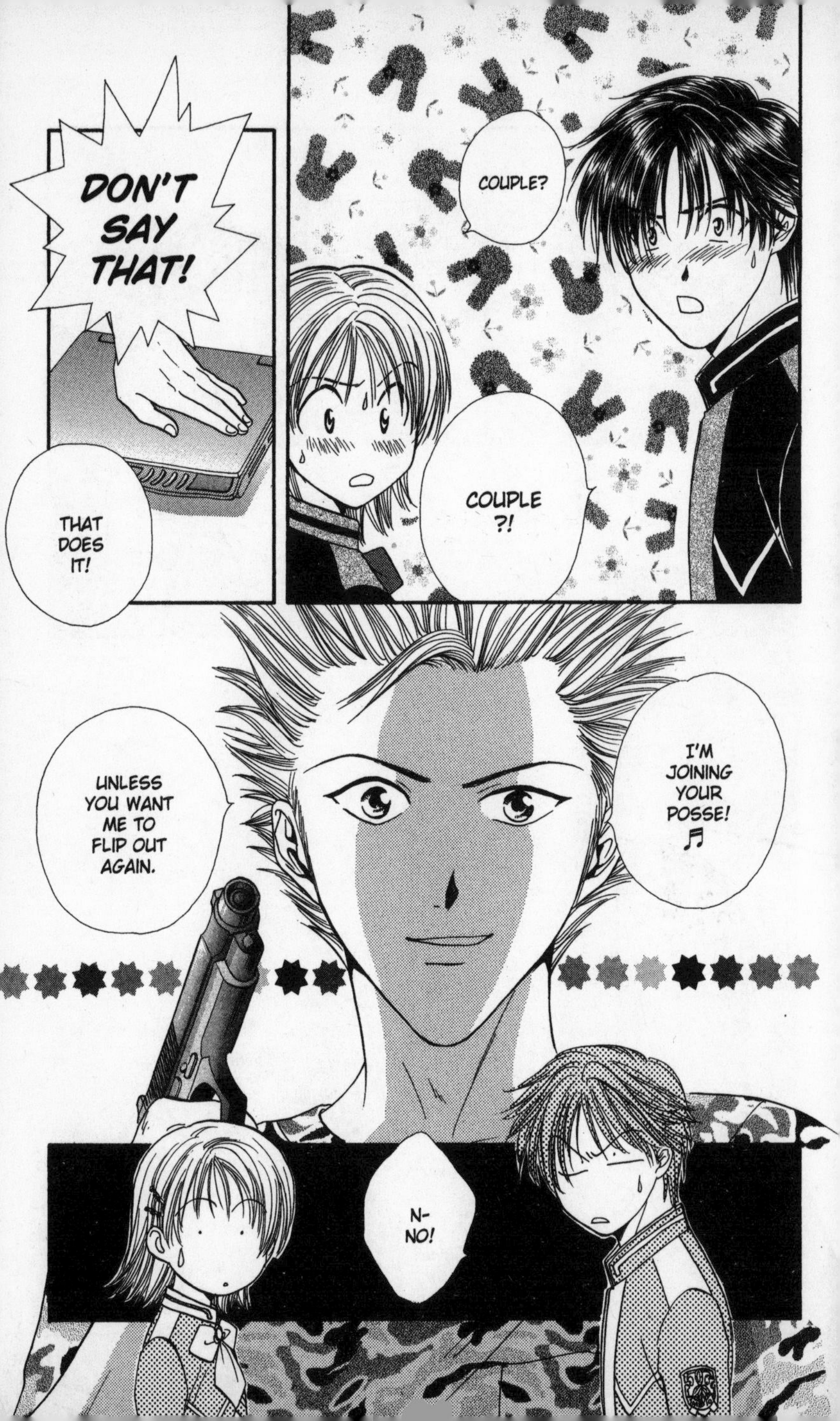
COUPLE?
COUPLE?!
DON'T SAY THAT!
THAT DOES IT!
I'M JOINING YOUR POSSE! ♬
UNLESS YOU WANT ME TO FLIP OUT AGAIN.
N-NO!

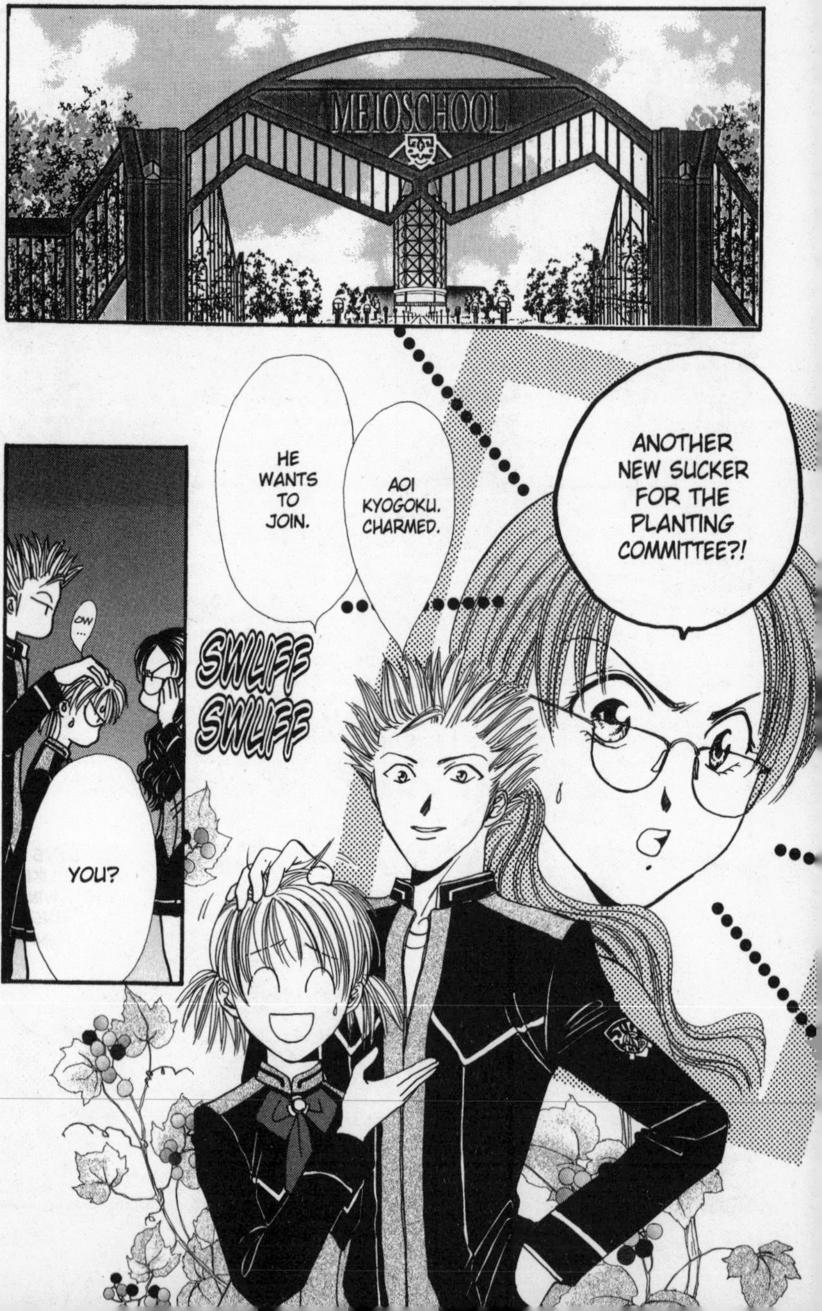
MEIOSCHOOL
ANOTHER NEW SUCKER FOR THE PLANTING COMMITTEE?!
AOI KYOGOKU. CHARMED.
HE WANTS TO JOIN.
SWUFF SWUFF
OW ...
YOU?

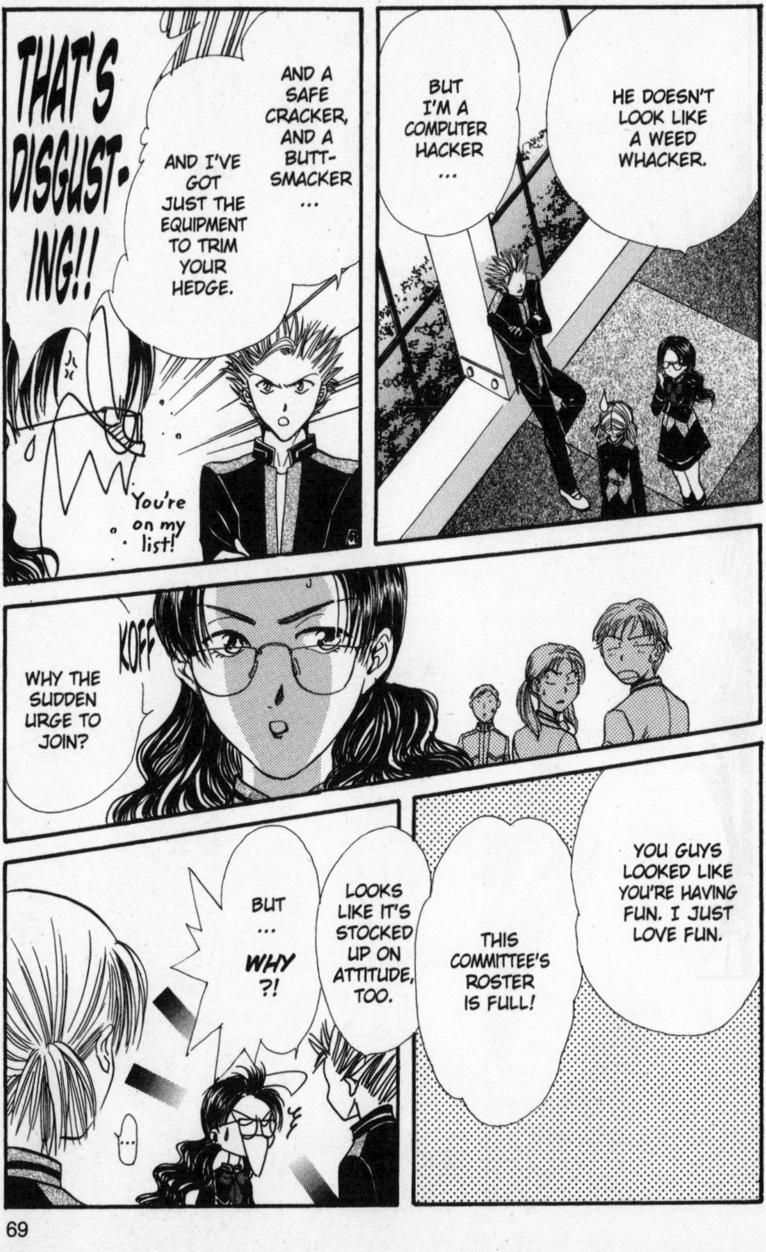
HE DOESN'T LOOK LIKE A WEED WHACKER.
BUT I'M A COMPUTER HACKER ...
AND A SAFE CRACKER, AND A BUTT-SMACKER ...
AND I'VE GOT JUST THE EQUIPMENT TO TRIM YOUR HEDGE.
THAT'S DISGUSTING!!
You're on my list!
KOFF
WHY THE SUDDEN URGE TO JOIN?
YOU GUYS LOOKED LIKE YOU'RE HAVING FUN. I JUST LOVE FUN.
THIS COMMITTEE'S ROSTER IS FULL!
LOOKS LIKE IT'S STOCKED UP ON ATTITUDE, TOO.
BUT ... WHY ?!
...

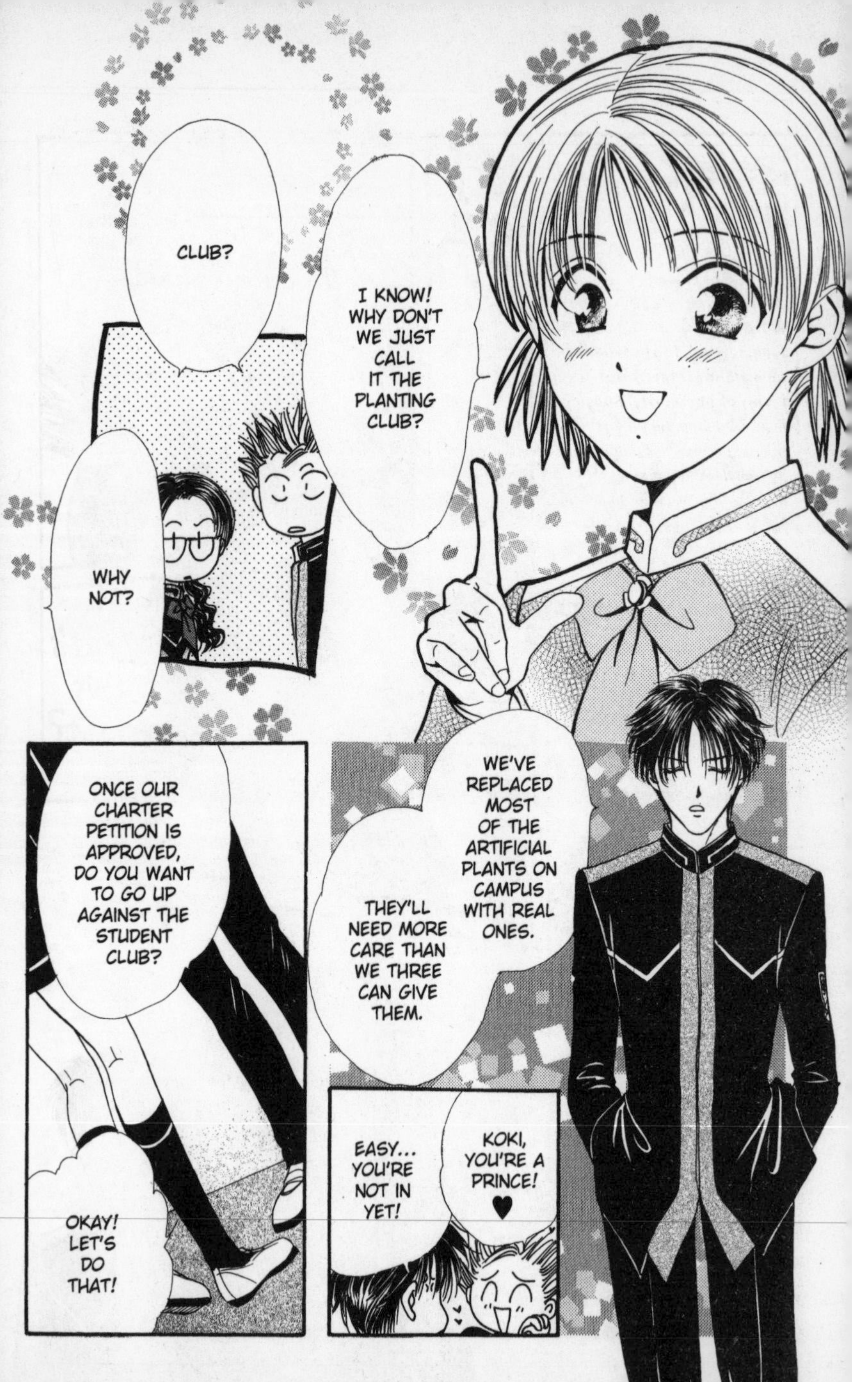
I KNOW! WHY DON'T WE JUST CALL IT THE PLANTING CLUB?
CLUB?
WHY NOT?
WE'VE REPLACED MOST OF THE ARTIFICIAL PLANTS ON CAMPUS WITH REAL ONES.
THEY'LL NEED MORE CARE THAN WE THREE CAN GIVE THEM.
KOKI, YOU'RE A PRINCE! ♥
EASY... YOU'RE NOT IN YET!
ONCE OUR CHARTER PETITION IS APPROVED, DO YOU WANT TO GO UP AGAINST THE STUDENT CLUB?
OKAY! LET'S DO THAT!

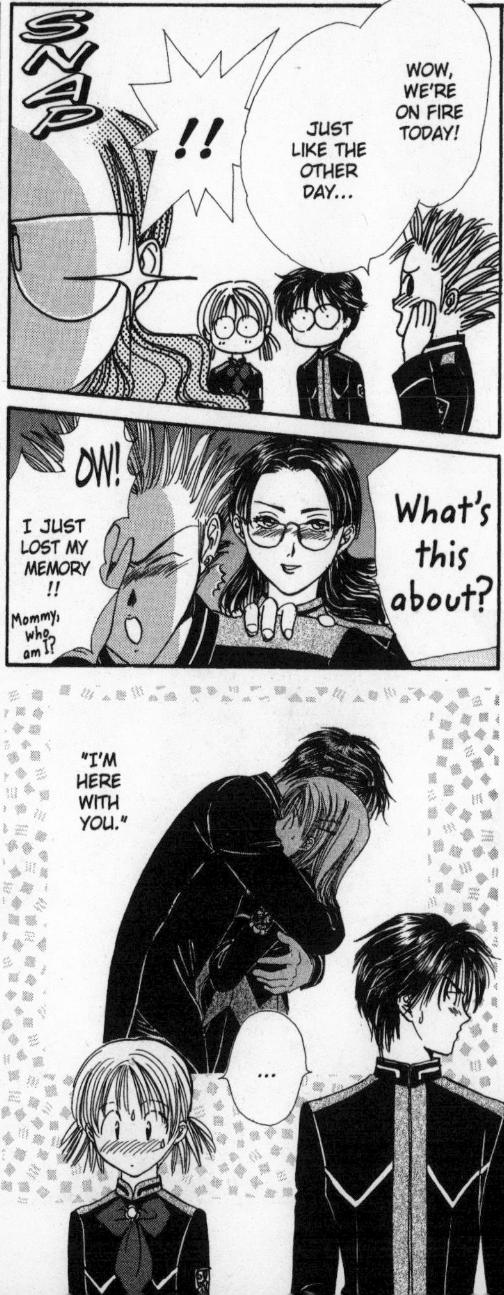
WOW, WE'RE ON FIRE TODAY!
JUST LIKE THE OTHER DAY...
!!
SNAP
What's this about?
OW!
I JUST LOST MY MEMORY !!
Mommy, who am I?
"I'M HERE WITH YOU."
...

I always wanted to draw Tanpopo as a flighty, peace-loving type, so that's why she's that way. But there are people who say they love her and that makes me happy. This is the first Watase character of this type... (well, that's true for all my characters.) But in terms of popularity, Kugyo is tops. In a way, he's a first for me, a "serious" young man. At first, he appears cool, and I've drawn many characters like that. But what makes "Scoop" different is his love of flowers and plants. (smile)

The most fun characters for me to draw are Tsuki and Aoi (Flippy). [smile] Aoi's attitude is a little strange at times, kind of aggressive (he flips out).

For some reason, Tsuki has a lot of fans. Where did that refined side of her go?

And in this story, an airhead girl appears. Actually, drawing Uchimura is the most fun. Especially her eyes!! Drawing her eyelashes with my 0.8 pen makes me wonder, "What am I doing?" (smile) Hmm... In real life people like her are pretty comic-like, aren't they? I think, "you show off too much, girl!!" I call her type "Reverse Panda." But after many days of fatigue and sleep-deprivation, I become a panda too. (Or a bear) Boo hoo!!!

Ow, my wrist hurts. I can't write anymore...

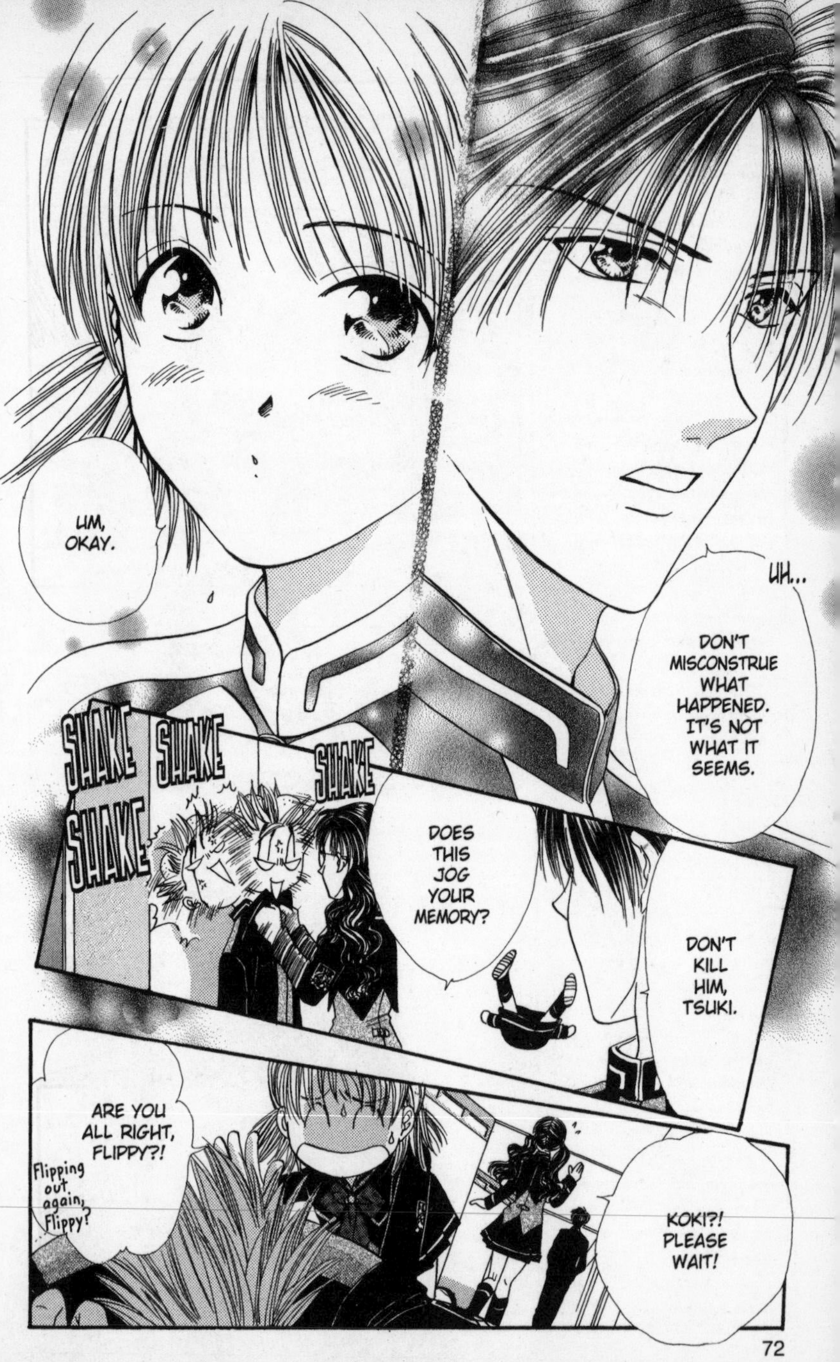
UH...
DON'T MISCONSTRUE WHAT HAPPENED. IT'S NOT WHAT IT SEEMS.
UM, OKAY.
DON'T KILL HIM, TSUKI.
DOES THIS JOG YOUR MEMORY?
SHAKE SHAKE SHAKE SHAKE
KOKI?! PLEASE WAIT!
ARE YOU ALL RIGHT, FLIPPY?!
Flipping out again, Flippy?

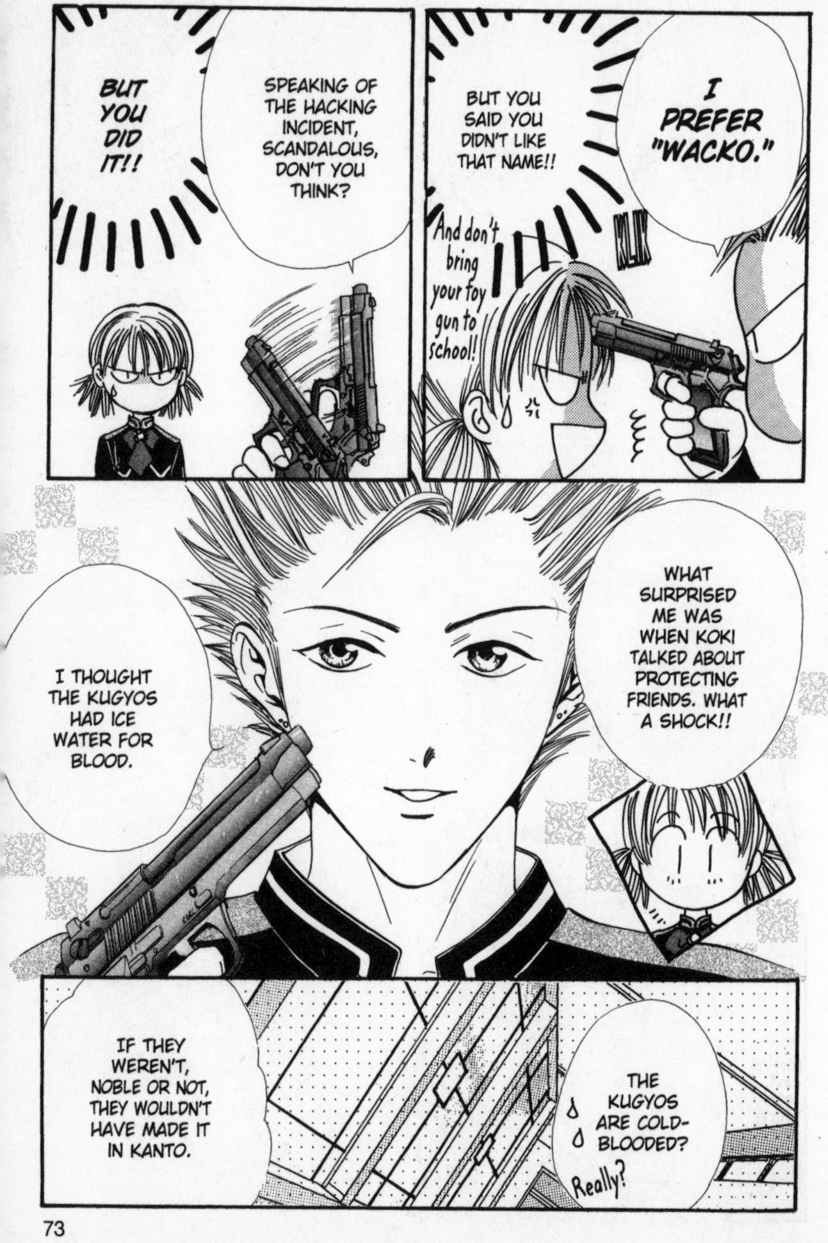
I PREFER "WACKO."
BUT YOU SAID YOU DIDN'T LIKE THAT NAME!!
And don't bring your toy gun to school!
SPEAKING OF THE HACKING INCIDENT, SCANDALOUS, DON'T YOU THINK?
BUT YOU DID IT!!
WHAT SURPRISED ME WAS WHEN KOKI TALKED ABOUT PROTECTING FRIENDS. WHAT A SHOCK!!
I THOUGHT THE KUGYOS HAD ICE WATER FOR BLOOD.
THE KUGYOS ARE COLD-BLOODED?
Really?
IF THEY WEREN'T, NOBLE OR NOT, THEY WOULDN'T HAVE MADE IT IN KANTO.

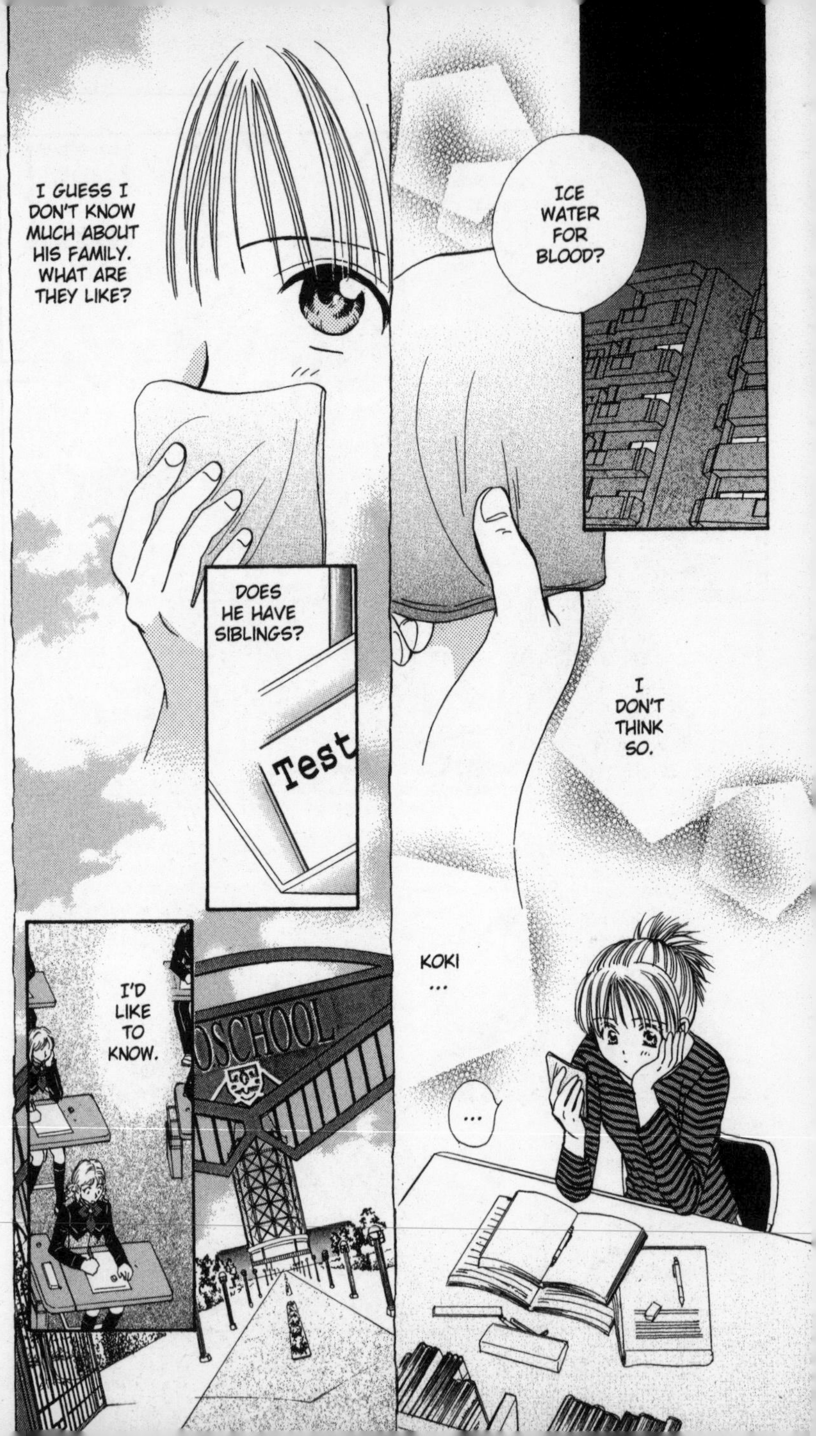
ICE WATER FOR BLOOD?
I DON'T THINK SO.
KOKI ...
...
I GUESS I DON'T KNOW MUCH ABOUT HIS FAMILY. WHAT ARE THEY LIKE?
DOES HE HAVE SIBLINGS?
Test
I'D LIKE TO KNOW.

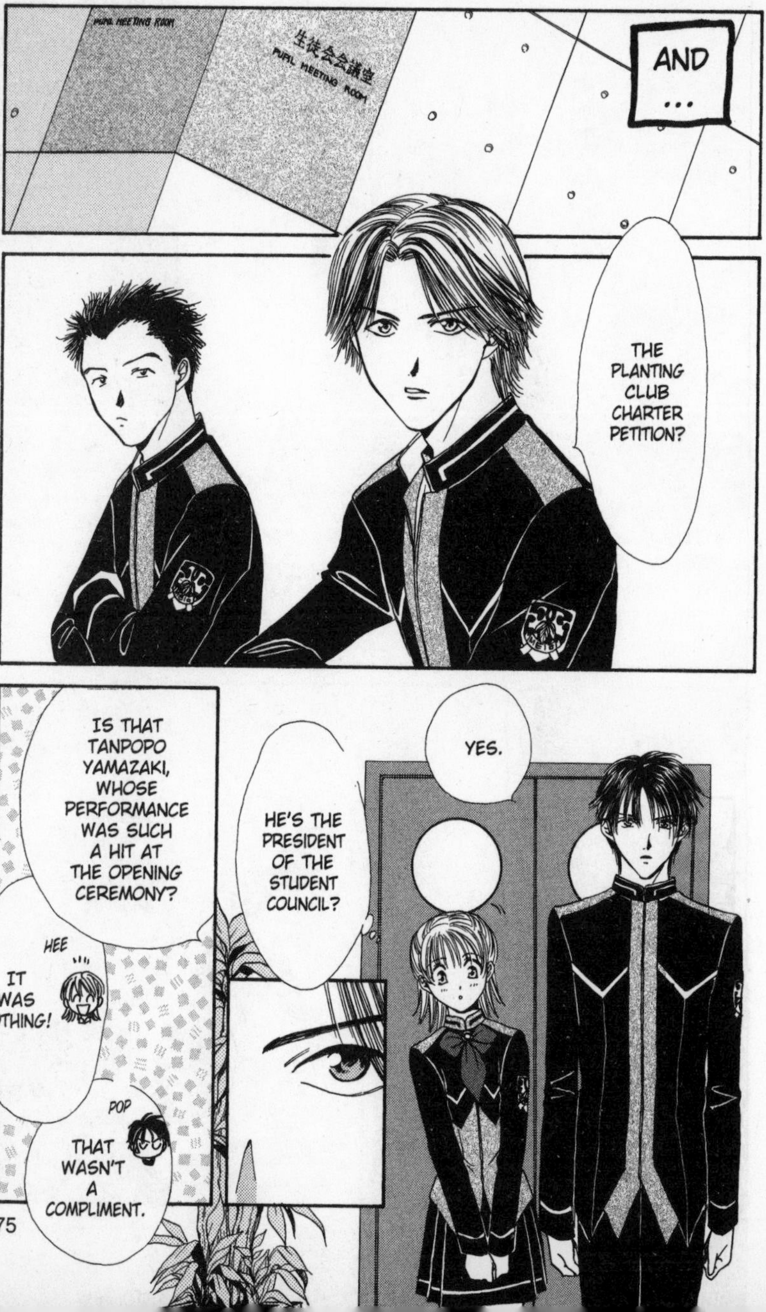
生徒会会議室
PUPIL MEETING ROOM
AND ...
THE PLANTING CLUB CHARTER PETITION?
YES.
HE'S THE PRESIDENT OF THE STUDENT COUNCIL?
IS THAT TANPOPO YAMAZAKI, WHOSE PERFORMANCE WAS SUCH A HIT AT THE OPENING CEREMONY?
HEE
IT WAS NOTHING!
POP
THAT WASN'T A COMPLIMENT.

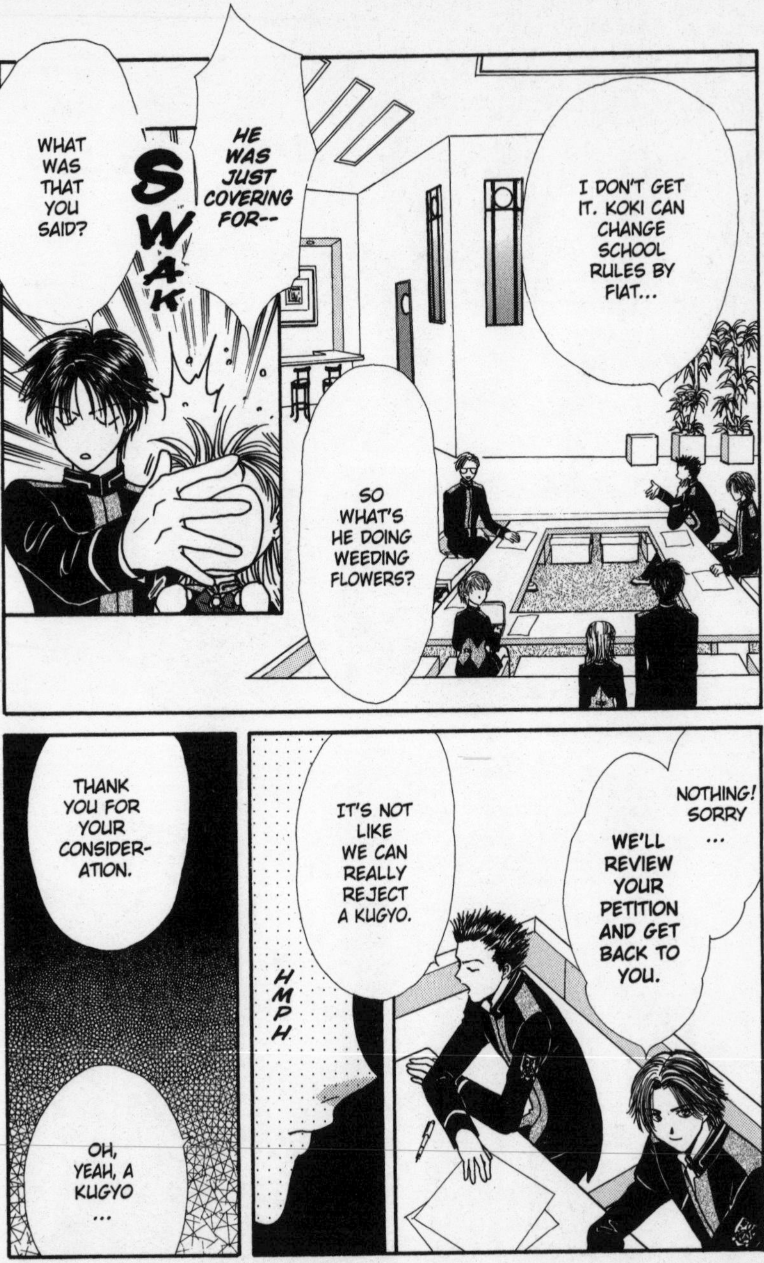
I DON'T GET IT. KOKI CAN CHANGE SCHOOL RULES BY FIAT...
SO WHAT'S HE DOING WEEDING FLOWERS?
HE WAS JUST COVERING FOR--
SWAK
WHAT WAS THAT YOU SAID?
NOTHING! SORRY ...
WE'LL REVIEW YOUR PETITION AND GET BACK TO YOU.
IT'S NOT LIKE WE CAN REALLY REJECT A KUGYO.
HMPH
THANK YOU FOR YOUR CONSIDERATION.
OH, YEAH, A KUGYO ...

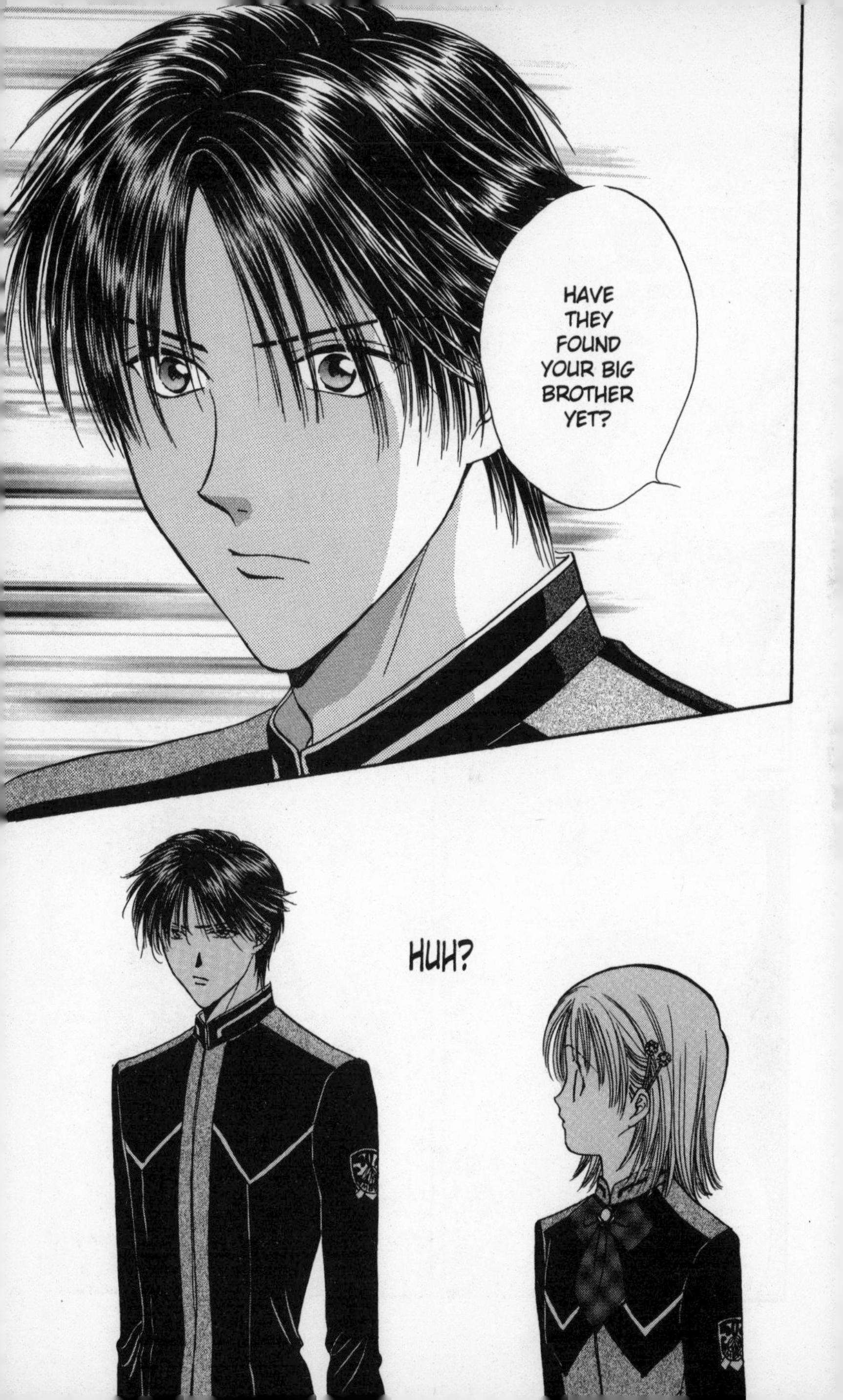
HAVE THEY FOUND YOUR BIG BROTHER YET?
HUH?

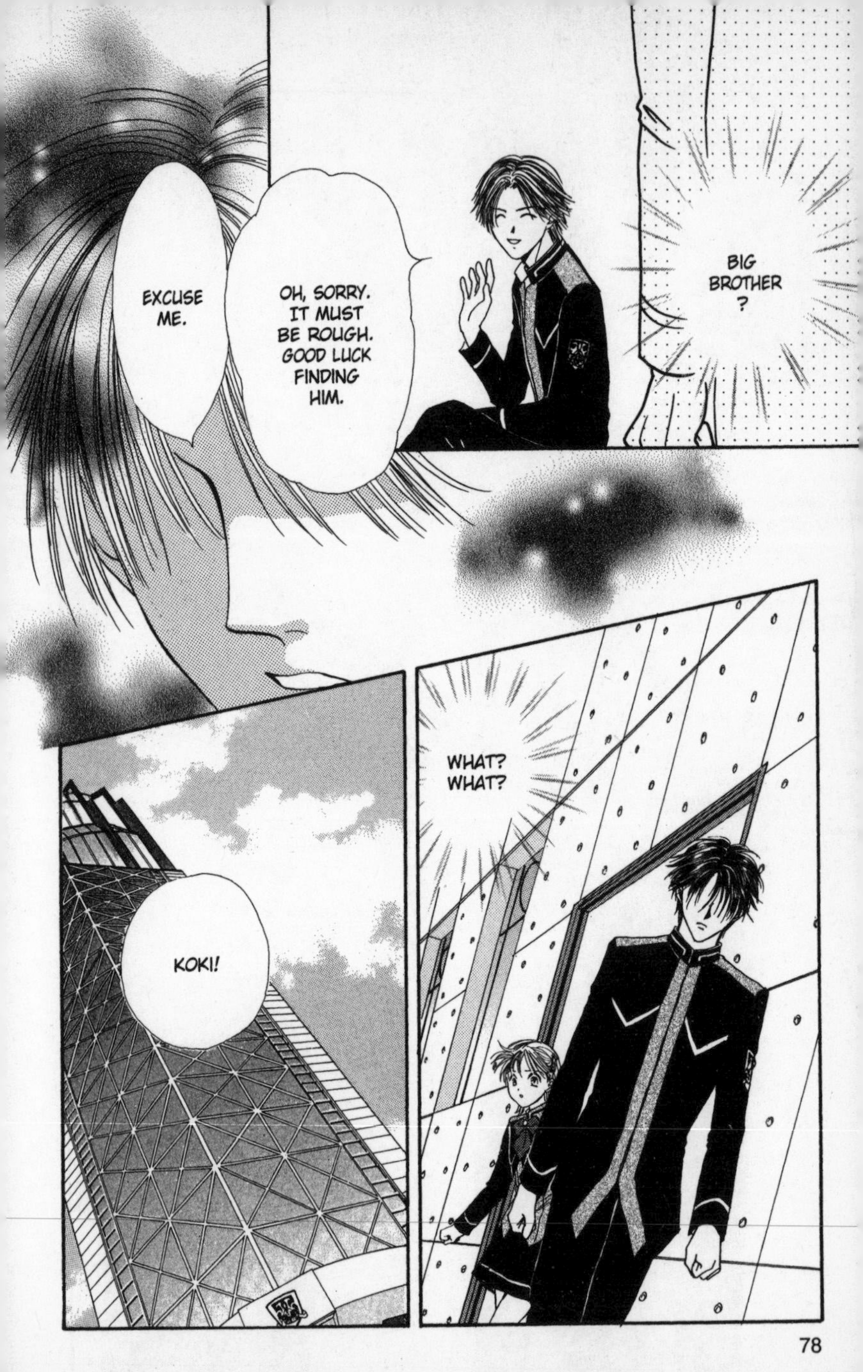
BIG BROTHER ?
OH, SORRY. IT MUST BE ROUGH. GOOD LUCK FINDING HIM.
EXCUSE ME.
WHAT? WHAT?
KOKI!

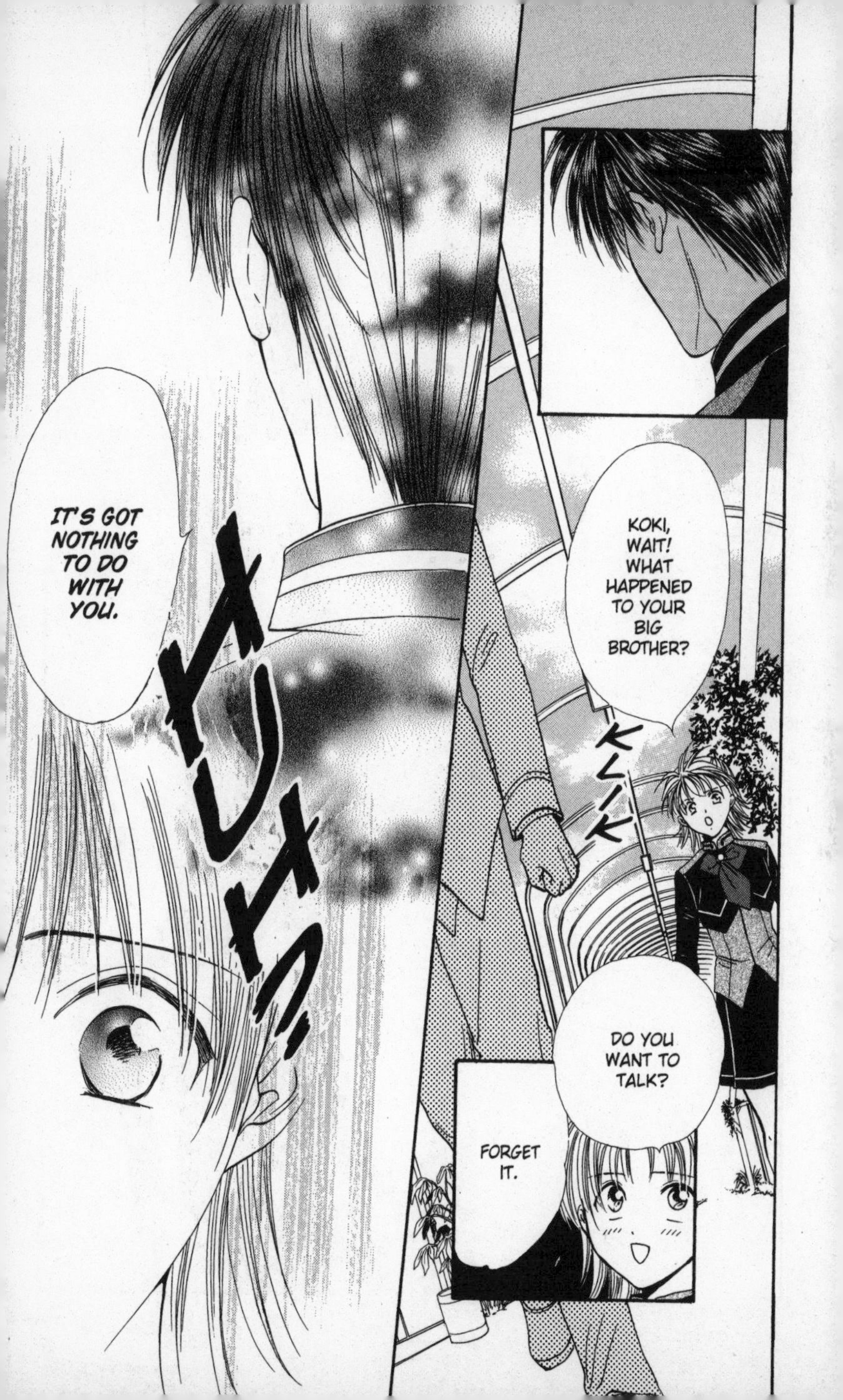
KOKI, WAIT! WHAT HAPPENED TO YOUR BIG BROTHER?
KLIK
DO YOU WANT TO TALK?
FORGET IT.
IT'S GOT NOTHING TO DO WITH YOU.

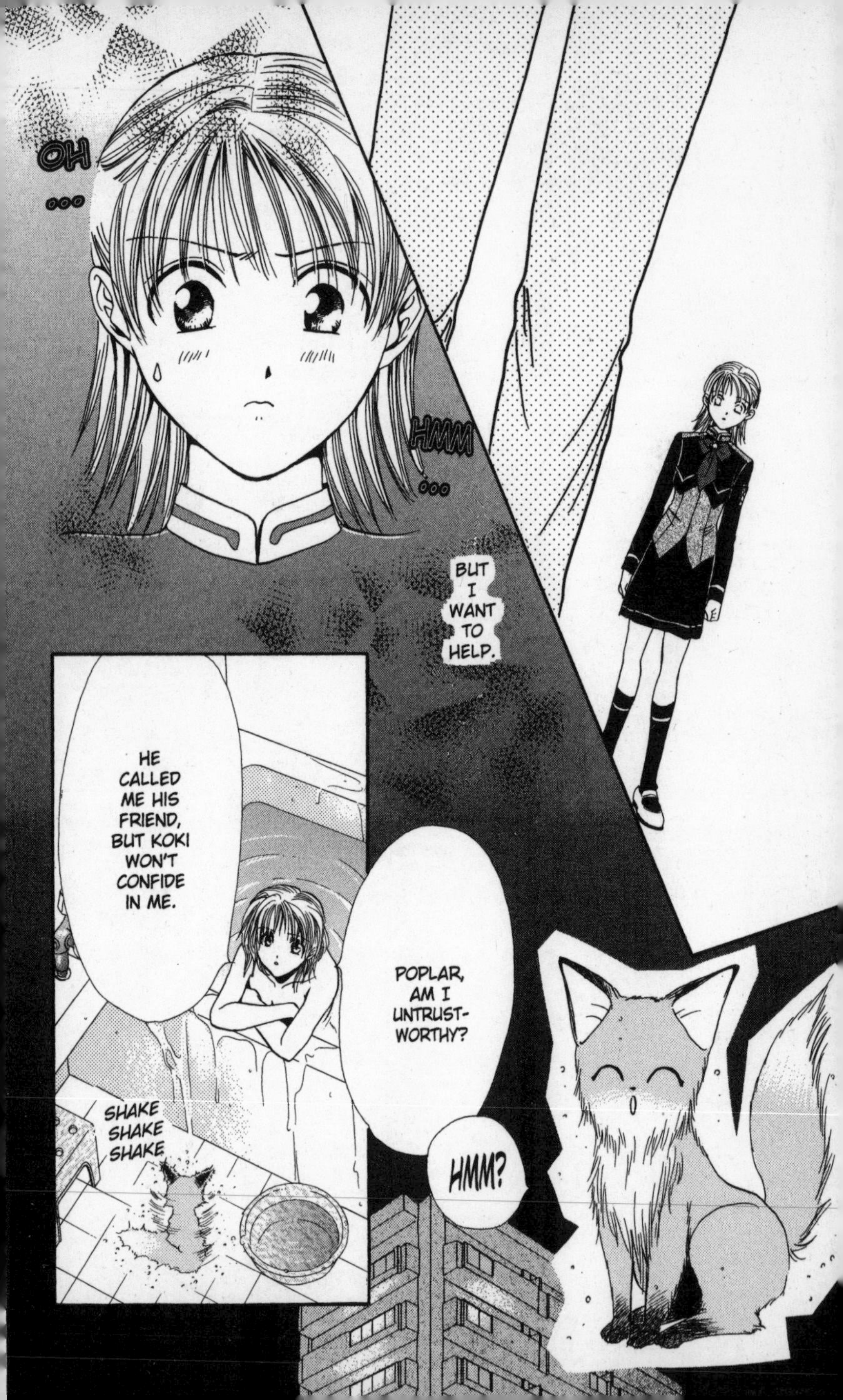
OH...
HMM...
BUT I WANT TO HELP.
HE CALLED ME HIS FRIEND, BUT KOKI WON'T CONFIDE IN ME.
SHAKE SHAKE SHAKE
POPLAR, AM I UNTRUST-WORTHY?
HMM?

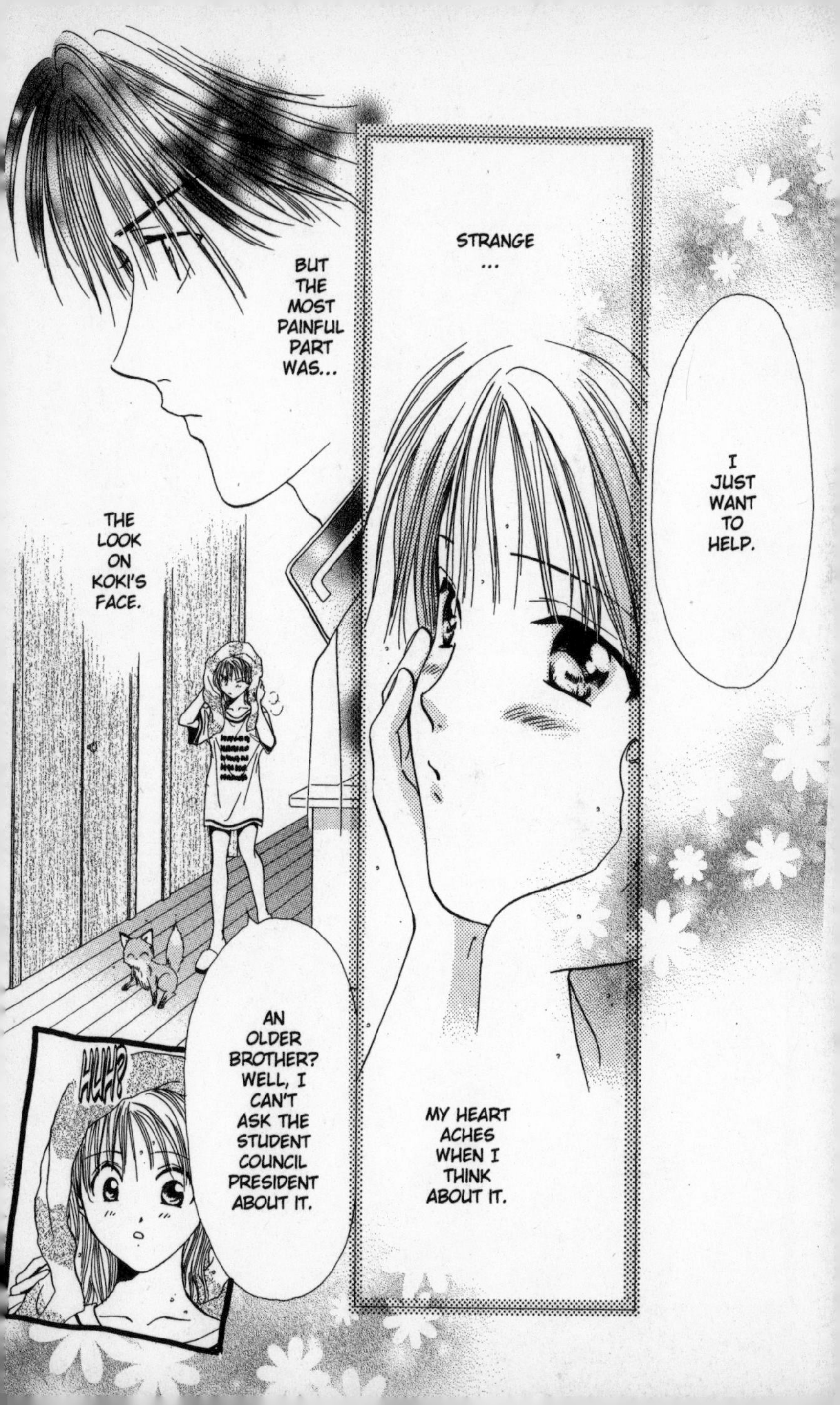
I JUST WANT TO HELP.
STRANGE ...
MY HEART ACHES WHEN I THINK ABOUT IT.
BUT THE MOST PAINFUL PART WAS...
THE LOOK ON KOKI'S FACE.
AN OLDER BROTHER? WELL, I CAN'T ASK THE STUDENT COUNCIL PRESIDENT ABOUT IT.
HUH?

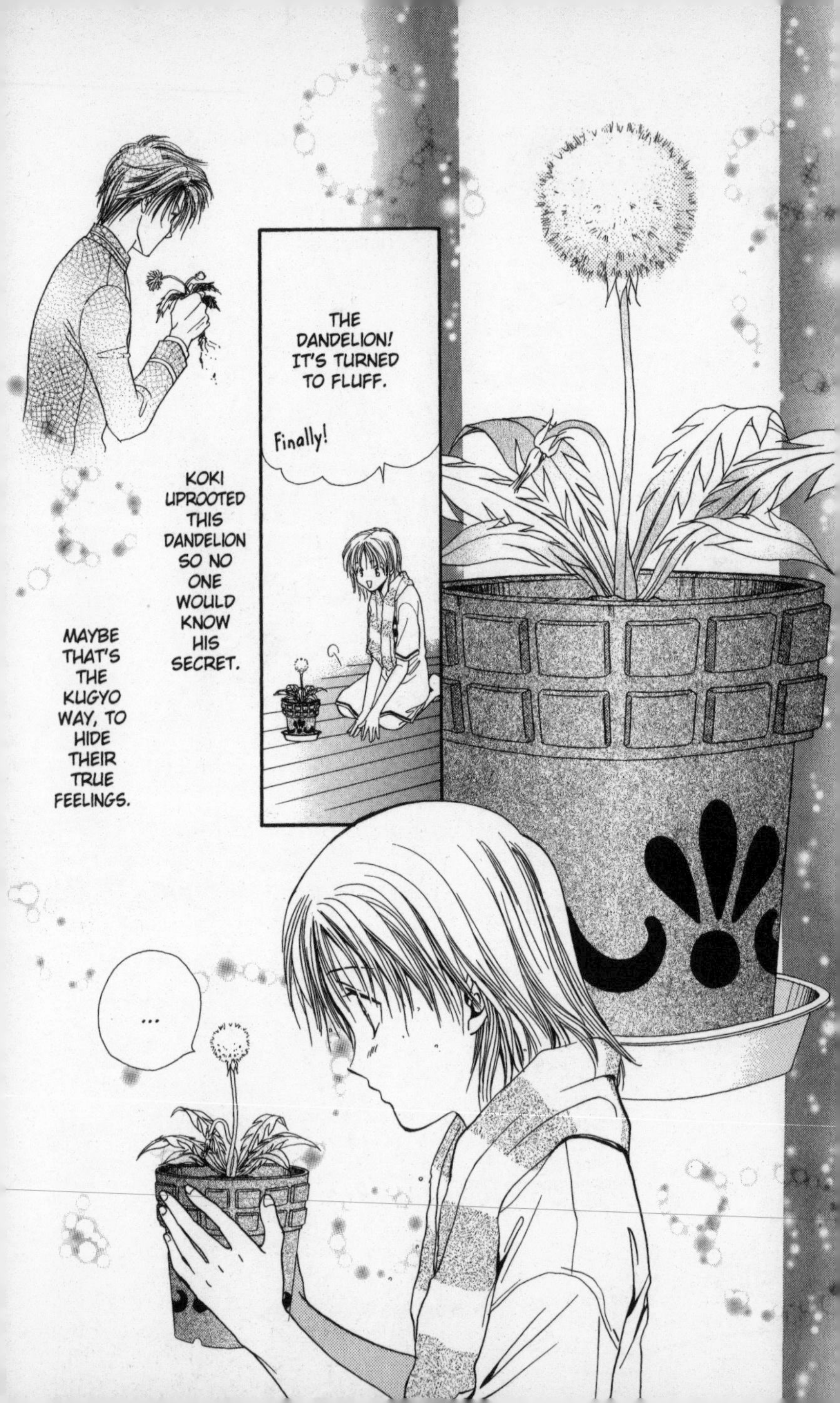
THE DANDELION! IT'S TURNED TO FLUFF.
Finally!
KOKI UPROOTED THIS DANDELION SO NO ONE WOULD KNOW HIS SECRET.
MAYBE THAT'S THE KUGYO WAY, TO HIDE THEIR TRUE FEELINGS.
...

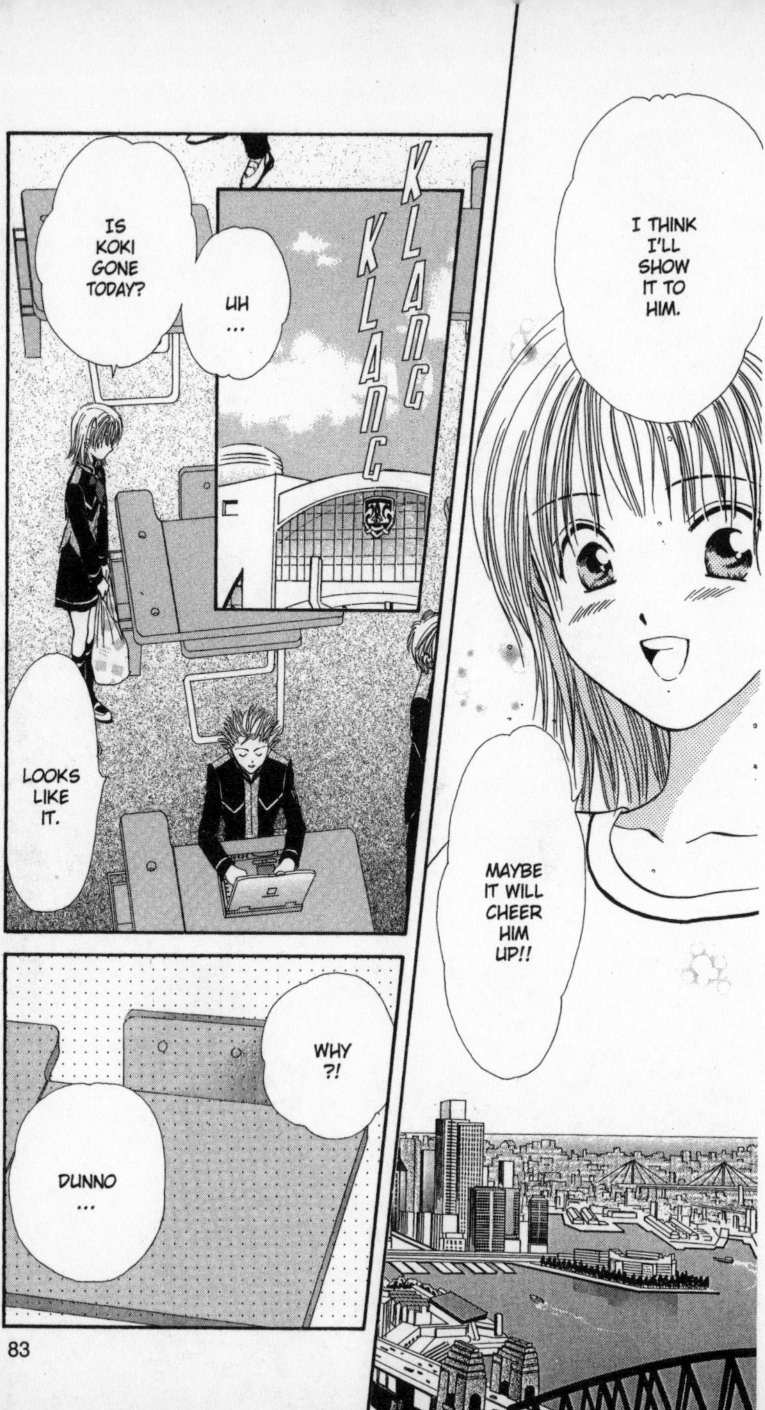
I THINK I'LL SHOW IT TO HIM.
MAYBE IT WILL CHEER HIM UP!!
KLANG
KLANG
IS KOKI GONE TODAY?
UH ...
LOOKS LIKE IT.
WHY ?!
DUNNO ...

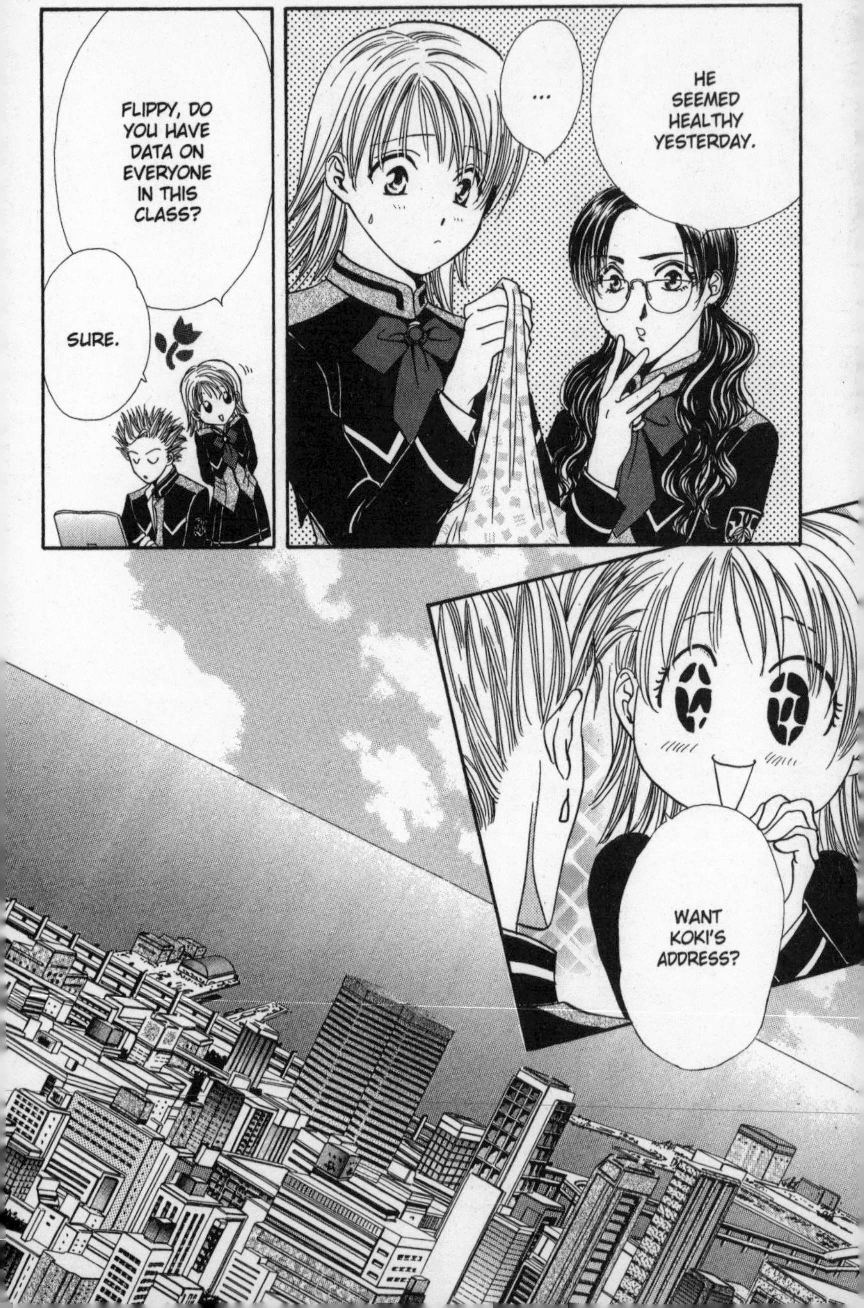
HE SEEMED HEALTHY YESTERDAY.
...
FLIPPY, DO YOU HAVE DATA ON EVERYONE IN THIS CLASS?
SURE.
WANT KOKI'S ADDRESS?

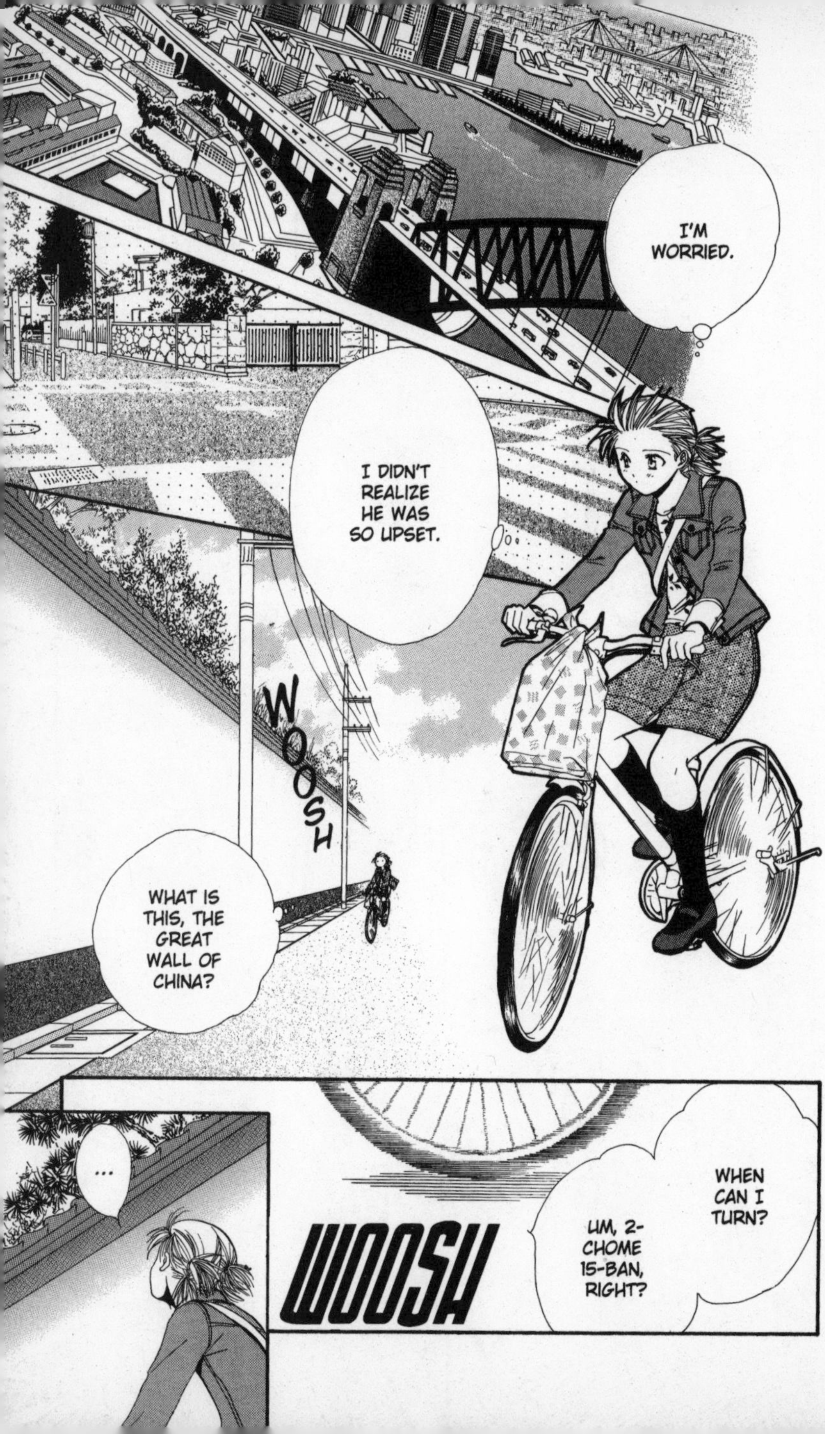
I'M WORRIED.
I DIDN'T REALIZE HE WAS SO UPSET.
WOOSH
WHAT IS THIS, THE GREAT WALL OF CHINA?
WHEN CAN I TURN?
UM, 2-CHOME 15-BAN, RIGHT?
WOOSH
...

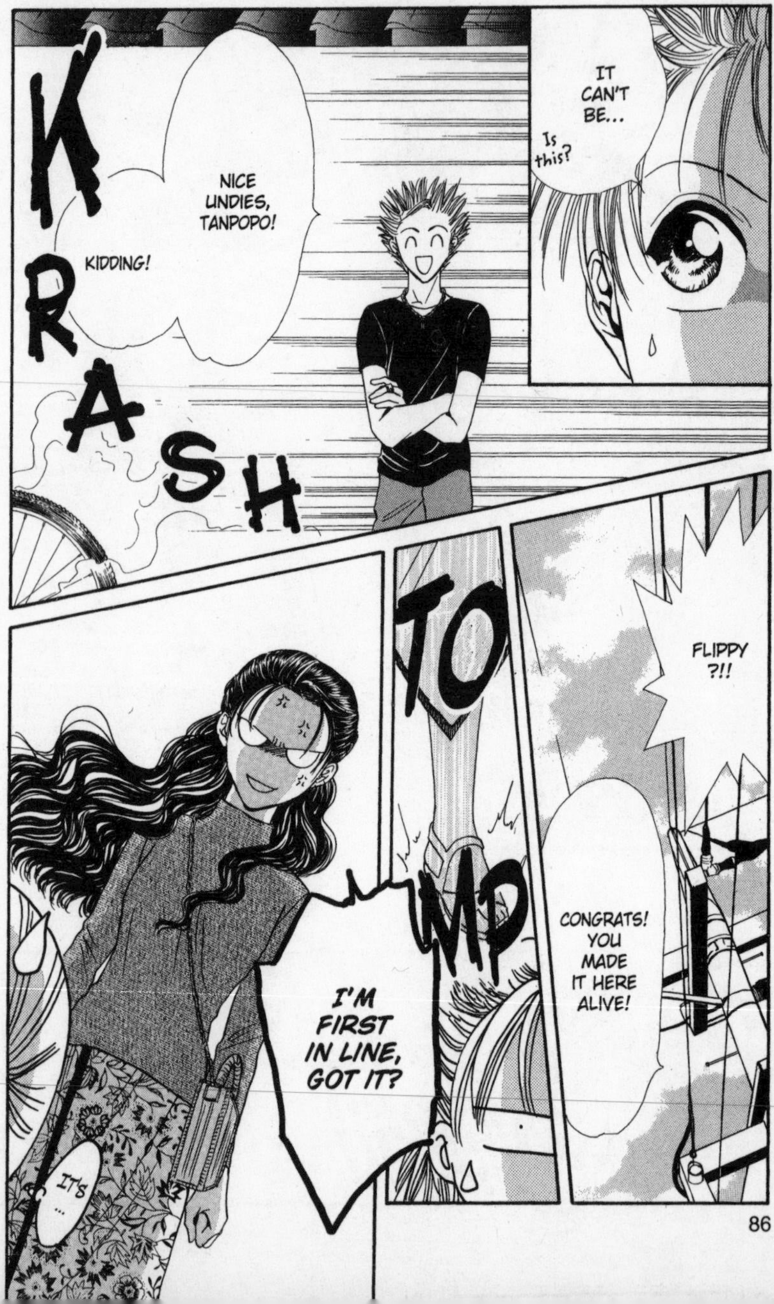
IT CAN'T BE...
Is this?
NICE UNDIES, TANPOPO!
KIDDING!
KRASH
FLIPPY ?!!
CONGRATS! YOU MADE IT HERE ALIVE!
TOMP
I'M FIRST IN LINE, GOT IT?
It's ...

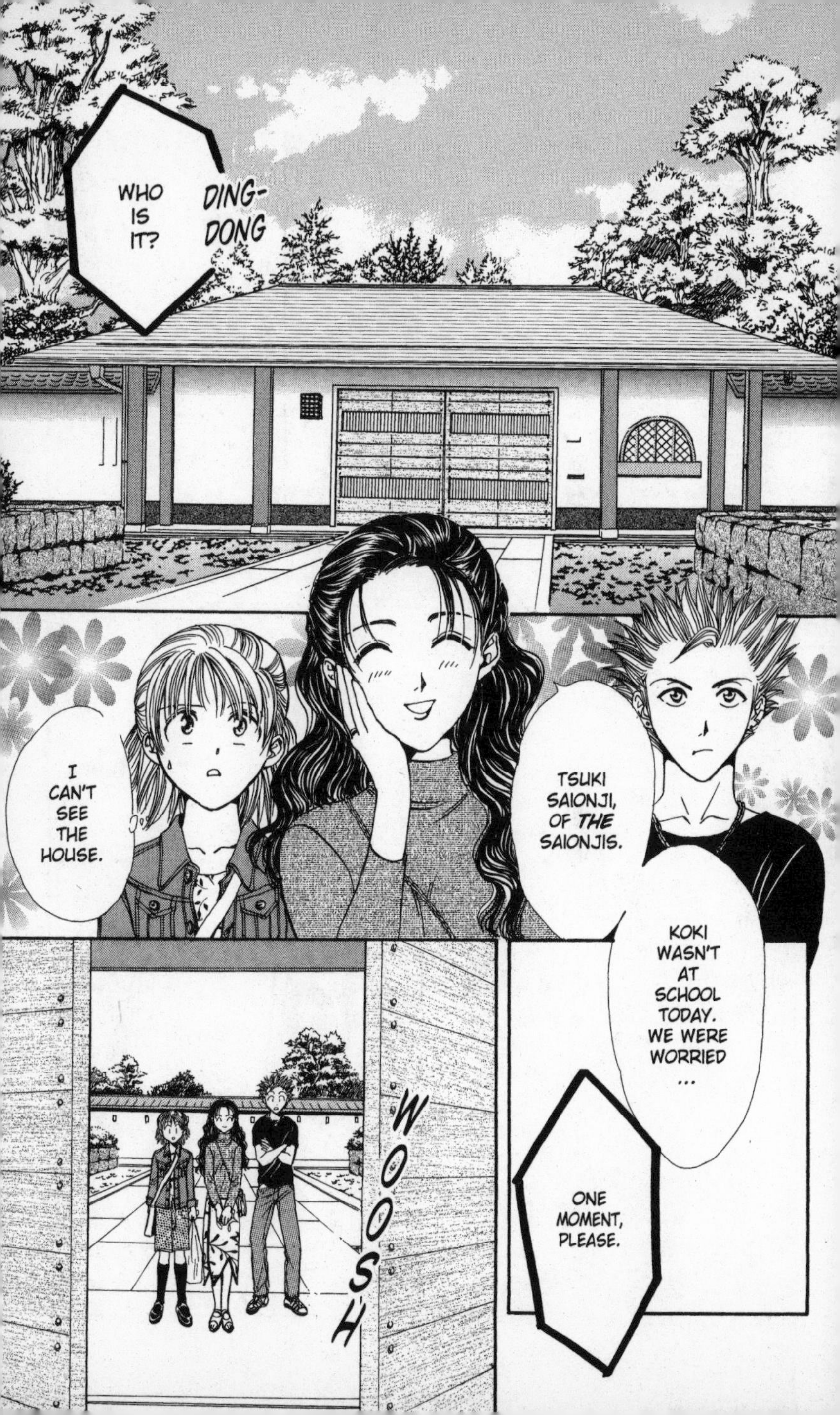
DING-DONG
WHO IS IT?
TSUKI SAIONJI, OF *THE* SAIONJIS.
I CAN'T SEE THE HOUSE.
KOKI WASN'T AT SCHOOL TODAY. WE WERE WORRIED ...
ONE MOMENT, PLEASE.
WOOSH

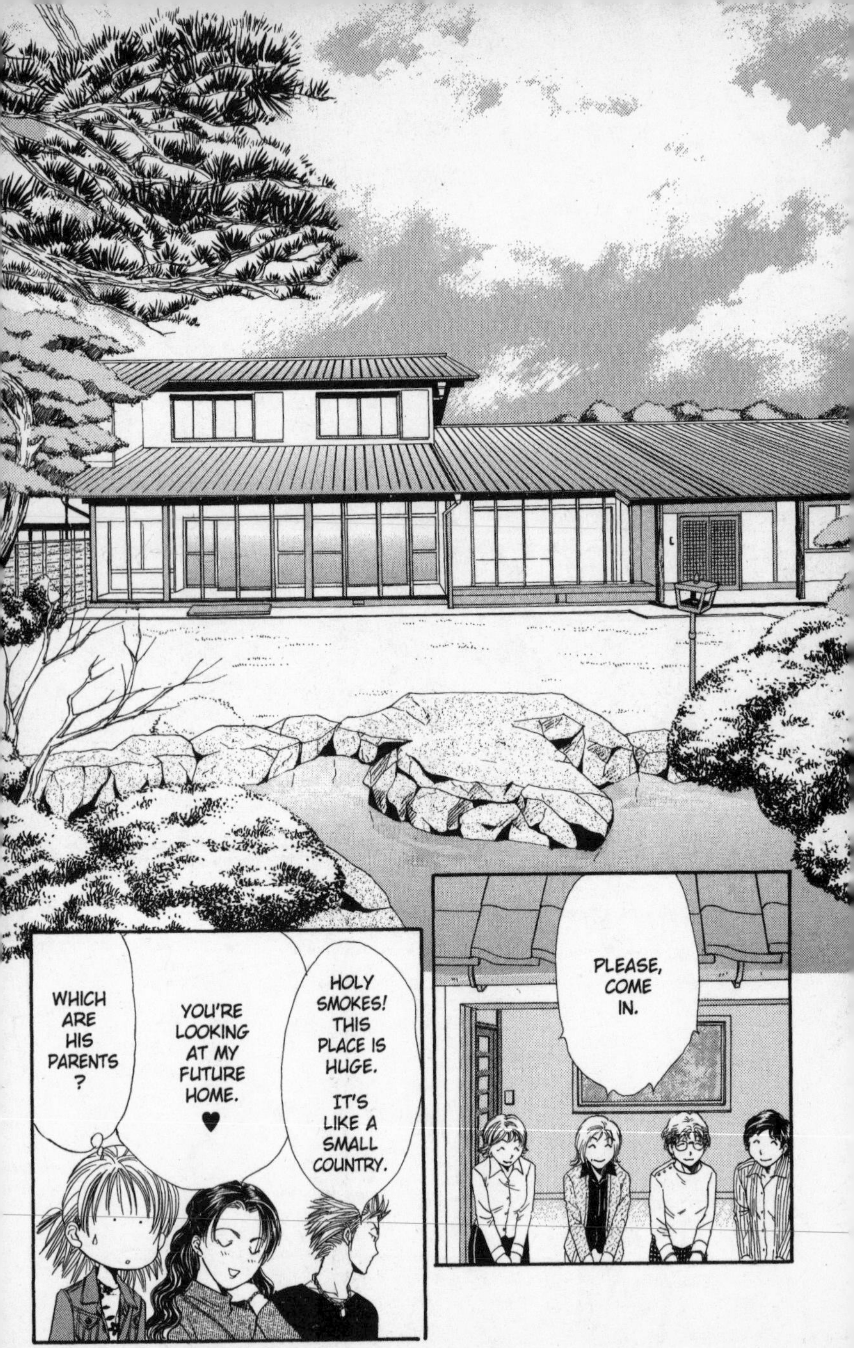
PLEASE, COME IN.
HOLY SMOKES! THIS PLACE IS HUGE.
IT'S LIKE A SMALL COUNTRY.
YOU'RE LOOKING AT MY FUTURE HOME. ♥
WHICH ARE HIS PARENTS?

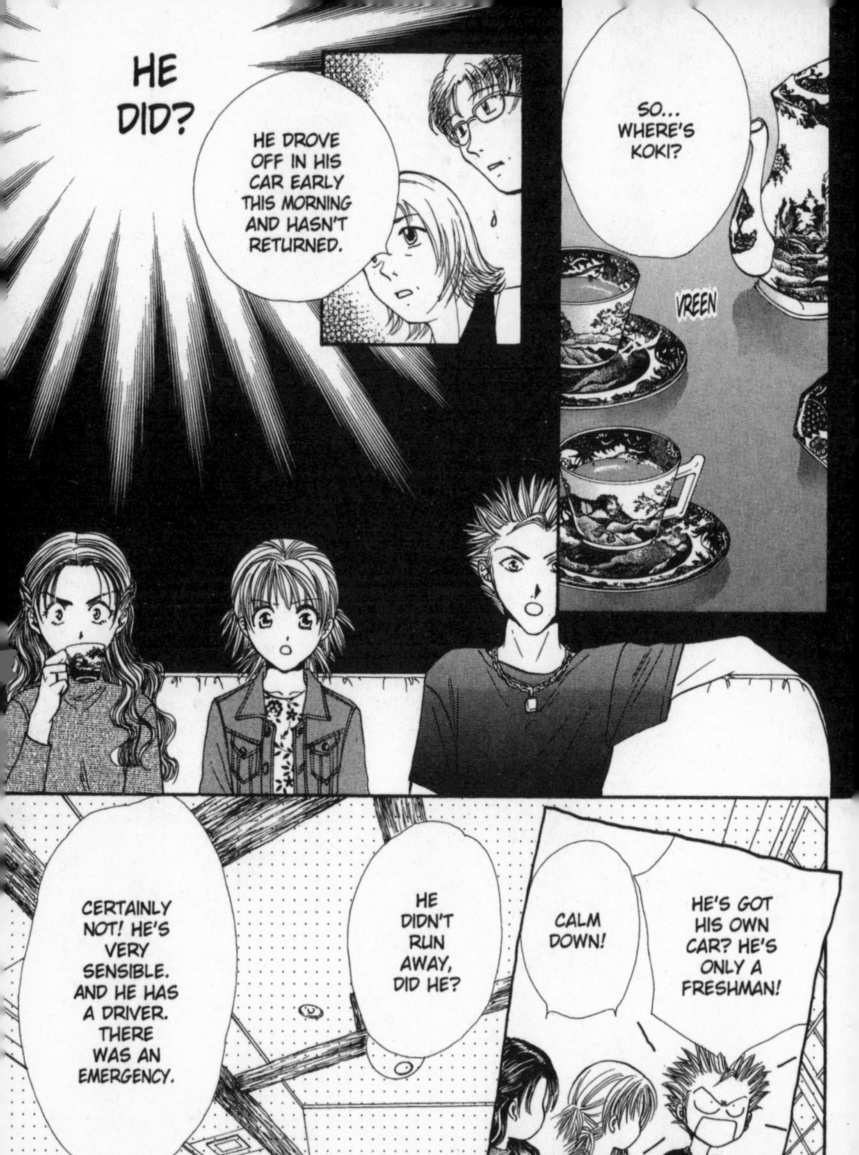
SO... WHERE'S KOKI?
VREEN
HE DROVE OFF IN HIS CAR EARLY THIS MORNING AND HASN'T RETURNED.
HE DID?
HE'S GOT HIS OWN CAR? HE'S ONLY A FRESHMAN!
CALM DOWN!
HE DIDN'T RUN AWAY, DID HE?
CERTAINLY NOT! HE'S VERY SENSIBLE. AND HE HAS A DRIVER. THERE WAS AN EMERGENCY.

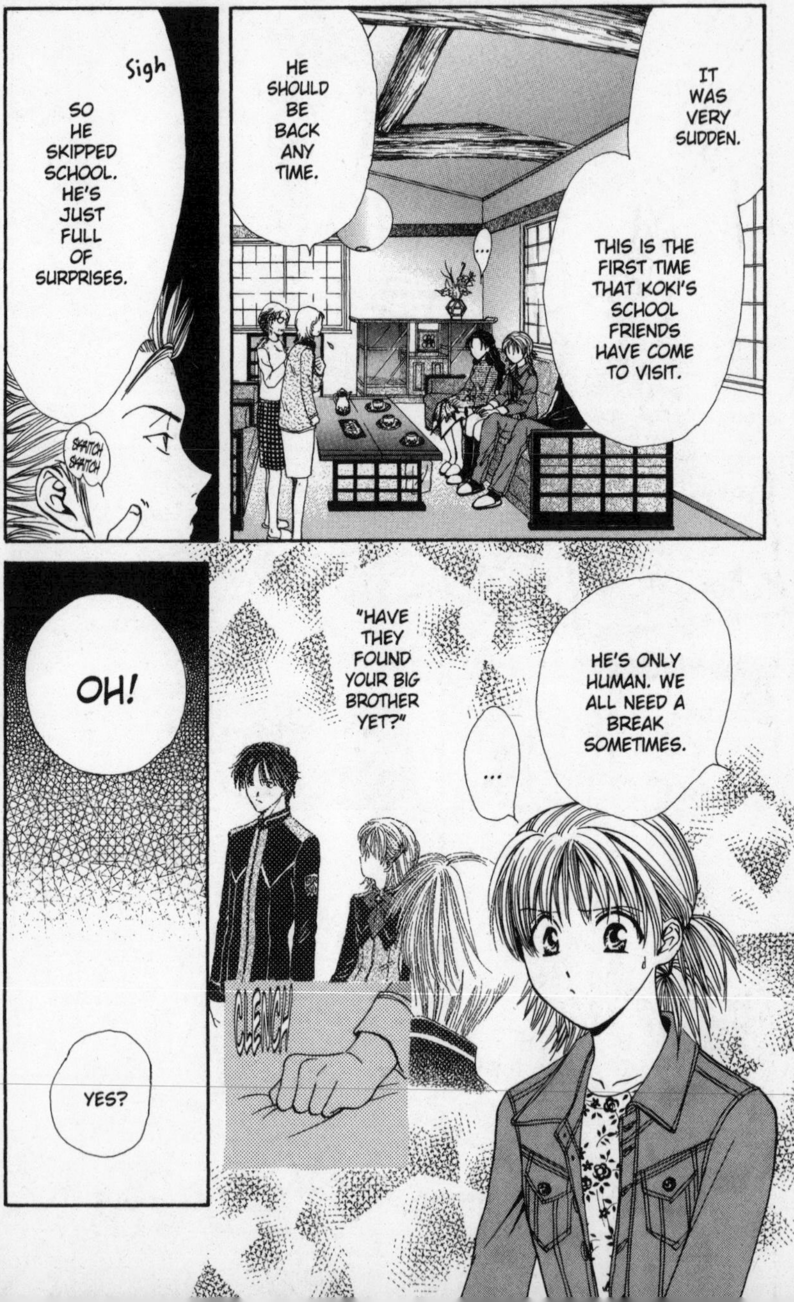
IT WAS VERY SUDDEN.
THIS IS THE FIRST TIME THAT KOKI'S SCHOOL FRIENDS HAVE COME TO VISIT.
...
HE SHOULD BE BACK ANY TIME.
Sigh
SO HE SKIPPED SCHOOL. HE'S JUST FULL OF SURPRISES.
SKRITCH SKRITCH
HE'S ONLY HUMAN. WE ALL NEED A BREAK SOMETIMES.
...
"HAVE THEY FOUND YOUR BIG BROTHER YET?"
CLENCH
OH!
YES?

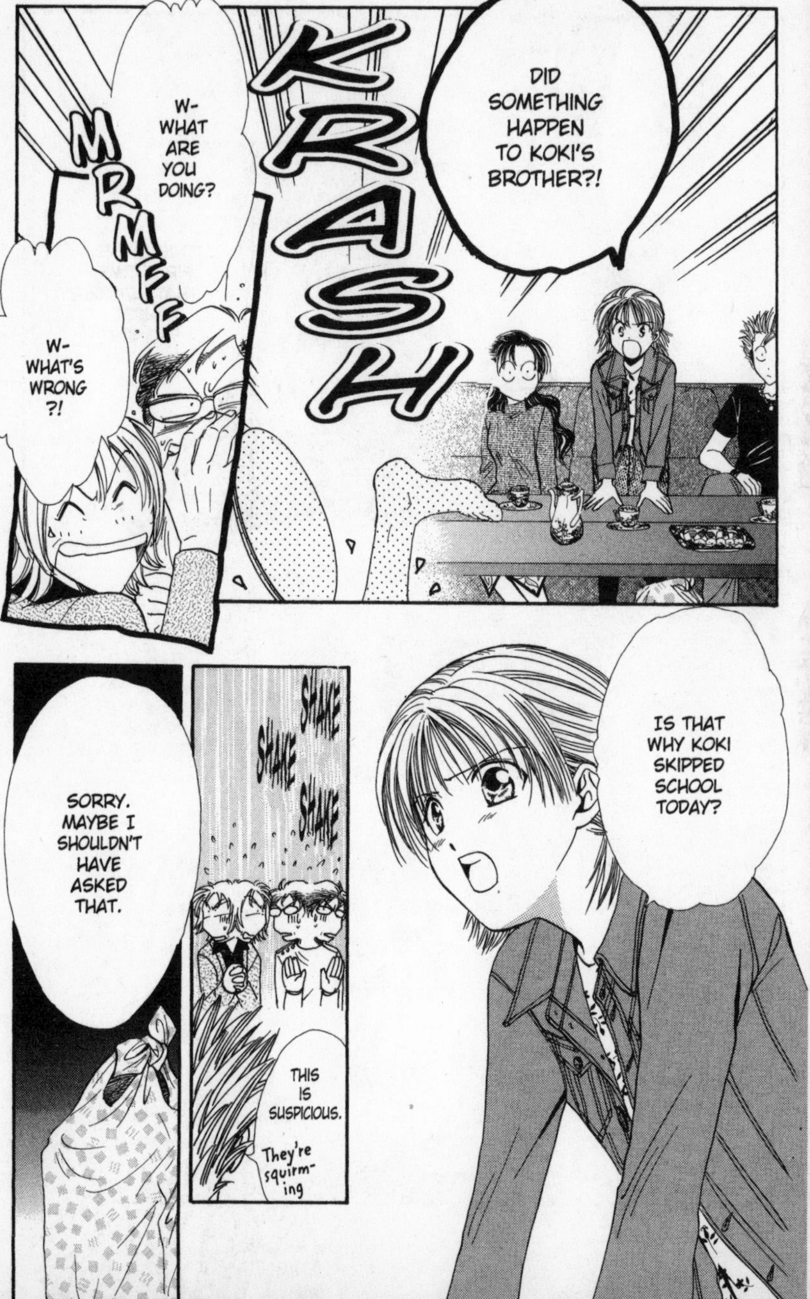
DID SOMETHING HAPPEN TO KOKI'S BROTHER?!
KRASH
W-WHAT ARE YOU DOING?
MRMFF
W-WHAT'S WRONG?!
IS THAT WHY KOKI SKIPPED SCHOOL TODAY?
SHAKE SHAKE
SHAKE SHAKE
THIS IS SUSPICIOUS.
They're squirming
SORRY. MAYBE I SHOULDN'T HAVE ASKED THAT.

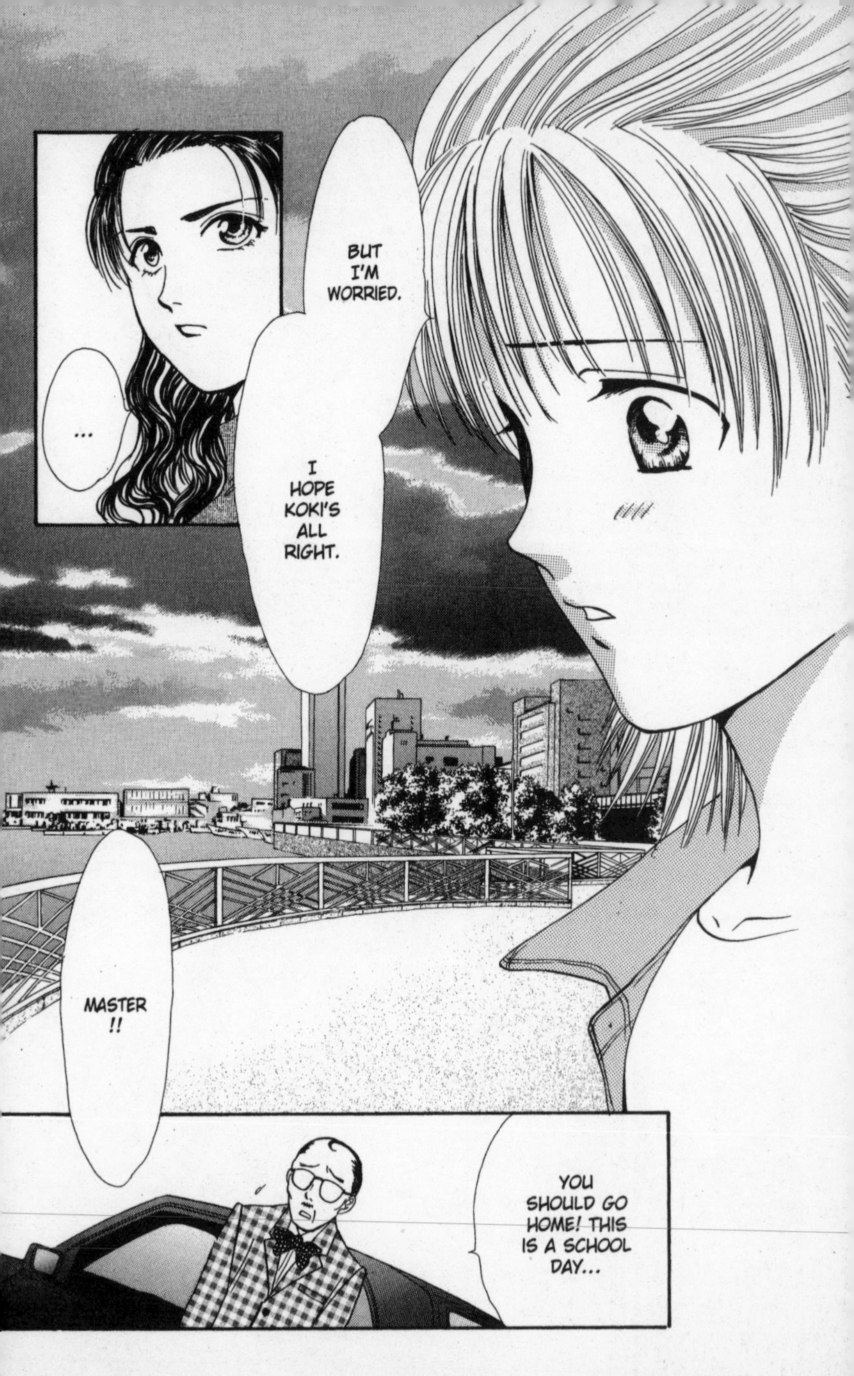
BUT I'M WORRIED.
I HOPE KOKI'S ALL RIGHT.
...
MASTER !!
YOU SHOULD GO HOME! THIS IS A SCHOOL DAY...

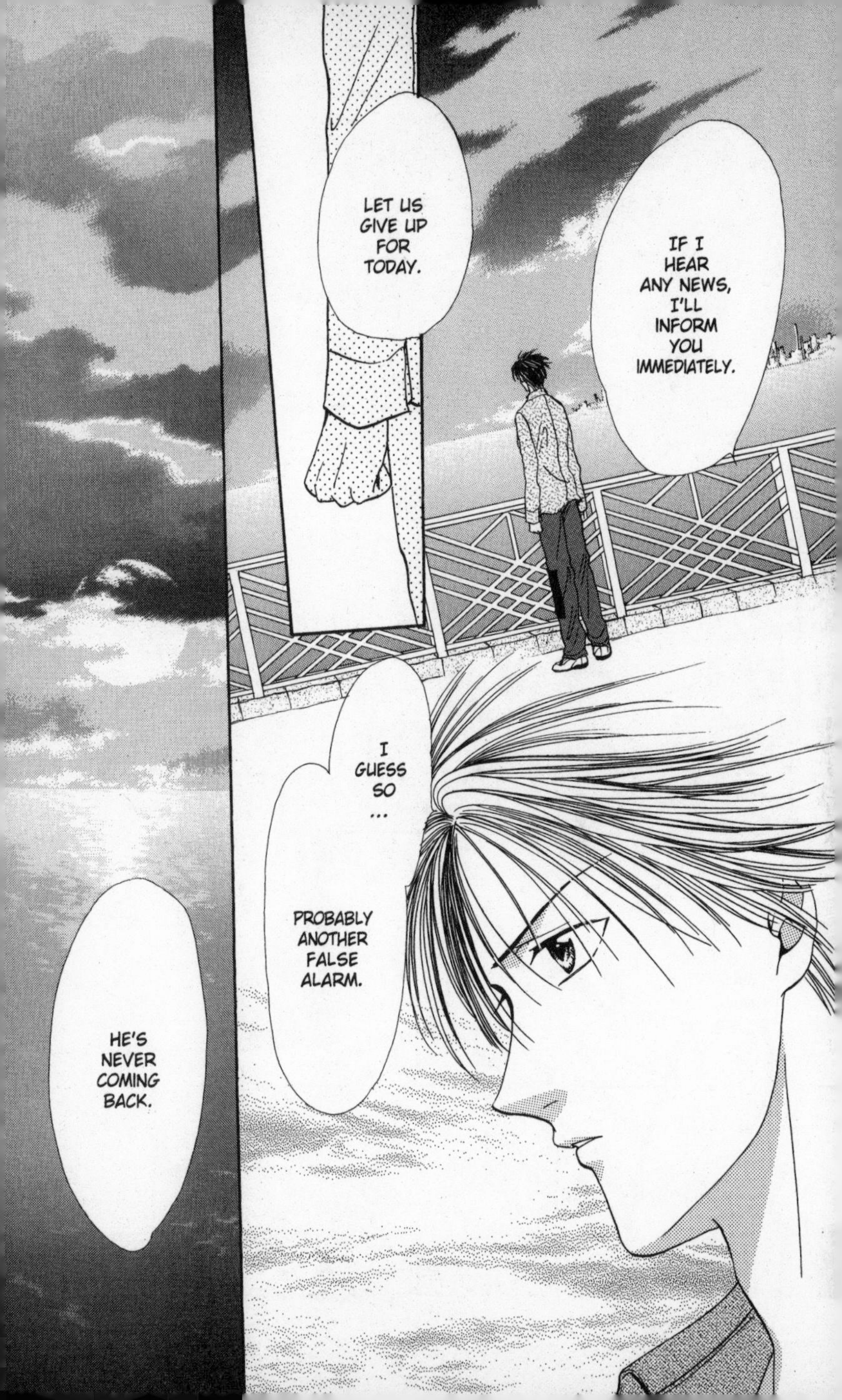
IF I HEAR ANY NEWS, I'LL INFORM YOU IMMEDIATELY.
LET US GIVE UP FOR TODAY.
I GUESS SO ...
PROBABLY ANOTHER FALSE ALARM.
HE'S NEVER COMING BACK.

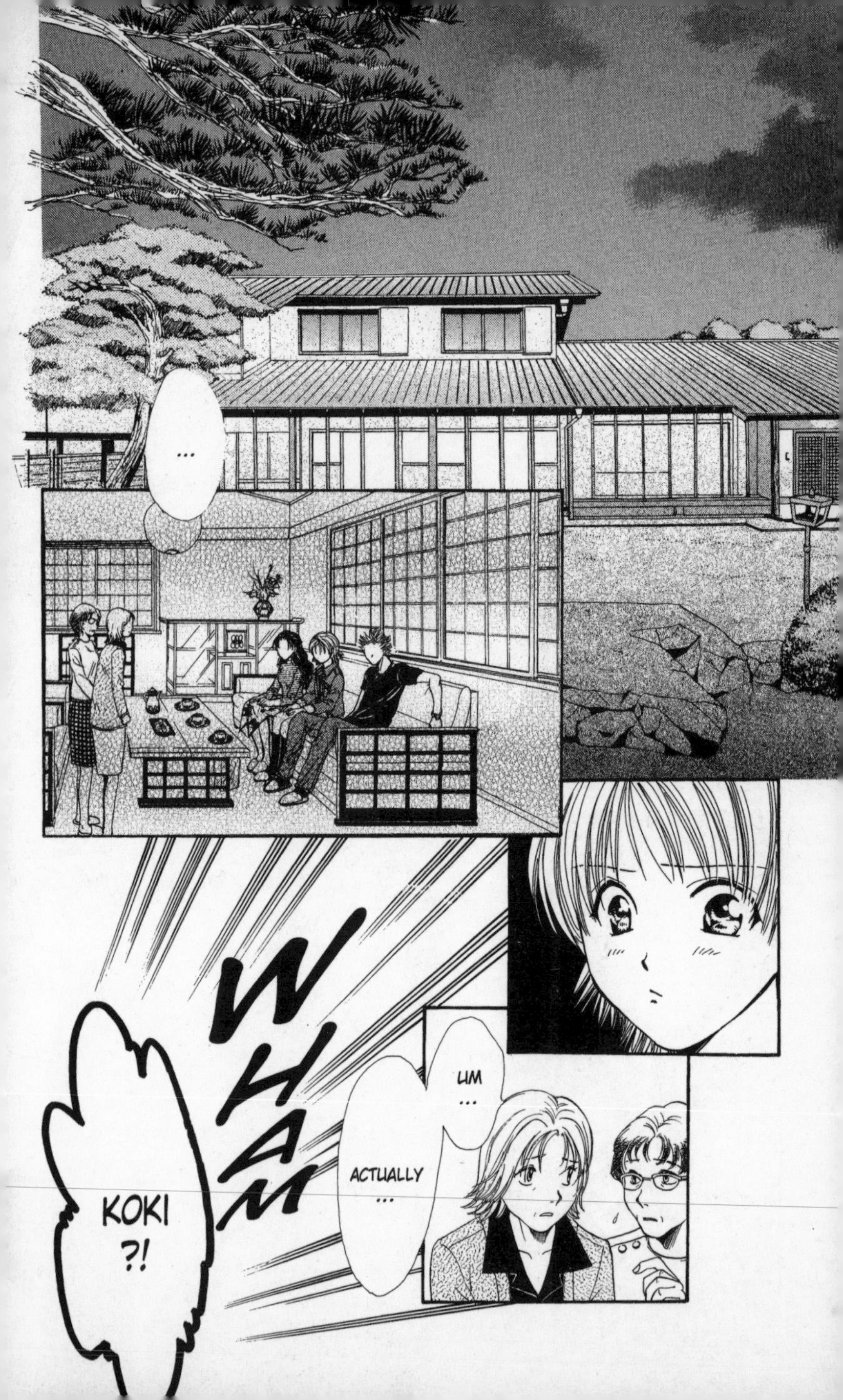
...
UM ...
ACTUALLY ...
WHAM
KOKI ?!

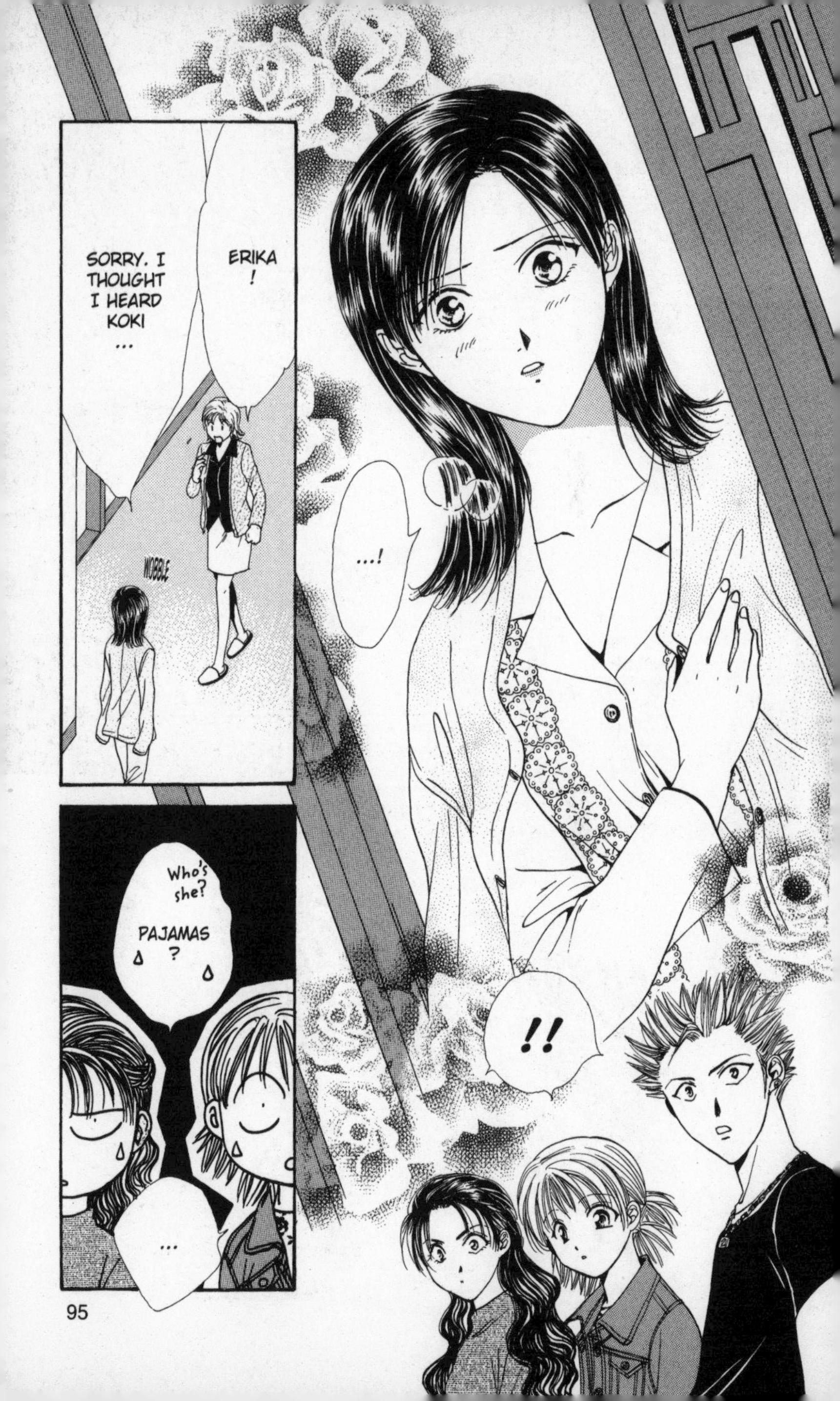

...!
!!
ERIKA !
SORRY. I THOUGHT I HEARD KOKI ...
WOBBLE
Who's she? PAJAMAS ?
...

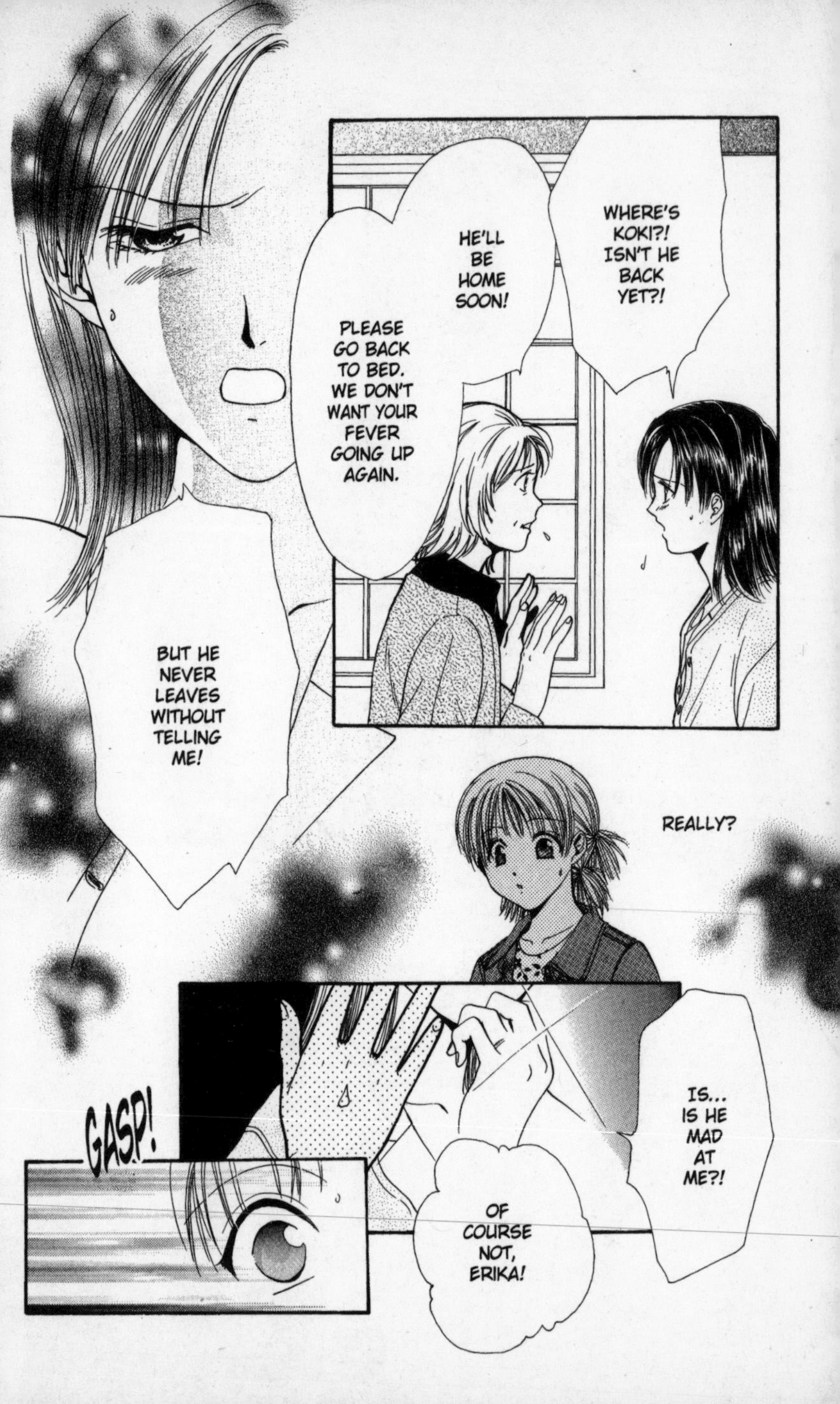
WHERE'S KOKI?! ISN'T HE BACK YET?!
HE'LL BE HOME SOON!
PLEASE GO BACK TO BED. WE DON'T WANT YOUR FEVER GOING UP AGAIN.
BUT HE NEVER LEAVES WITHOUT TELLING ME!
REALLY?
IS... IS HE MAD AT ME?!
OF COURSE NOT, ERIKA!
GASP!

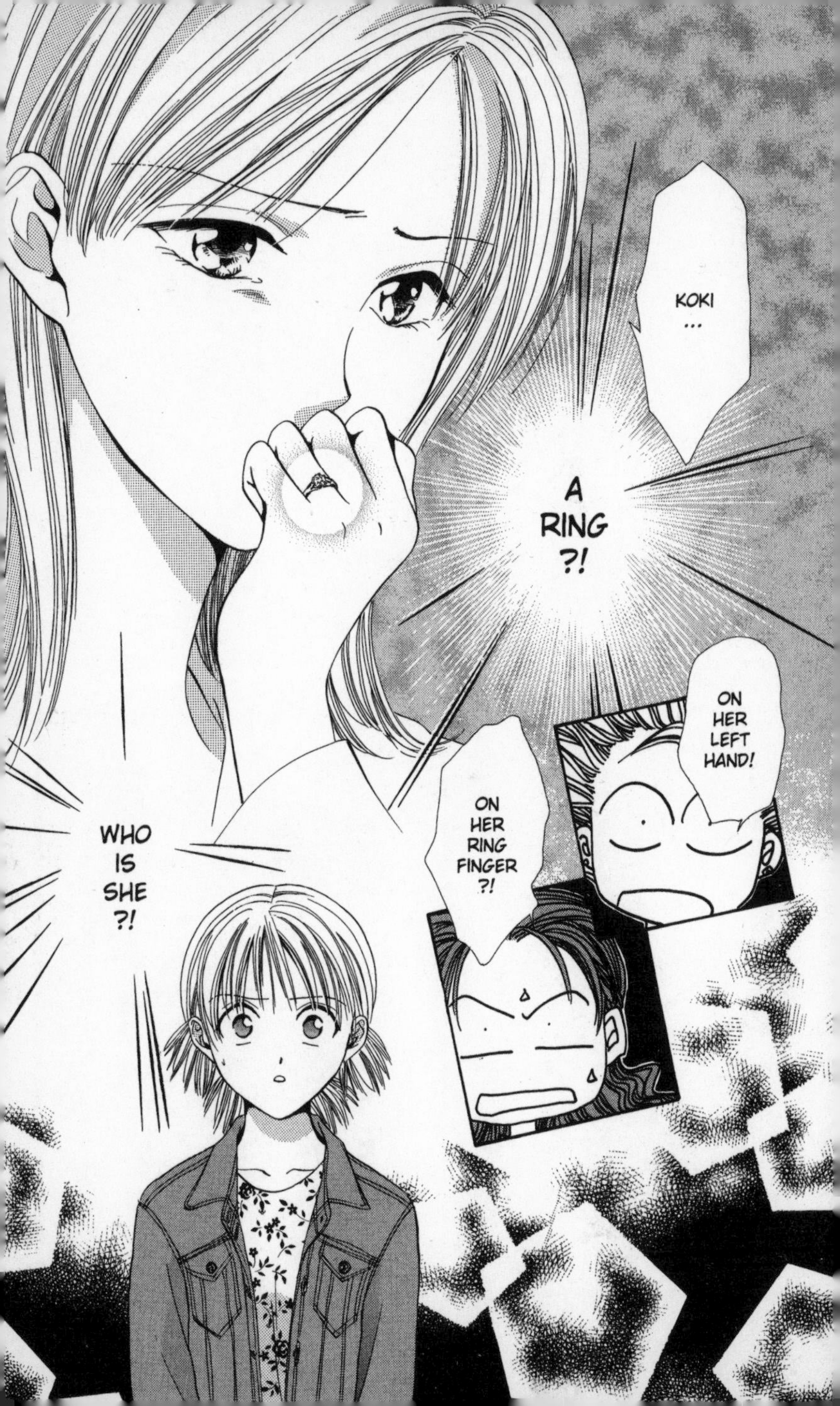
KOKI ...
A RING ?!
ON HER LEFT HAND!
ON HER RING FINGER ?!
WHO IS SHE ?!

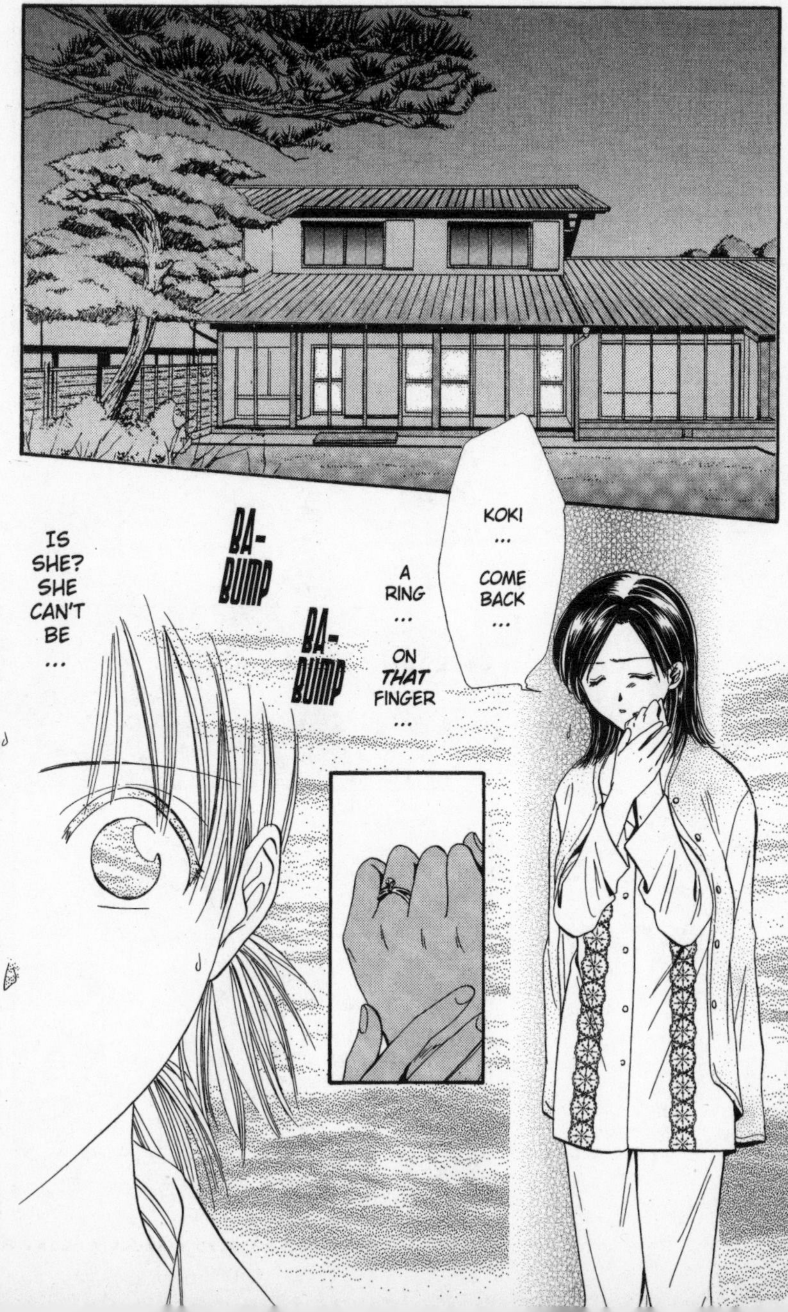
KOKI ... COME BACK ...
A RING ... ON THAT FINGER ...
BA-BUMP
BA-BUMP
IS SHE? SHE CAN'T BE ...

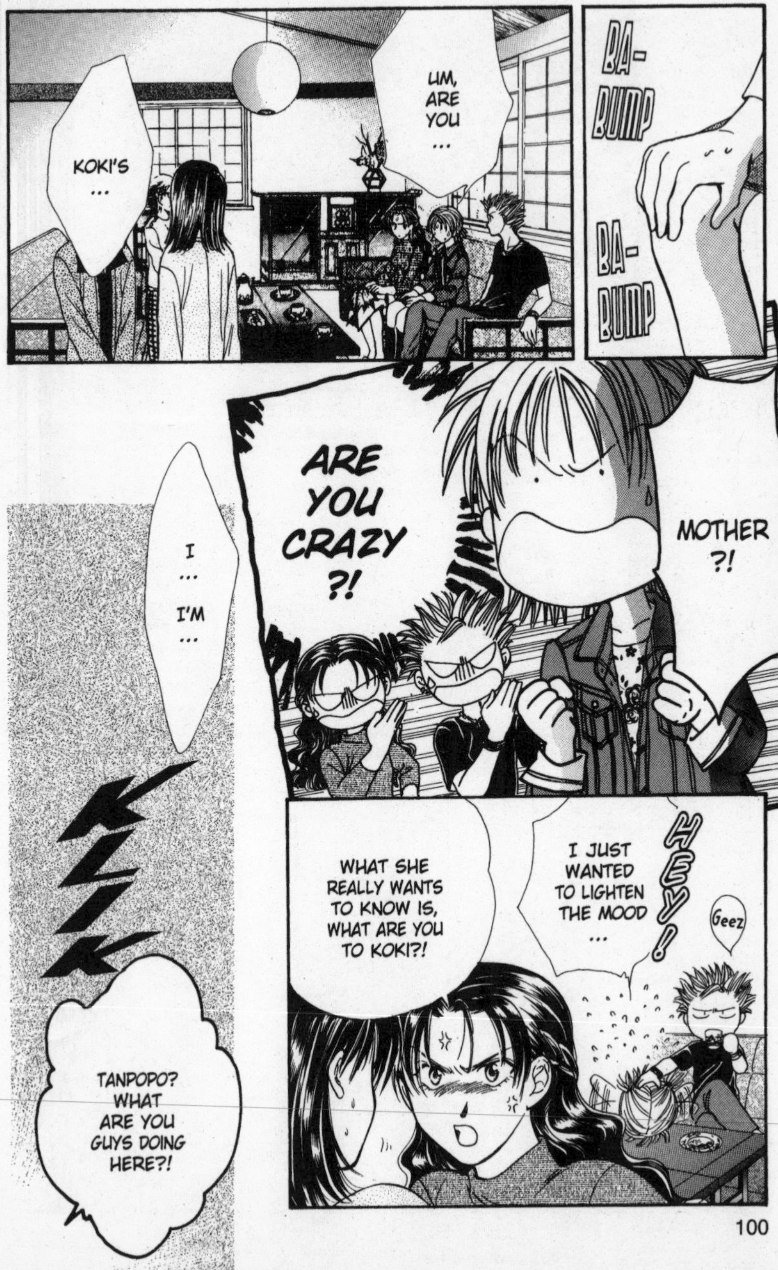
BA-BUMP
BA-BUMP
UM, ARE YOU ...
KOKI'S ...
MOTHER ?!
ARE YOU CRAZY ?!
HEY!
I JUST WANTED TO LIGHTEN THE MOOD ...
WHAT SHE REALLY WANTS TO KNOW IS, WHAT ARE YOU TO KOKI?!
Geez
I ... I'M ...
KLIK
TANPOPO? WHAT ARE YOU GUYS DOING HERE?!

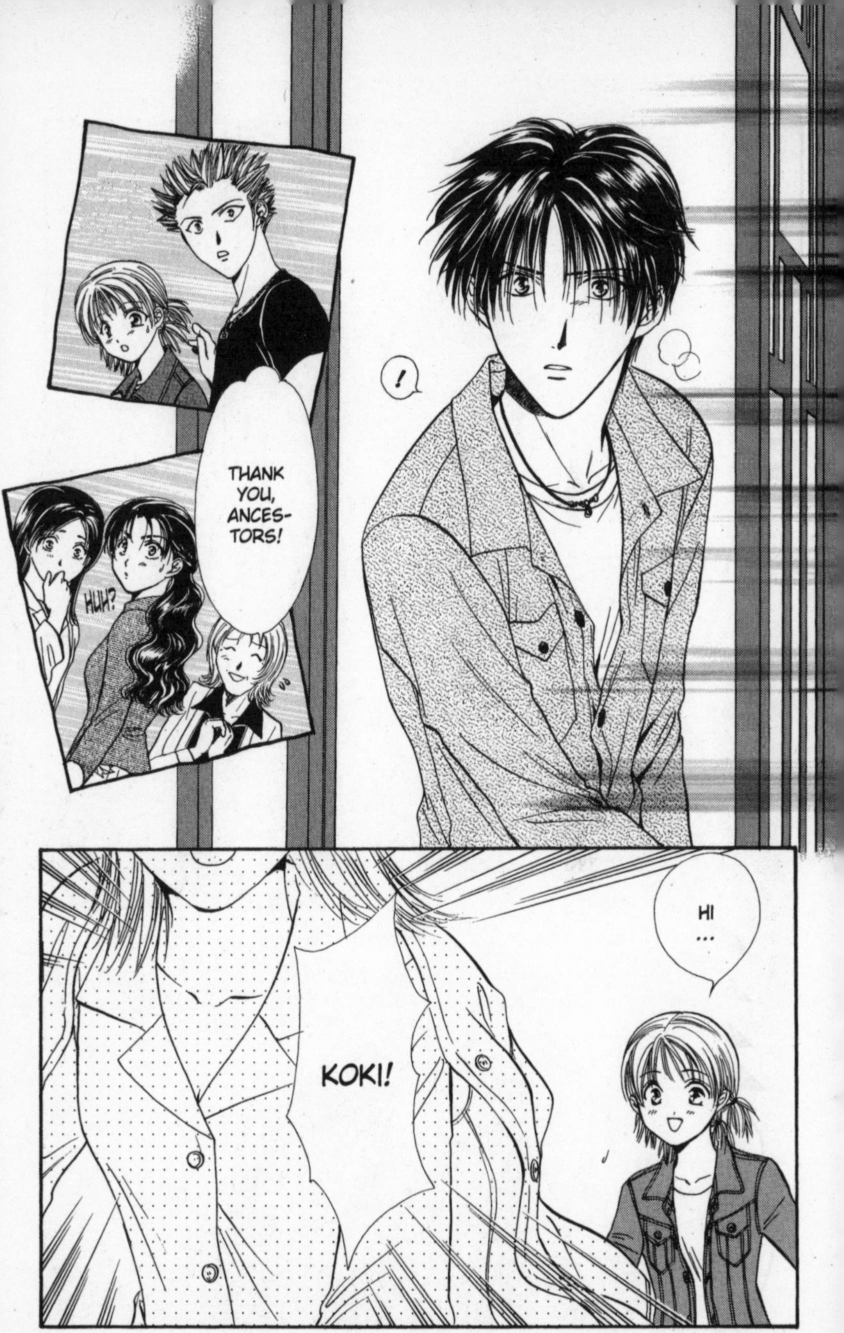
!
THANK YOU, ANCESTORS!
HUH?
HI ...
KOKI!

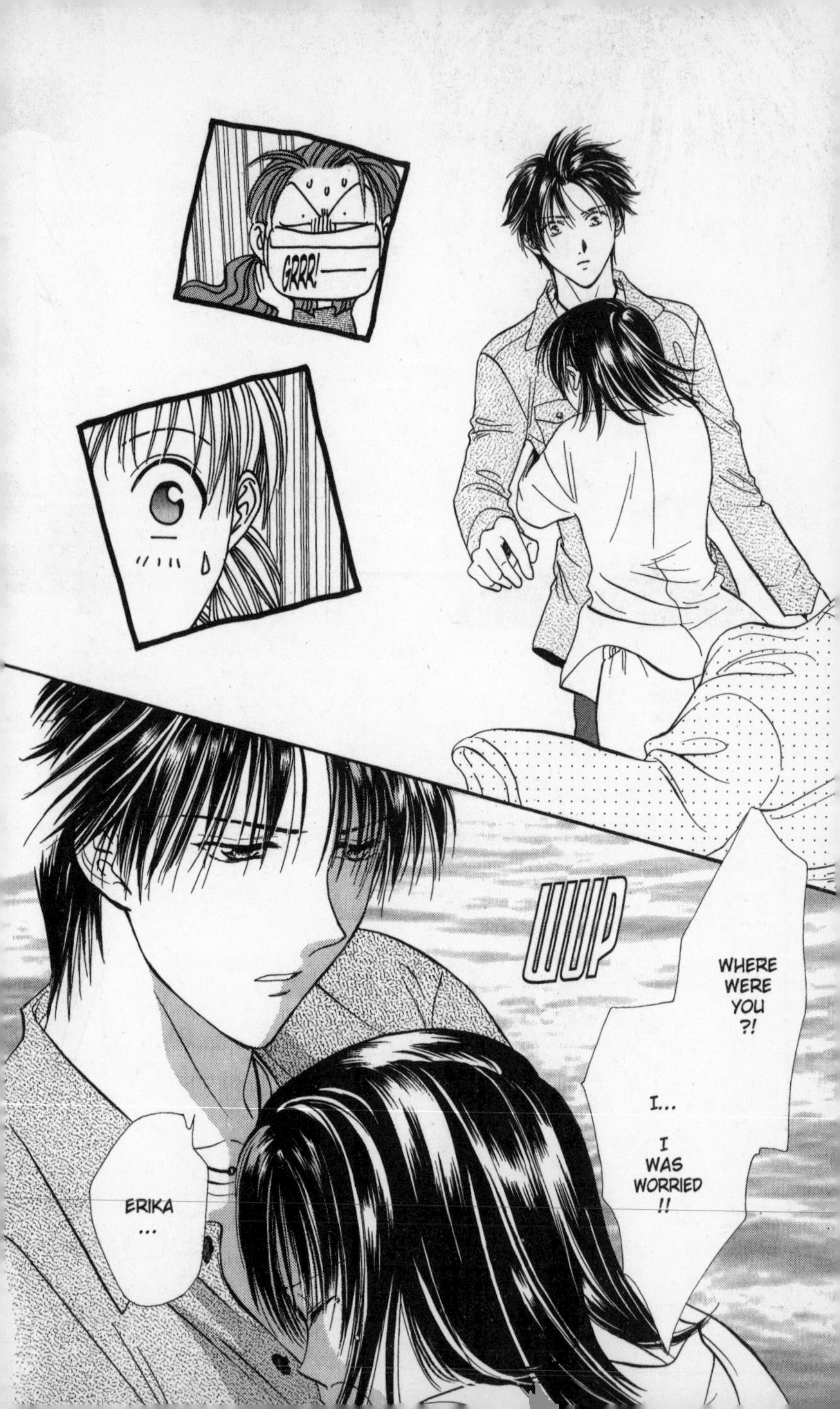
GRRR!
WUP
WHERE WERE YOU ?!
I... I WAS WORRIED !!
ERIKA ...

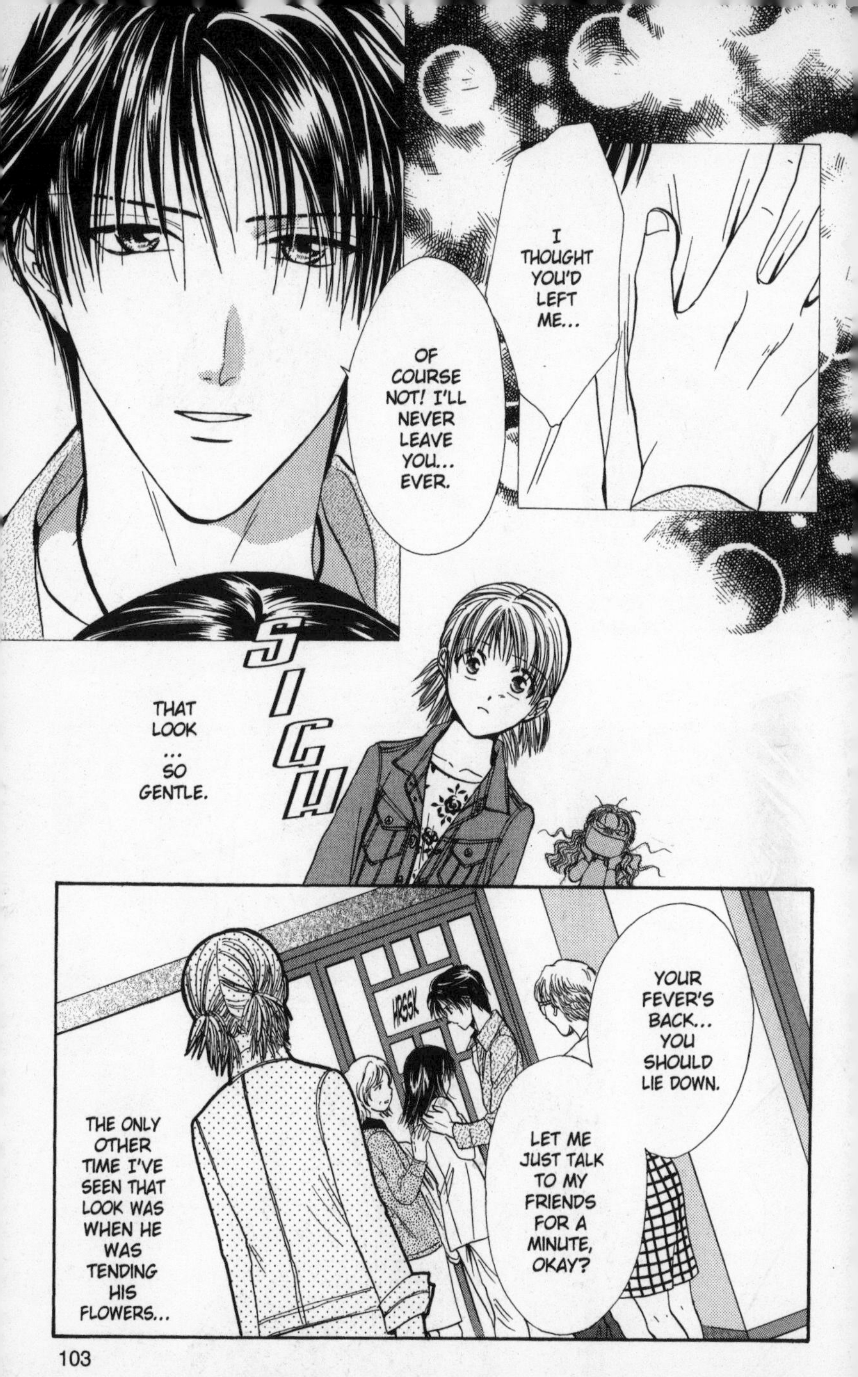
I THOUGHT YOU'D LEFT ME...
OF COURSE NOT! I'LL NEVER LEAVE YOU... EVER.
SIGH
THAT LOOK ... SO GENTLE.
YOUR FEVER'S BACK... YOU SHOULD LIE DOWN.
HRSSK
LET ME JUST TALK TO MY FRIENDS FOR A MINUTE, OKAY?
THE ONLY OTHER TIME I'VE SEEN THAT LOOK WAS WHEN HE WAS TENDING HIS FLOWERS...

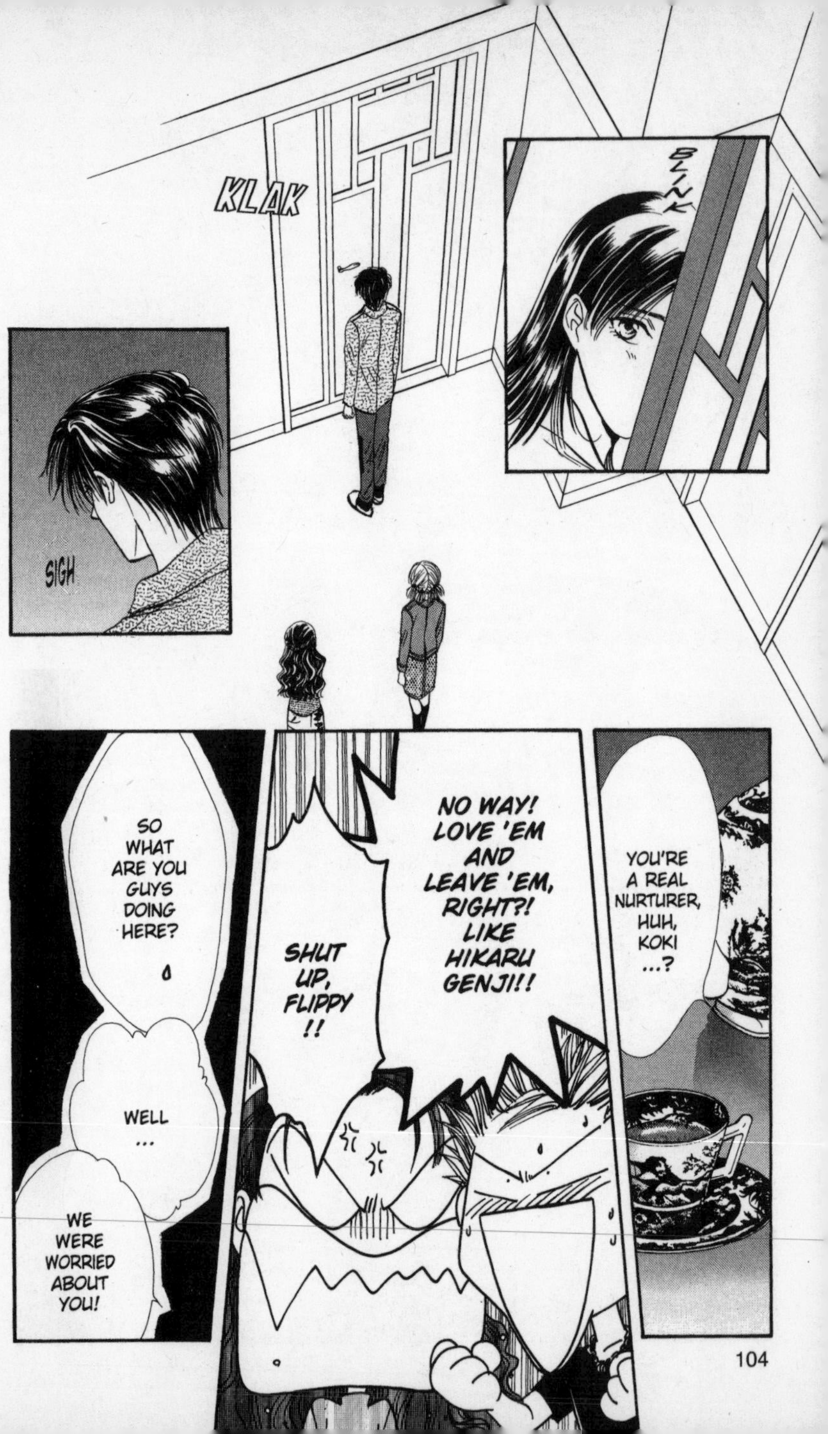
KLAK
BLINK
SIGH
YOU'RE A REAL NURTURER, HUH, KOKI ...?
NO WAY! LOVE 'EM AND LEAVE 'EM, RIGHT?! LIKE HIKARU GENJI!!
SHUT UP, FLIPPY !!
SO WHAT ARE YOU GUYS DOING HERE?
WELL ...
WE WERE WORRIED ABOUT YOU!

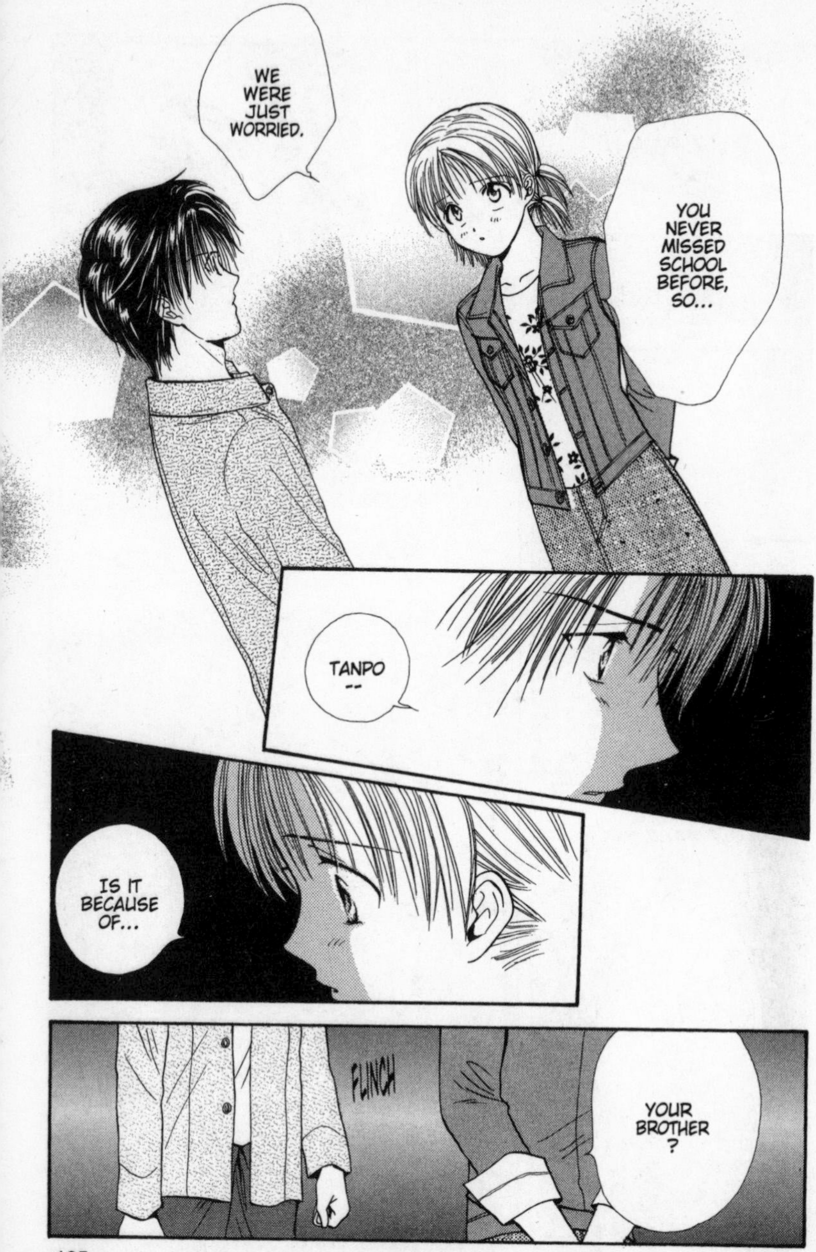
YOU NEVER MISSED SCHOOL BEFORE, SO...
WE WERE JUST WORRIED.
TANPO --
IS IT BECAUSE OF...
YOUR BROTHER ?
FLINCH

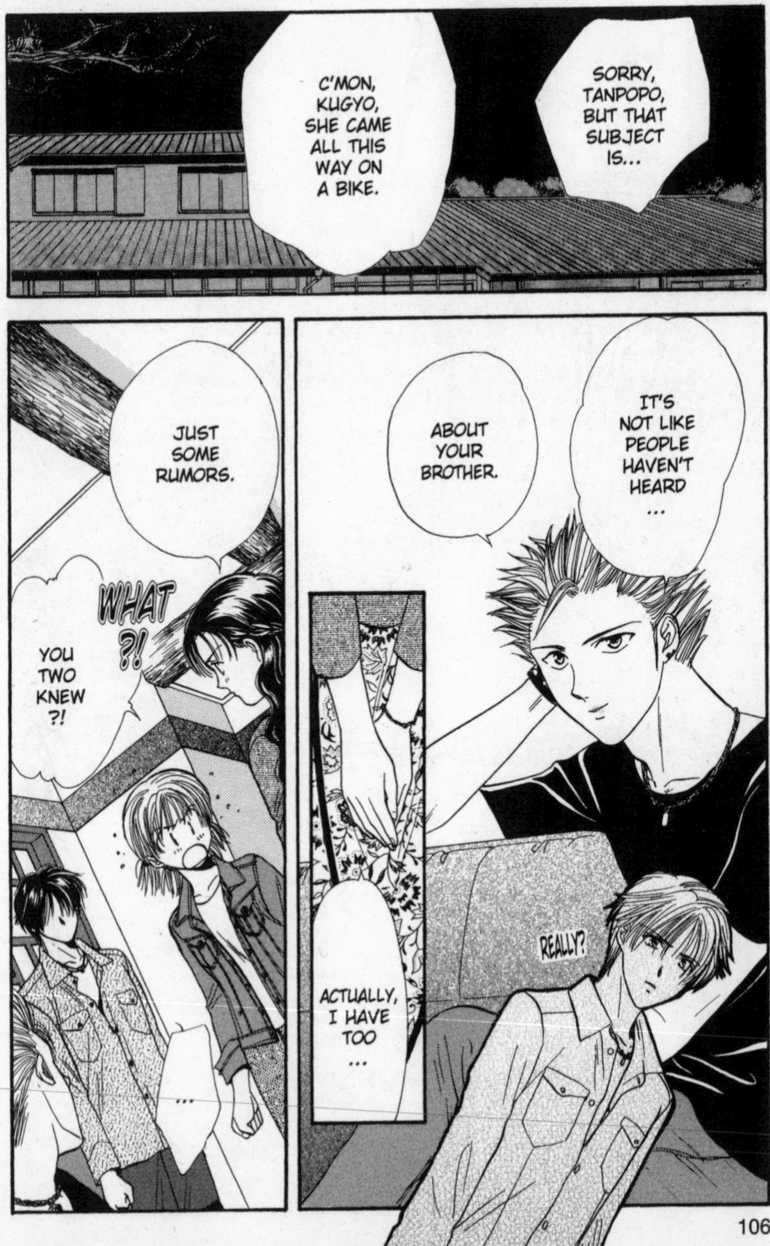
SORRY, TANPOPO, BUT THAT SUBJECT IS...
C'MON, KUGYO, SHE CAME ALL THIS WAY ON A BIKE.
IT'S NOT LIKE PEOPLE HAVEN'T HEARD ...
ABOUT YOUR BROTHER.
REALLY?
ACTUALLY, I HAVE TOO ...
JUST SOME RUMORS.
WHAT ?!
YOU TWO KNEW ?!
...

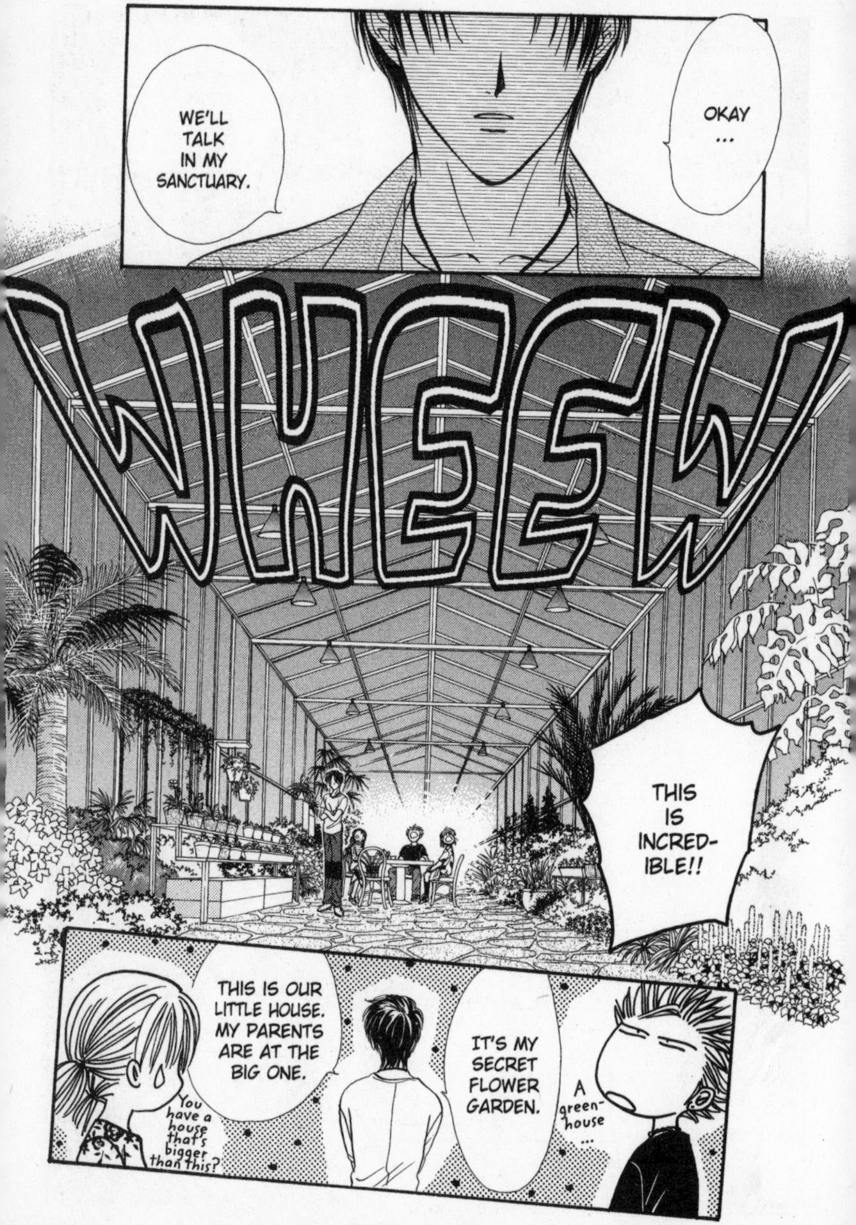
OKAY ...
WE'LL TALK IN MY SANCTUARY.
WHEEW
THIS IS INCREDIBLE!!
A greenhouse ...
IT'S MY SECRET FLOWER GARDEN.
THIS IS OUR LITTLE HOUSE. MY PARENTS ARE AT THE BIG ONE.
You have a house that's bigger than this?

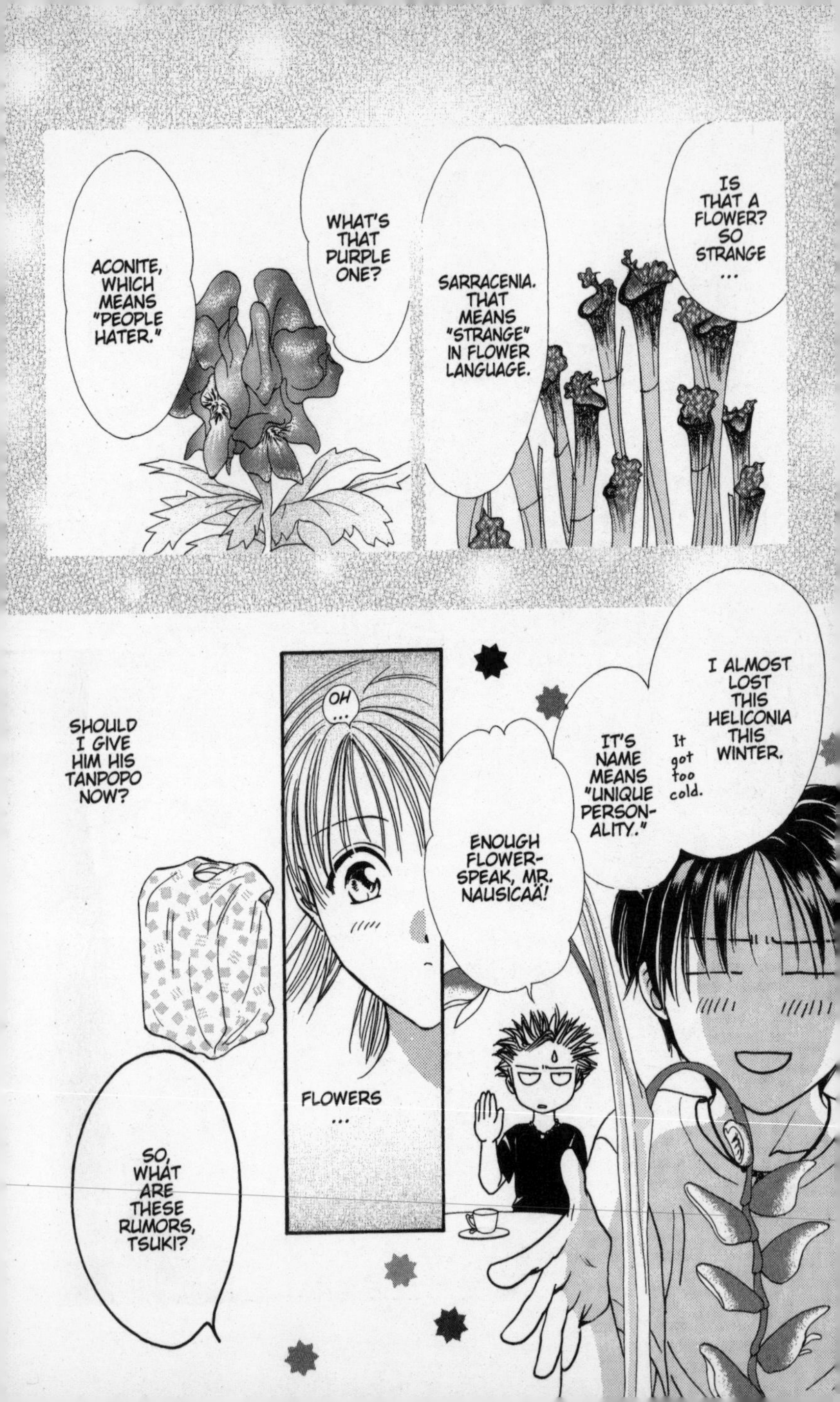
IS THAT A FLOWER? SO STRANGE ...
SARRACENIA. THAT MEANS "STRANGE" IN FLOWER LANGUAGE.
WHAT'S THAT PURPLE ONE?
ACONITE, WHICH MEANS "PEOPLE HATER."
I ALMOST LOST THIS HELICONIA THIS WINTER.
It got too cold.
IT'S NAME MEANS "UNIQUE PERSONALITY."
ENOUGH FLOWER-SPEAK, MR. NAUSICAÄ!
OH ...
FLOWERS ...
SHOULD I GIVE HIM HIS TANPOPO NOW?
SO, WHAT ARE THESE RUMORS, TSUKI?

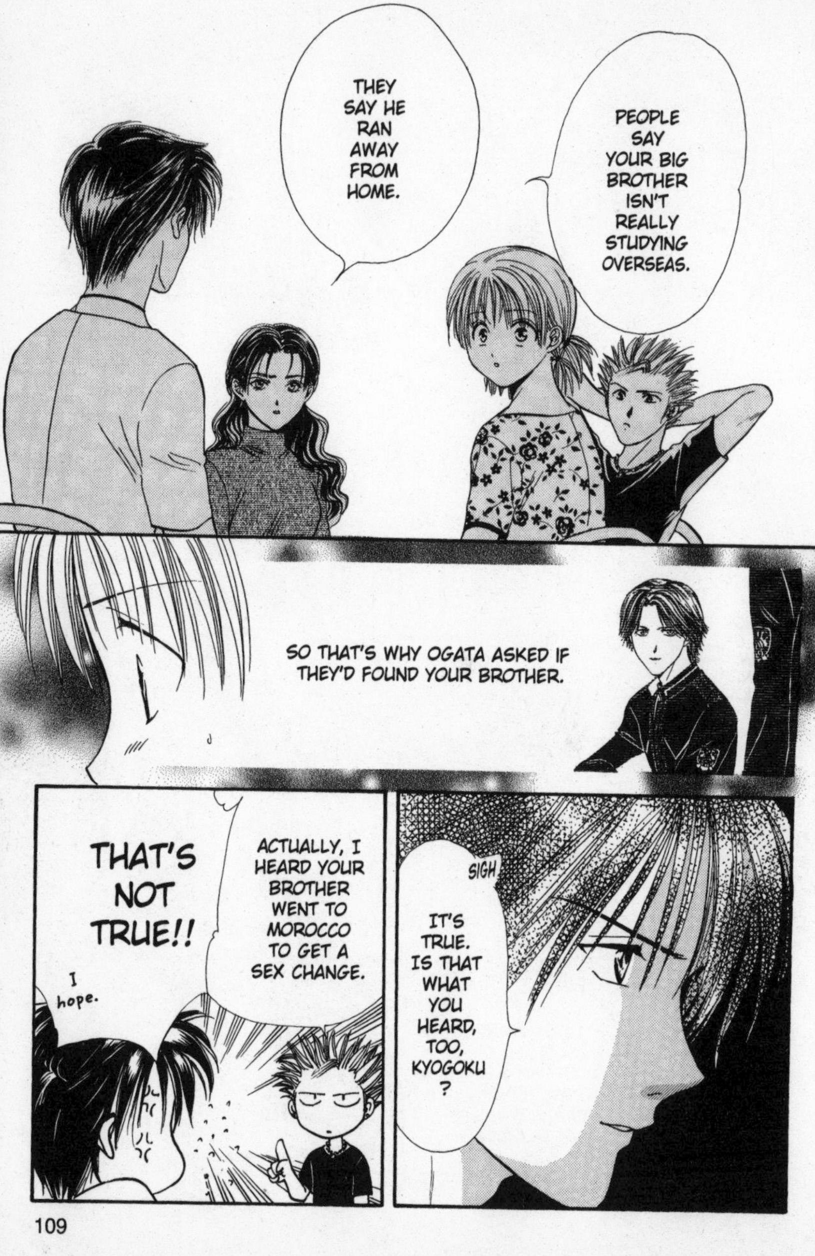

PEOPLE SAY YOUR BIG BROTHER ISN'T REALLY STUDYING OVERSEAS.
THEY SAY HE RAN AWAY FROM HOME.
SO THAT'S WHY OGATA ASKED IF THEY'D FOUND YOUR BROTHER.
SIGH
IT'S TRUE. IS THAT WHAT YOU HEARD, TOO, KYOGOKU?
ACTUALLY, I HEARD YOUR BROTHER WENT TO MOROCCO TO GET A SEX CHANGE.
THAT'S NOT TRUE!!
I hope.

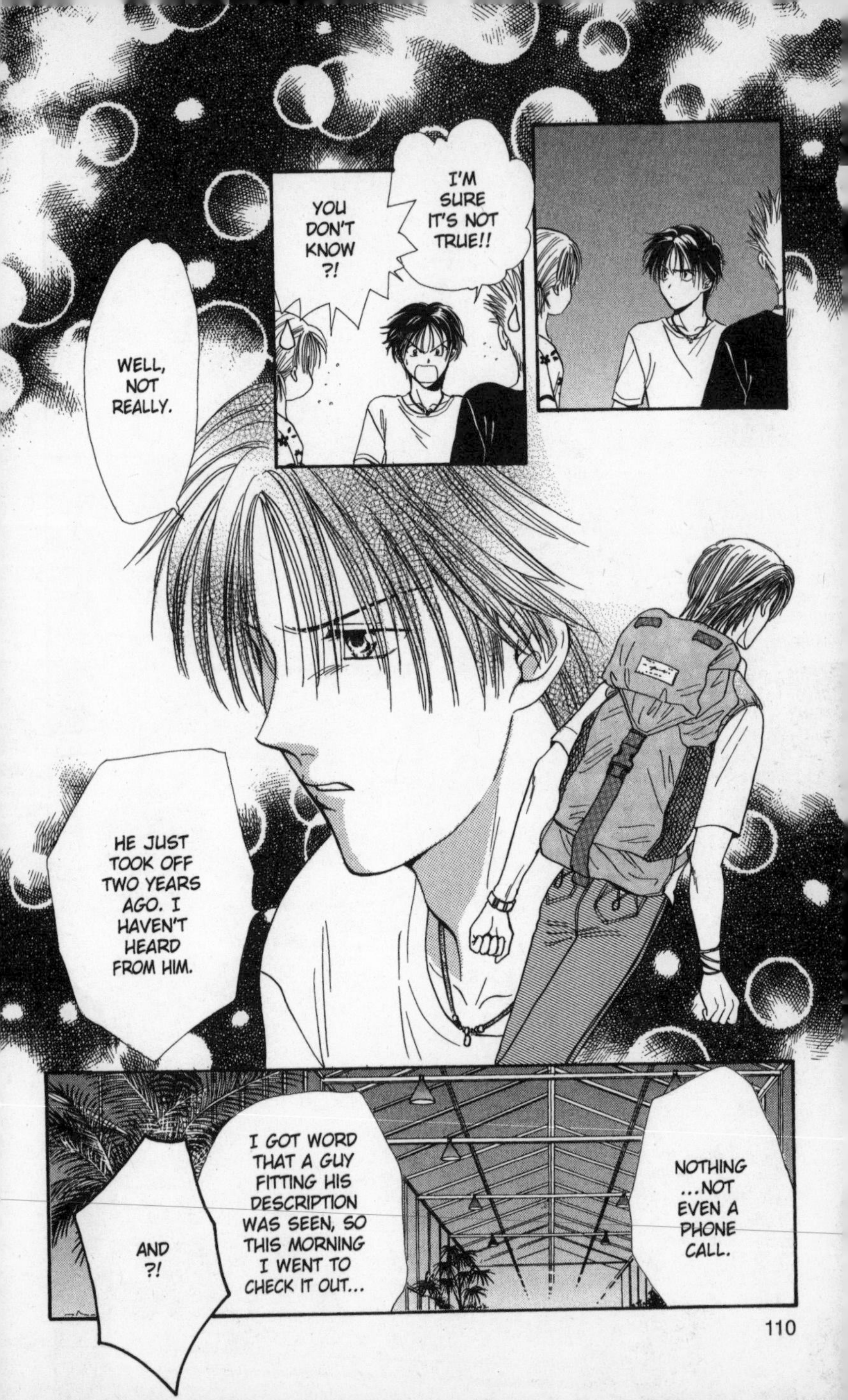
I'M SURE IT'S NOT TRUE!!
YOU DON'T KNOW ?!
WELL, NOT REALLY.
HE JUST TOOK OFF TWO YEARS AGO. I HAVEN'T HEARD FROM HIM.
NOTHING ...NOT EVEN A PHONE CALL.
I GOT WORD THAT A GUY FITTING HIS DESCRIPTION WAS SEEN, SO THIS MORNING I WENT TO CHECK IT OUT...
AND ?!

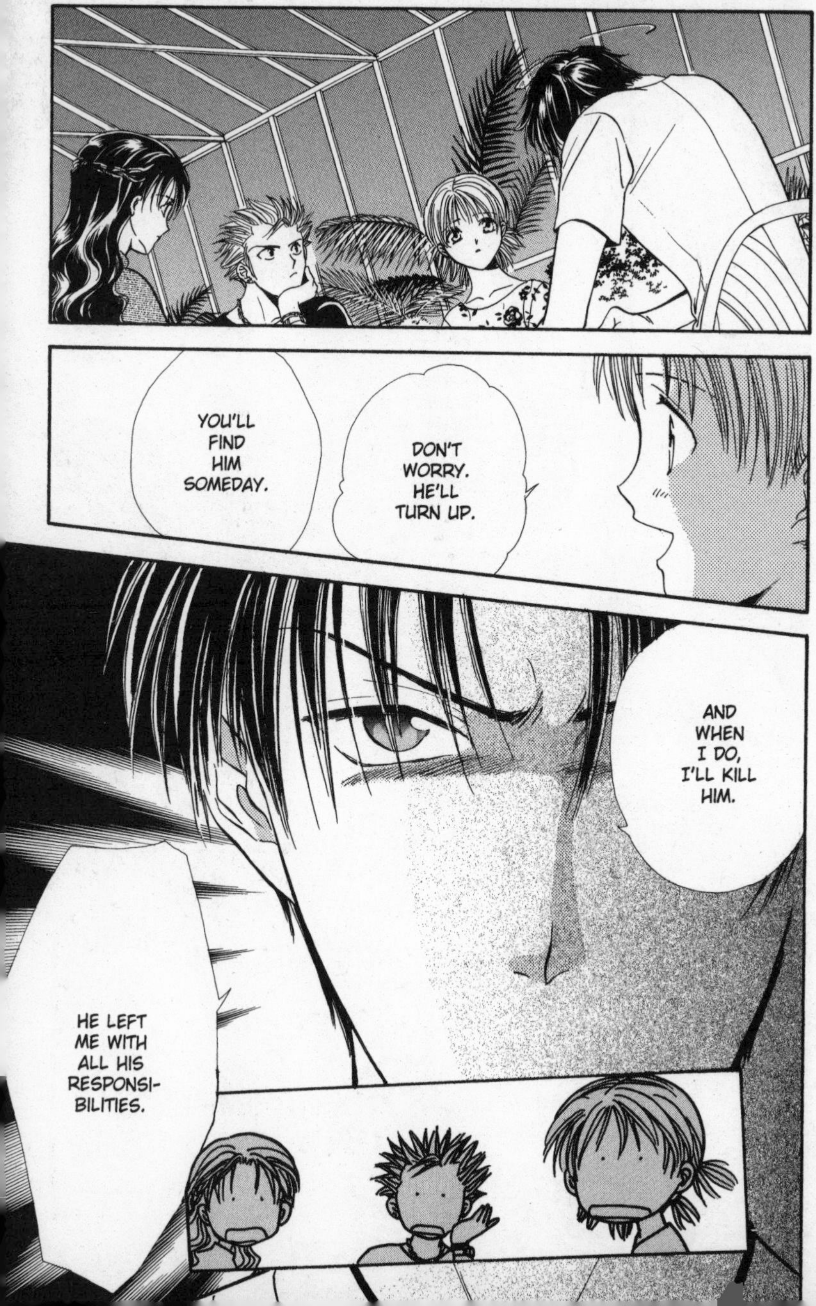
DON'T WORRY. HE'LL TURN UP.
YOU'LL FIND HIM SOMEDAY.
AND WHEN I DO, I'LL KILL HIM.
HE LEFT ME WITH ALL HIS RESPONSIBILITIES.

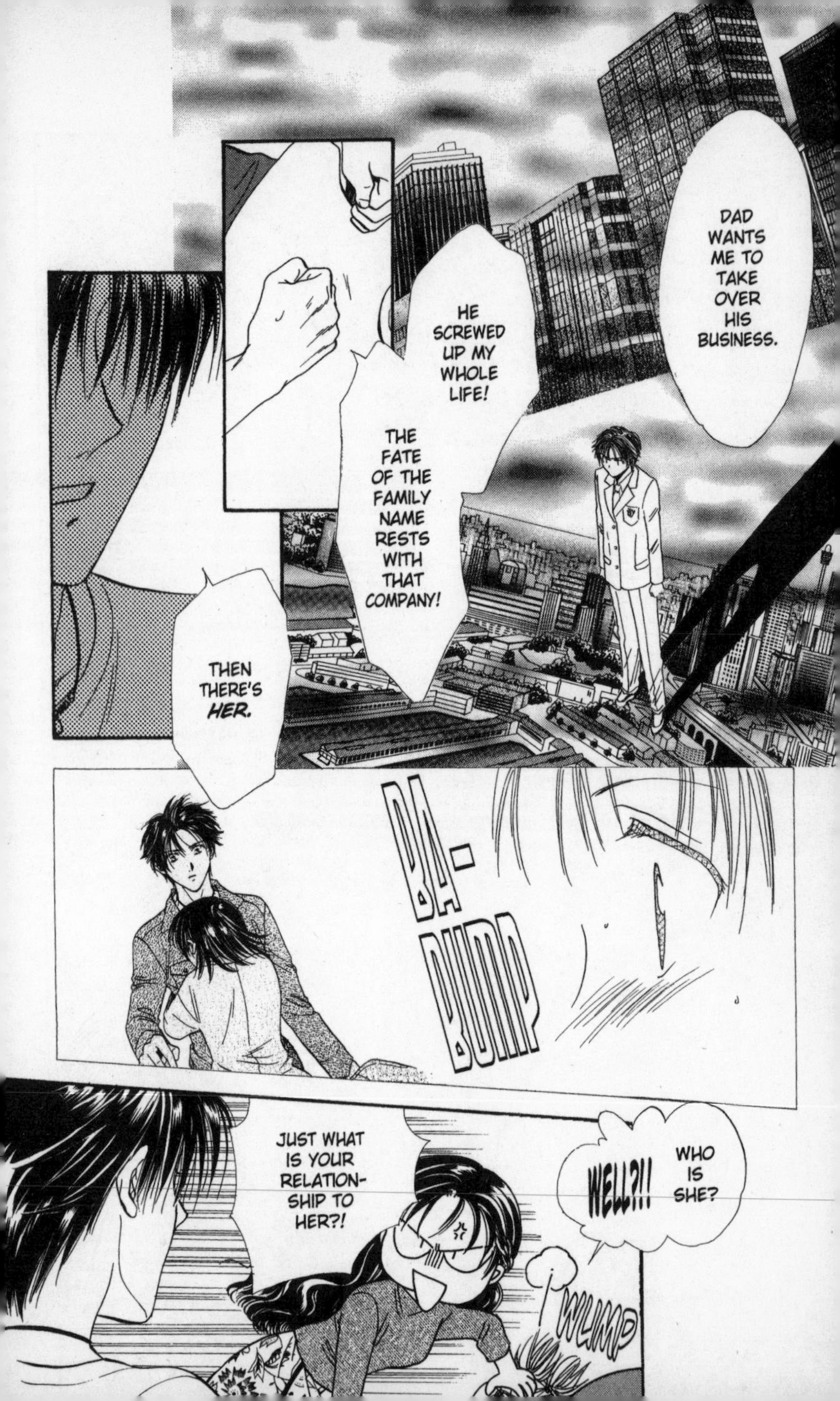
DAD WANTS ME TO TAKE OVER HIS BUSINESS.
HE SCREWED UP MY WHOLE LIFE!
THE FATE OF THE FAMILY NAME RESTS WITH THAT COMPANY!
THEN THERE'S *HER.*
BA-BUMP
WHO IS SHE?
WELL?!!
JUST WHAT IS YOUR RELATIONSHIP TO HER?!
WUMP

Poplar is the first animal character I've done in a long time. Tanpopo was raised in Hokkaido, so I thought a fox would be good. But this is not a **Northern** fox! Huh? Those are the only kind, you say? I think you're wrong!! (hmph) This is a comic and the creator makes the rules! (But my characters really are alive, somehow.)

As for real foxes, they have a parasite living inside of them called echinococcosis, so if you do somehow find one, don't pet it like Tanpopo does Poplar! (This is fiction, after all!!)

My assistant told me something scary once. Although echinococcosis is supposed to be found only in foxes, it has evolved and can live in dogs and--worse still--humans?! Once introduced into a human body, it can destroy the lungs!! Really, it's happened to a some people!! You have to have surgery! Aaagh! Hokkaido, are you all right? It's just a matter of time before it crosses over to Honshu, right?

Wow, foxes have it rough (or maybe not), but we've got it rougher!!! Animals evolve and get stronger, but what about humans? (Hey! I can use this storyline in **Ayashi no Ceres**!!!)

Aaah! And speaking of parasites... (I have some really nasty stories...)

ERIKA IS ...

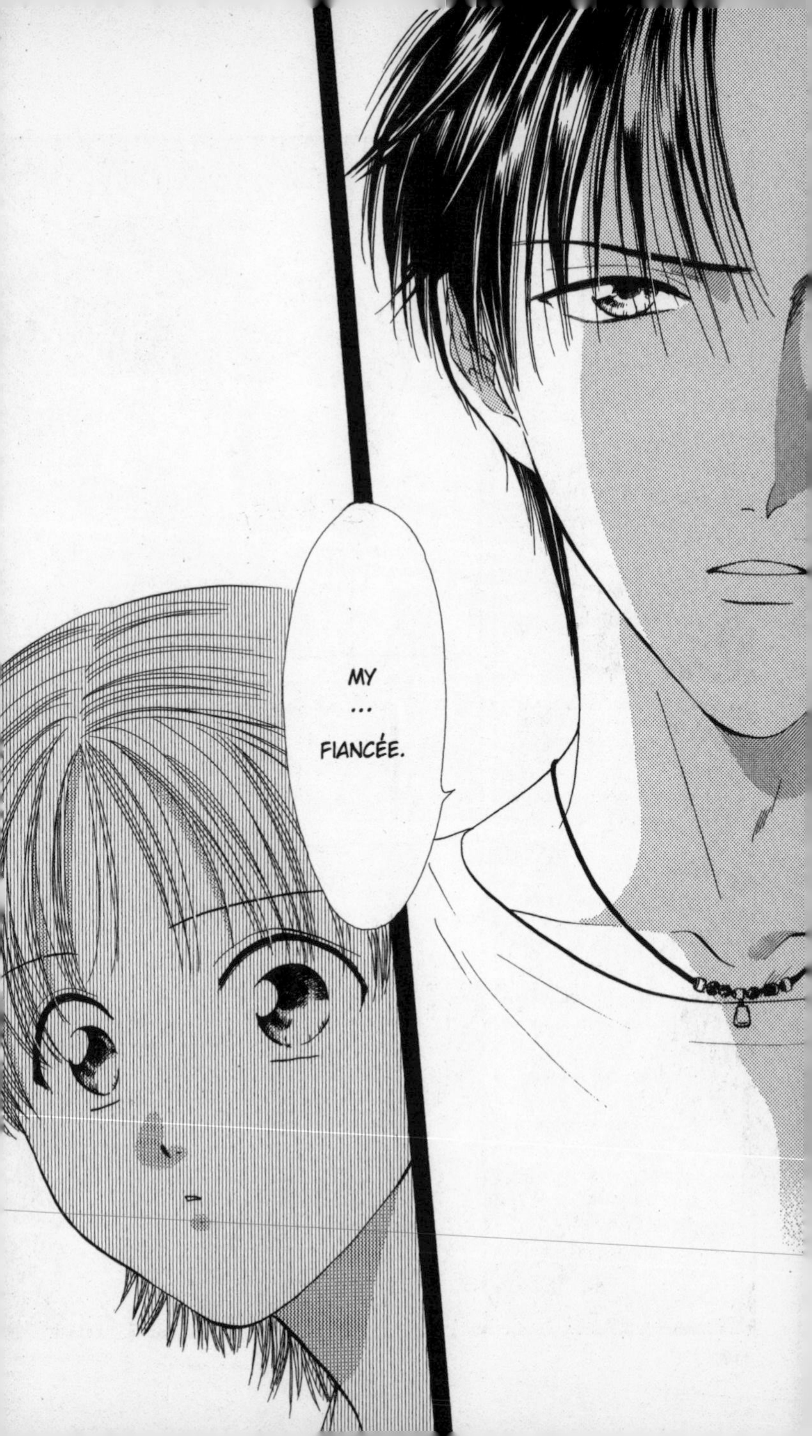
MY ... FIANCÉE.

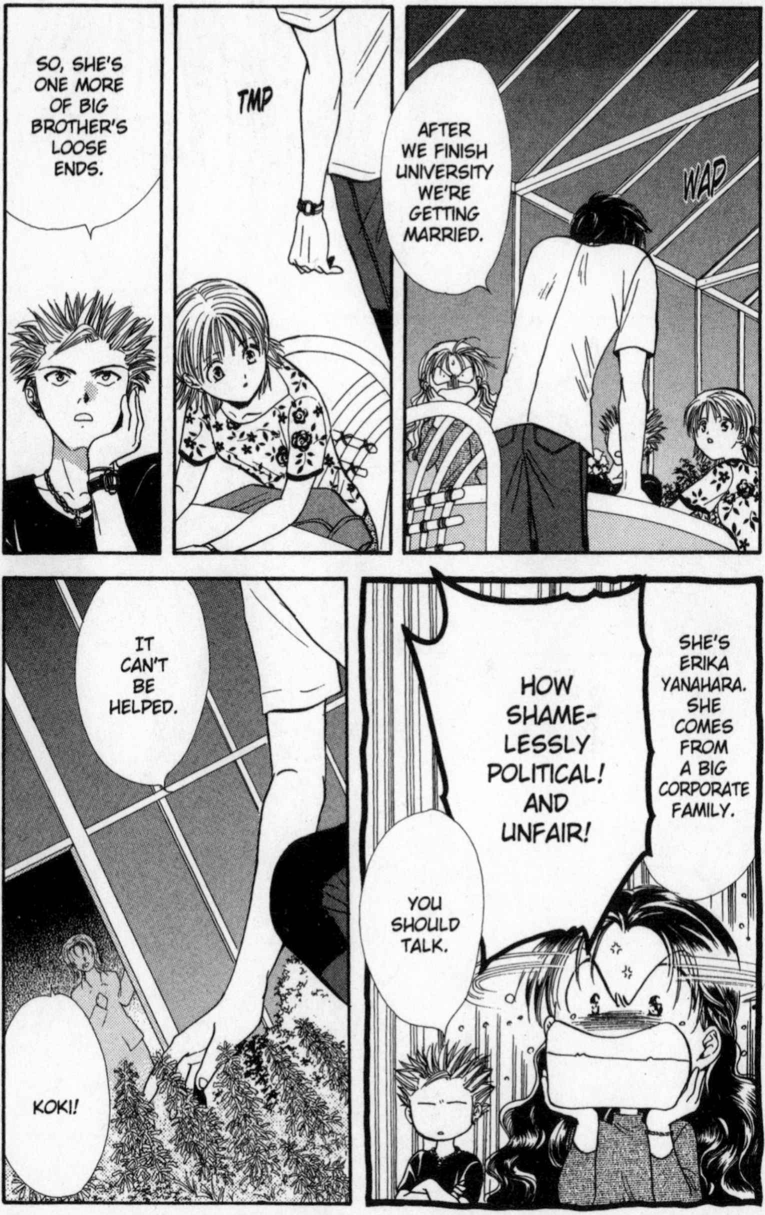
AFTER WE FINISH UNIVERSITY WE'RE GETTING MARRIED.
WAP
TMP
SO, SHE'S ONE MORE OF BIG BROTHER'S LOOSE ENDS.
SHE'S ERIKA YANAHARA. SHE COMES FROM A BIG CORPORATE FAMILY.
HOW SHAME-LESSLY POLITICAL! AND UNFAIR!
YOU SHOULD TALK.
IT CAN'T BE HELPED.
KOKI!

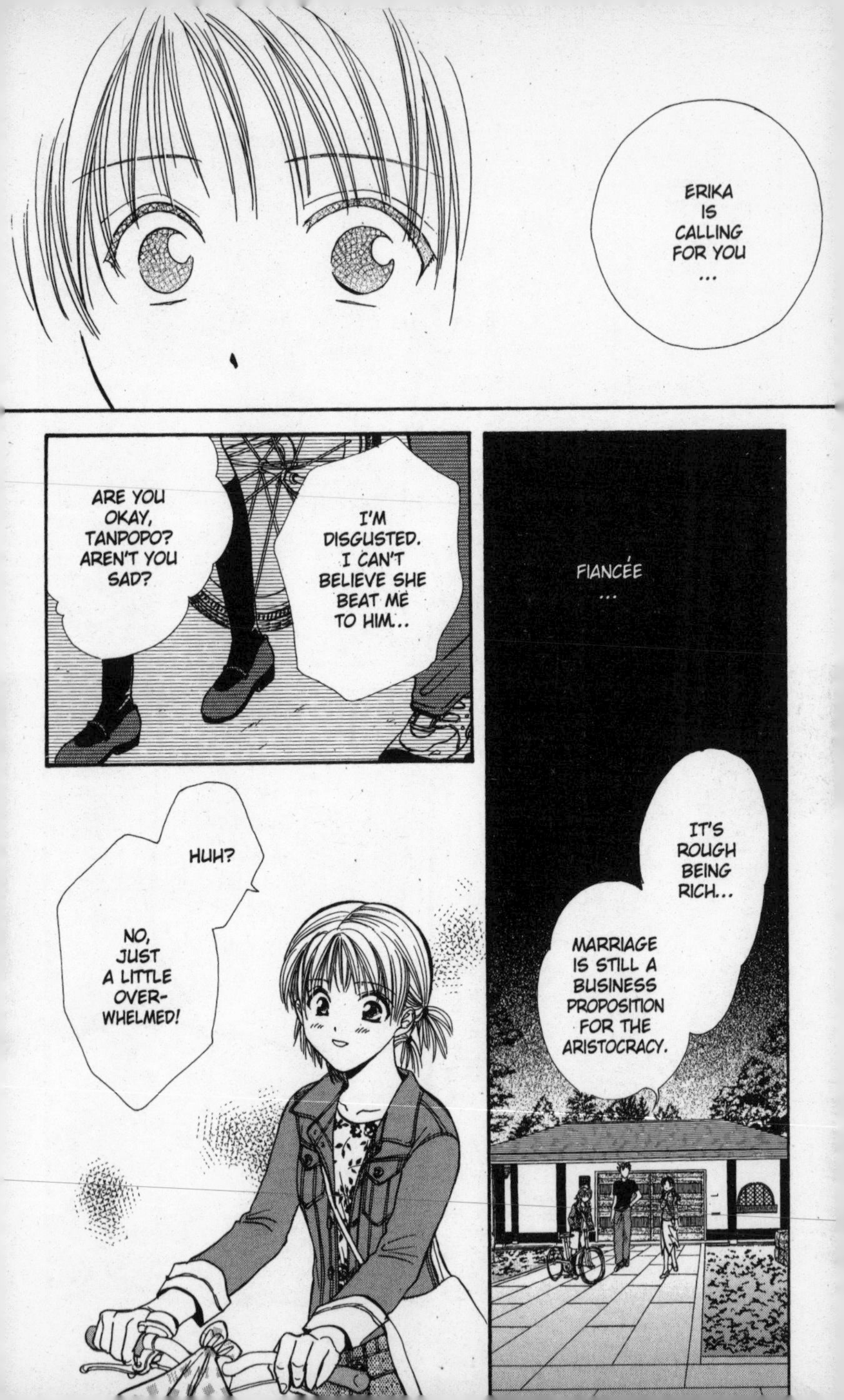
ERIKA IS CALLING FOR YOU ...
FIANCÉE ...
IT'S ROUGH BEING RICH...
MARRIAGE IS STILL A BUSINESS PROPOSITION FOR THE ARISTOCRACY.
I'M DISGUSTED. I CAN'T BELIEVE SHE BEAT ME TO HIM...
ARE YOU OKAY, TANPOPO? AREN'T YOU SAD?
HUH?
NO, JUST A LITTLE OVER-WHELMED!

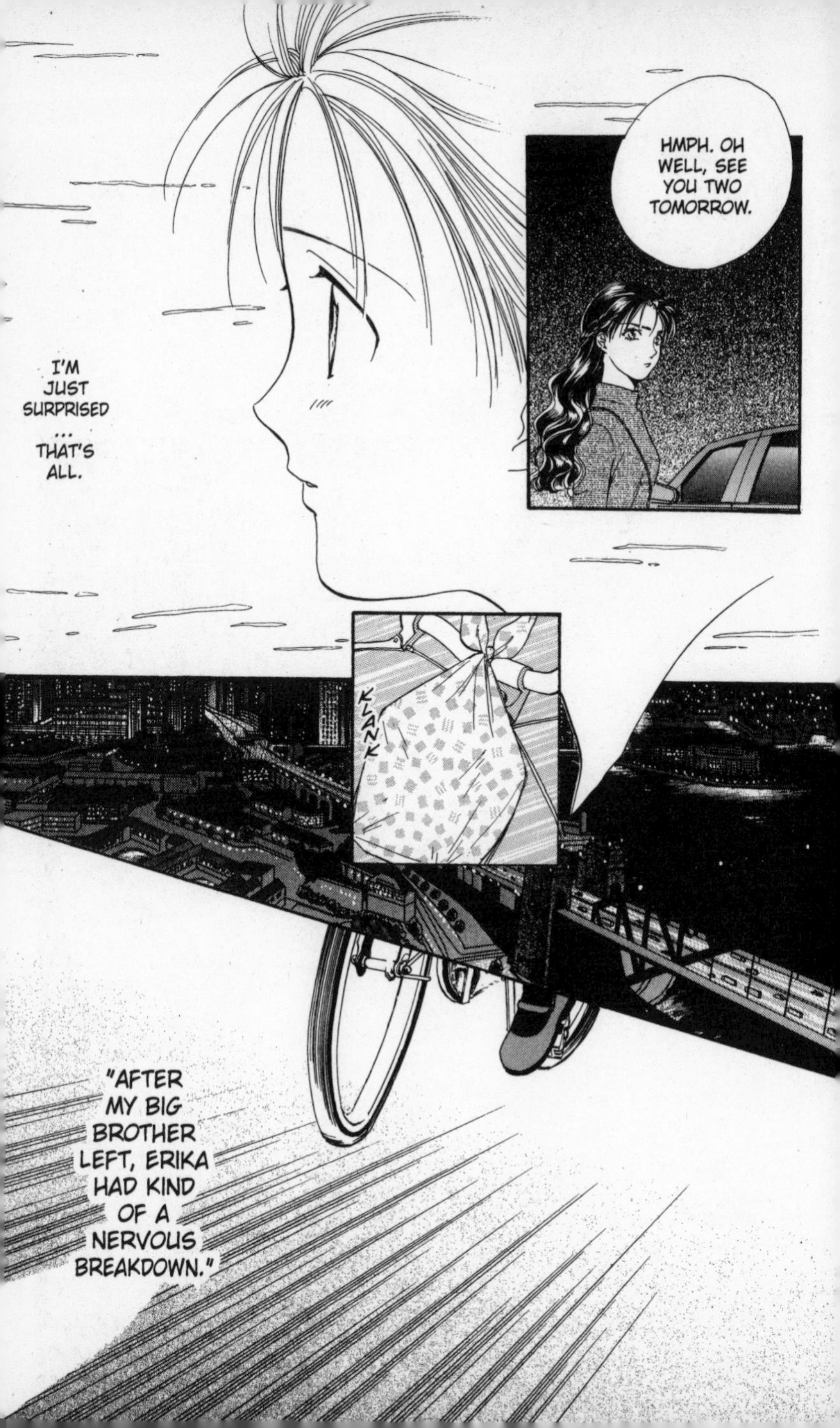
HMPH. OH WELL, SEE YOU TWO TOMORROW.
I'M JUST SURPRISED ... THAT'S ALL.
KLANK
"AFTER MY BIG BROTHER LEFT, ERIKA HAD KIND OF A NERVOUS BREAKDOWN."

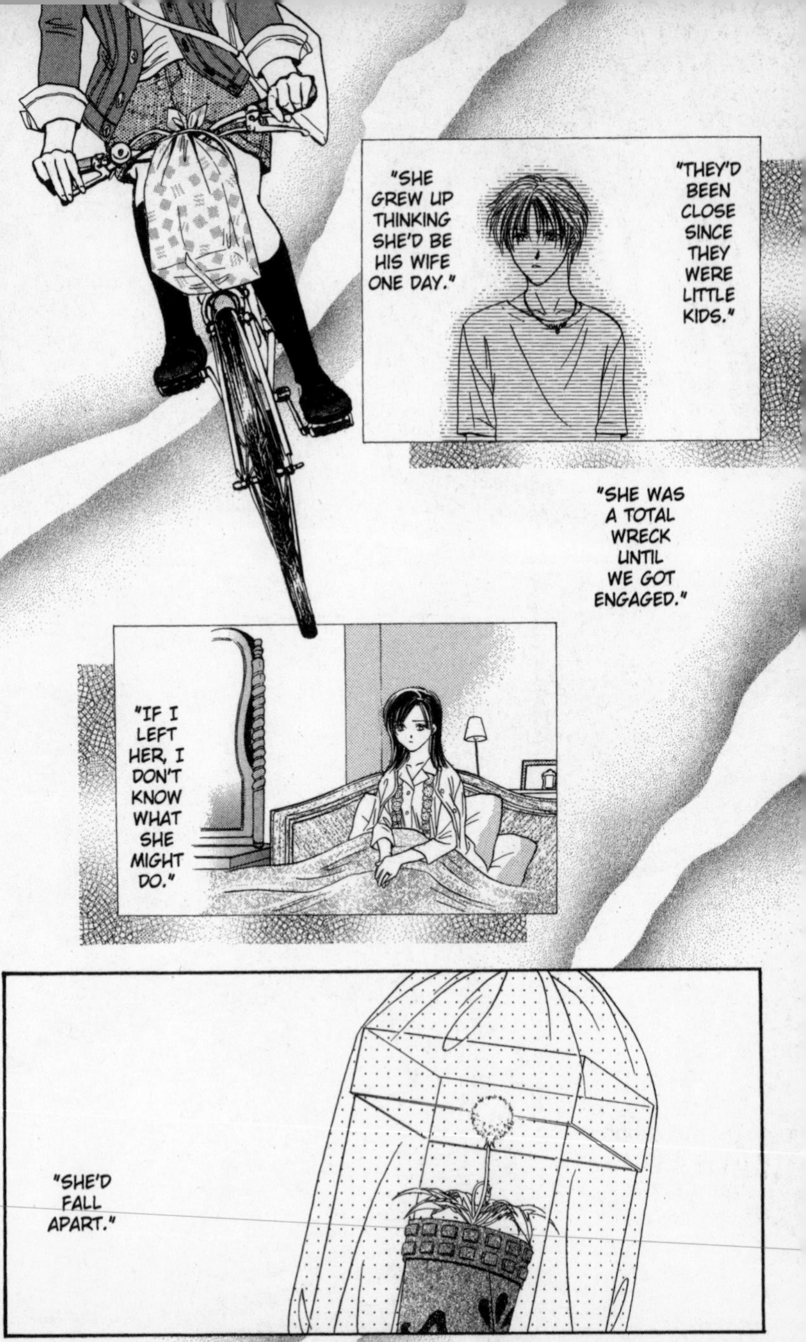
"THEY'D BEEN CLOSE SINCE THEY WERE LITTLE KIDS."
"SHE GREW UP THINKING SHE'D BE HIS WIFE ONE DAY."
"SHE WAS A TOTAL WRECK UNTIL WE GOT ENGAGED."
"IF I LEFT HER, I DON'T KNOW WHAT SHE MIGHT DO."
"SHE'D FALL APART."

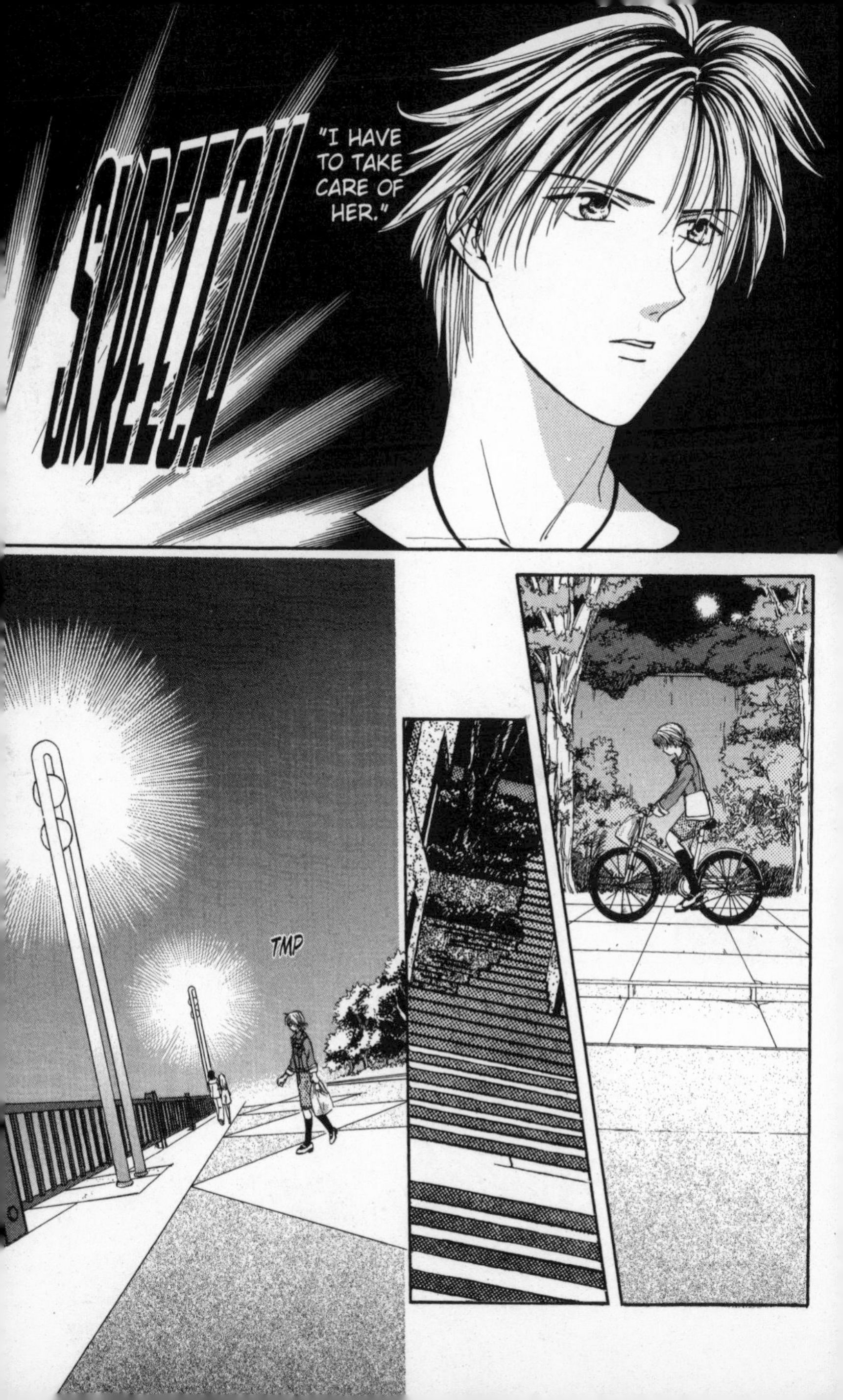
"I HAVE TO TAKE CARE OF HER."
SKREECH
TMP

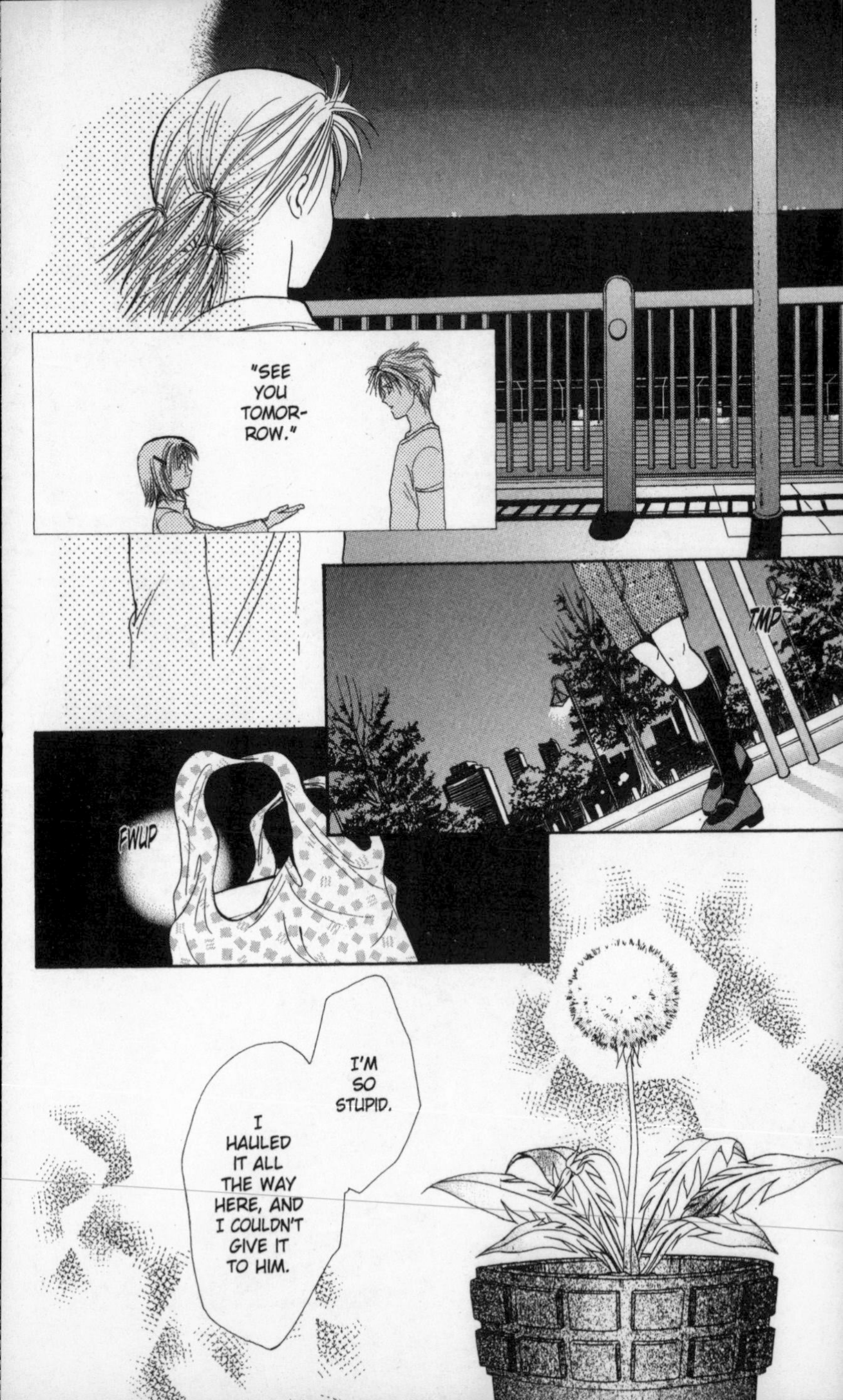
"SEE YOU TOMORROW."
TMP
FWUP
I'M SO STUPID.
I HAULED IT ALL THE WAY HERE, AND I COULDN'T GIVE IT TO HIM.

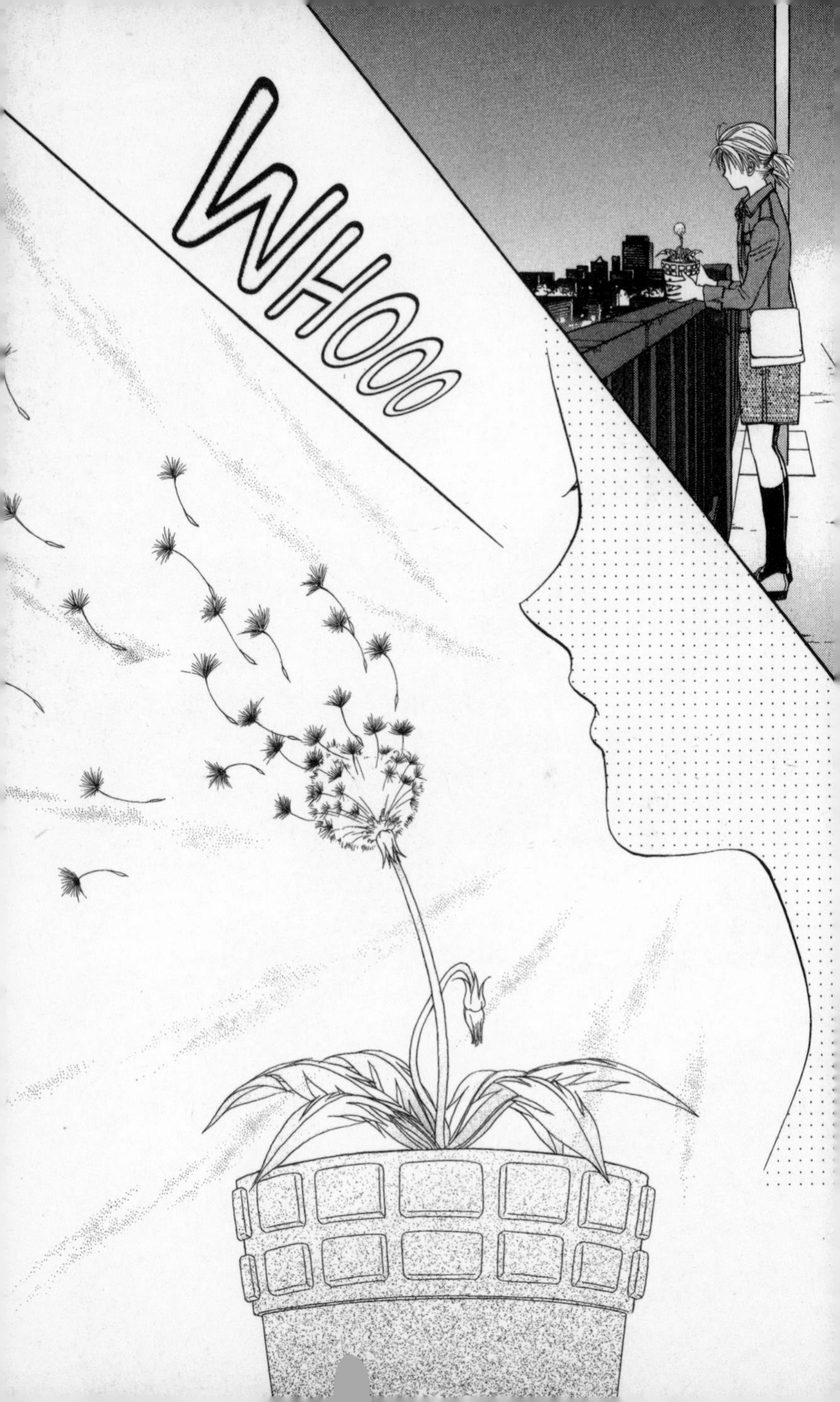
WHOOO

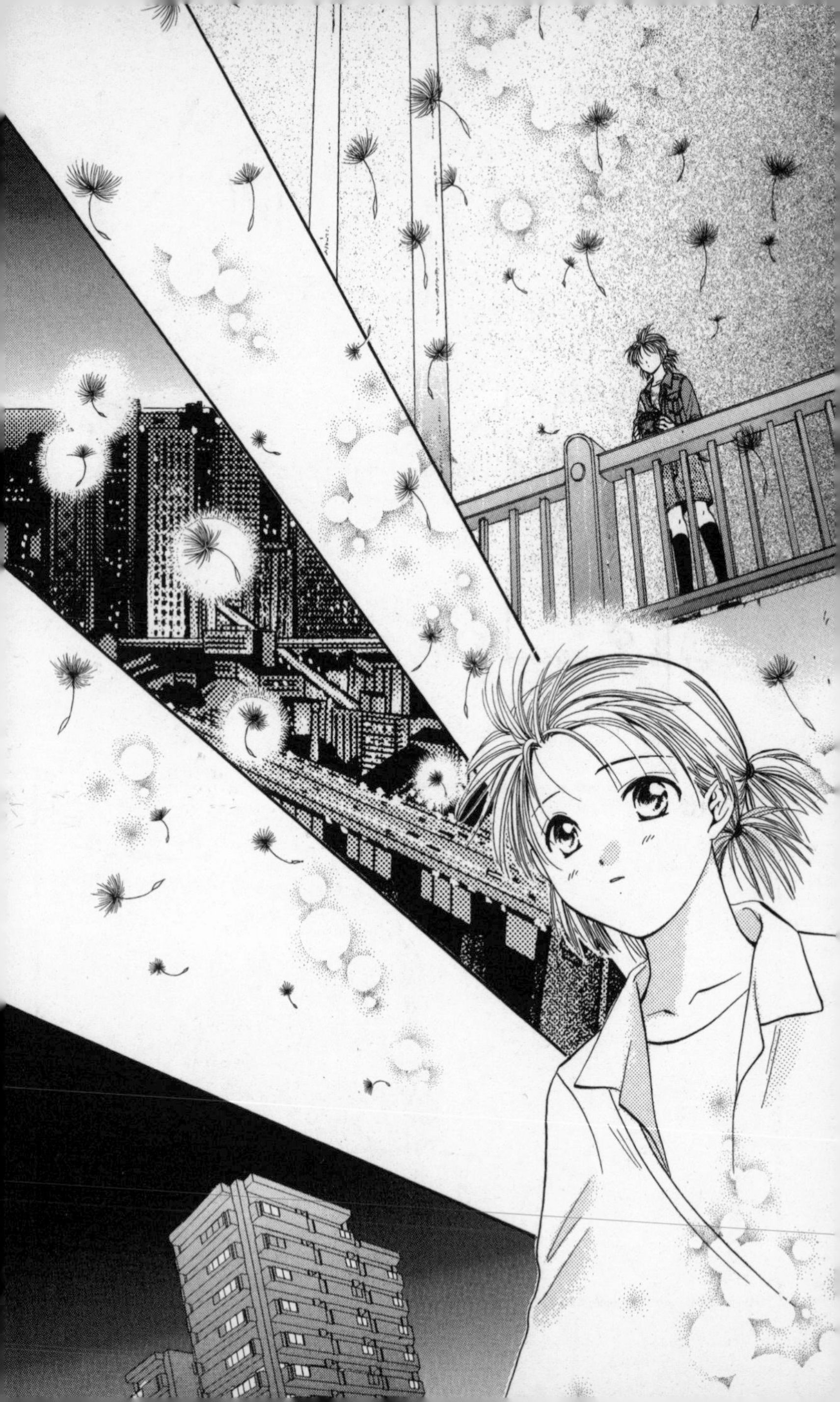

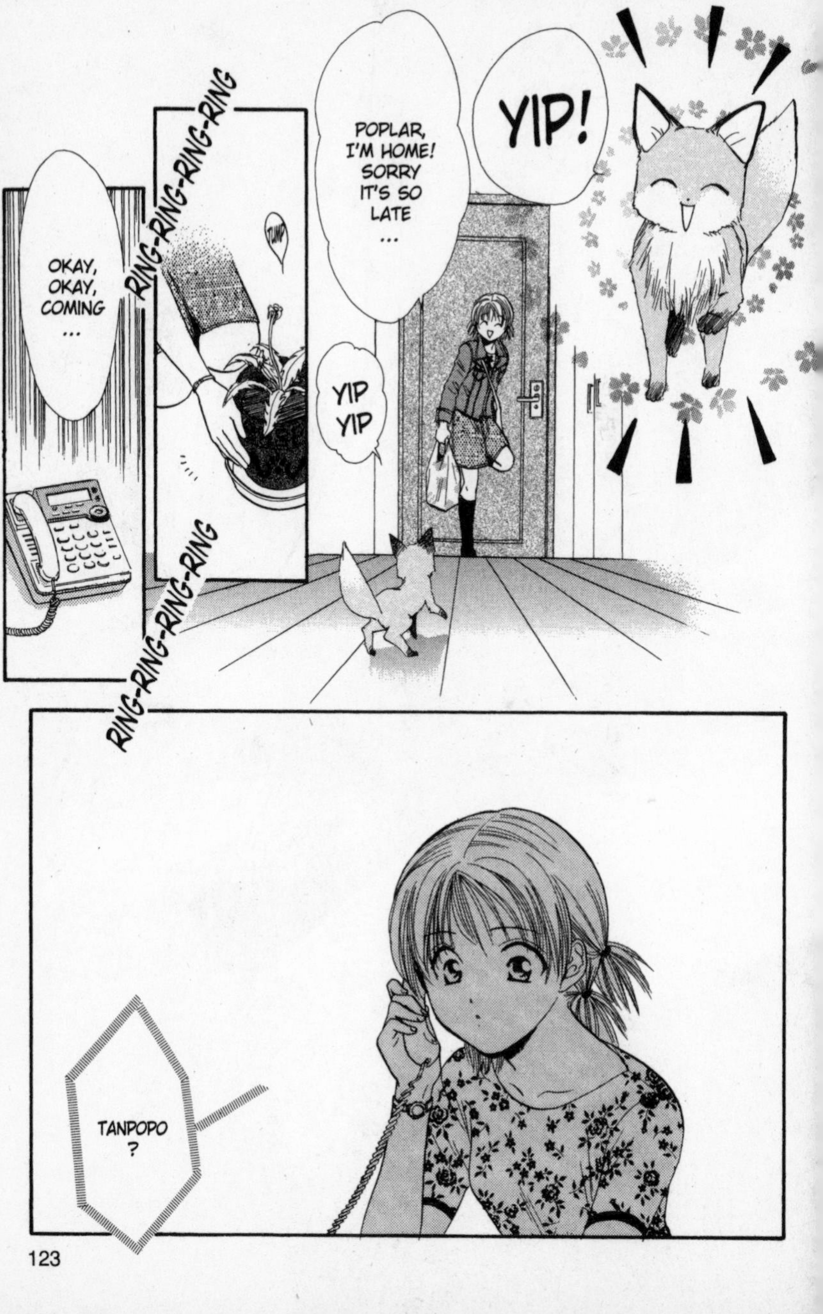
YIP!
POPLAR, I'M HOME! SORRY IT'S SO LATE ...
YIP YIP
RING-RING-RING-RING
RING-RING-RING-RING
OKAY, OKAY, COMING ...
TANPOPO ?

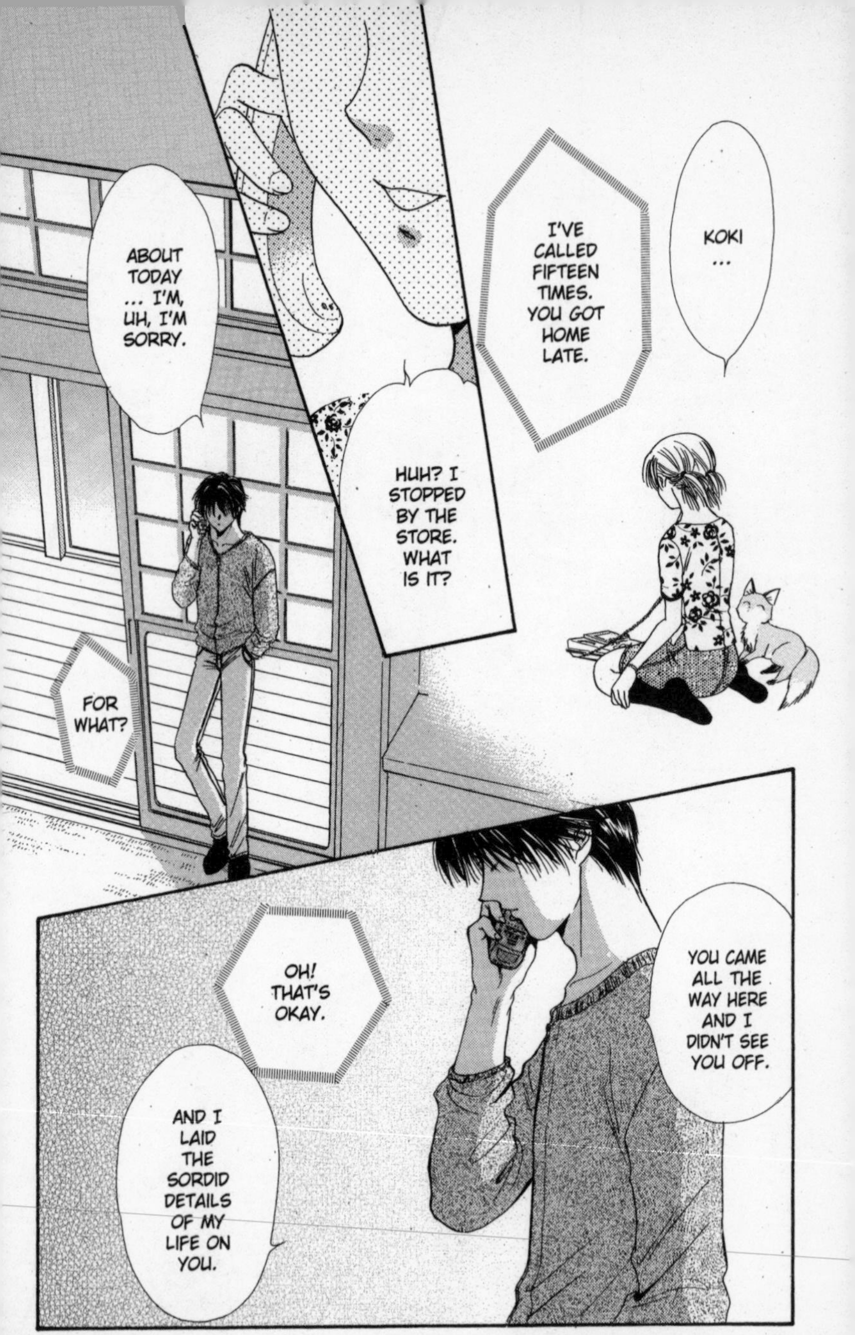
KOKI ...
I'VE CALLED FIFTEEN TIMES. YOU GOT HOME LATE.
HUH? I STOPPED BY THE STORE. WHAT IS IT?
ABOUT TODAY ... I'M, UH, I'M SORRY.
FOR WHAT?
YOU CAME ALL THE WAY HERE AND I DIDN'T SEE YOU OFF.
OH! THAT'S OKAY.
AND I LAID THE SORDID DETAILS OF MY LIFE ON YOU.

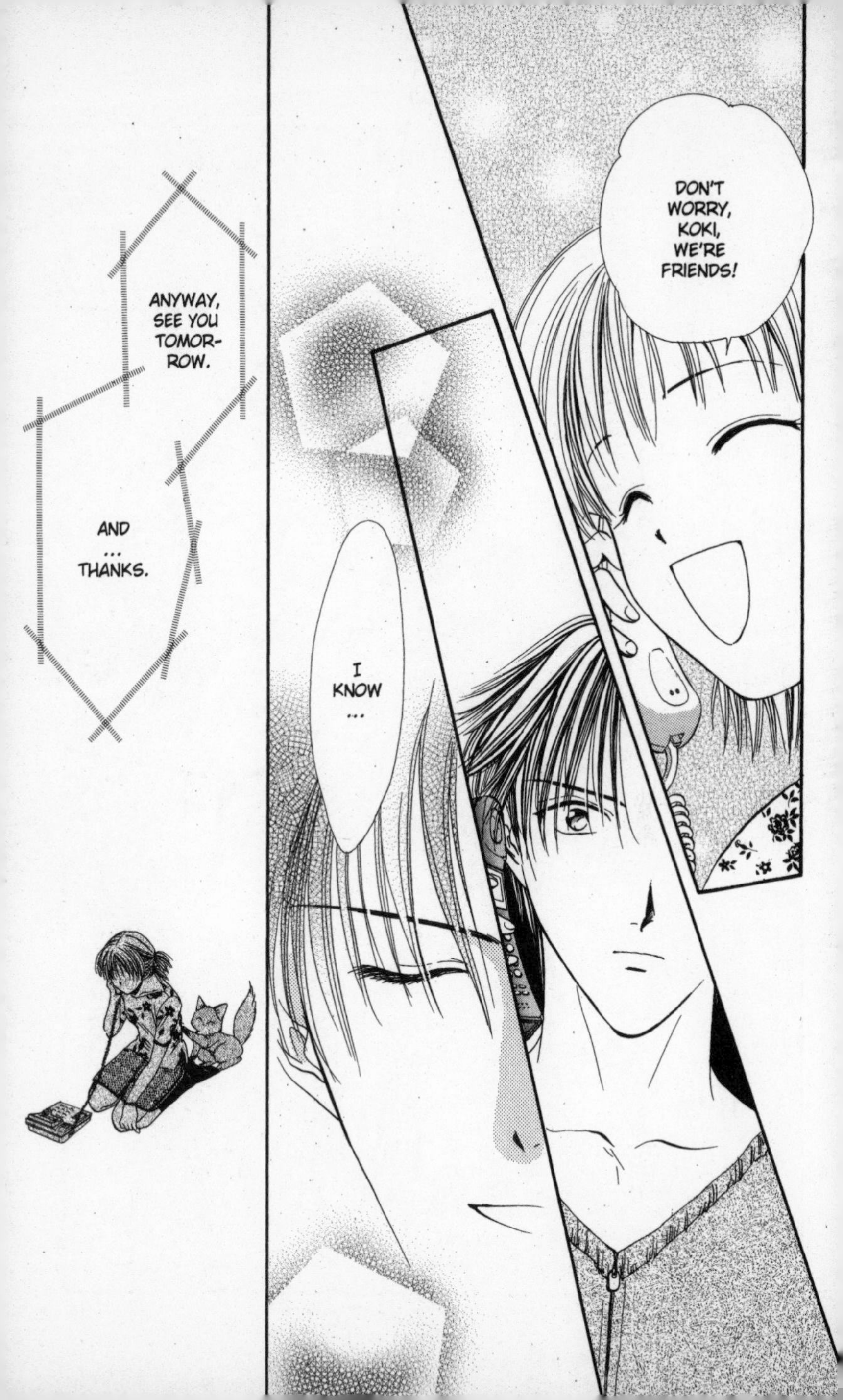
DON'T WORRY, KOKI, WE'RE FRIENDS!
I KNOW ...
ANYWAY, SEE YOU TOMOR-ROW.
AND ... THANKS.

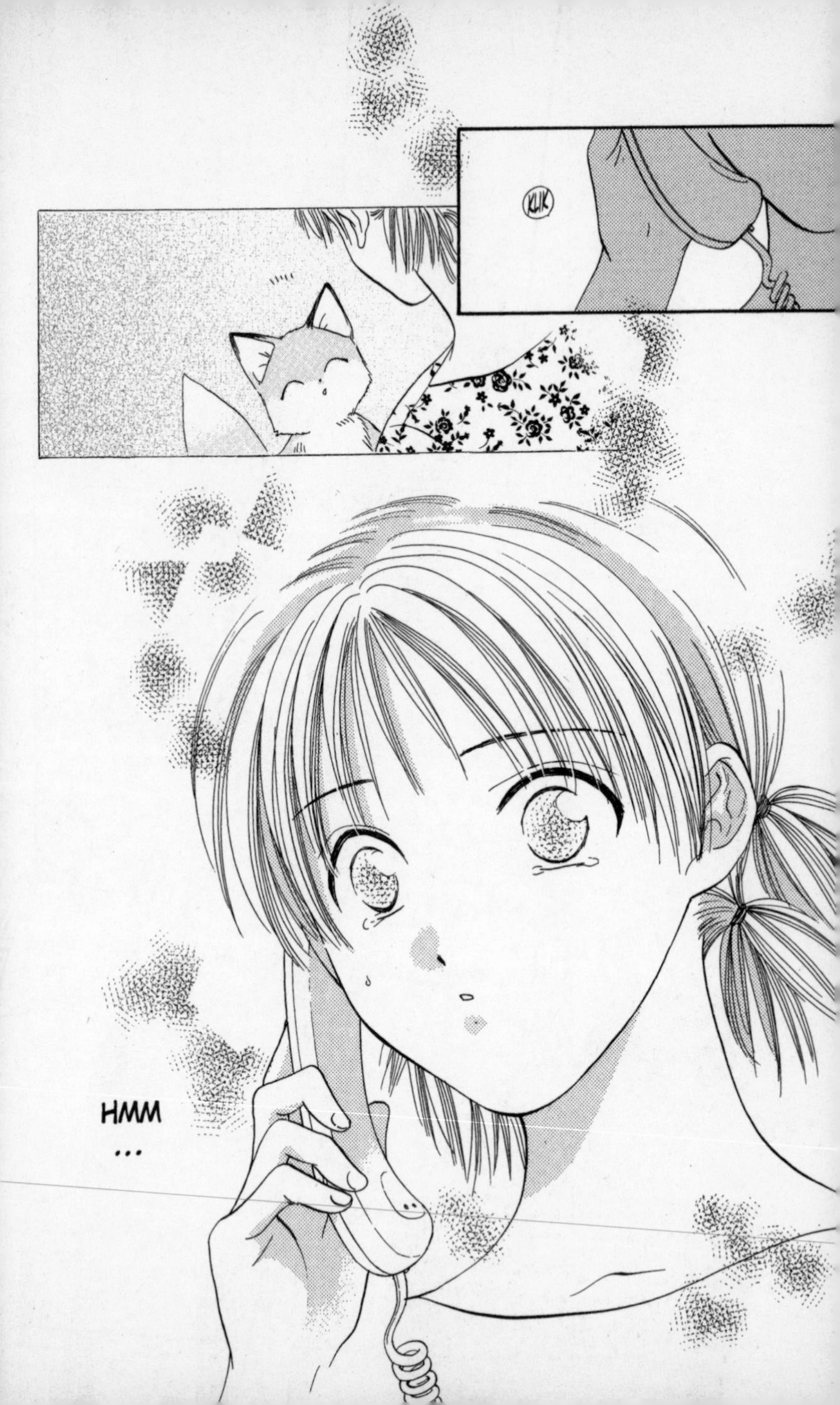
KLIK
HMM
...

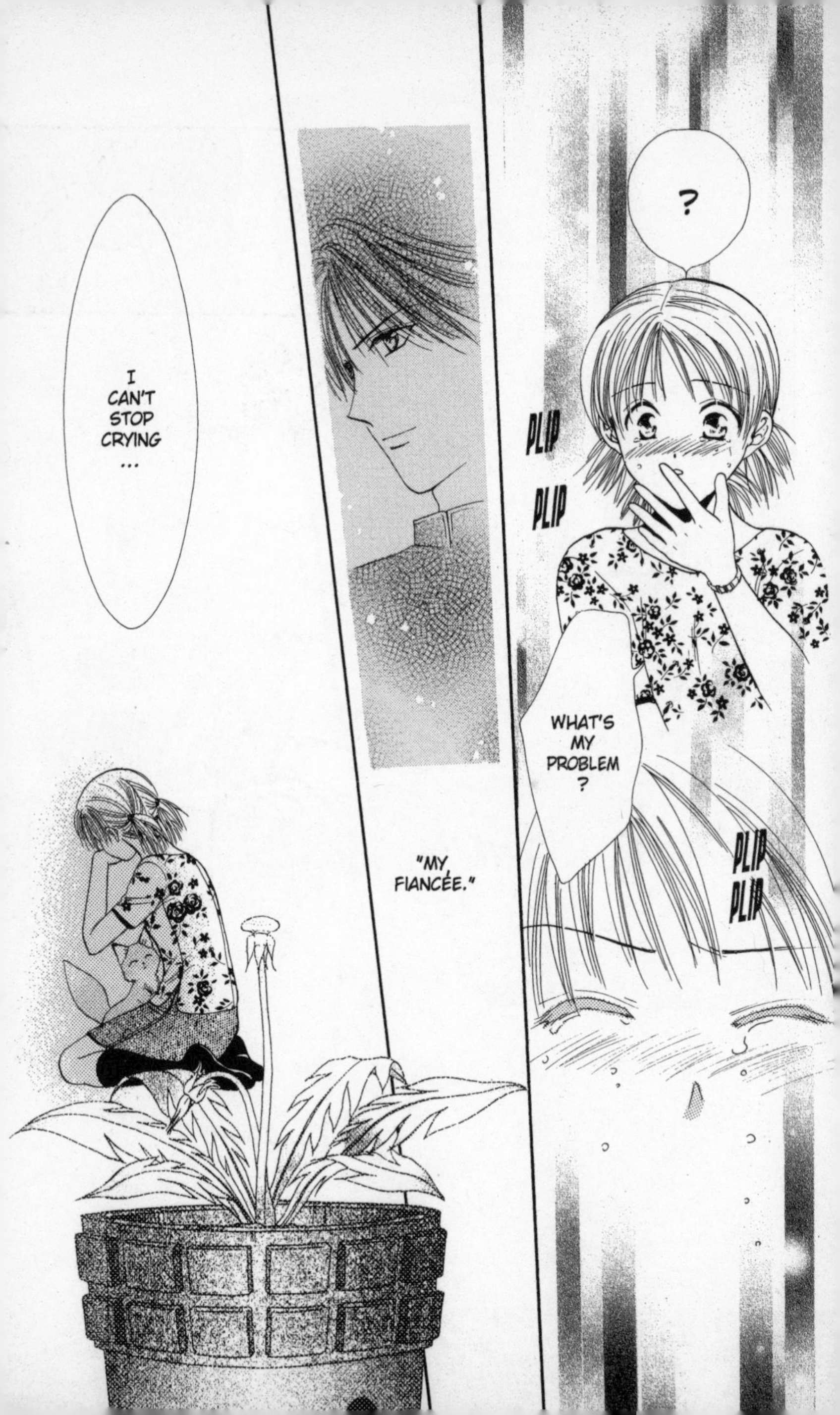
?
PLIP
PLIP
WHAT'S MY PROBLEM ?
PLIP PLIP
"MY, FIANCÉE."
I CAN'T STOP CRYING ...

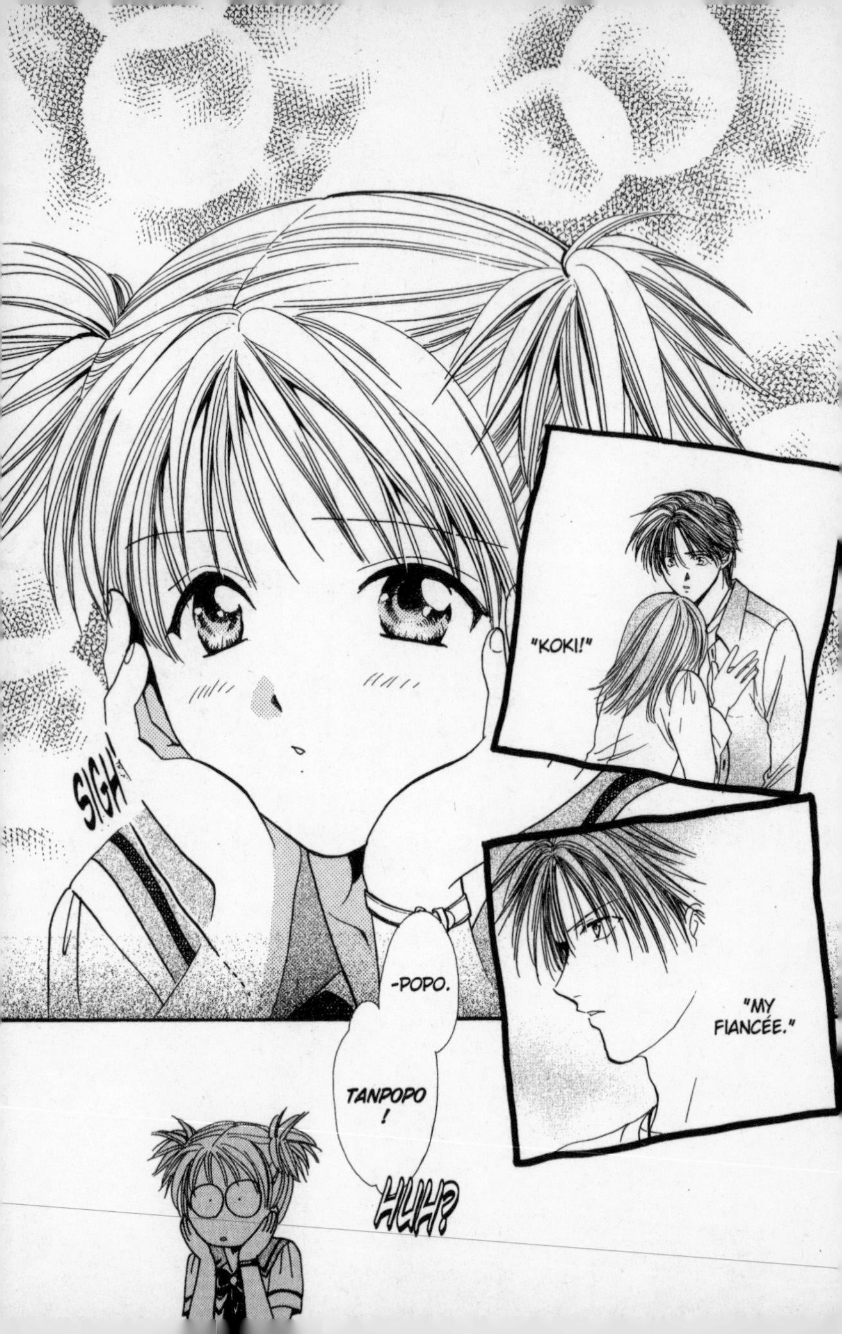
SIGH
"KOKI!"
"MY FIANCÉE."
TANPOPO!
-POPO.
HUH?

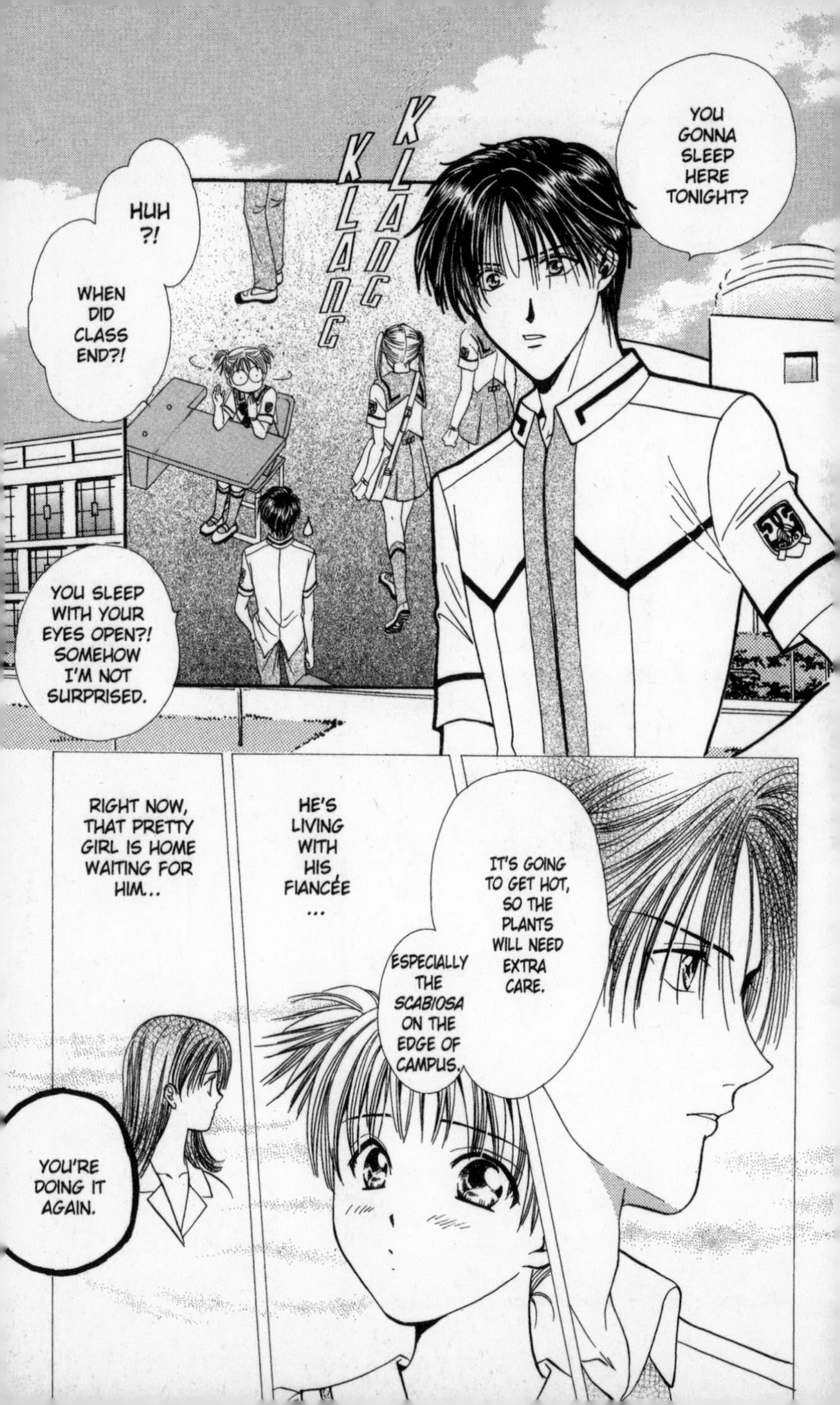

YOU GONNA SLEEP HERE TONIGHT?
KLANG
KLANG
HUH?!
WHEN DID CLASS END?!
YOU SLEEP WITH YOUR EYES OPEN?! SOMEHOW I'M NOT SURPRISED.
IT'S GOING TO GET HOT, SO THE PLANTS WILL NEED EXTRA CARE.
ESPECIALLY THE SCABIOSA ON THE EDGE OF CAMPUS.
HE'S LIVING WITH HIS FIANCÉE ...
RIGHT NOW, THAT PRETTY GIRL IS HOME WAITING FOR HIM...
YOU'RE DOING IT AGAIN.

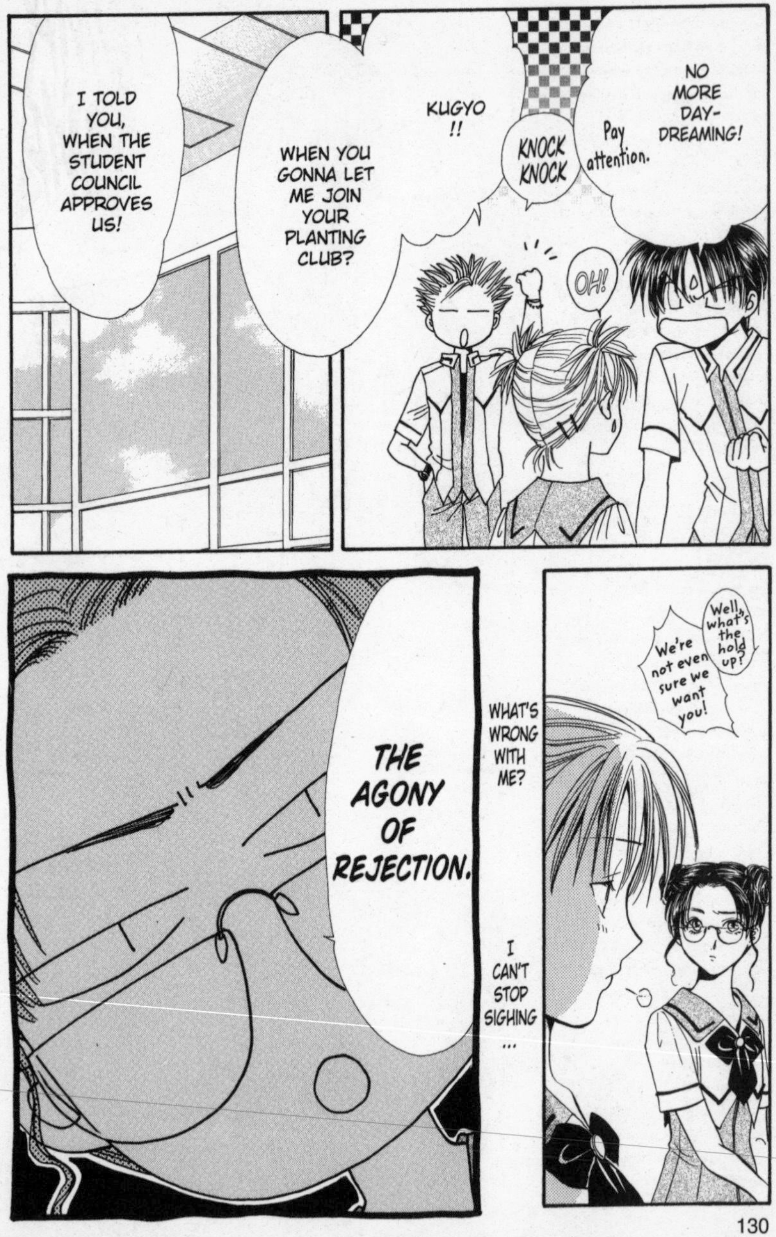

NO MORE DAY-DREAMING!
Pay attention.
KNOCK KNOCK
OH!
KUGYO !!
WHEN YOU GONNA LET ME JOIN YOUR PLANTING CLUB?
I TOLD YOU, WHEN THE STUDENT COUNCIL APPROVES US!
Well, what's the hold up?
We're not even sure we want you!
WHAT'S WRONG WITH ME?
I CAN'T STOP SIGHING ...
THE AGONY OF REJECTION.

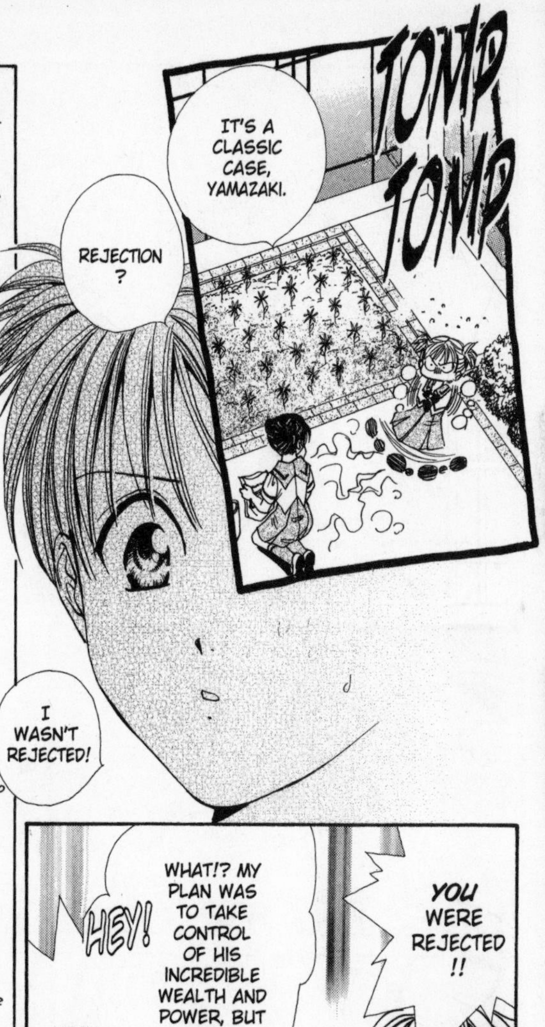
TOMP TOMP
IT'S A CLASSIC CASE, YAMAZAKI.
REJECTION?
I WASN'T REJECTED!
YOU WERE REJECTED!!
WHAT!? MY PLAN WAS TO TAKE CONTROL OF HIS INCREDIBLE WEALTH AND POWER, BUT THEN...
HEY!
THIS ISN'T ABOUT ME!!

Once a squid was going to make an appearance on our dinner table. My mom was just about to prepare it, when she discovered "The Thing!!" It wriggled briefly to the surface of the squid, then squirmed back inside. (Goose bumps)

My mom thought, "Gyaa!!" and then decided, "I'm never going to eat squid again!!" After hearing that, I also developed an aversion to squid. (I never really liked seafood anyway.)

Long ago, I was snacking on a bag of candy, when I noticed there was a big centipede or caterpillar thing with a head like I've never seen in the bag. I was disgusted! Wow! I felt like I'd seen Godzilla or Mothra! (What **was** that thing?) I threw it away on the spot, but it still bothers me to this day!!!

Ugh, just writing this gives me the creeps... Sorry, such an unpleasant subject. Let's all be careful, okay?

The other day, I was talking to my assistant and some others about this subject and what a commotion it caused. The horror stories they told... There was one about a cockroach wing that was found in some restaurant food. (I had some spoiled food brought to me once.) Hmm...Just because it's a shop, doesn't mean it's safe. You really have to be careful or risk having an unpleasant experience. If the kitchen looks dirty you should leave immediately.

And you should always wash vegetables thoroughly in hot water or else! It's scary enough already...

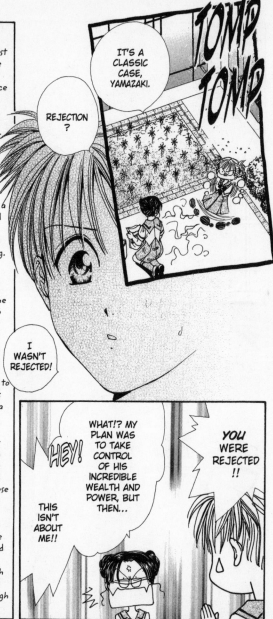

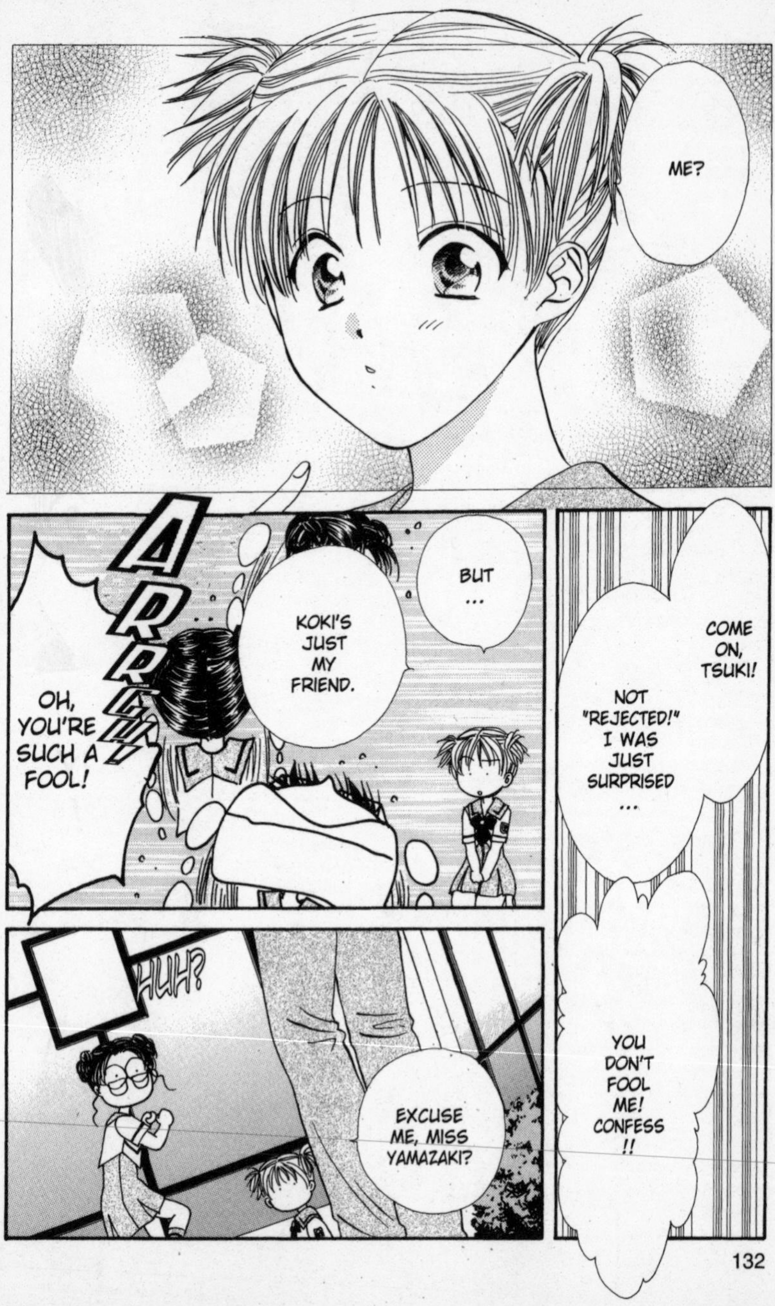

ME?
COME ON, TSUKI!
NOT "REJECTED!" I WAS JUST SURPRISED ...
YOU DON'T FOOL ME! CONFESS !!
BUT ...
KOKI'S JUST MY FRIEND.
OH, YOU'RE SUCH A FOOL!
HUH?
EXCUSE ME, MISS YAMAZAKI?

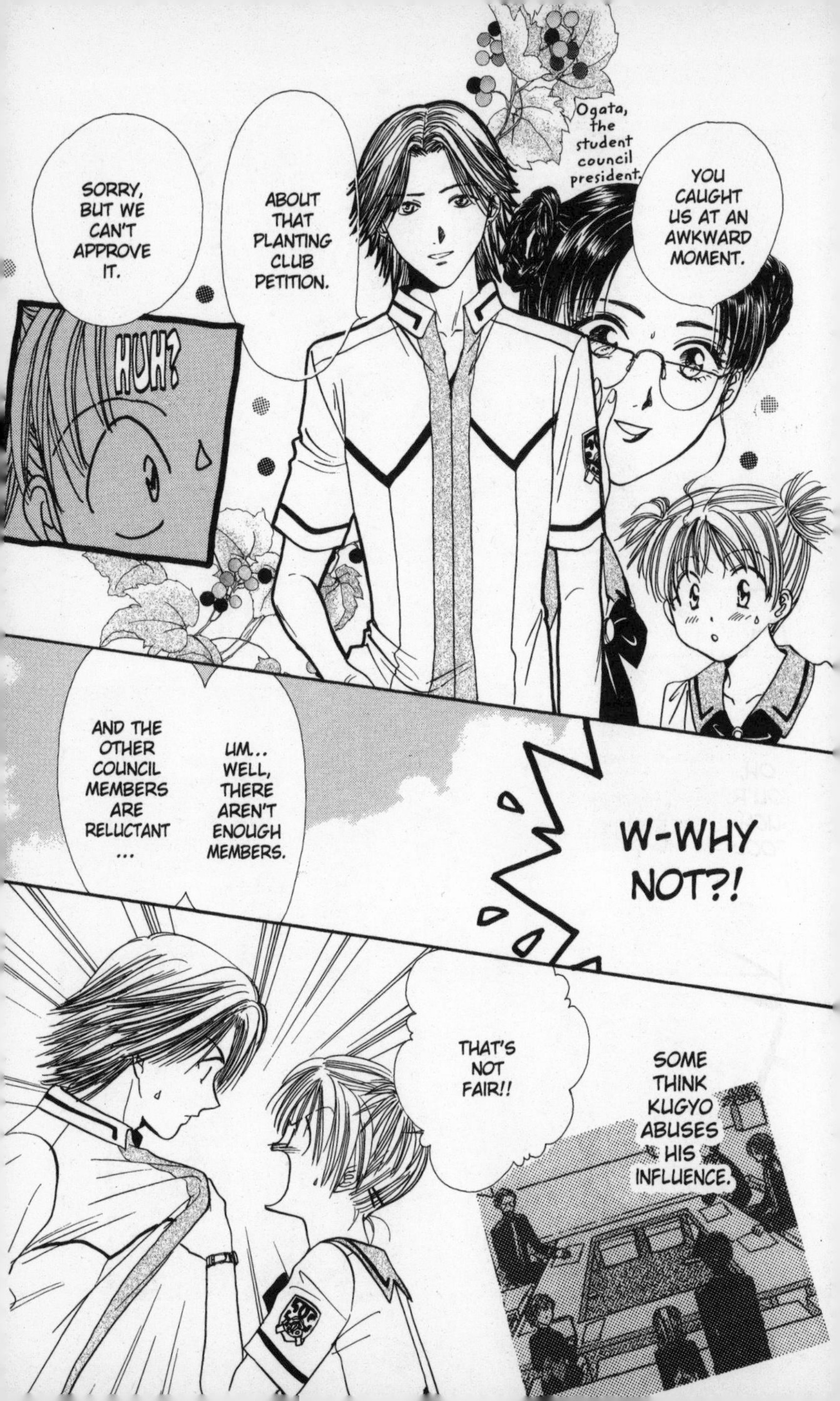
Ogata, the student council president.
YOU CAUGHT US AT AN AWKWARD MOMENT.
ABOUT THAT PLANTING CLUB PETITION.
SORRY, BUT WE CAN'T APPROVE IT.
HUH?
W-WHY NOT?!
UM... WELL, THERE AREN'T ENOUGH MEMBERS.
AND THE OTHER COUNCIL MEMBERS ARE RELUCTANT ...
SOME THINK KUGYO ABUSES HIS INFLUENCE.
THAT'S NOT FAIR!!

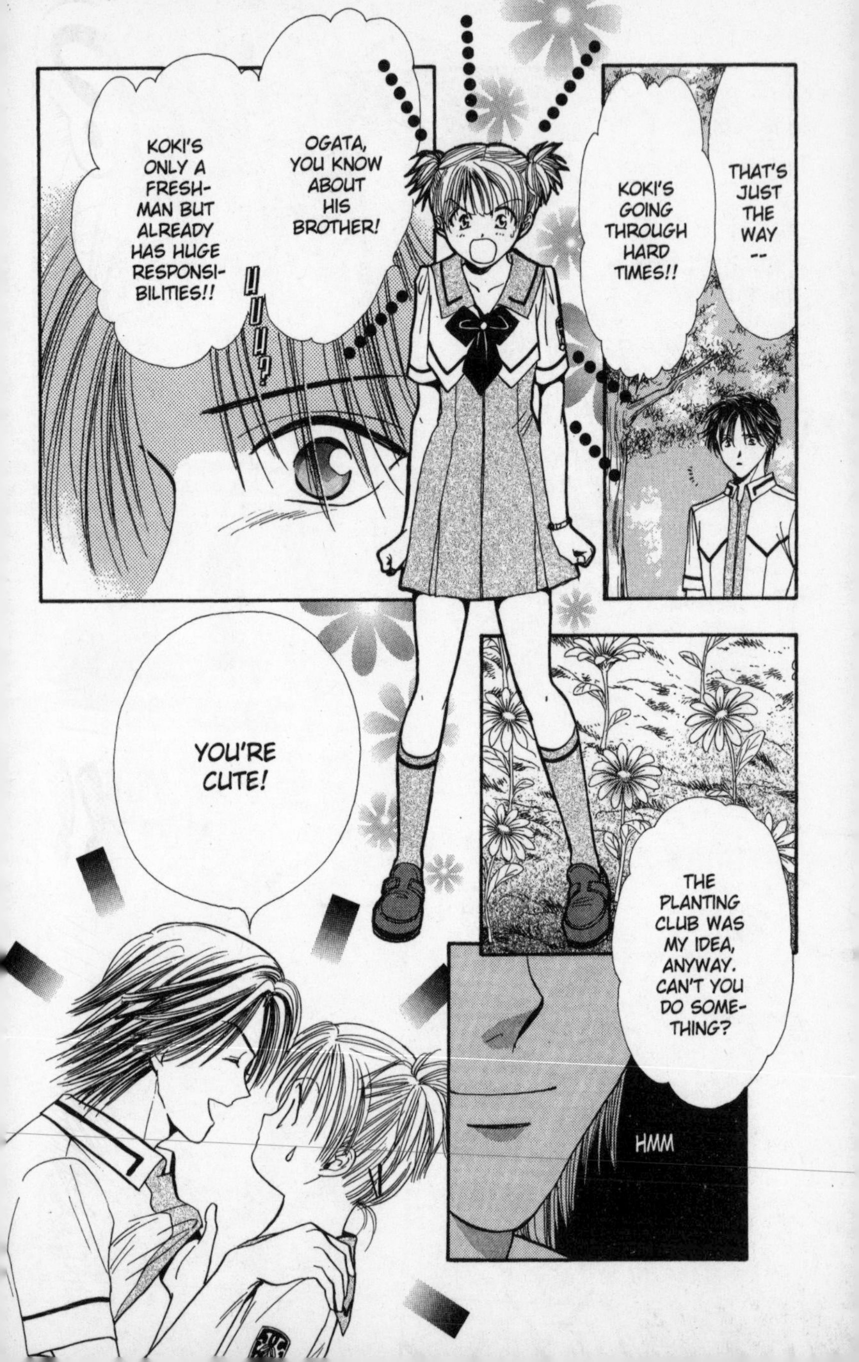
THAT'S JUST THE WAY --
KOKI'S GOING THROUGH HARD TIMES!!
OGATA, YOU KNOW ABOUT HIS BROTHER!
KOKI'S ONLY A FRESHMAN BUT ALREADY HAS HUGE RESPONSIBILITIES!!
THE PLANTING CLUB WAS MY IDEA, ANYWAY. CAN'T YOU DO SOMETHING?
HMM
YOU'RE CUTE!

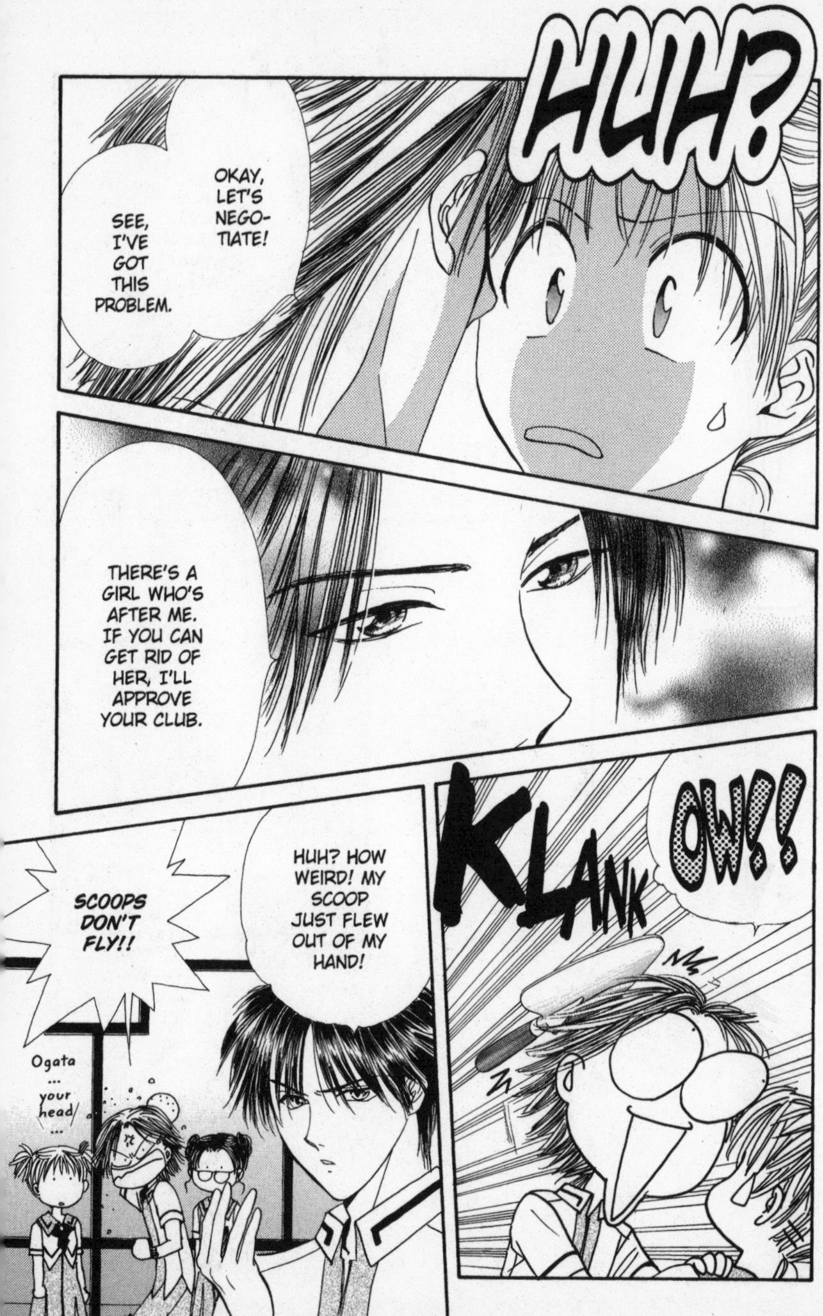
HUH?
OKAY, LET'S NEGO-TIATE!
SEE, I'VE GOT THIS PROBLEM.
THERE'S A GIRL WHO'S AFTER ME. IF YOU CAN GET RID OF HER, I'LL APPROVE YOUR CLUB.
OW!!
KLANK
HUH? HOW WEIRD! MY SCOOP JUST FLEW OUT OF MY HAND!
SCOOPS DON'T FLY!!
Ogata ... your head ...

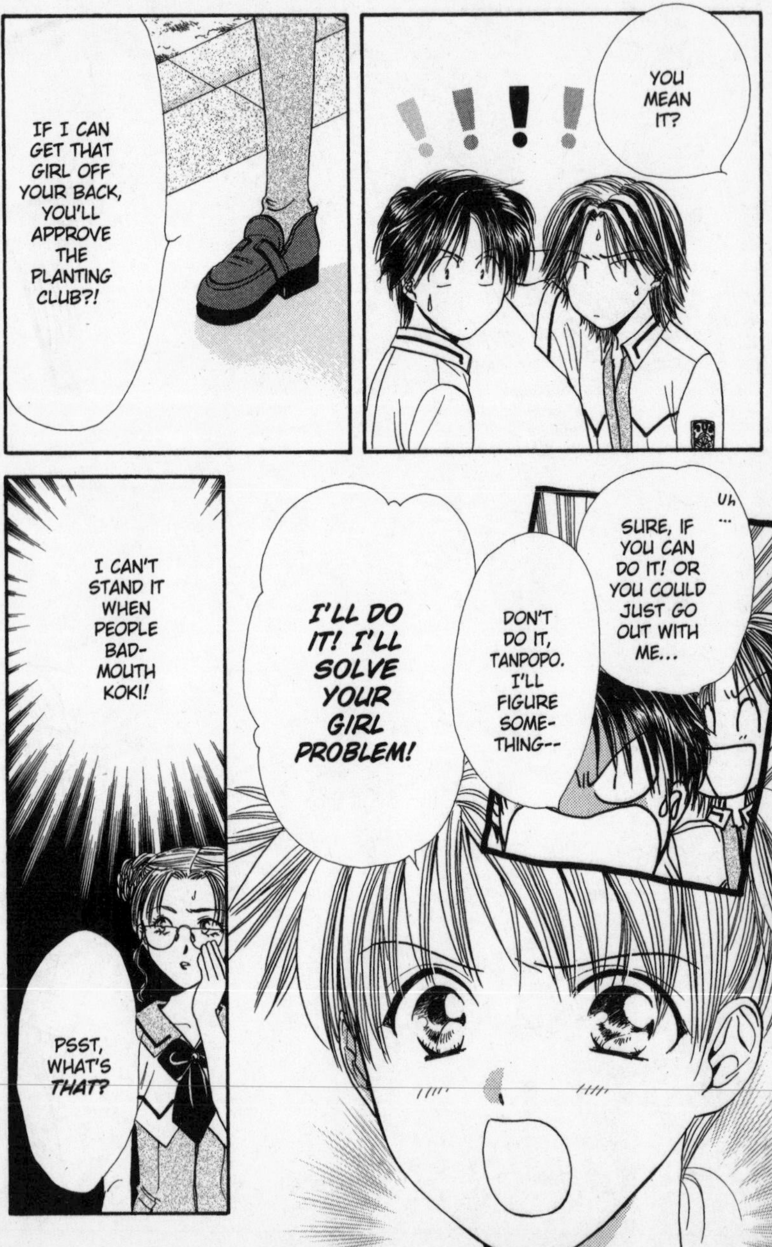
!!!!
YOU MEAN IT?
IF I CAN GET THAT GIRL OFF YOUR BACK, YOU'LL APPROVE THE PLANTING CLUB?!
Uh ...
SURE, IF YOU CAN DO IT! OR YOU COULD JUST GO OUT WITH ME...
DON'T DO IT, TANPOPO. I'LL FIGURE SOME-THING--
I'LL DO IT! I'LL SOLVE YOUR GIRL PROBLEM!
I CAN'T STAND IT WHEN PEOPLE BAD-MOUTH KOKI!
PSST, WHAT'S THAT?

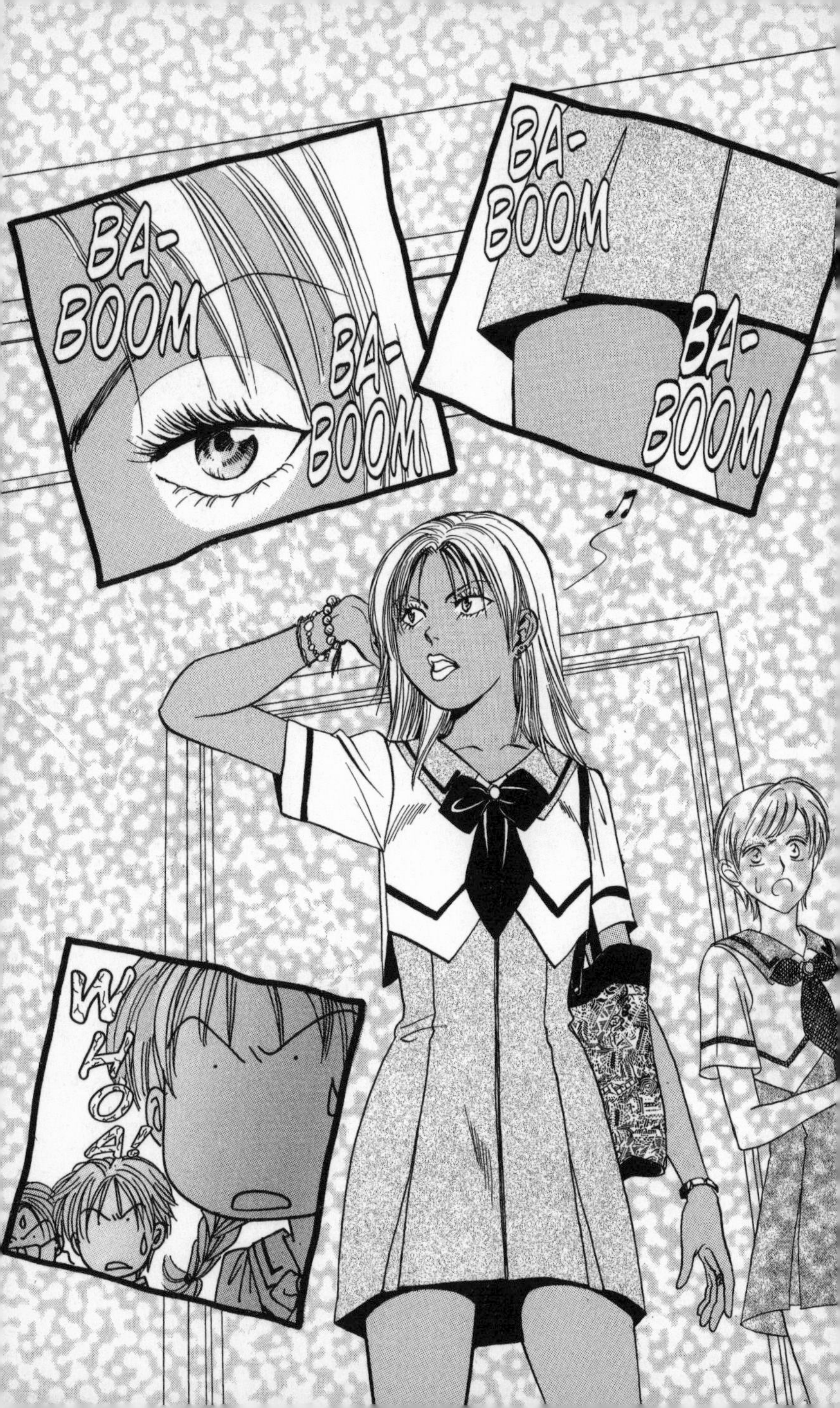
BA-BOOM
BA-BOOM
BA-BOOM
BA-BOOM
WHOA!

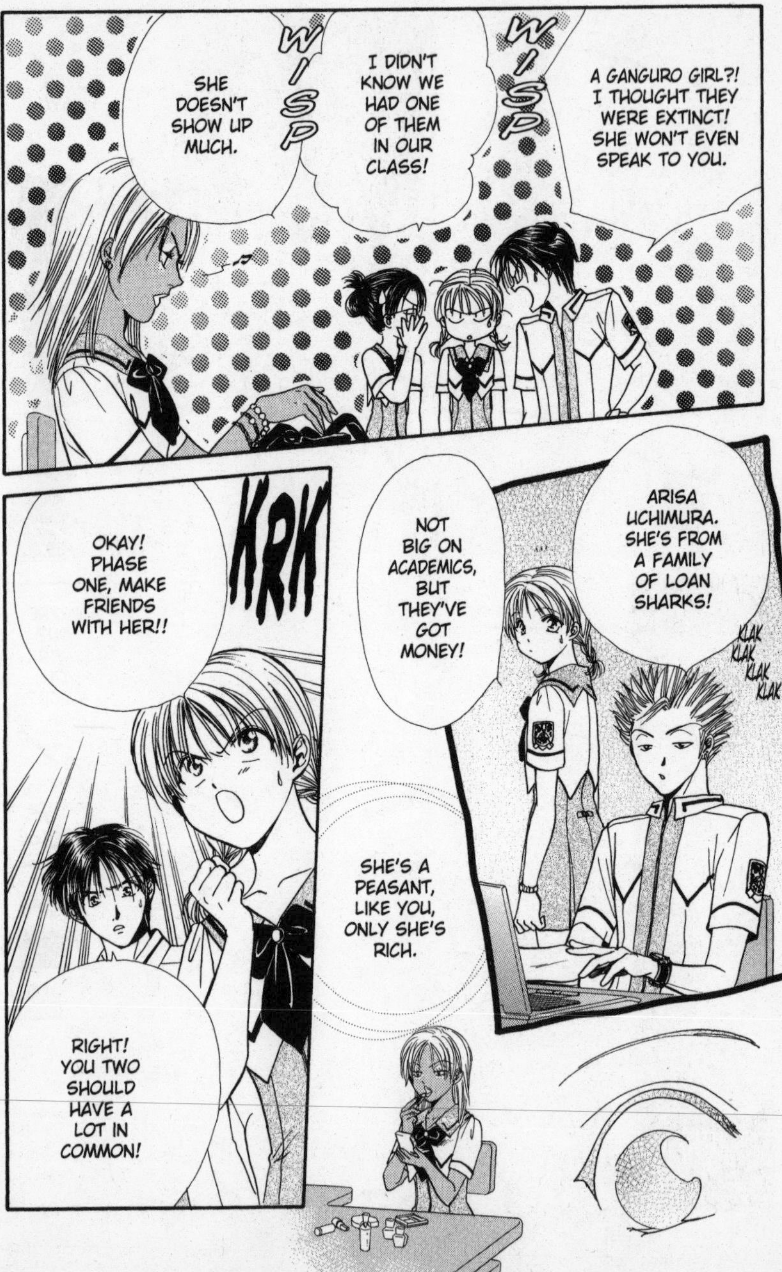
A GANGURO GIRL?! I THOUGHT THEY WERE EXTINCT! SHE WON'T EVEN SPEAK TO YOU.
WISP
I DIDN'T KNOW WE HAD ONE OF THEM IN OUR CLASS!
WISP
SHE DOESN'T SHOW UP MUCH.
ARISA UCHIMURA. SHE'S FROM A FAMILY OF LOAN SHARKS!
KLAK KLAK KLAK KLAK
NOT BIG ON ACADEMICS, BUT THEY'VE GOT MONEY!
SHE'S A PEASANT, LIKE YOU, ONLY SHE'S RICH.
KRK
OKAY! PHASE ONE, MAKE FRIENDS WITH HER!!
RIGHT! YOU TWO SHOULD HAVE A LOT IN COMMON!

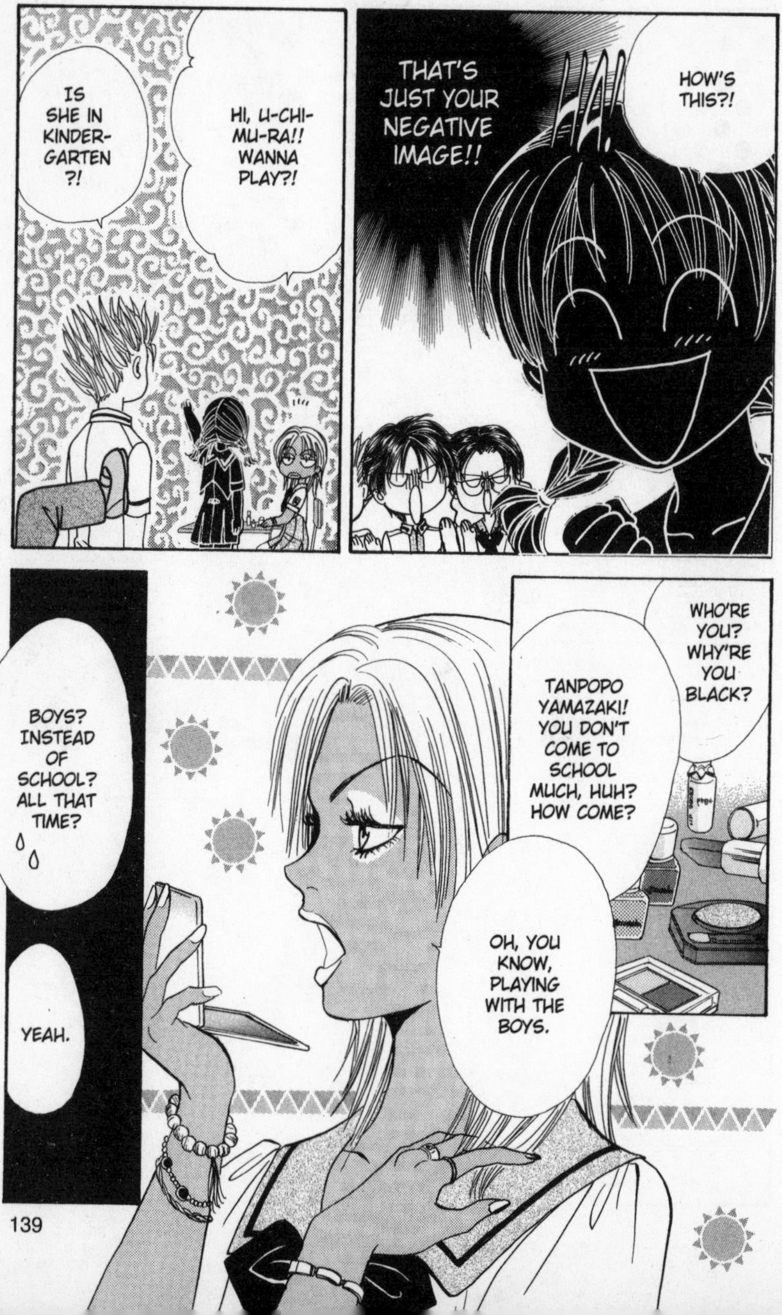
HOW'S THIS?!
THAT'S JUST YOUR NEGATIVE IMAGE!!
HI, U-CHI-MU-RA!! WANNA PLAY?!
IS SHE IN KINDER-GARTEN?!
WHO'RE YOU? WHY'RE YOU BLACK?
TANPOPO YAMAZAKI! YOU DON'T COME TO SCHOOL MUCH, HUH? HOW COME?
OH, YOU KNOW, PLAYING WITH THE BOYS.
BOYS? INSTEAD OF SCHOOL? ALL THAT TIME?
YEAH.

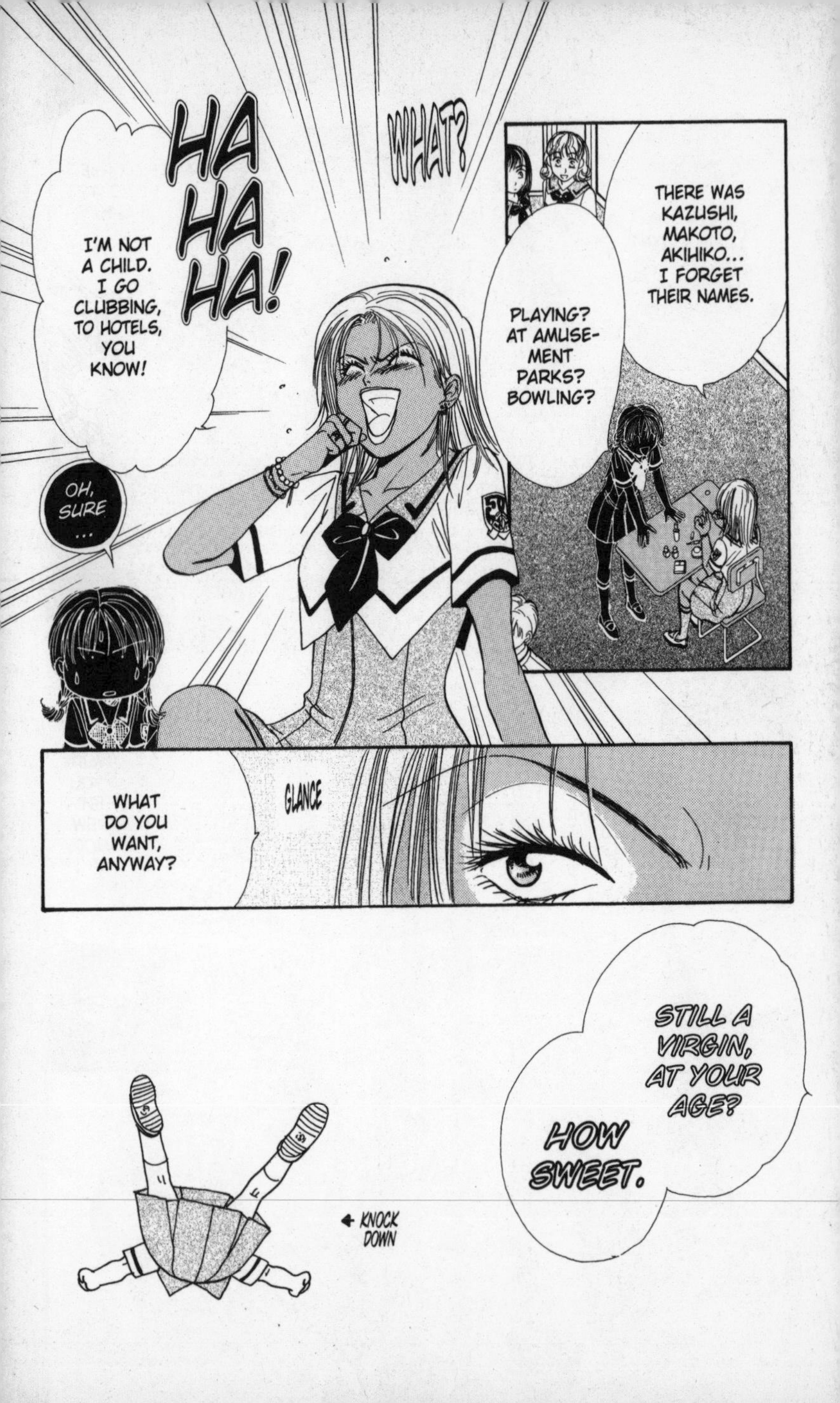
THERE WAS KAZUSHI, MAKOTO, AKIHIKO... I FORGET THEIR NAMES.
PLAYING? AT AMUSEMENT PARKS? BOWLING?
WHAT?
HA HA HA!
I'M NOT A CHILD. I GO CLUBBING, TO HOTELS, YOU KNOW!
OH, SURE...
GLANCE
WHAT DO YOU WANT, ANYWAY?
STILL A VIRGIN, AT YOUR AGE?
HOW SWEET.
KNOCK DOWN

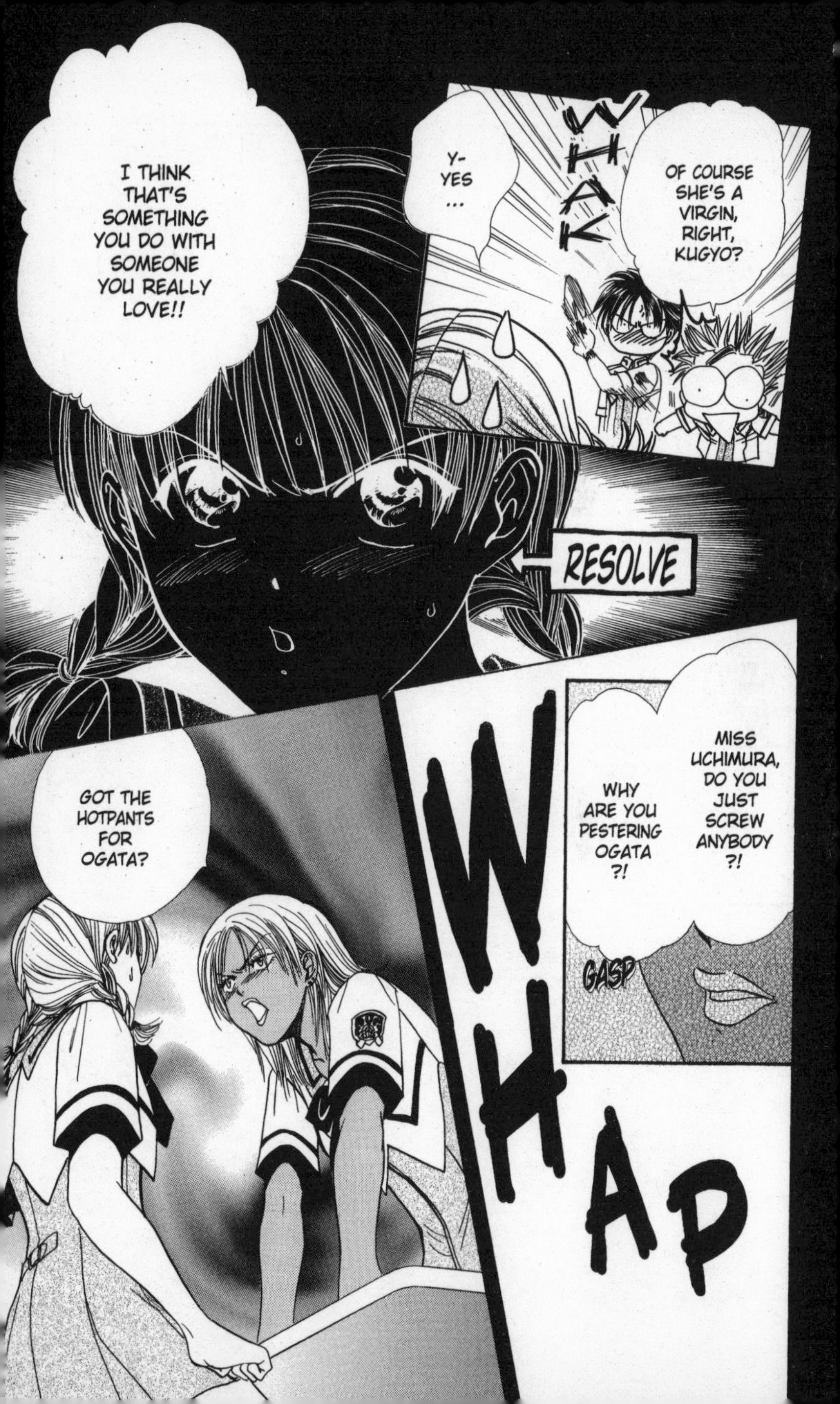
OF COURSE SHE'S A VIRGIN, RIGHT, KUGYO?
WHAK
Y-YES ...
I THINK THAT'S SOMETHING YOU DO WITH SOMEONE YOU REALLY LOVE!!
RESOLVE
MISS UCHIMURA, DO YOU JUST SCREW ANYBODY ?!
WHY ARE YOU PESTERING OGATA ?!
GASP
WHAP
GOT THE HOTPANTS FOR OGATA?

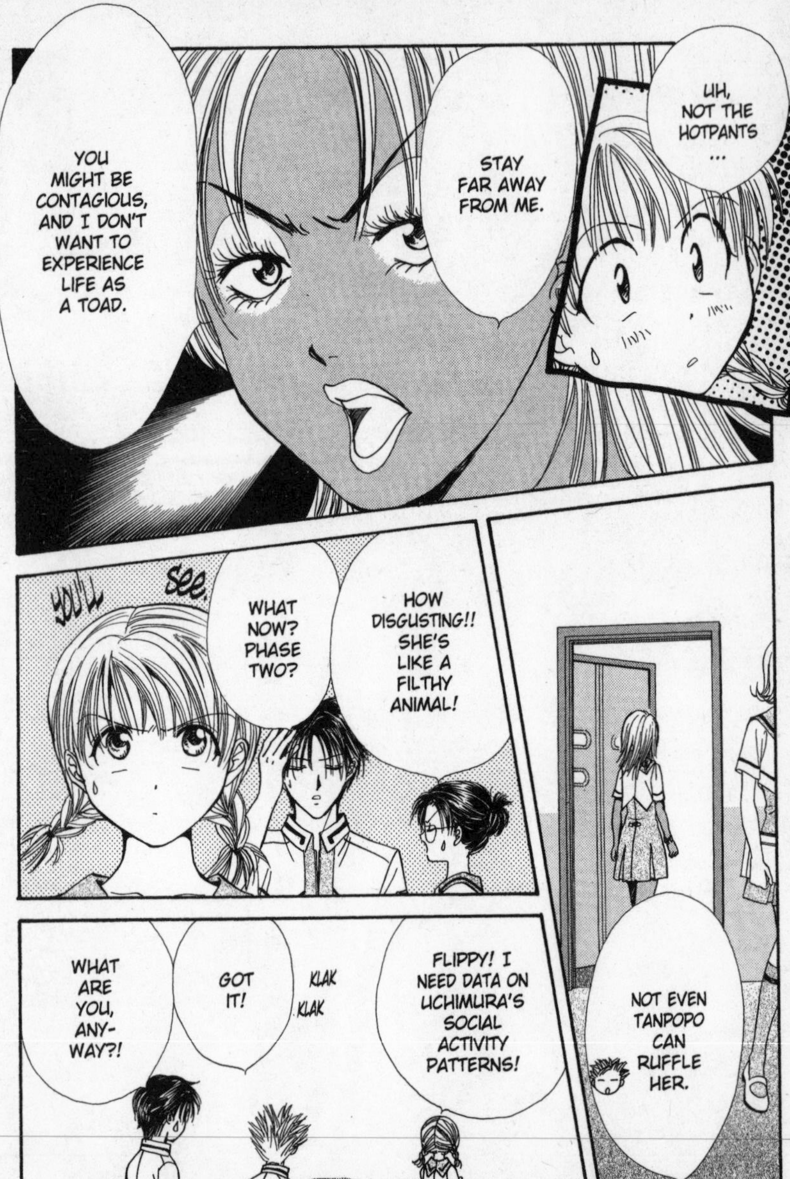

UH, NOT THE HOTPANTS ...
STAY FAR AWAY FROM ME.
YOU MIGHT BE CONTAGIOUS, AND I DON'T WANT TO EXPERIENCE LIFE AS A TOAD.
NOT EVEN TANPOPO CAN RUFFLE HER.
HOW DISGUSTING!! SHE'S LIKE A FILTHY ANIMAL!
WHAT NOW? PHASE TWO?
YOU'LL see.
FLIPPY! I NEED DATA ON UCHIMURA'S SOCIAL ACTIVITY PATTERNS!
KLAK
KLAK
GOT IT!
WHAT ARE YOU, ANY-WAY?!

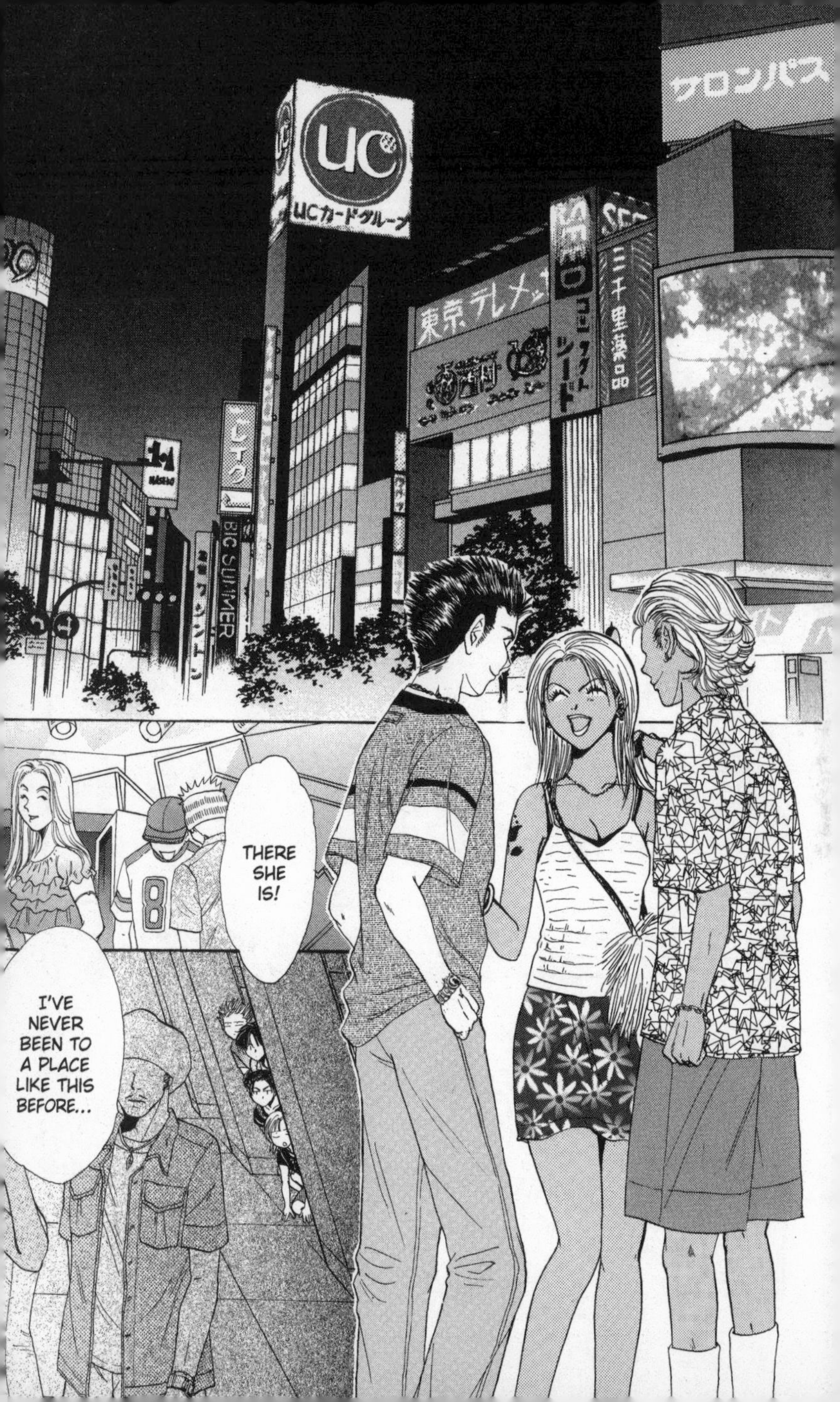

サロンパス
UC
UCカードグループ
三千里薬品
BIG SUMMER
THERE SHE IS!
I'VE NEVER BEEN TO A PLACE LIKE THIS BEFORE...

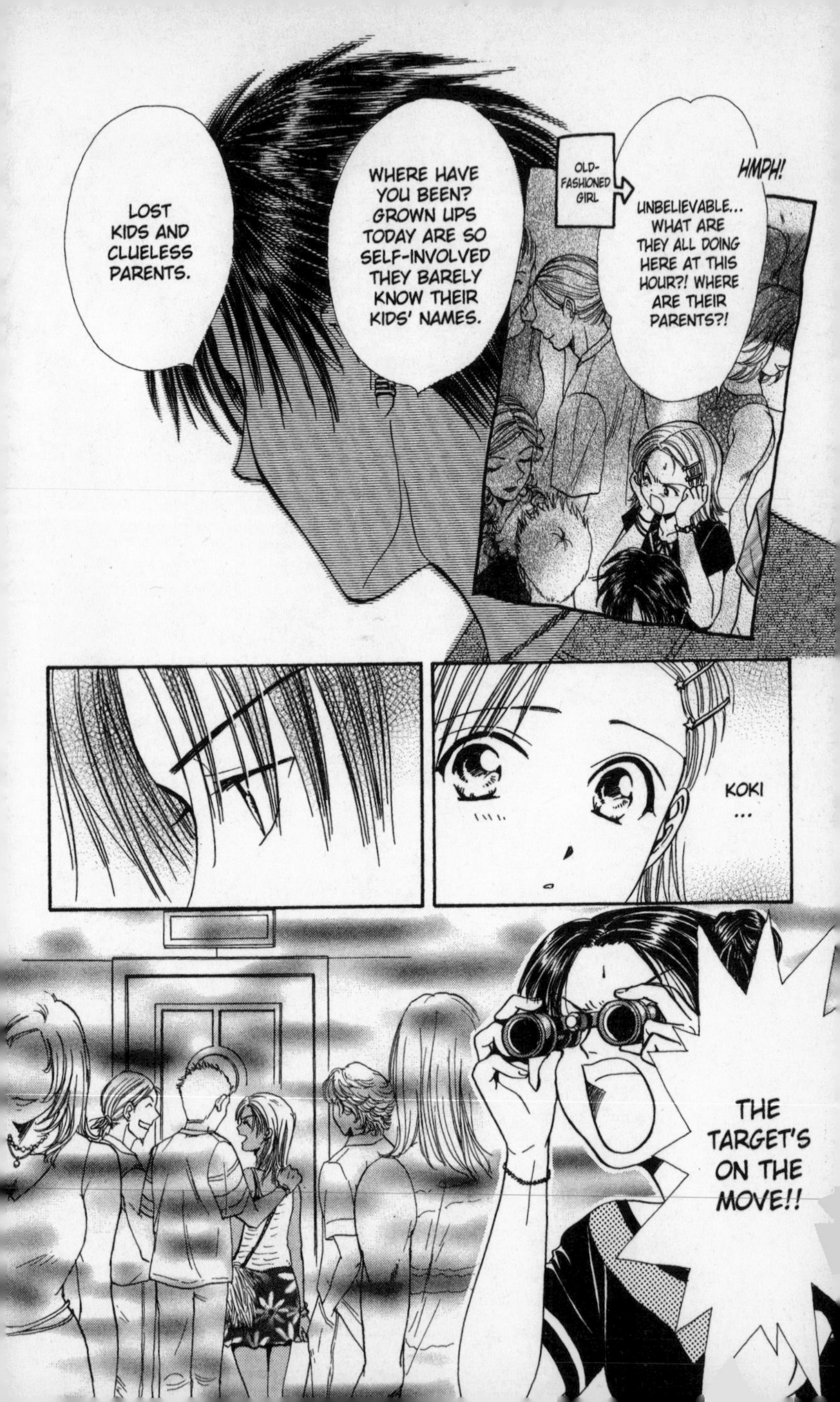
HMPH!
UNBELIEVABLE... WHAT ARE THEY ALL DOING HERE AT THIS HOUR?! WHERE ARE THEIR PARENTS?!
OLD-FASHIONED GIRL
WHERE HAVE YOU BEEN? GROWN UPS TODAY ARE SO SELF-INVOLVED THEY BARELY KNOW THEIR KIDS' NAMES.
LOST KIDS AND CLUELESS PARENTS.
KOKI ...
THE TARGET'S ON THE MOVE!!

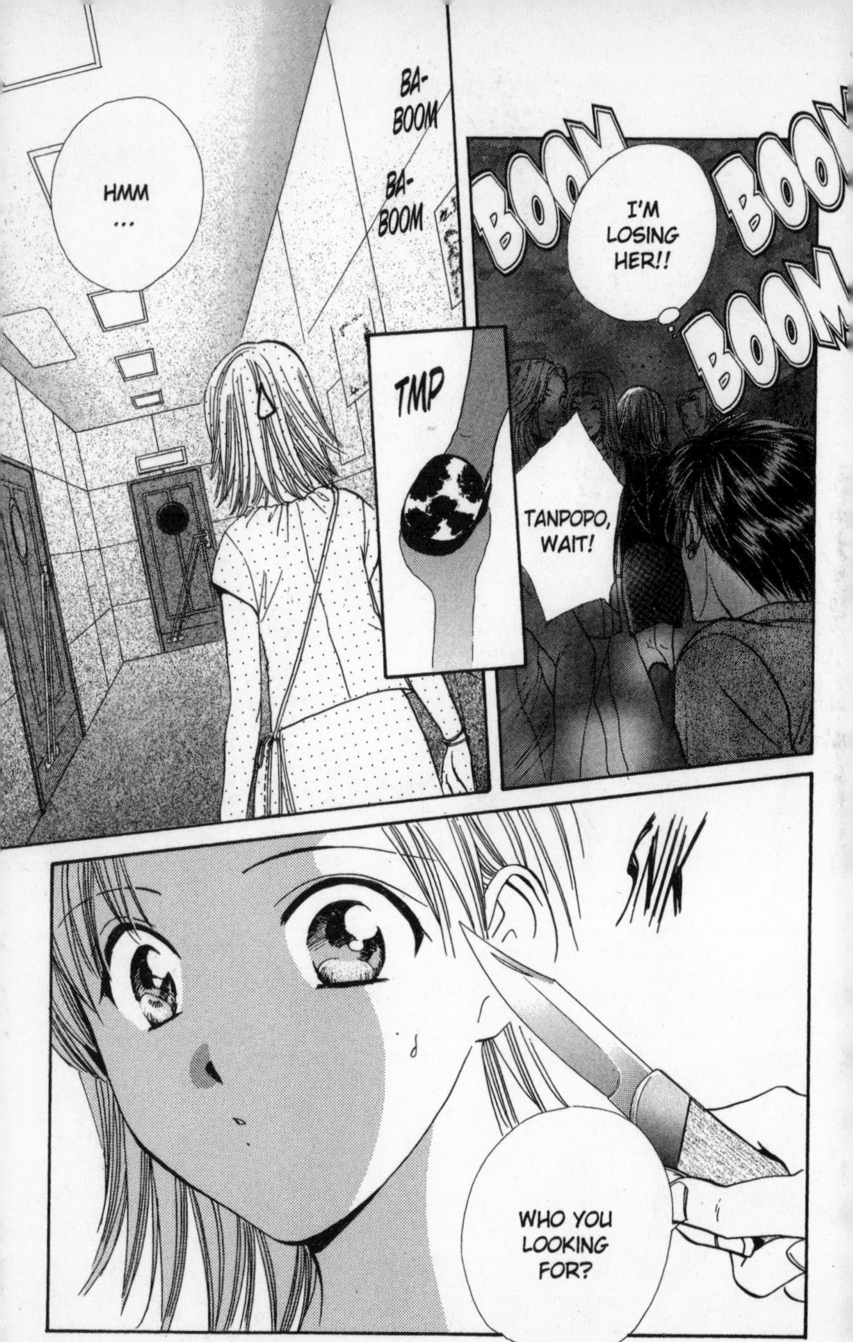
BOOM BOOM BOOM
I'M LOSING HER!!
TANPOPO, WAIT!
TMP
BA-BOOM
BA-BOOM
HMM ...
SNK
WHO YOU LOOKING FOR?

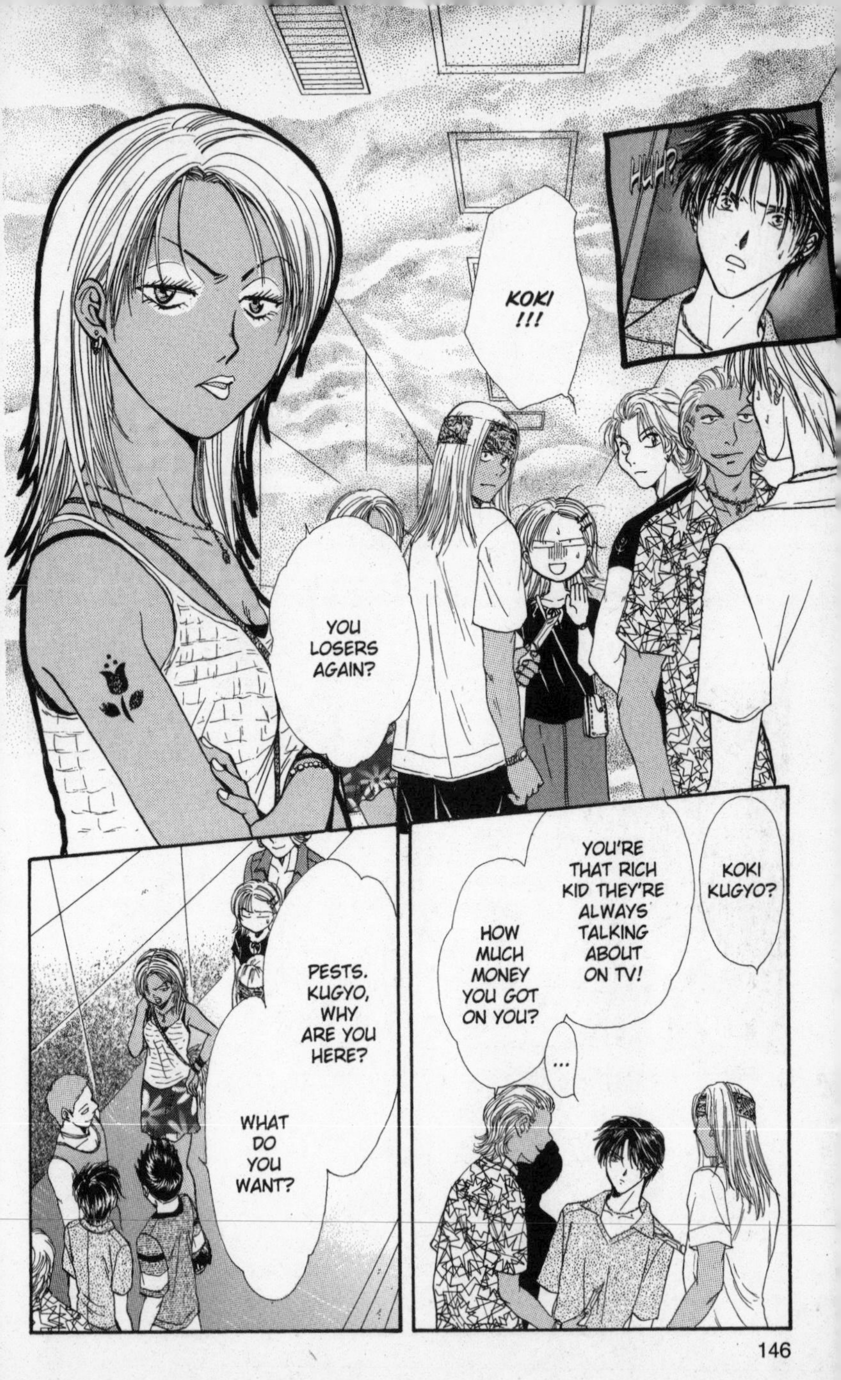
KOKI !!!
HUH?
YOU LOSERS AGAIN?
KOKI KUGYO?
YOU'RE THAT RICH KID THEY'RE ALWAYS TALKING ABOUT ON TV!
HOW MUCH MONEY YOU GOT ON YOU?
...
PESTS. KUGYO, WHY ARE YOU HERE?
WHAT DO YOU WANT?

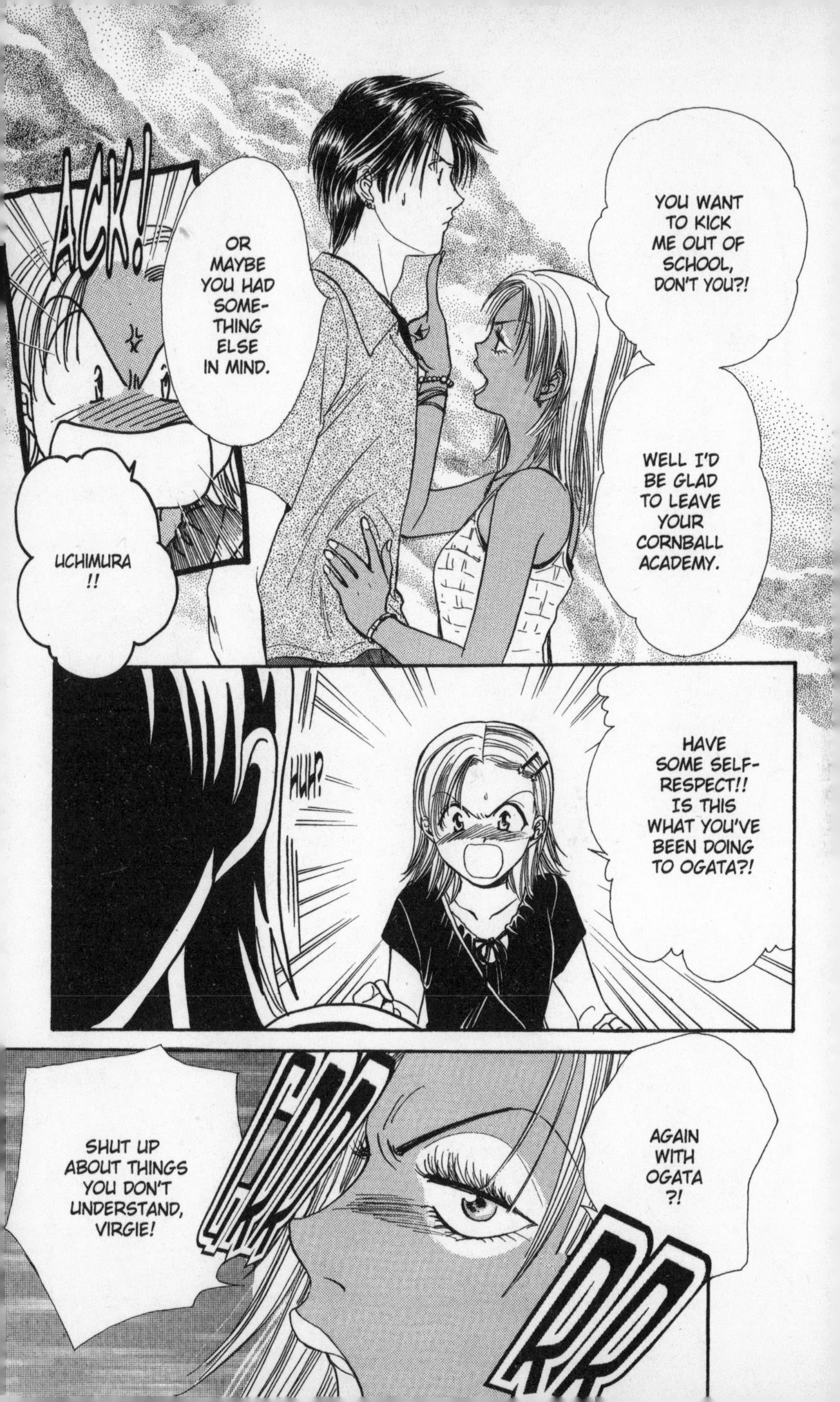
YOU WANT TO KICK ME OUT OF SCHOOL, DON'T YOU?!
WELL I'D BE GLAD TO LEAVE YOUR CORNBALL ACADEMY.
OR MAYBE YOU HAD SOME-THING ELSE IN MIND.
ACK!
UCHIMURA !!
HAVE SOME SELF-RESPECT!! IS THIS WHAT YOU'VE BEEN DOING TO OGATA?!
HUH?
AGAIN WITH OGATA ?!
SHUT UP ABOUT THINGS YOU DON'T UNDERSTAND, VIRGIE!

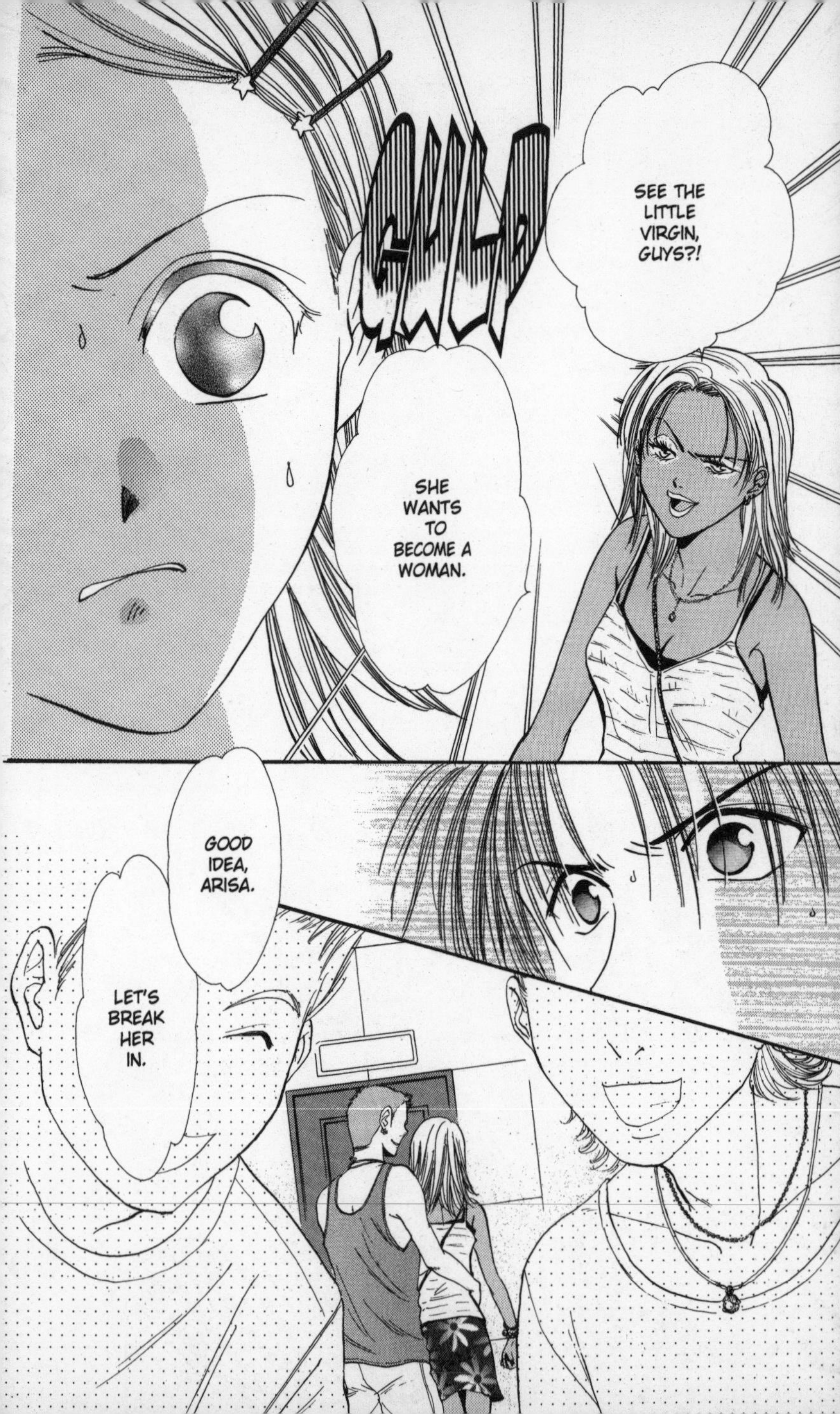
SEE THE LITTLE VIRGIN, GUYS?!
SHE WANTS TO BECOME A WOMAN.
GOOD IDEA, ARISA.
LET'S BREAK HER IN.

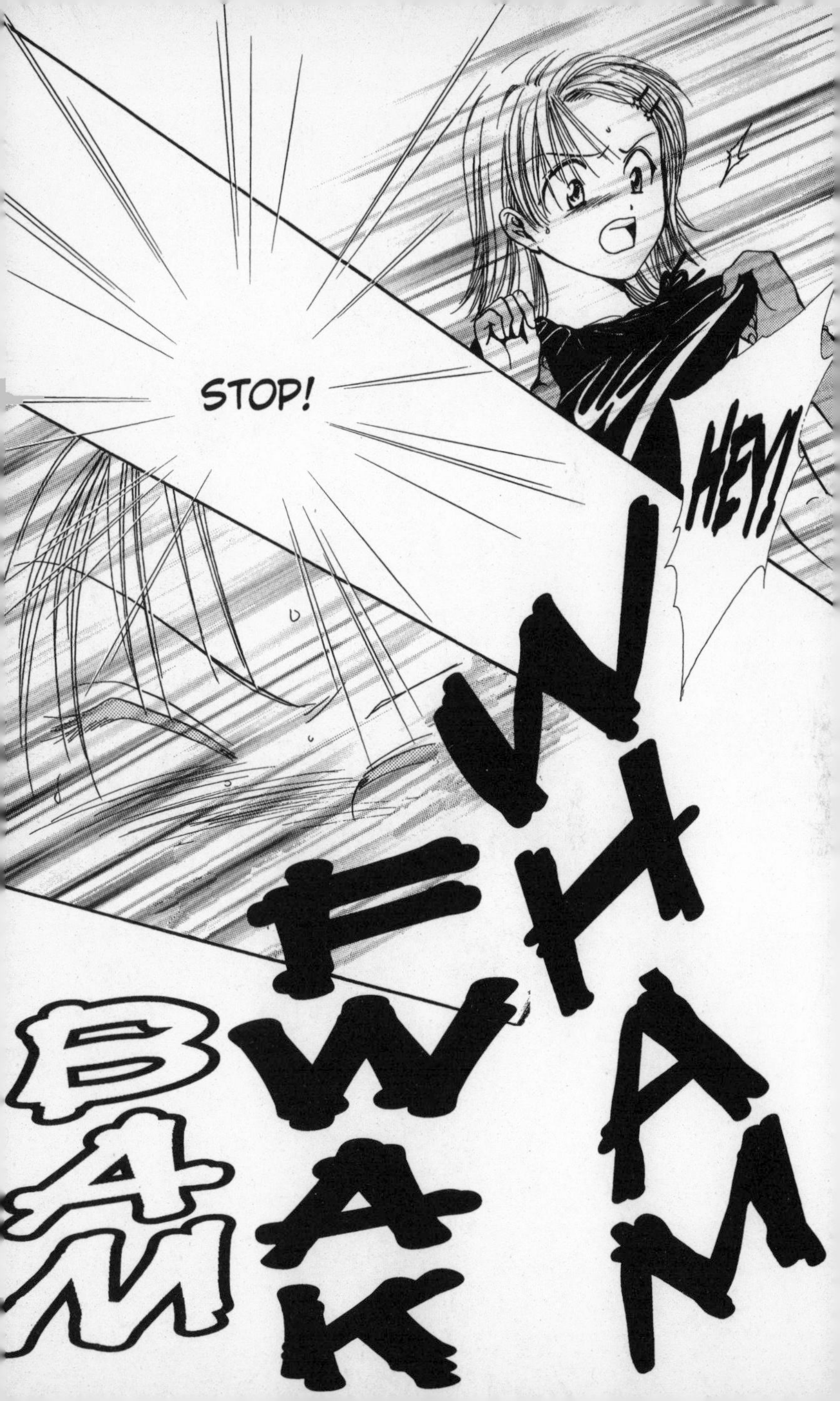

HEY!
STOP!
WHAM
WHAK
BAM

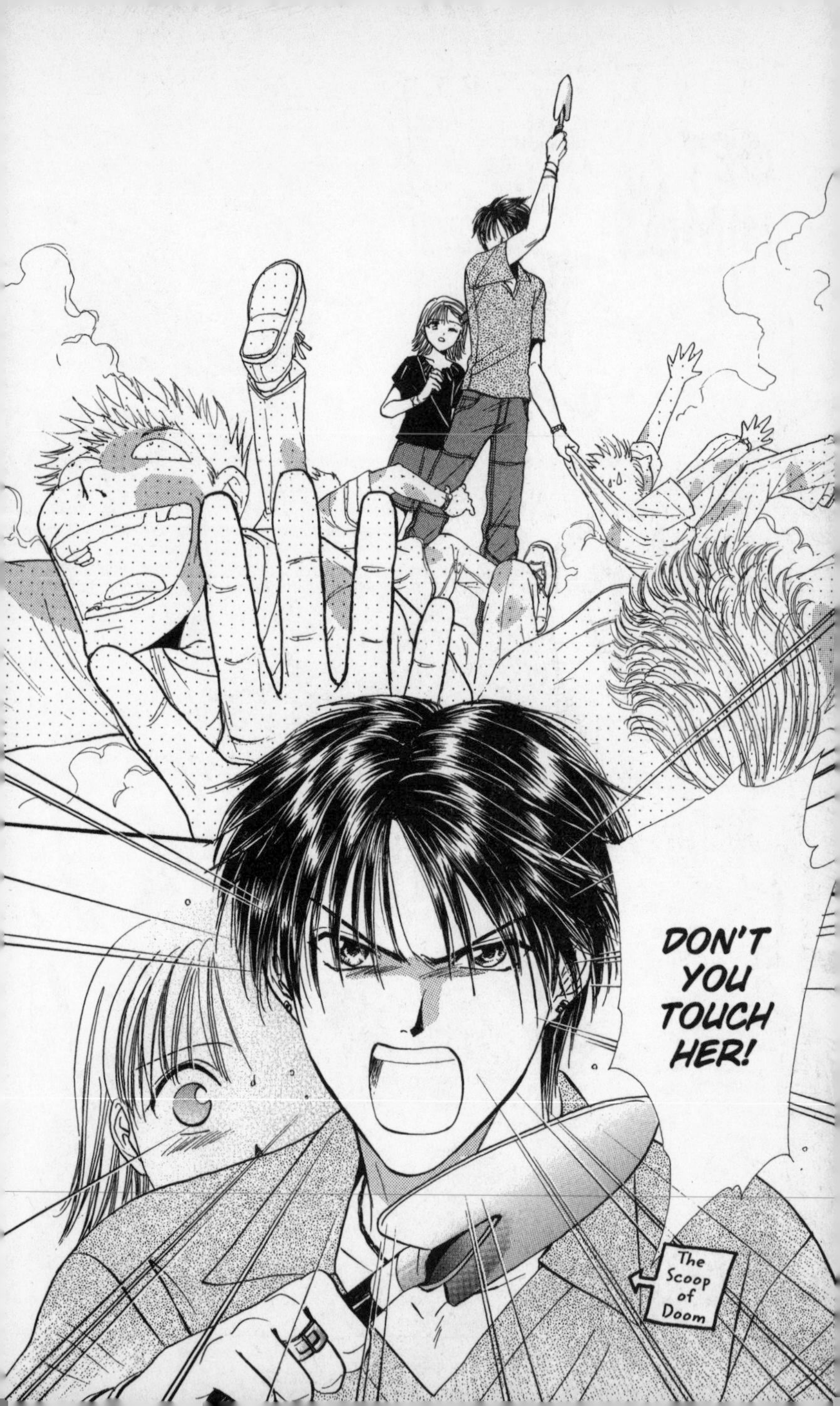
DON'T YOU TOUCH HER!
The Scoop of Doom

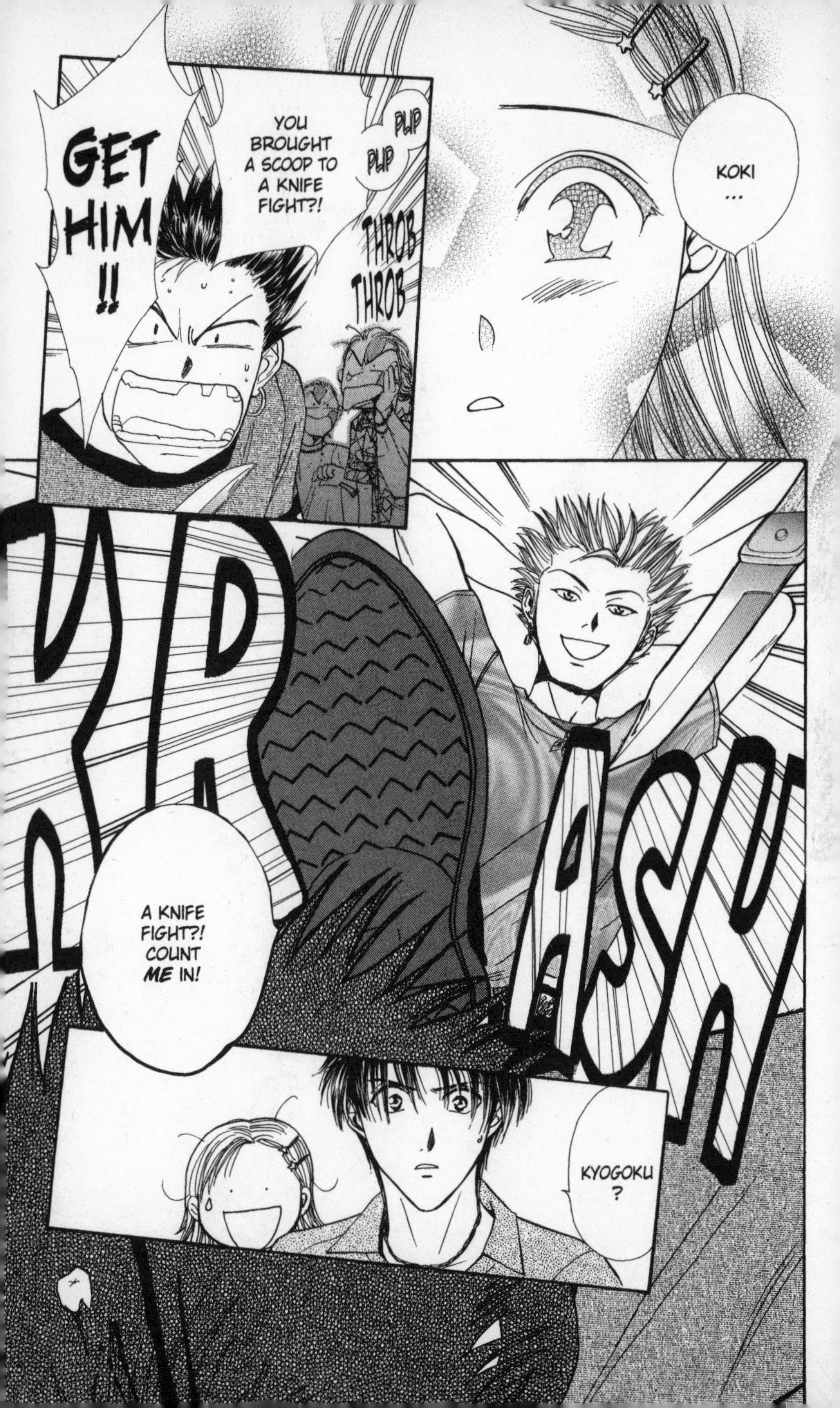
KOKI ...
PLIP PLIP
YOU BROUGHT A SCOOP TO A KNIFE FIGHT?!
THROB THROB
GET HIM !!
A KNIFE FIGHT?! COUNT *ME* IN!
KYOGOKU ?

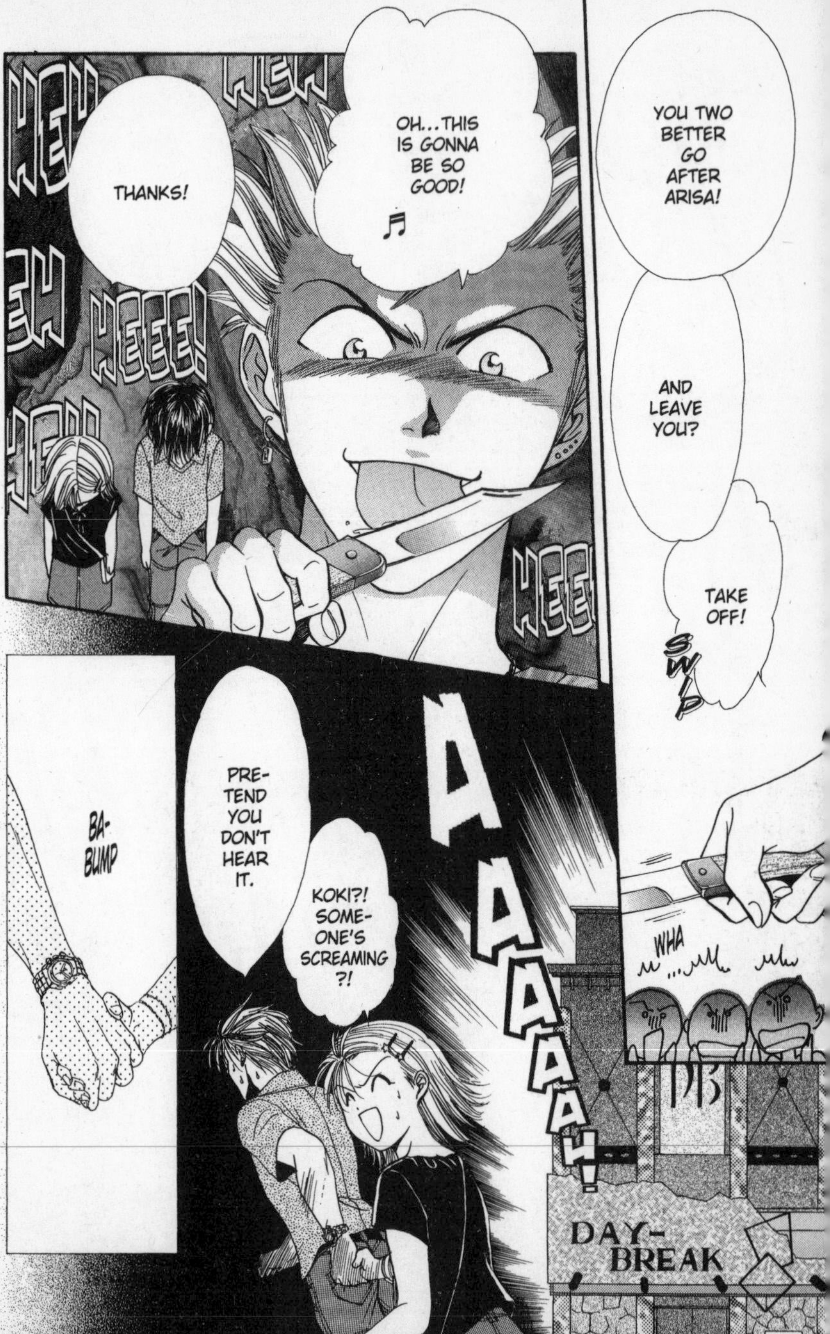
YOU TWO BETTER GO AFTER ARISA!
AND LEAVE YOU?
TAKE OFF!
SWIP
OH...THIS IS GONNA BE SO GOOD! ♬
THANKS!
HEH HEEE!
WHA...
AAAAAAH!
KOKI?! SOME-ONE'S SCREAMING?!
PRE-TEND YOU DON'T HEAR IT.
DAY-BREAK
BA-BUMP

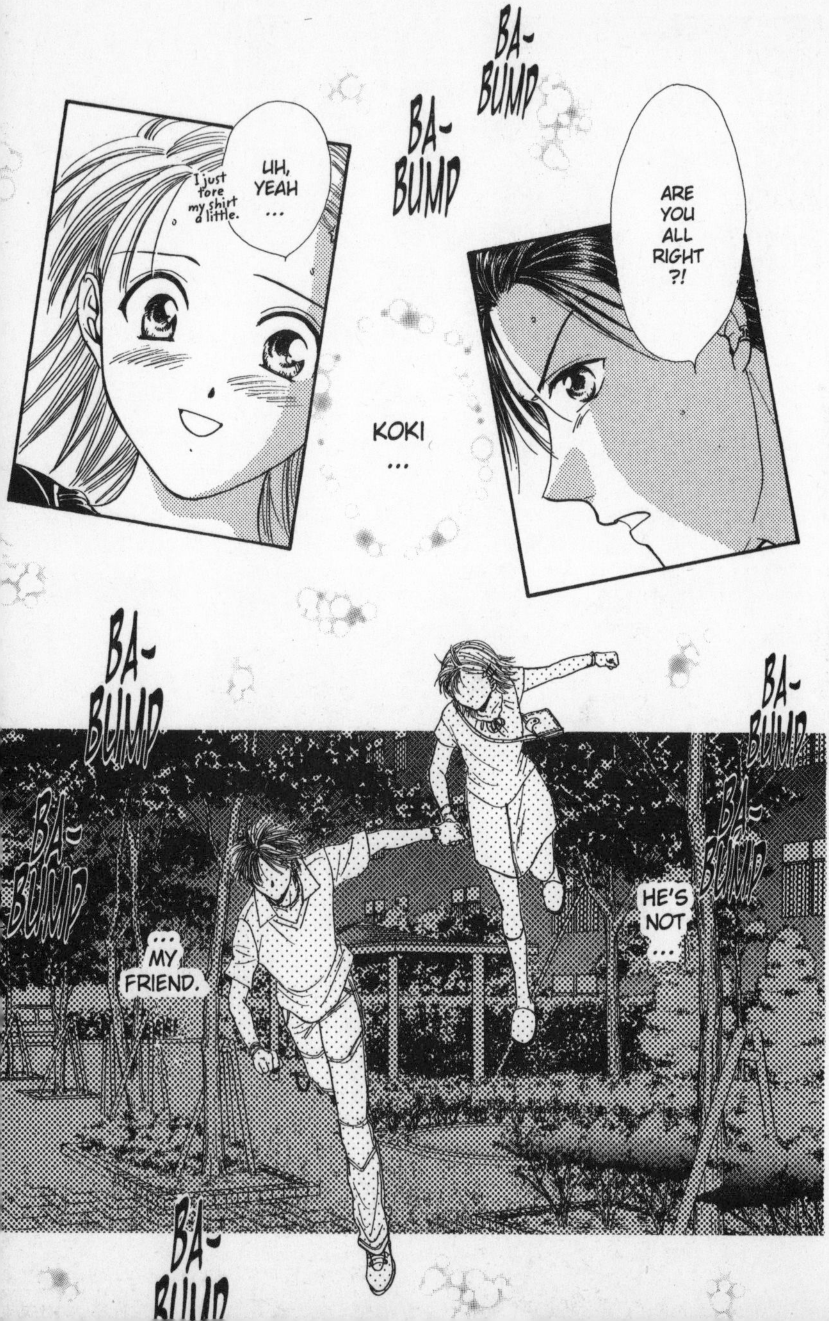
BA-BUMP
BA-BUMP
ARE YOU ALL RIGHT?!
UH, YEAH ...
I just tore my shirt a little.
KOKI ...
BA-BUMP
BA-BUMP
HE'S NOT ...
BA-BUMP
BA-BUMP
... MY FRIEND.
BA-

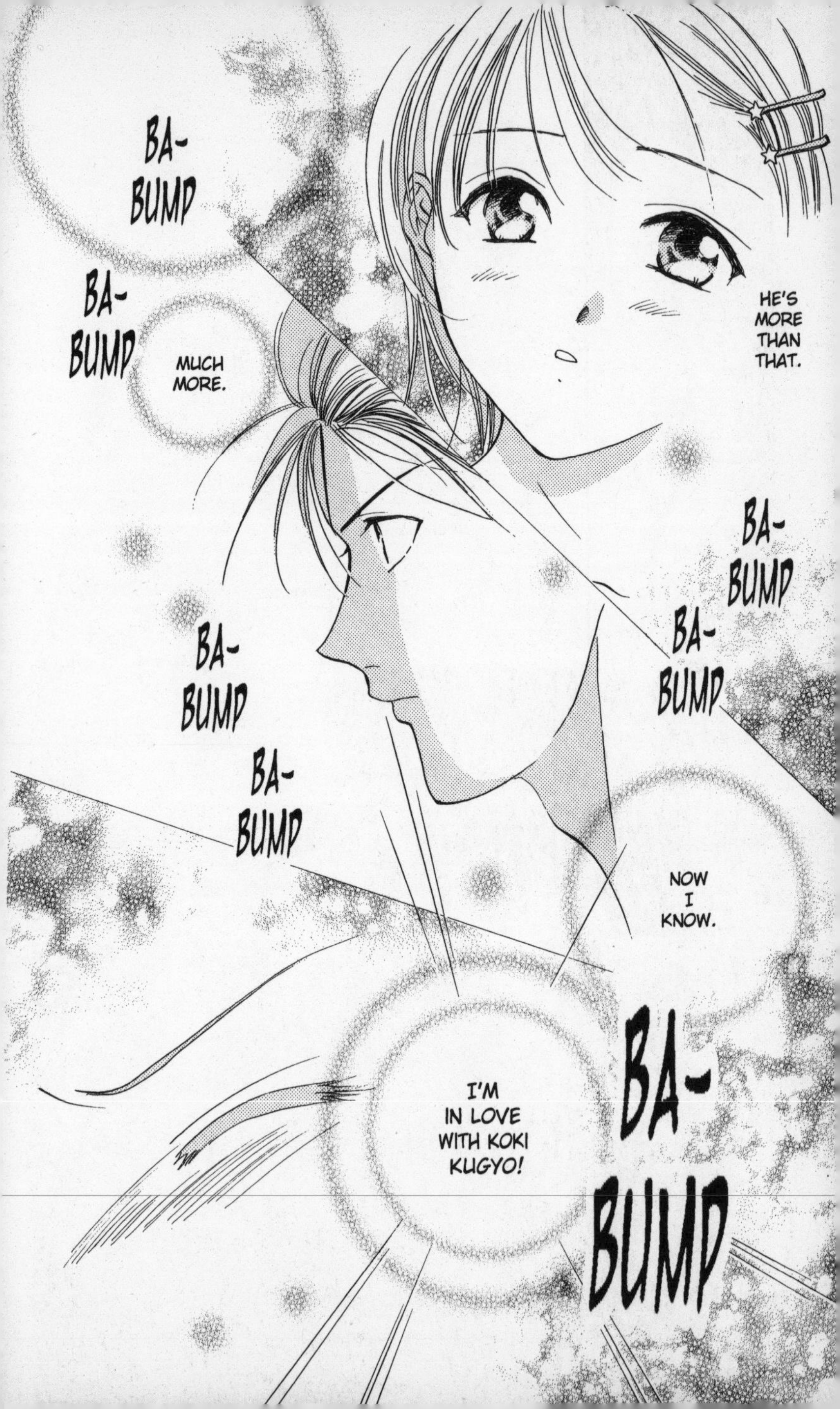
HE'S MORE THAN THAT.
BA-BUMP
BA-BUMP
MUCH MORE.
BA-BUMP
BA-BUMP
BA-BUMP
BA-BUMP
NOW I KNOW.
I'M IN LOVE WITH KOKI KUGYO!
BA-BUMP

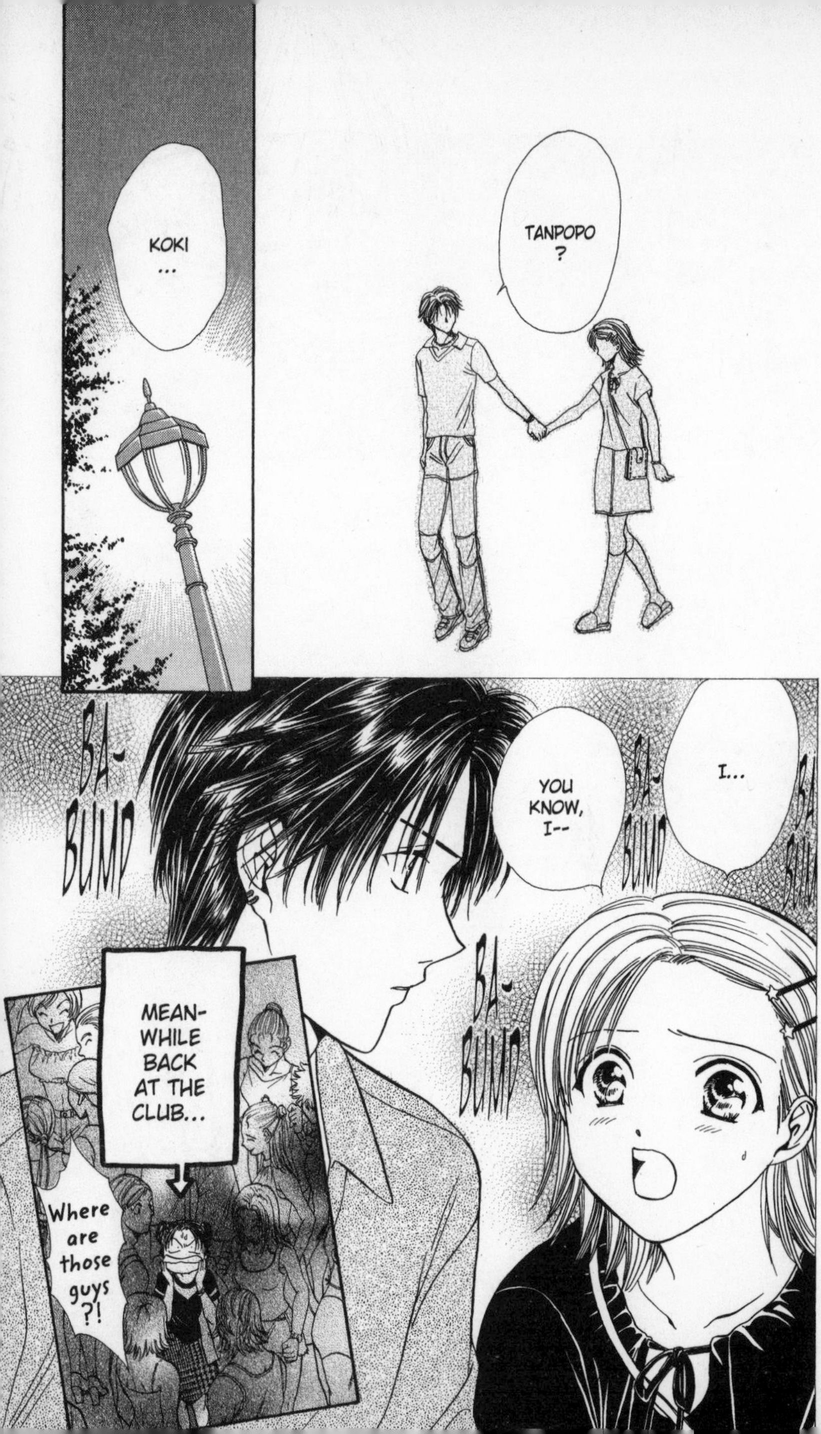
TANPOPO ?
KOKI ...
BA-BUMP
I...
BA-BUMP
YOU KNOW, I--
BA-BUMP
BA-BUMP
MEAN-WHILE BACK AT THE CLUB...
Where are those guys ?!

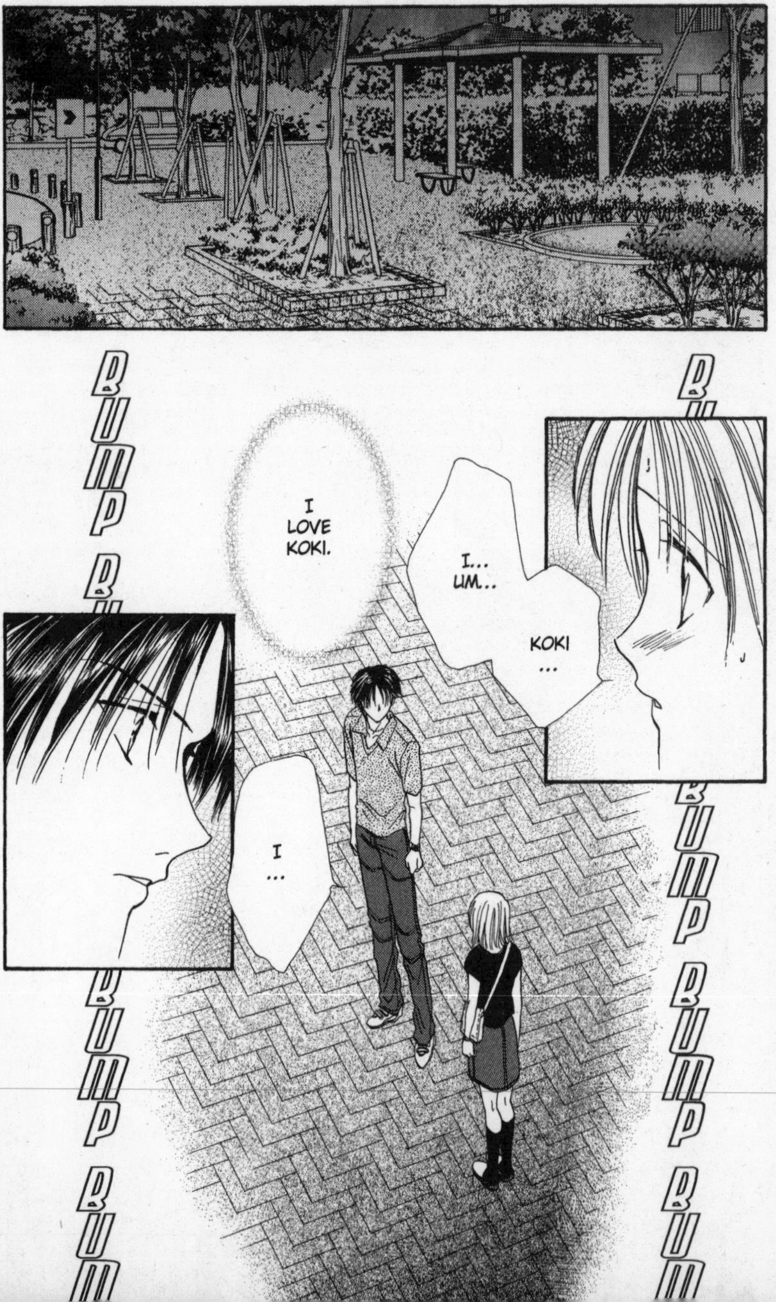
BUMP BUMP BUMP BUM
I... UM..
KOKI ...
I LOVE KOKI.
I ...
BUMP BUMP BUMP BUM

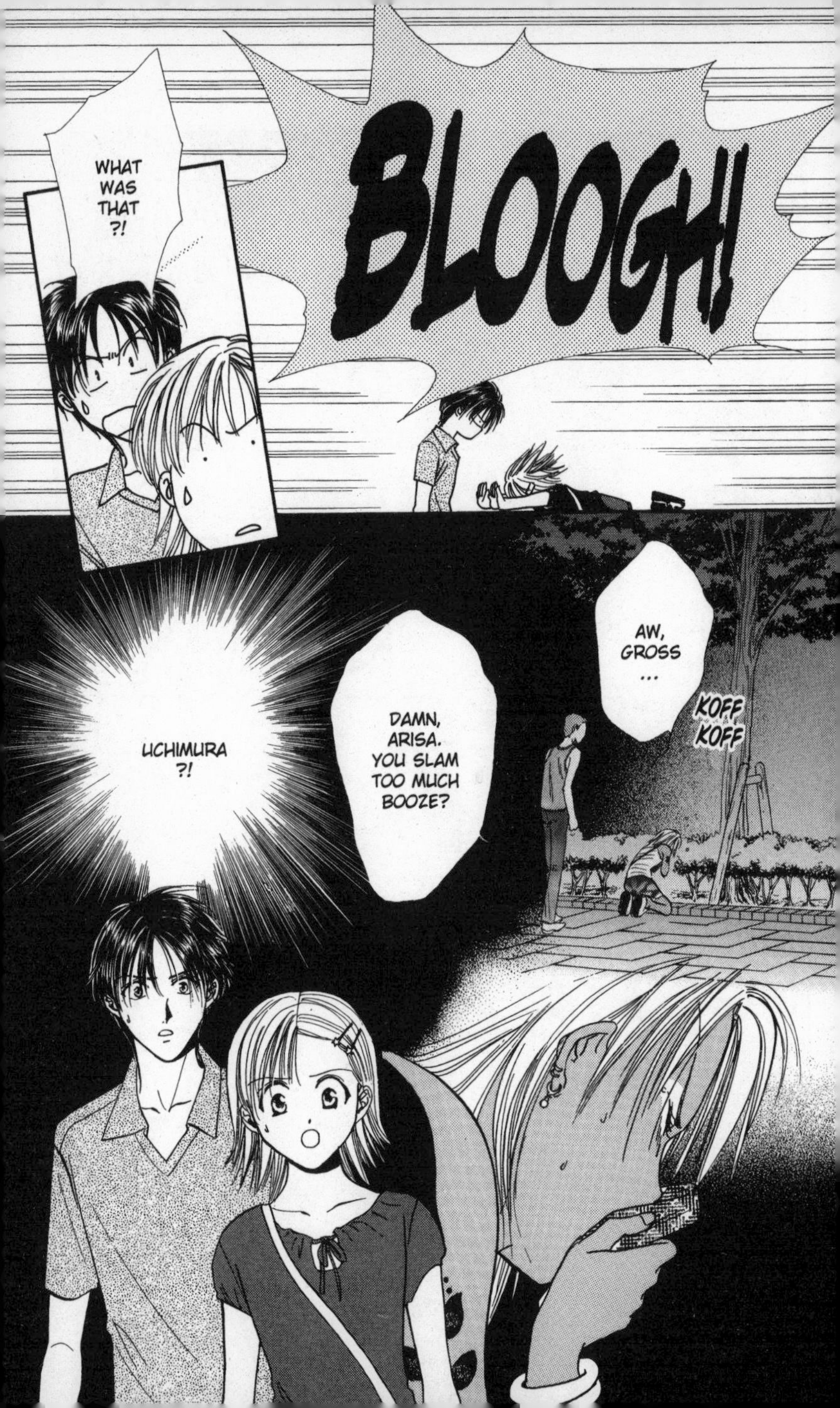
BLOOGH!
WHAT WAS THAT ?!
AW, GROSS ...
KOFF KOFF
DAMN, ARISA. YOU SLAM TOO MUCH BOOZE?
UCHIMURA ?!

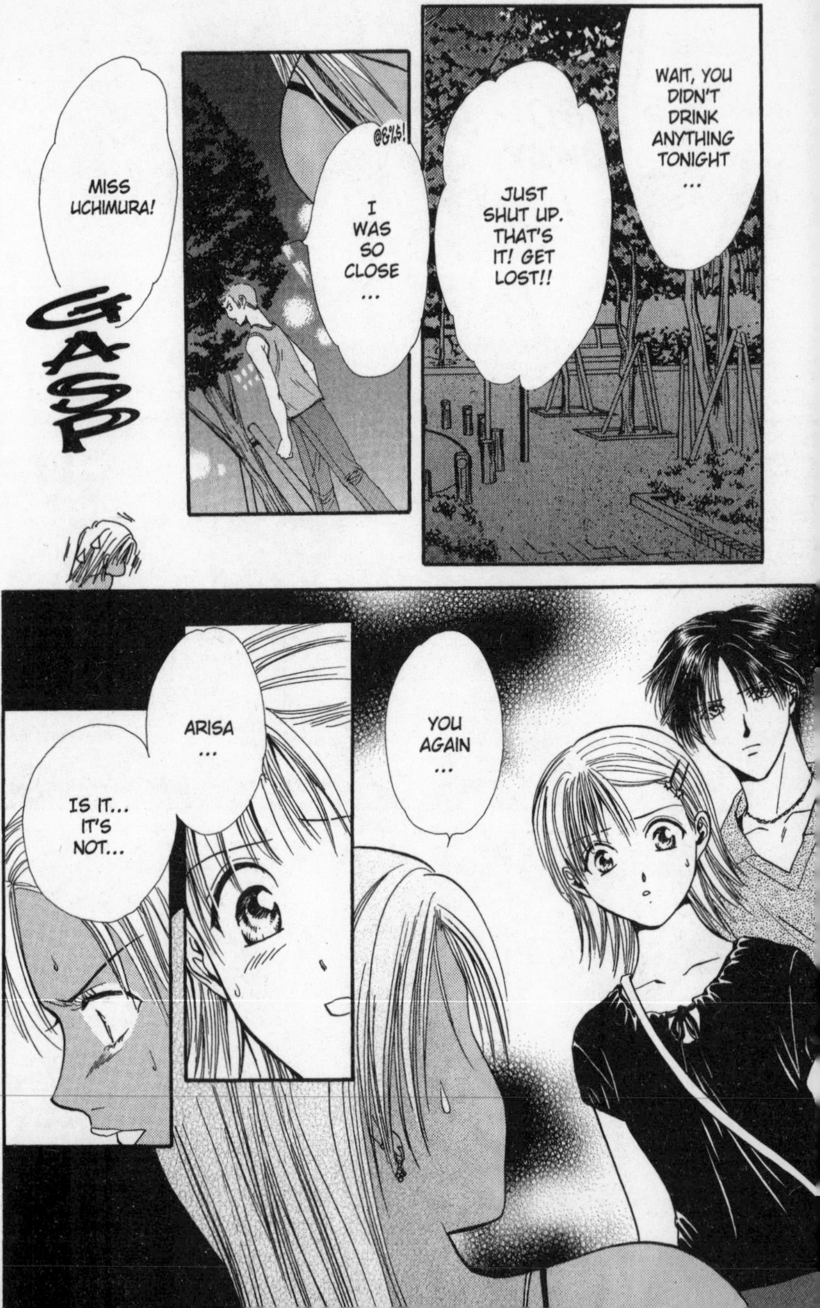
WAIT, YOU DIDN'T DRINK ANYTHING TONIGHT ...
JUST SHUT UP. THAT'S IT! GET LOST!!
@&%$!
I WAS SO CLOSE ...
MISS UCHIMURA!
GASP
YOU AGAIN ...
ARISA ...
IS IT... IT'S NOT...

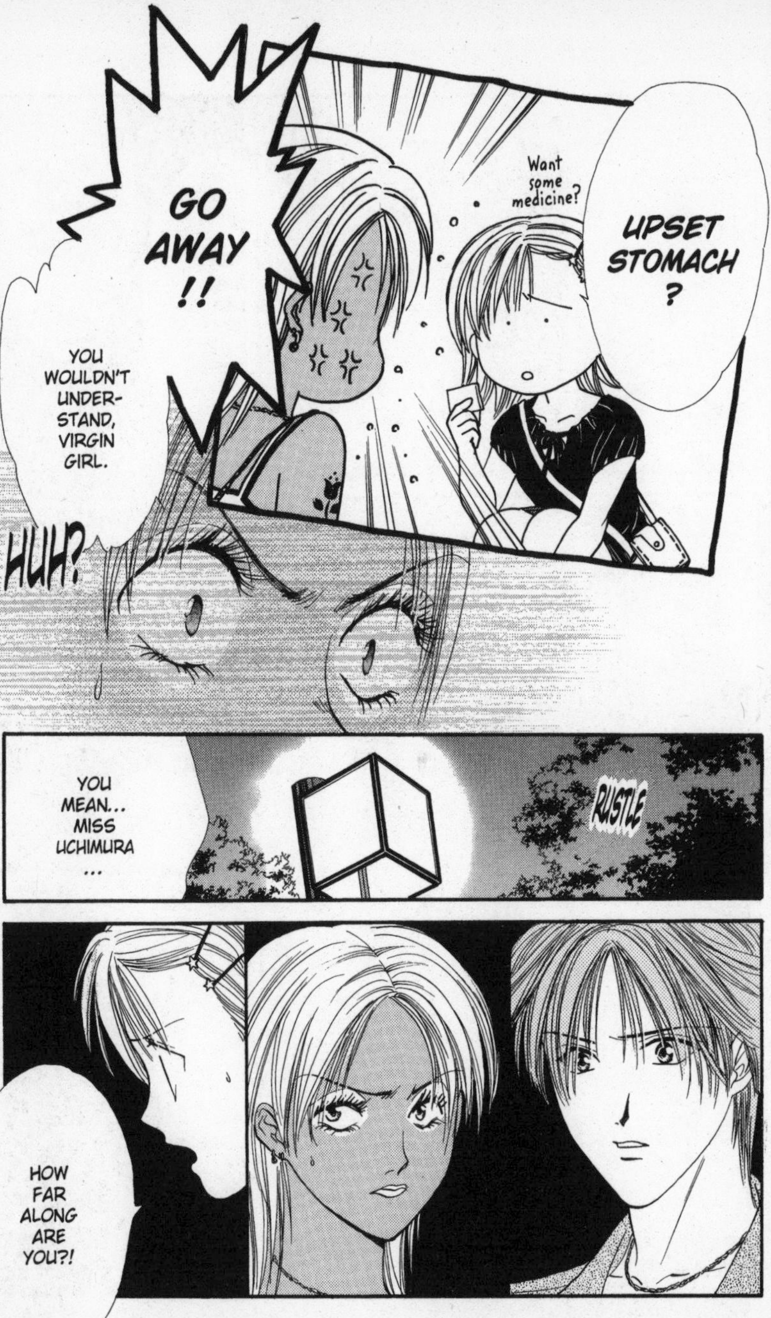
UPSET STOMACH ?
Want some medicine?
GO AWAY !!
YOU WOULDN'T UNDER-STAND, VIRGIN GIRL.
HUH?
RUSTLE
YOU MEAN... MISS UCHIMURA ...
HOW FAR ALONG ARE YOU?!

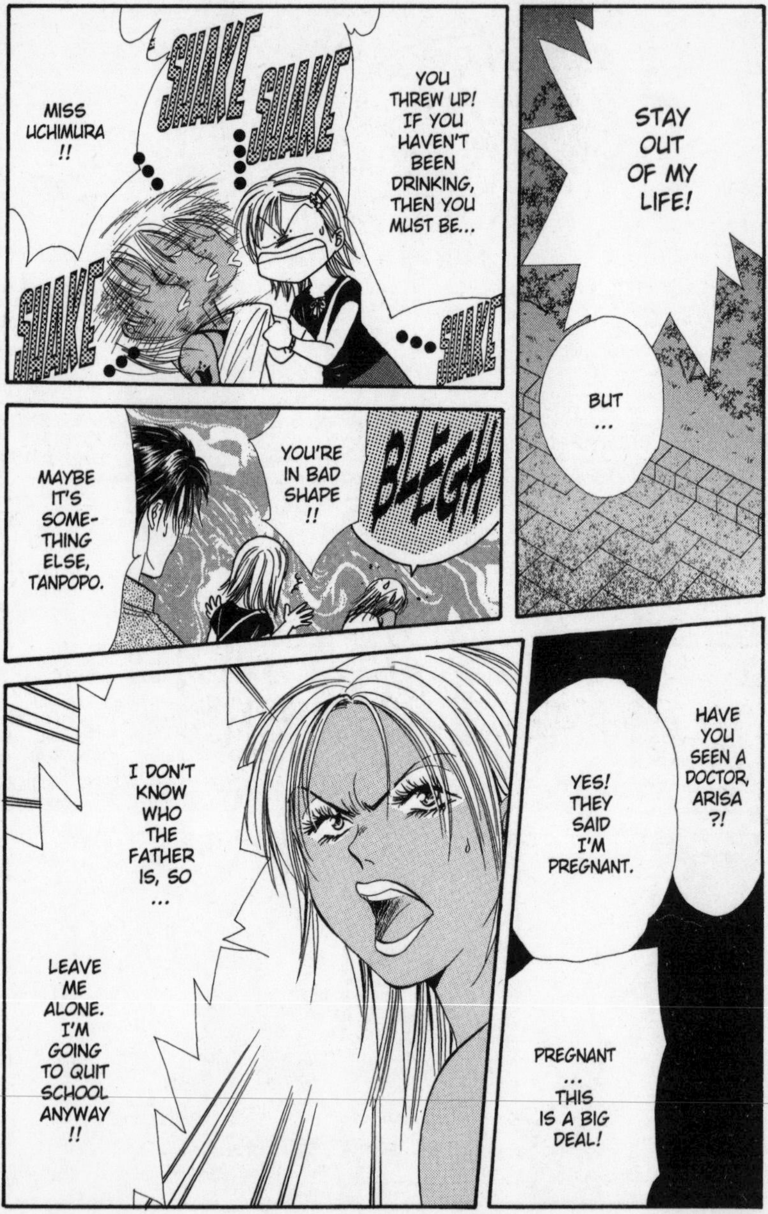
STAY OUT OF MY LIFE!
BUT ...
SHAKE
YOU THREW UP! IF YOU HAVEN'T BEEN DRINKING, THEN YOU MUST BE...
SHAKE
SHAKE
MISS UCHIMURA !!
SHAKE
BLEGH
YOU'RE IN BAD SHAPE !!
MAYBE IT'S SOME-THING ELSE, TANPOPO.
HAVE YOU SEEN A DOCTOR, ARISA ?!
YES! THEY SAID I'M PREGNANT.
PREGNANT ... THIS IS A BIG DEAL!
I DON'T KNOW WHO THE FATHER IS, SO ...
LEAVE ME ALONE. I'M GOING TO QUIT SCHOOL ANYWAY !!

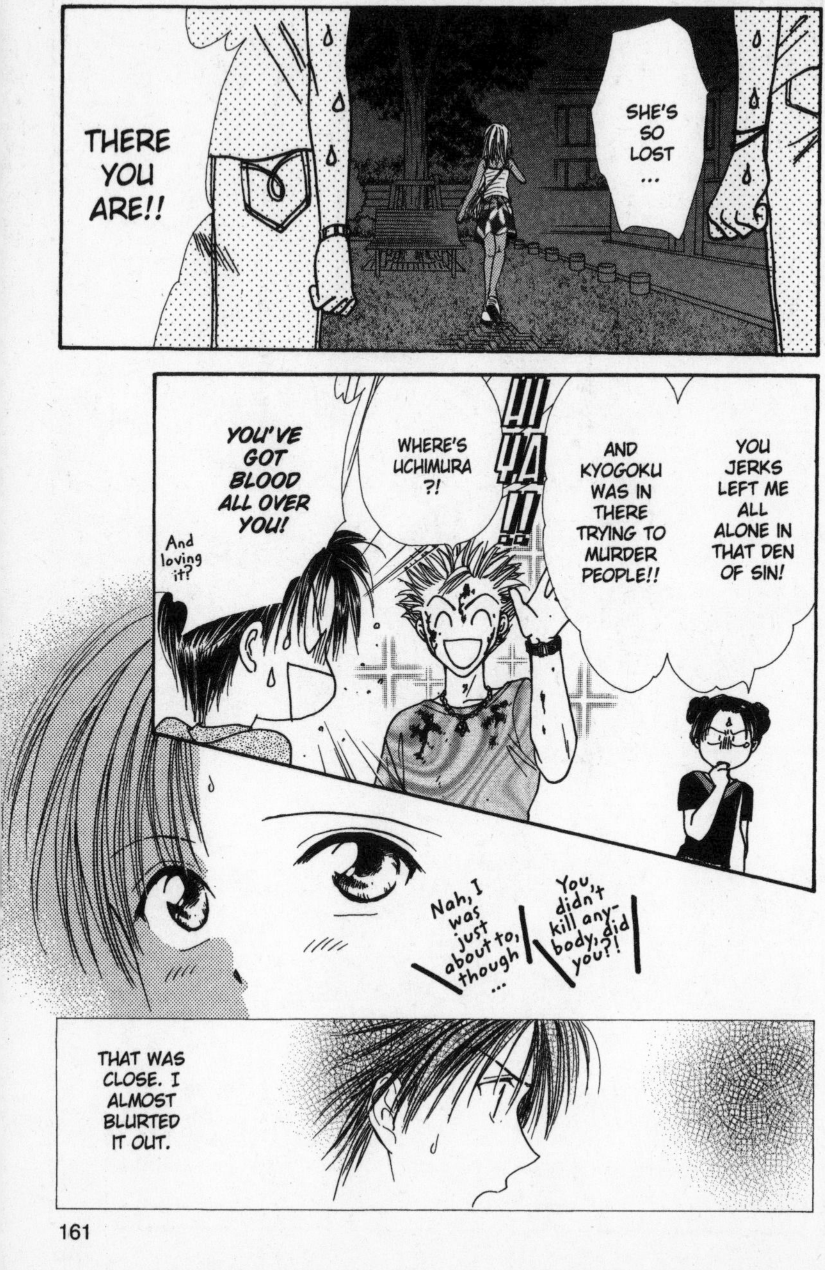
SHE'S SO LOST ...
THERE YOU ARE!!
YOU JERKS LEFT ME ALL ALONE IN THAT DEN OF SIN!
AND KYOGOKU WAS IN THERE TRYING TO MURDER PEOPLE!!
HIYA!!
WHERE'S UCHIMURA ?!
YOU'VE GOT BLOOD ALL OVER YOU!
And loving it?
You didn't kill anybody, did you?!
Nah, I was just about to, though ...
THAT WAS CLOSE. I ALMOST BLURTED IT OUT.

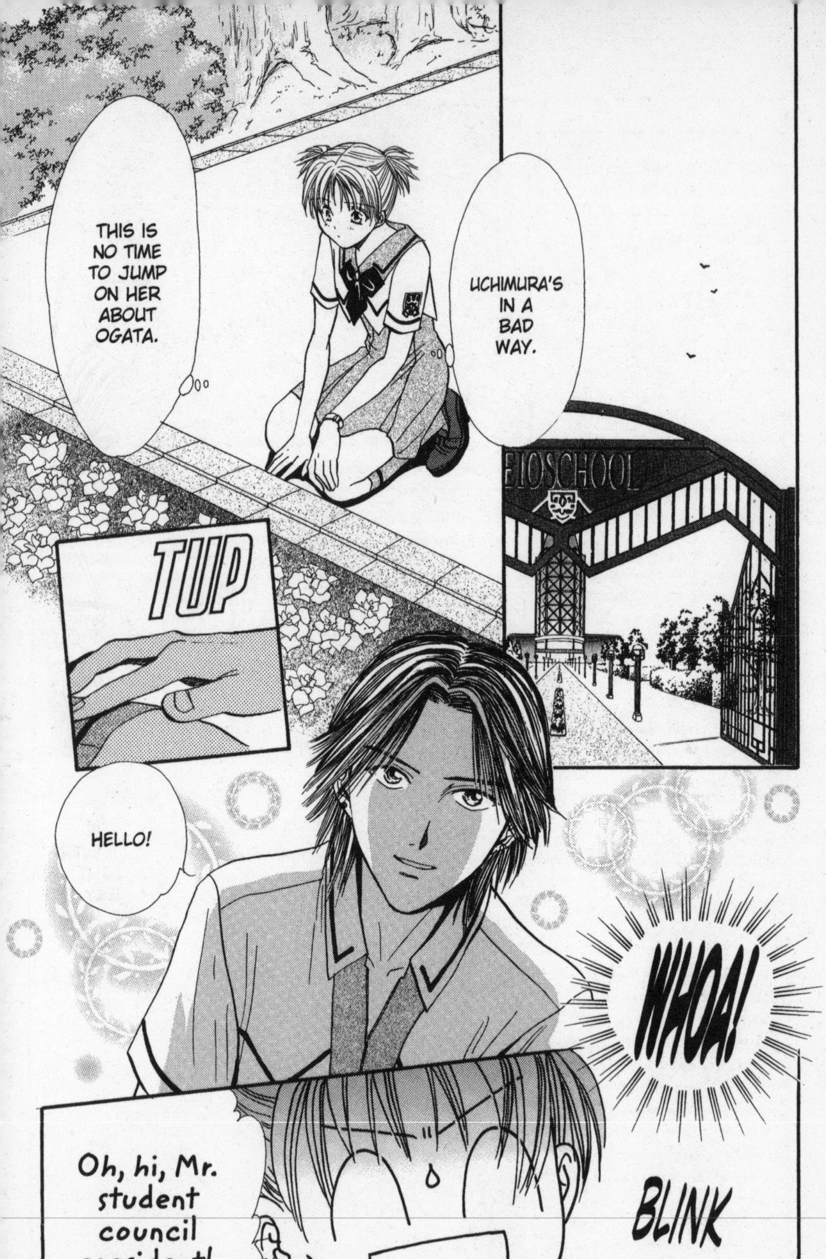

UCHIMURA'S IN A BAD WAY.
THIS IS NO TIME TO JUMP ON HER ABOUT OGATA.
TUP
HELLO!
WHOA!
BLINK
Oh, hi, Mr. student council president!

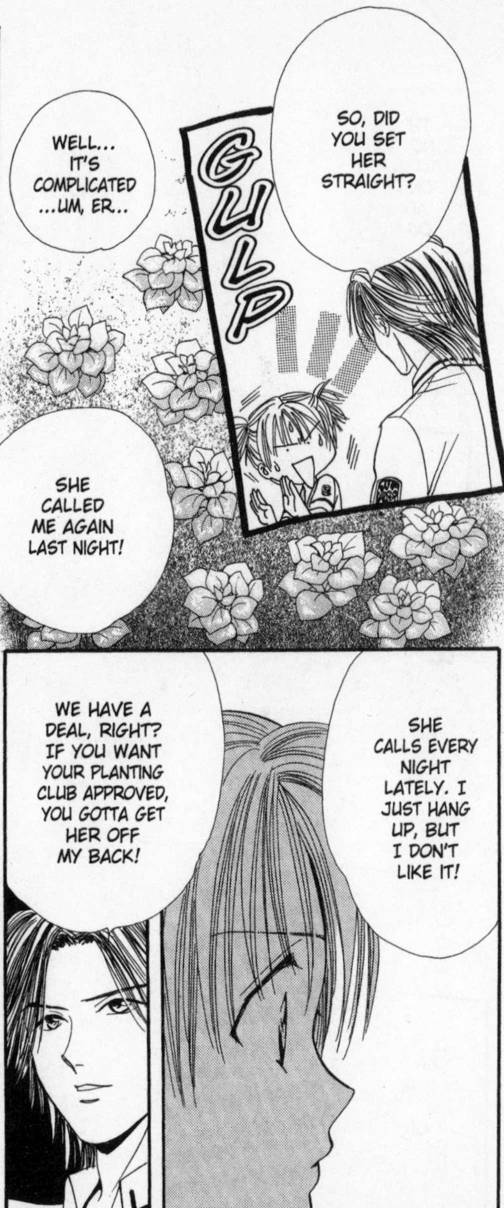
SO, DID YOU SET HER STRAIGHT?
GULP
WELL... IT'S COMPLICATED ...UM, ER...
SHE CALLED ME AGAIN LAST NIGHT!
SHE CALLS EVERY NIGHT LATELY. I JUST HANG UP, BUT I DON'T LIKE IT!
WE HAVE A DEAL, RIGHT? IF YOU WANT YOUR PLANTING CLUB APPROVED, YOU GOTTA GET HER OFF MY BACK!

Next! It's the second half of 2000 and just when I thought I had some free time--I don't. (Well, I guess I'm thankful...)

Besides **Imadoki!** I've been busy with lots of other projects. Last December, there was the soundtrack CD for **Ayashi no Ceres**, which I wrote about before, and the third **Ayashi no Ceres** novel, and the Postcard Book (**Fushigi Yûgi, Ayashi no Ceres**), and videos, etc. (smile)

Work is pouring in. Lots of sketch jobs. Those of you who say, "I can't go shopping in December!" I say, hey, you're lucky you still get New Year's gift money... Don't complain.

New Year's gift money. How nice. I don't get it anymore. (How old are you anyway?) And you don't send any.

For New Year's, I'd like to play those videos that are gathering dust. **Final Fantasy 9** isn't moving along... **Final Fantasy 8** isn't very popular (I stop in the middle and skip to the end!). If I don't get it, everyone around me says, "It's interesting!" But it is really good!

Speaking of interesting, I've recently gotten hooked on so-called children's books. I mean the kind that are like an actual novel. I'm hooked on the famous Harry Potter series. I really want book 3! Children around the world are putting their video games aside and getting hooked on these books. I hope Japan does the same. They're masterpieces that have revived the joy of reading, so if you haven't read them yet, please do!!

Ahh...Someday I hope I can create something like that. It won't be easy!

Anyway, until we meet again around February 2001 (oh!) in Book 3.

2000.10.22

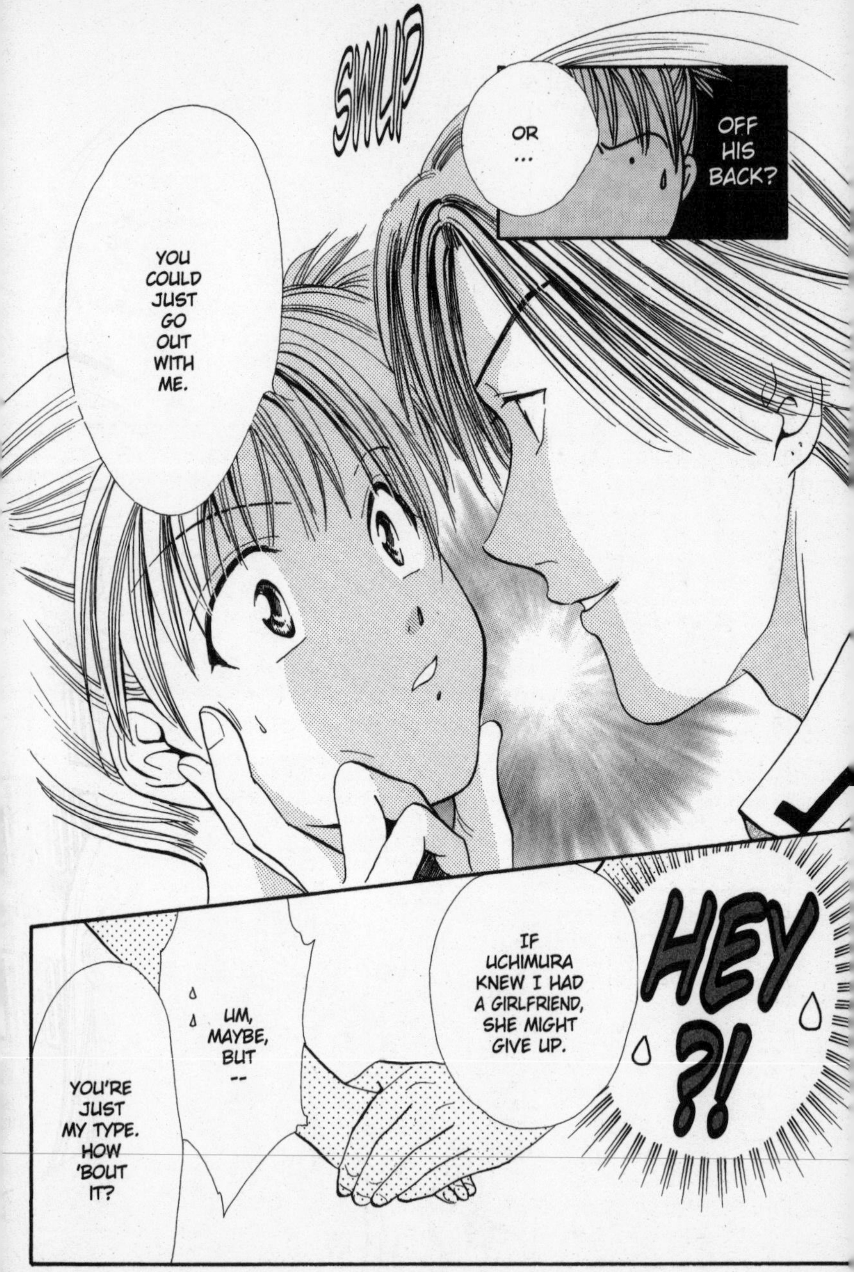
OFF HIS BACK?
OR ...
SWUP
YOU COULD JUST GO OUT WITH ME.
HEY ?!
IF UCHIMURA KNEW I HAD A GIRLFRIEND, SHE MIGHT GIVE UP.
UM, MAYBE, BUT --
YOU'RE JUST MY TYPE. HOW 'BOUT IT?

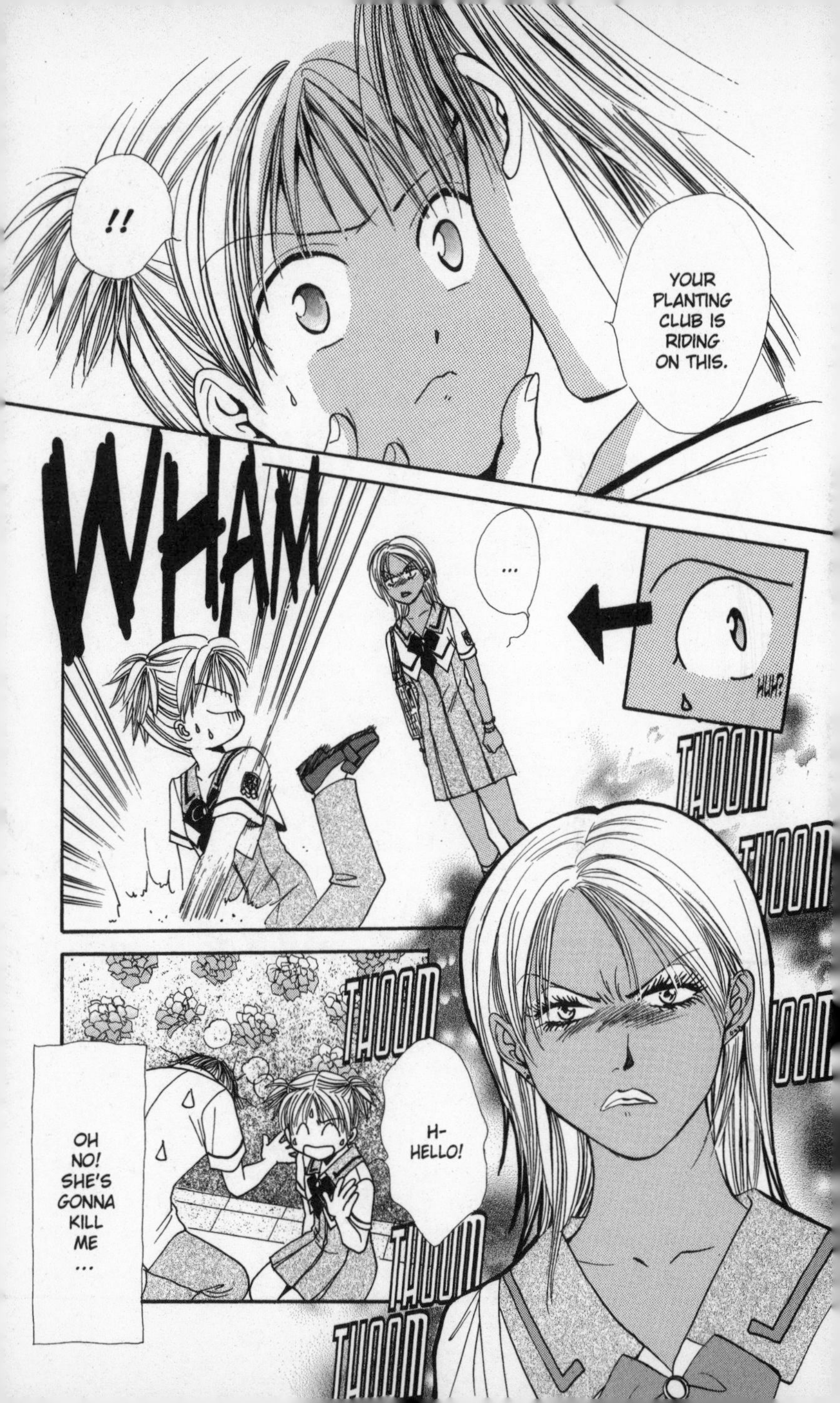
YOUR PLANTING CLUB IS RIDING ON THIS.
!!
HUH?
WHAM
...
THOOM
THOOM
THOOM
THOOM
THOOM
THOOM
H- HELLO!
OH NO! SHE'S GONNA KILL ME ...

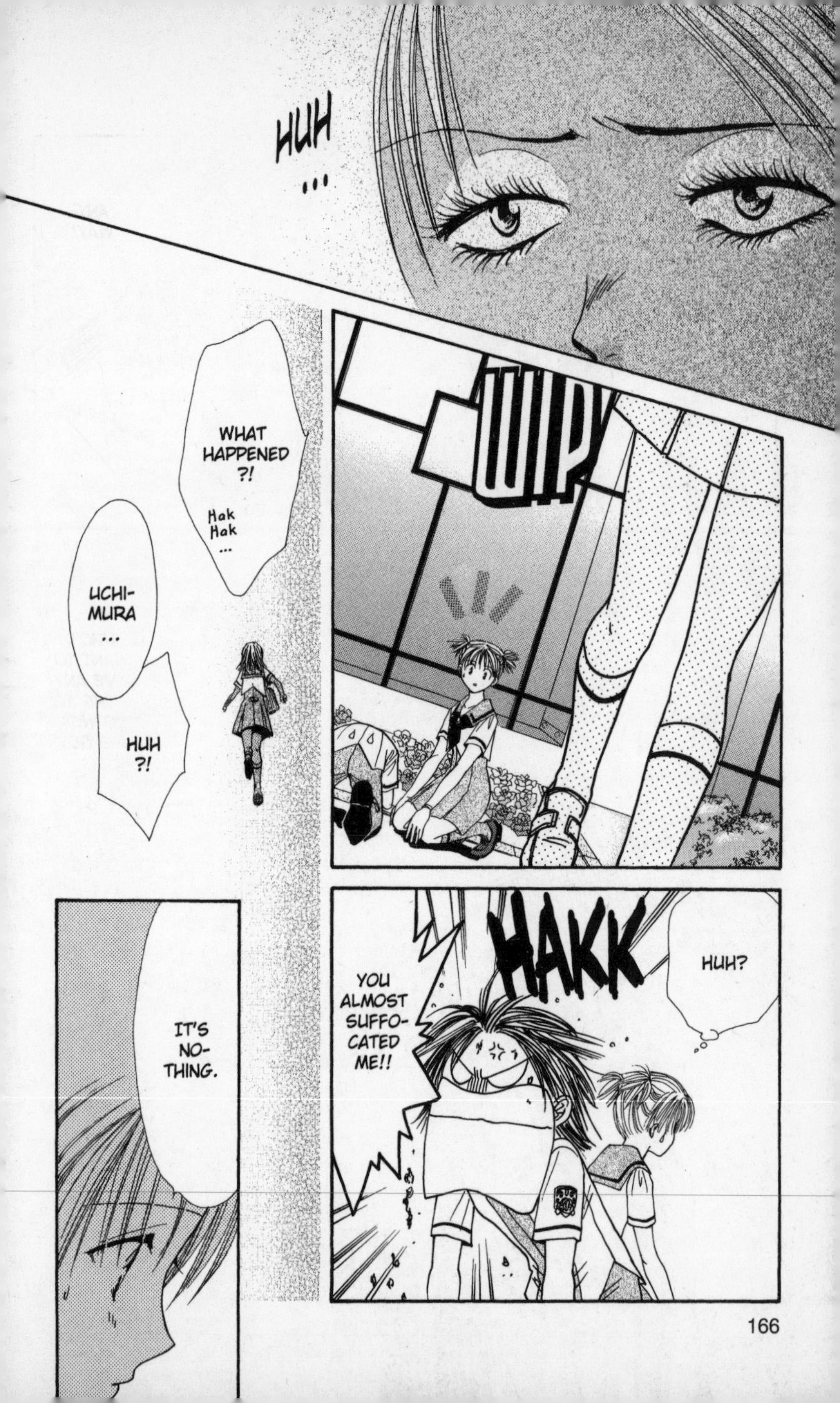
HUH ...
WIP
WHAT HAPPENED ?!
Hak Hak ...
UCHI-MURA ...
HUH ?!
HUH?
HAKK
YOU ALMOST SUFFO-CATED ME!!
IT'S NO-THING.

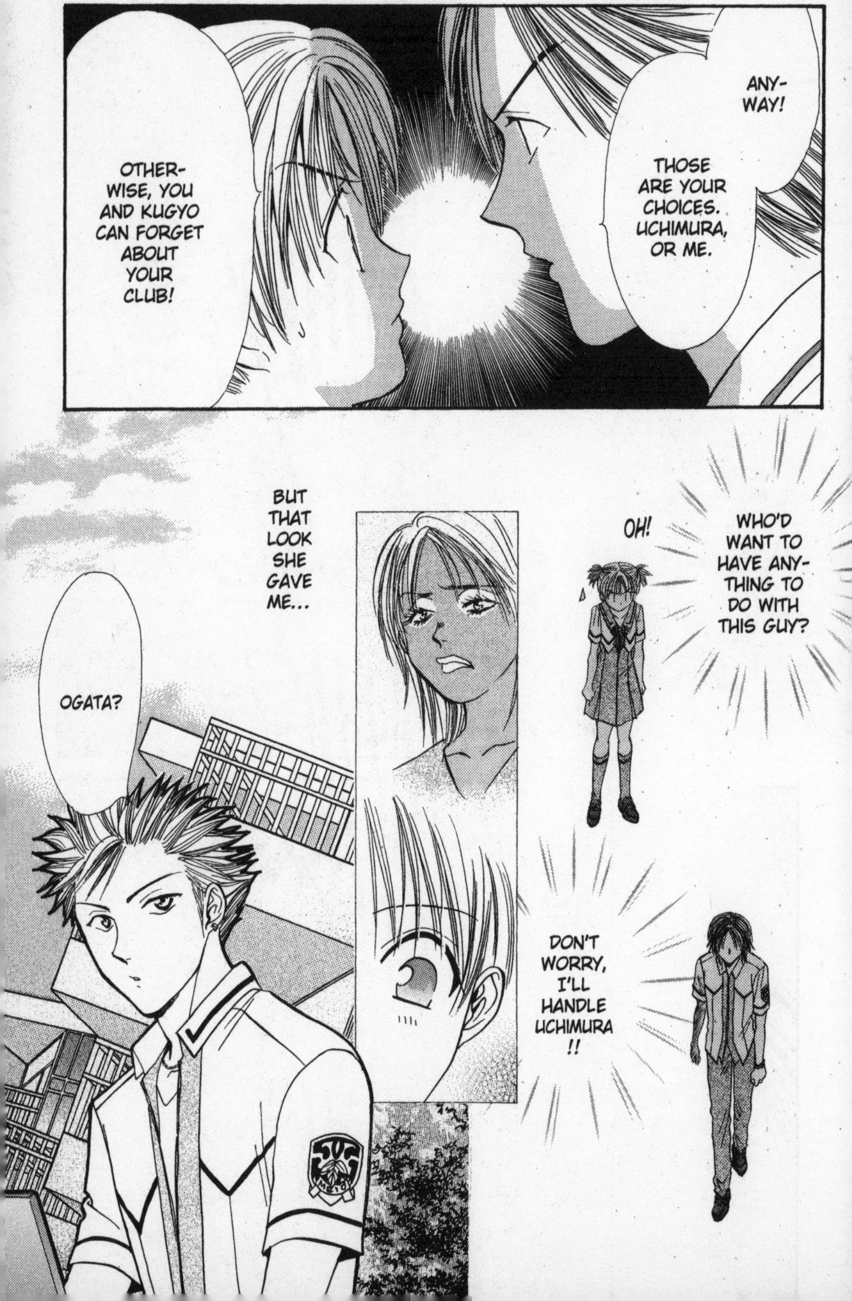
ANY-WAY!
THOSE ARE YOUR CHOICES. UCHIMURA, OR ME.
OTHER-WISE, YOU AND KUGYO CAN FORGET ABOUT YOUR CLUB!
WHO'D WANT TO HAVE ANY-THING TO DO WITH THIS GUY?
OH!
DON'T WORRY, I'LL HANDLE UCHIMURA !!
BUT THAT LOOK SHE GAVE ME...
OGATA?

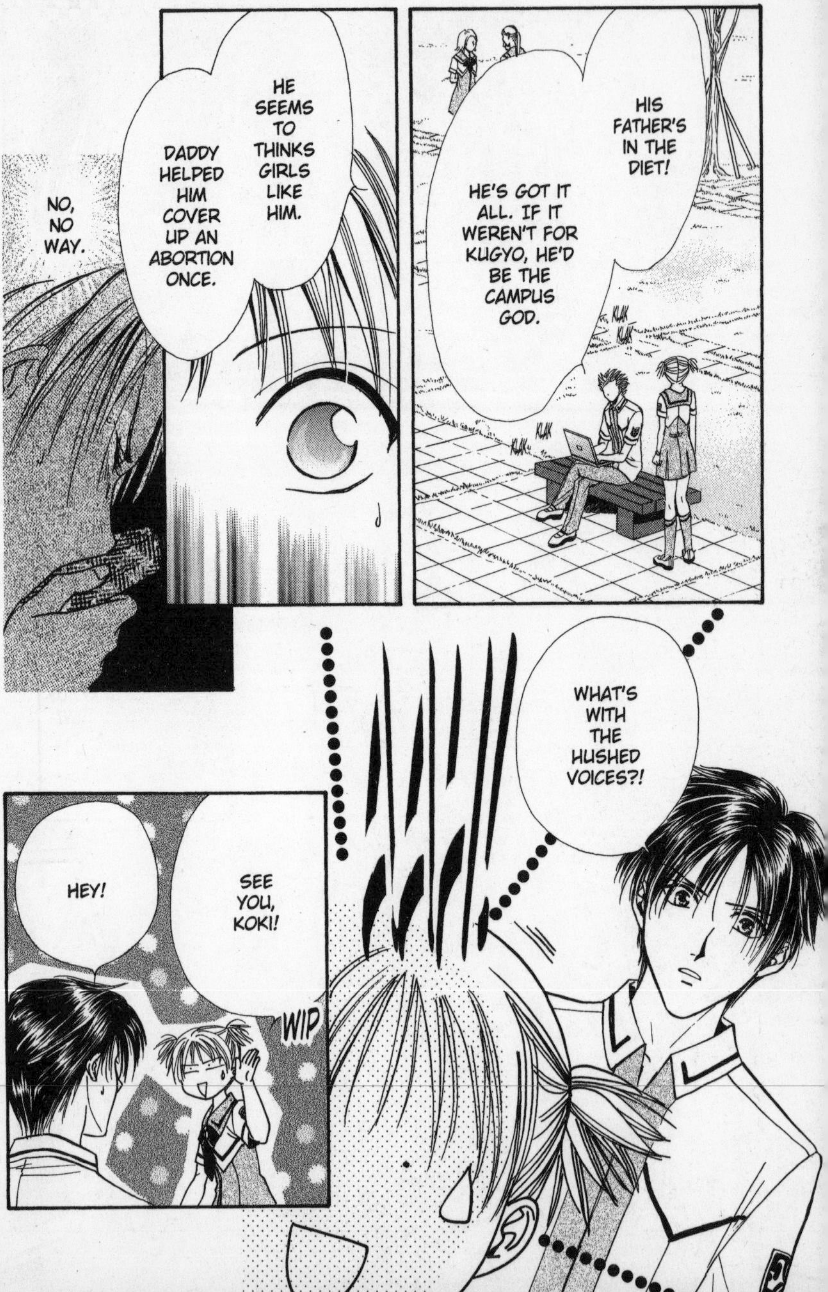
HIS FATHER'S IN THE DIET!
HE'S GOT IT ALL. IF IT WEREN'T FOR KUGYO, HE'D BE THE CAMPUS GOD.
KLAK KLAK
KLAK KLAK
HE SEEMS TO THINKS GIRLS LIKE HIM.
DADDY HELPED HIM COVER UP AN ABORTION ONCE.
NO, NO WAY.
WHAT'S WITH THE HUSHED VOICES?!
SEE YOU, KOKI!
HEY!
WIP

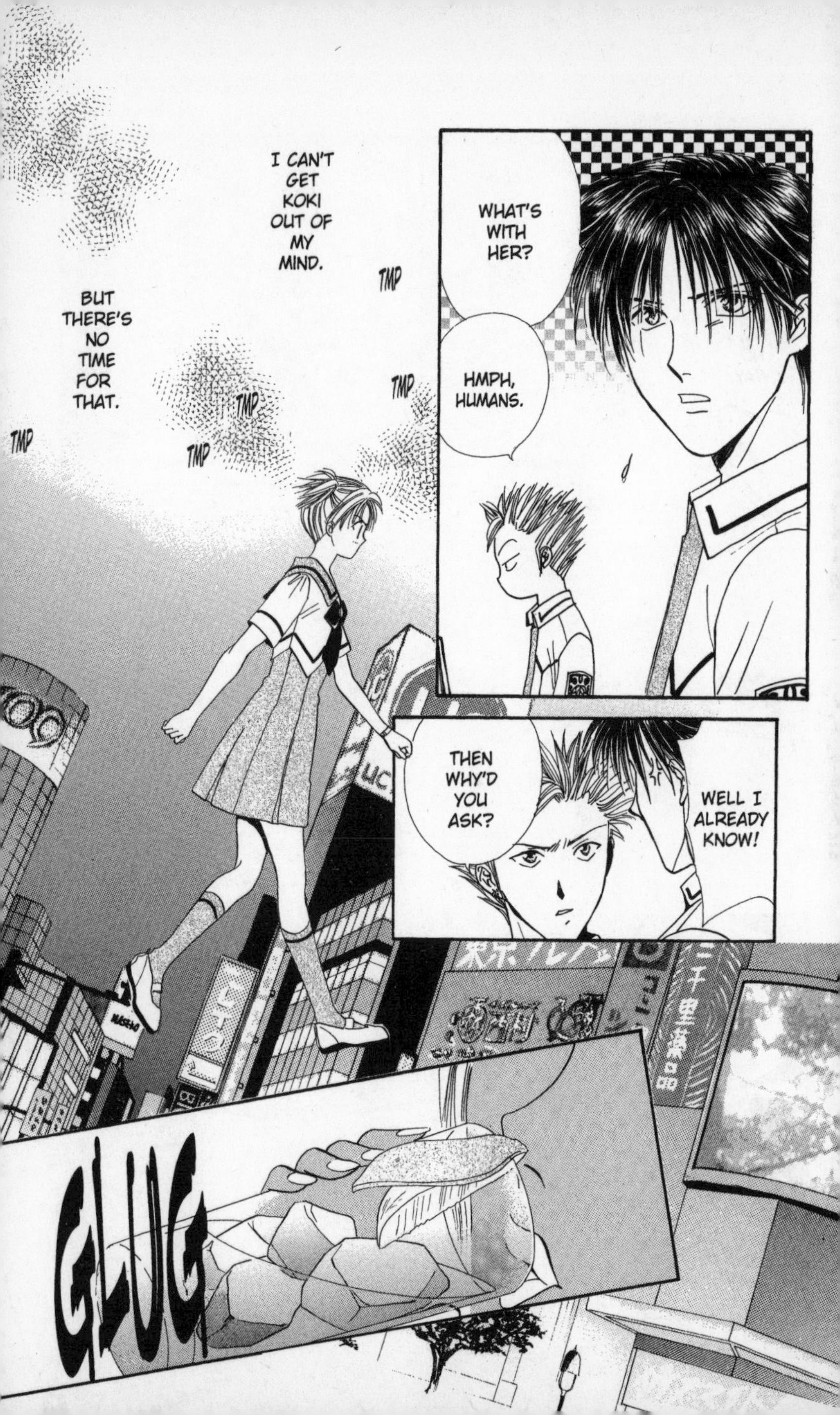

WHAT'S WITH HER?
HMPH, HUMANS.
WELL I ALREADY KNOW!
THEN WHY'D YOU ASK?
I CAN'T GET KOKI OUT OF MY MIND.
TMP
TMP
BUT THERE'S NO TIME FOR THAT.
TMP
TMP
TMP
GLUG

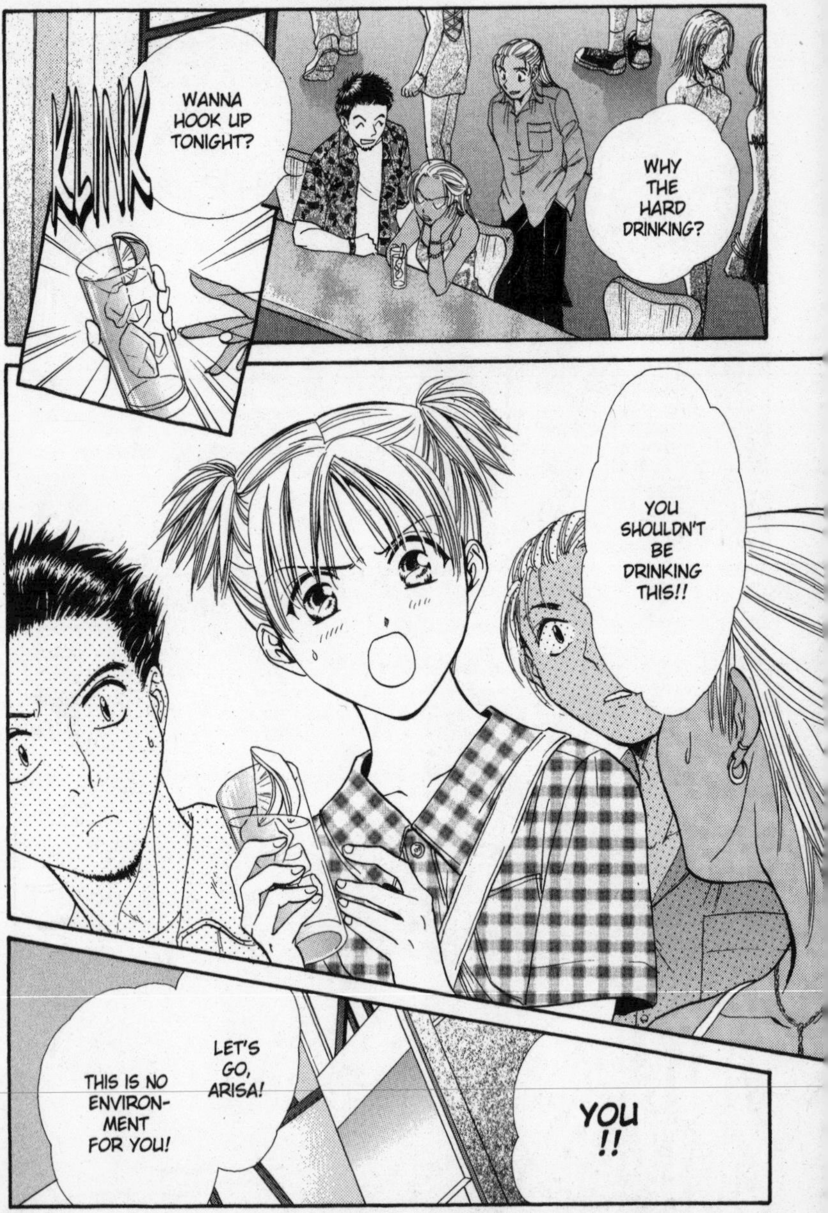
WHY THE HARD DRINKING?
WANNA HOOK UP TONIGHT?
KLINK
YOU SHOULDN'T BE DRINKING THIS!!
YOU!!
LET'S GO, ARISA!
THIS IS NO ENVIRON-MENT FOR YOU!

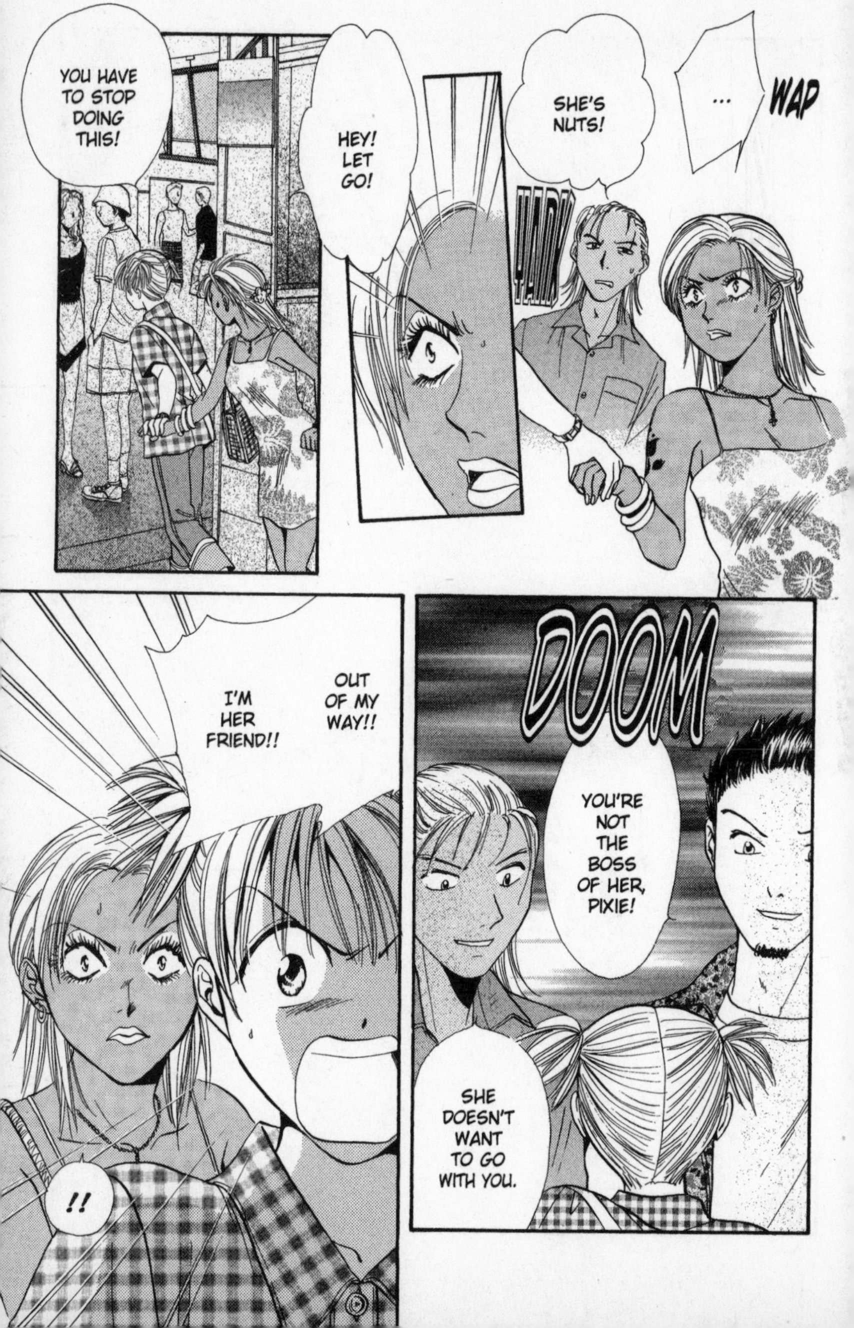

...
WAP
SHE'S NUTS!
YANK
HEY! LET GO!
YOU HAVE TO STOP DOING THIS!
DOOM
YOU'RE NOT THE BOSS OF HER, PIXIE!
SHE DOESN'T WANT TO GO WITH YOU.
OUT OF MY WAY!!
I'M HER FRIEND!!
!!

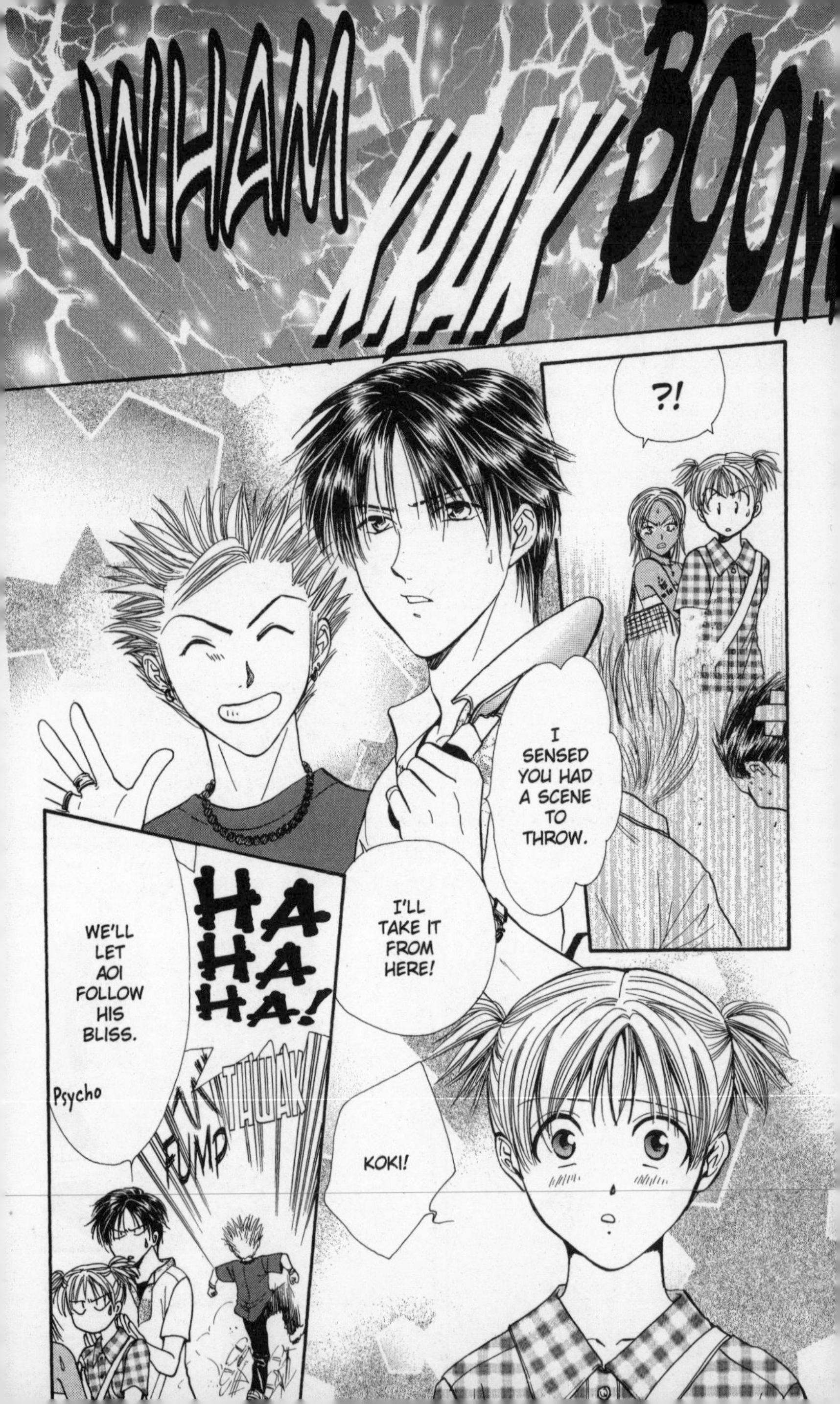

WHAM KRAK BOOM
?!
I SENSED YOU HAD A SCENE TO THROW.
I'LL TAKE IT FROM HERE!
HA HA HA!
WE'LL LET AOI FOLLOW HIS BLISS.
KOKI!
THWAK
FUMP
Psycho

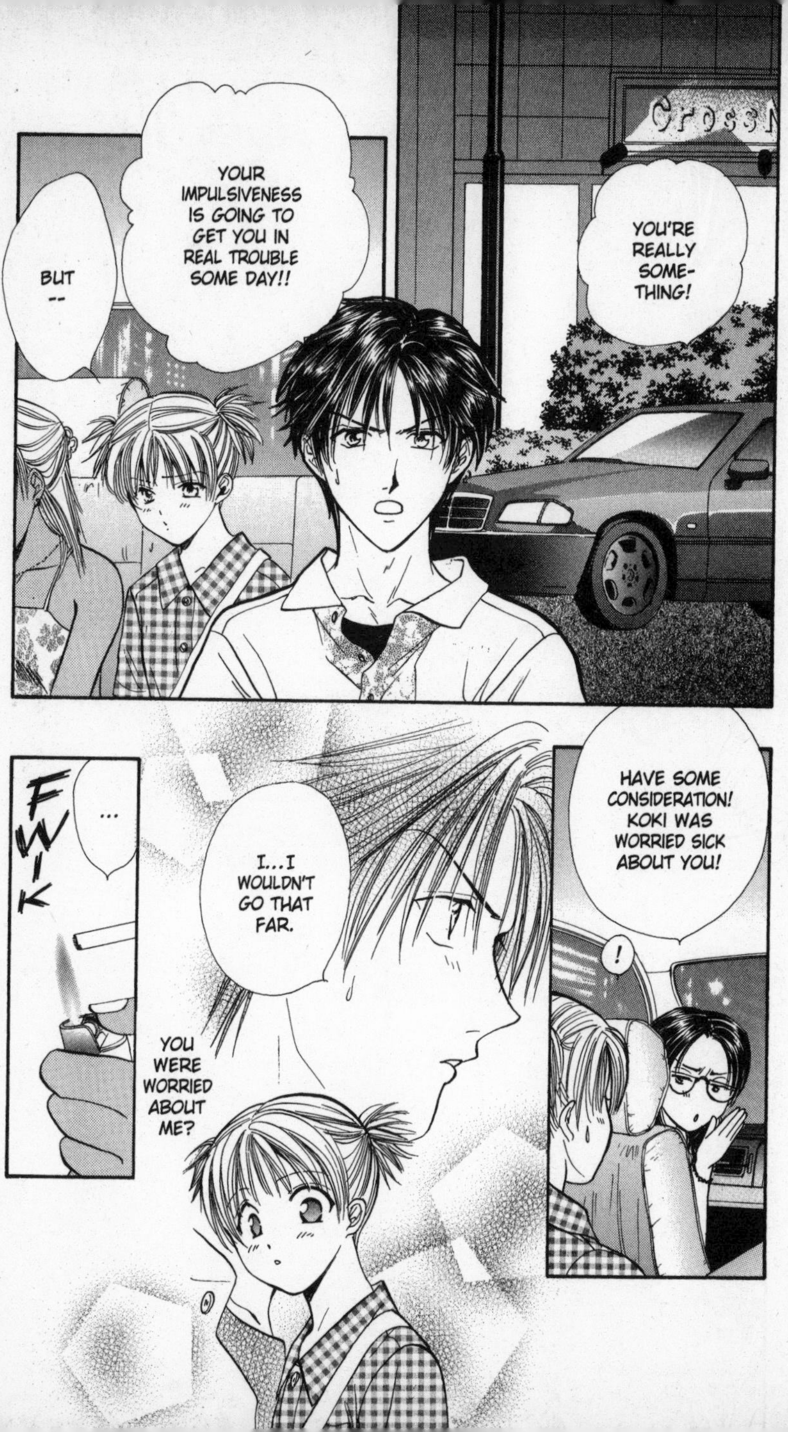
YOU'RE REALLY SOME-THING!
YOUR IMPULSIVENESS IS GOING TO GET YOU IN REAL TROUBLE SOME DAY!!
BUT --
HAVE SOME CONSIDERATION! KOKI WAS WORRIED SICK ABOUT YOU!
!
I...I WOULDN'T GO THAT FAR.
YOU WERE WORRIED ABOUT ME?
FWIK
...

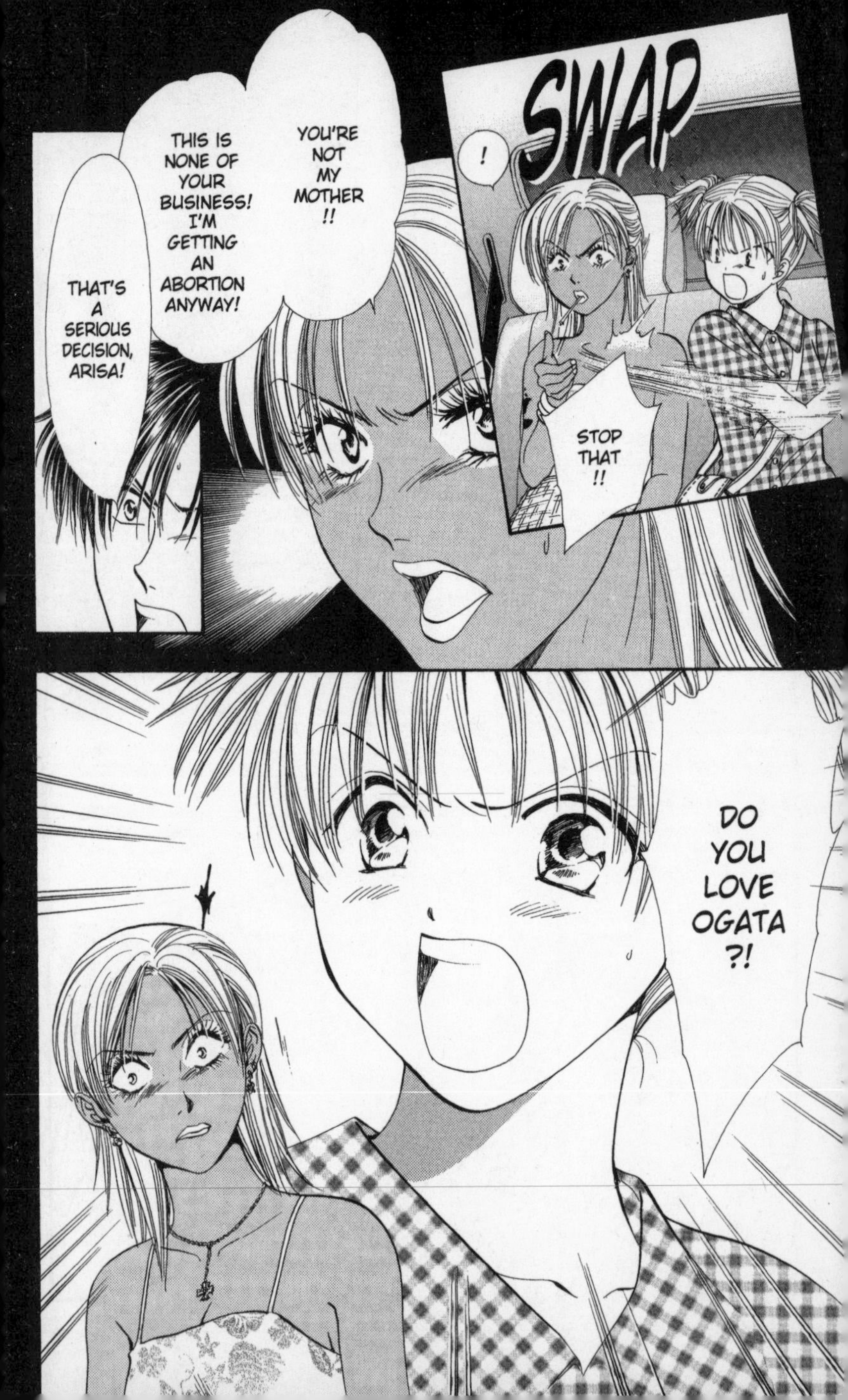
SWAP
!
STOP THAT !!
YOU'RE NOT MY MOTHER !!
THIS IS NONE OF YOUR BUSINESS! I'M GETTING AN ABORTION ANYWAY!
THAT'S A SERIOUS DECISION, ARISA!
DO YOU LOVE OGATA ?!

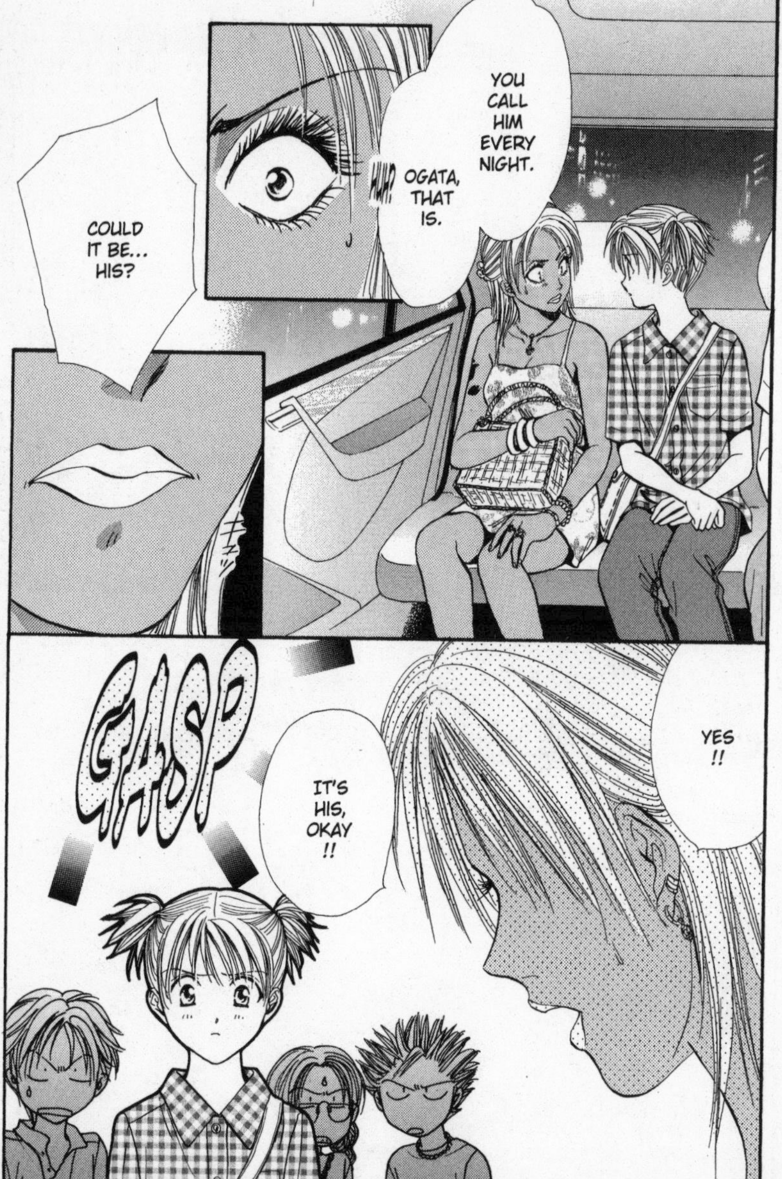

YOU CALL HIM EVERY NIGHT.
OGATA, THAT IS.
HUH?
COULD IT BE... HIS?
YES!!
IT'S HIS, OKAY!!
GASP

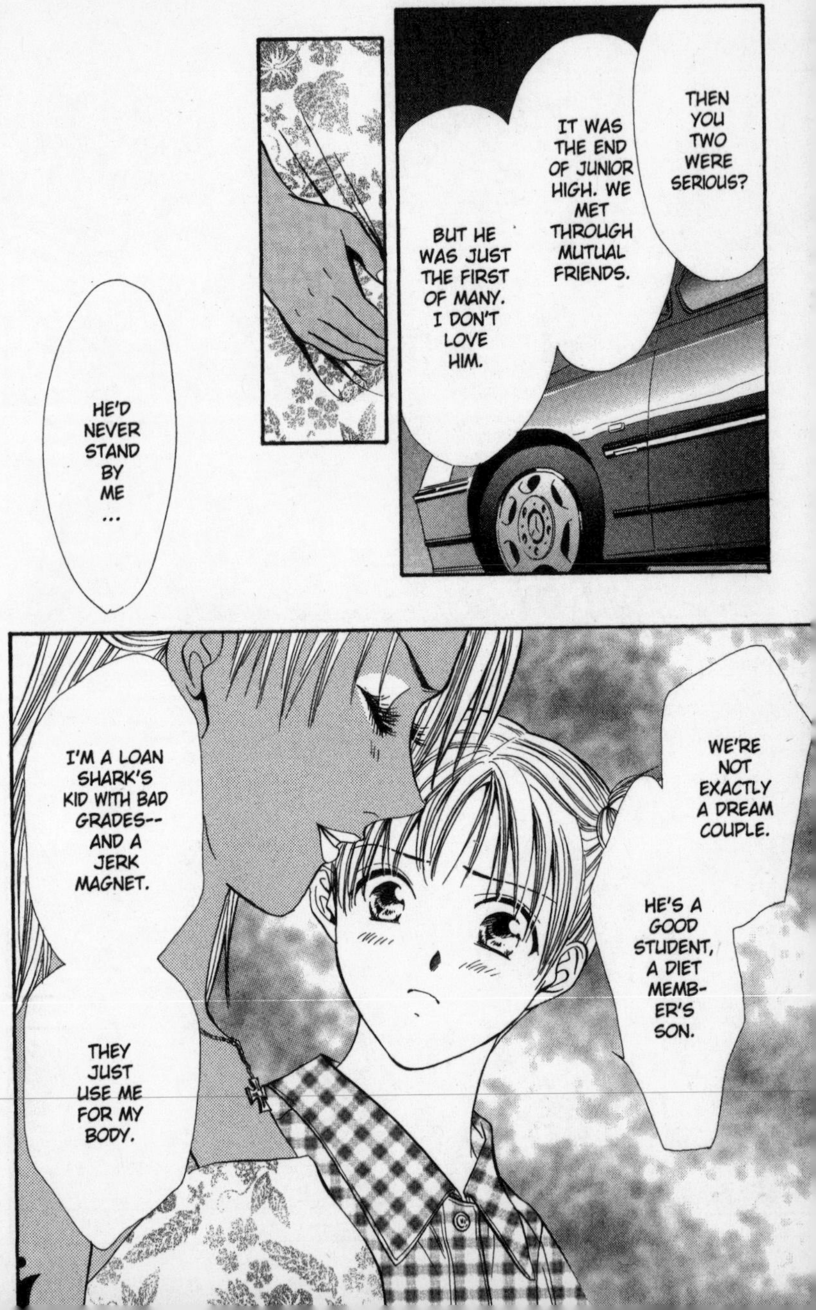
THEN YOU TWO WERE SERIOUS?
IT WAS THE END OF JUNIOR HIGH. WE MET THROUGH MUTUAL FRIENDS.
BUT HE WAS JUST THE FIRST OF MANY. I DON'T LOVE HIM.
HE'D NEVER STAND BY ME ...
WE'RE NOT EXACTLY A DREAM COUPLE.
HE'S A GOOD STUDENT, A DIET MEMB-ER'S SON.
I'M A LOAN SHARK'S KID WITH BAD GRADES-- AND A JERK MAGNET.
THEY JUST USE ME FOR MY BODY.

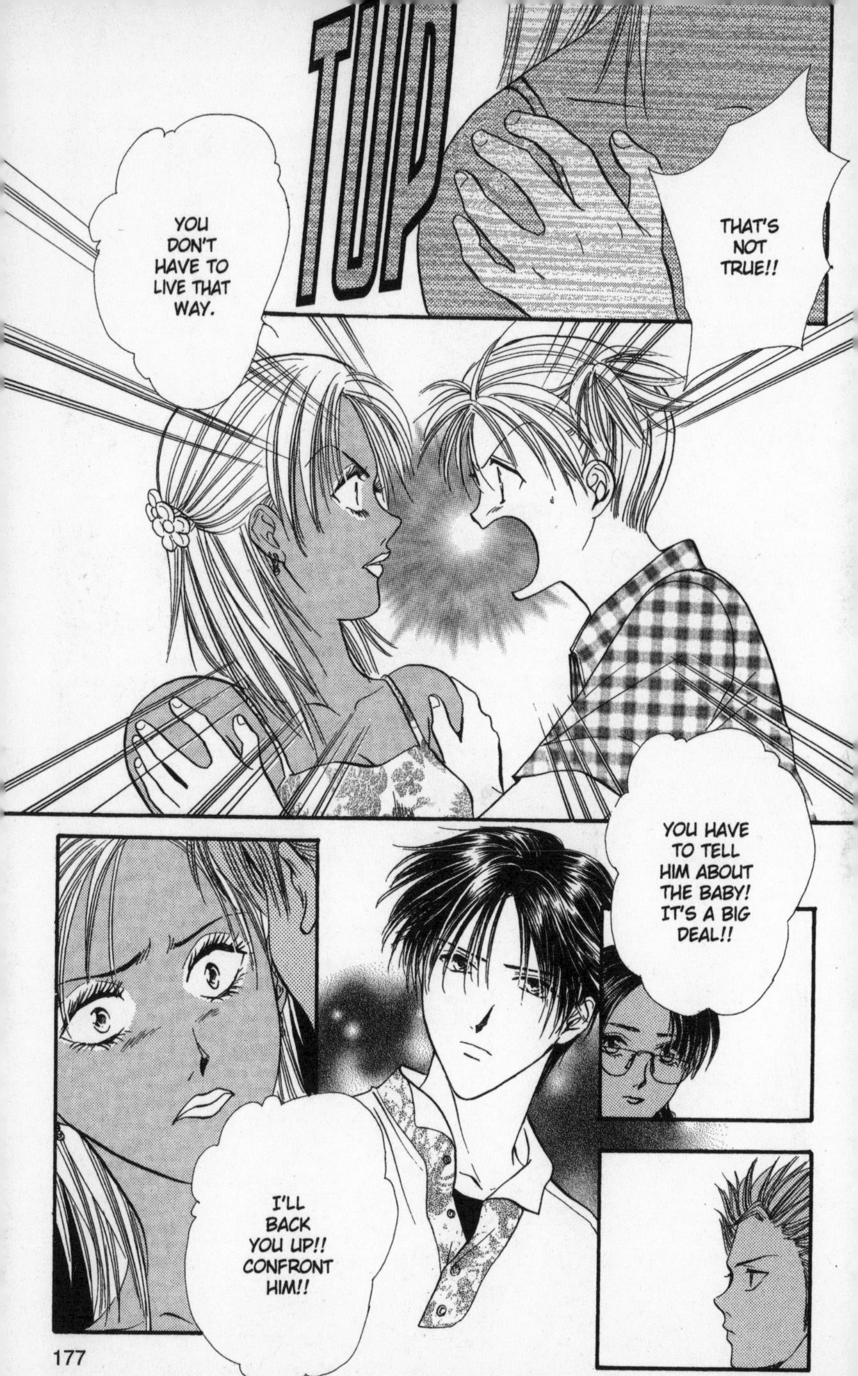
THAT'S NOT TRUE!!
TUP
YOU DON'T HAVE TO LIVE THAT WAY.
YOU HAVE TO TELL HIM ABOUT THE BABY! IT'S A BIG DEAL!!
I'LL BACK YOU UP!! CONFRONT HIM!!

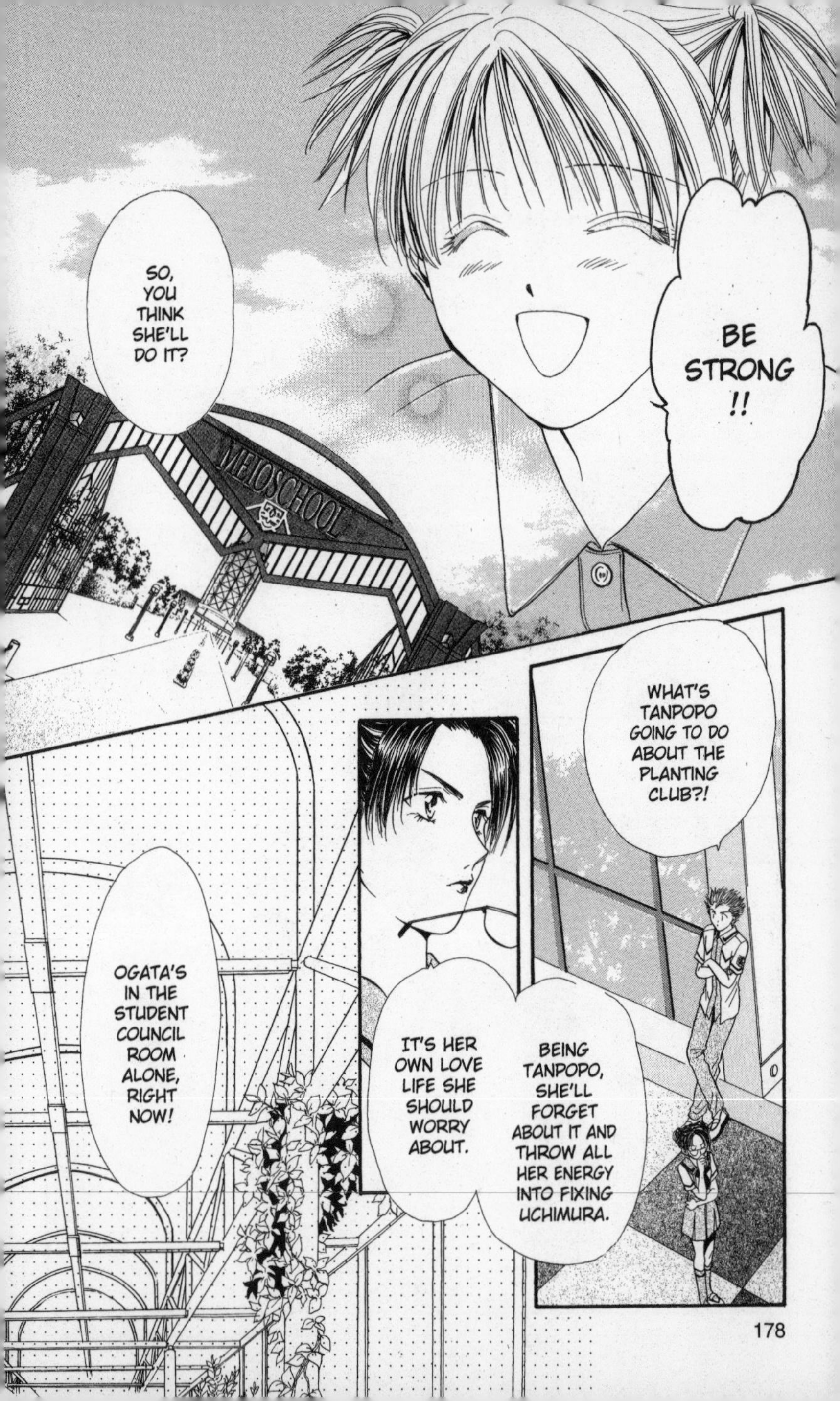

BE STRONG !!
SO, YOU THINK SHE'LL DO IT?
MEIOSCHOOL
WHAT'S TANPOPO GOING TO DO ABOUT THE PLANTING CLUB?!
BEING TANPOPO, SHE'LL FORGET ABOUT IT AND THROW ALL HER ENERGY INTO FIXING UCHIMURA.
IT'S HER OWN LOVE LIFE SHE SHOULD WORRY ABOUT.
OGATA'S IN THE STUDENT COUNCIL ROOM ALONE, RIGHT NOW!

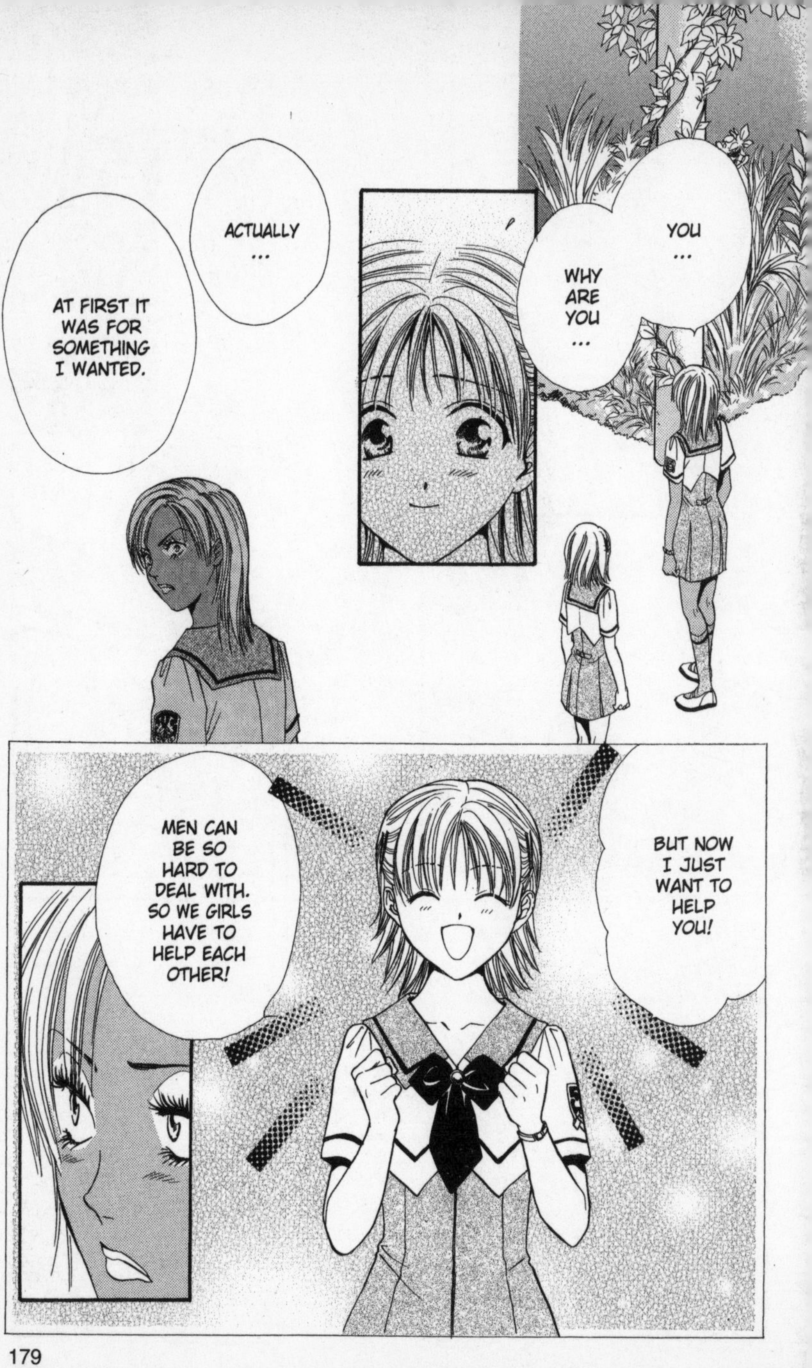
YOU ...
WHY ARE YOU ...
ACTUALLY ...
AT FIRST IT WAS FOR SOMETHING I WANTED.
BUT NOW I JUST WANT TO HELP YOU!
MEN CAN BE SO HARD TO DEAL WITH. SO WE GIRLS HAVE TO HELP EACH OTHER!

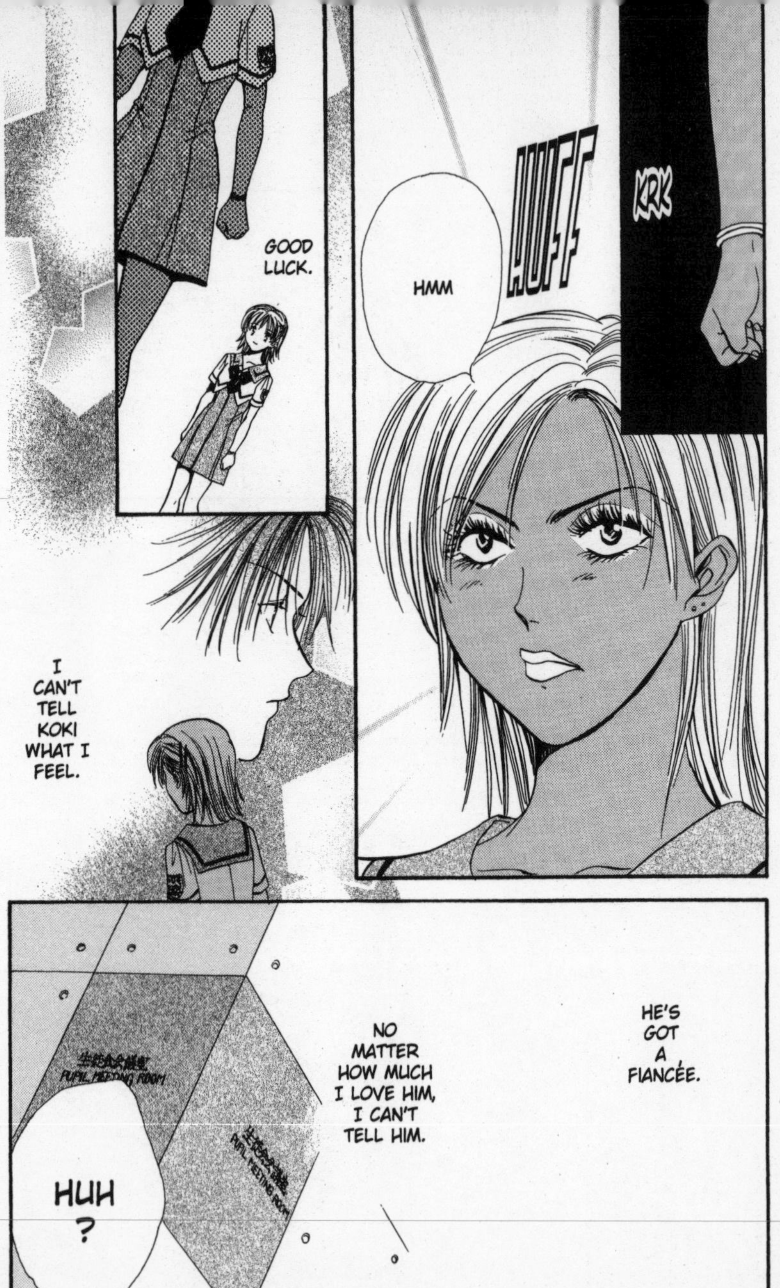
KRK
HUFF
HMM
GOOD LUCK.
I CAN'T TELL KOKI WHAT I FEEL.
HE'S GOT A FIANCÉE.
NO MATTER HOW MUCH I LOVE HIM, I CAN'T TELL HIM.
PUPIL MEETING ROOM
PUPIL MEETING ROOM
HUH?

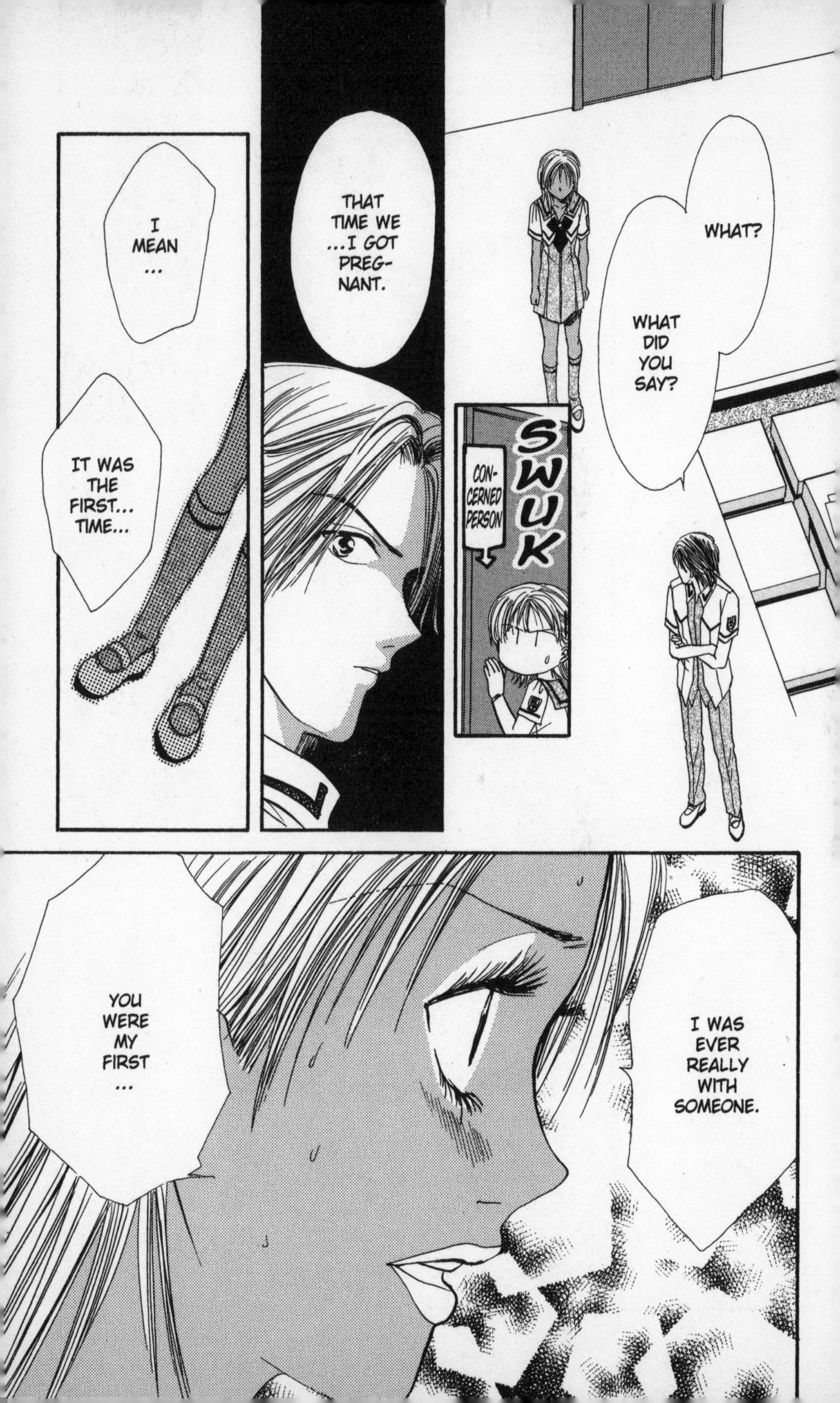

WHAT?
WHAT DID YOU SAY?
SWUK
CON-CERNED PERSON
THAT TIME WE ...I GOT PREG-NANT.
I MEAN ...
IT WAS THE FIRST... TIME...
YOU WERE MY FIRST ...
I WAS EVER REALLY WITH SOMEONE.

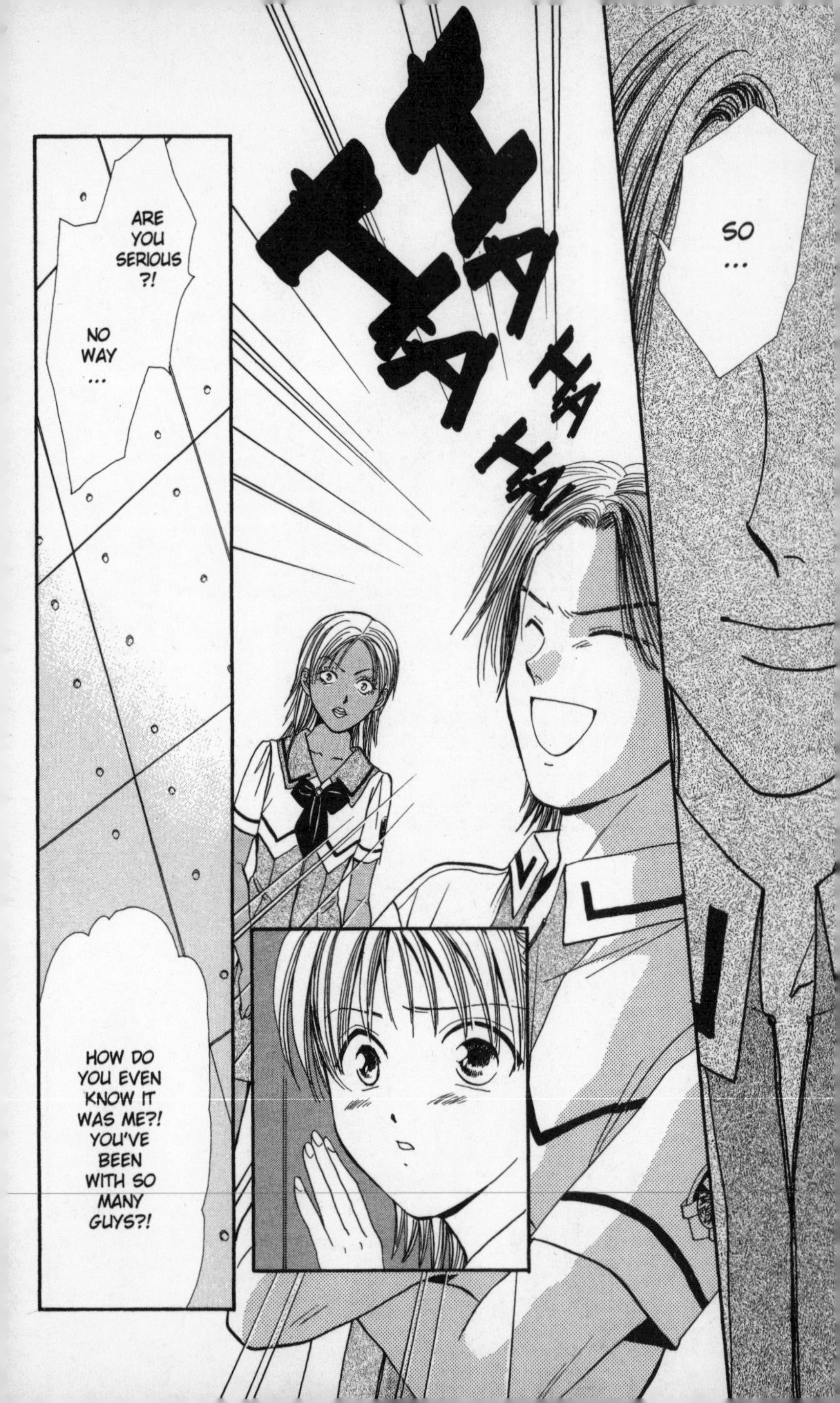
SO ...
HA HA
ARE YOU SERIOUS ?!
NO WAY ...
HOW DO YOU EVEN KNOW IT WAS ME?! YOU'VE BEEN WITH SO MANY GUYS?!

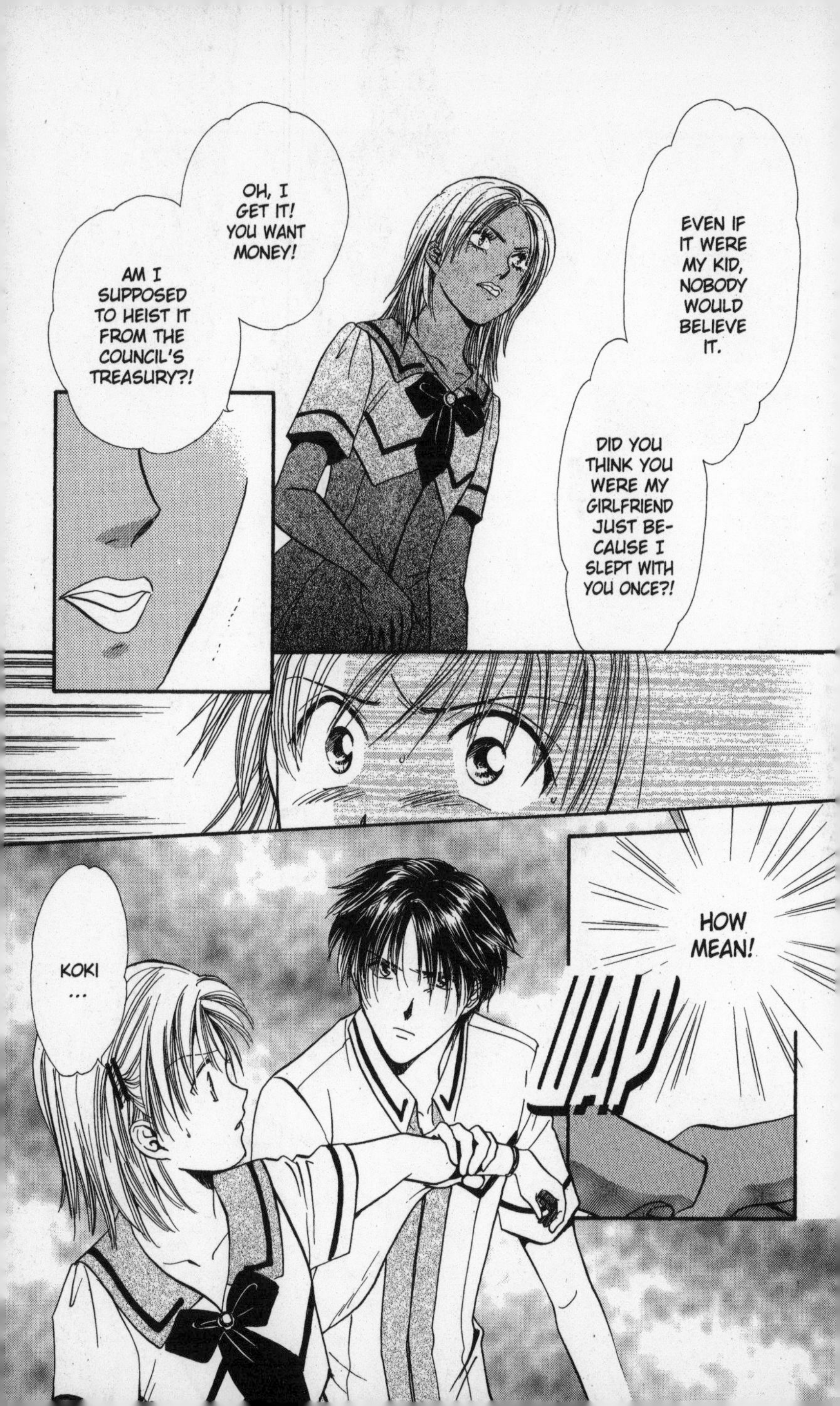
EVEN IF IT WERE MY KID, NOBODY WOULD BELIEVE IT.
DID YOU THINK YOU WERE MY GIRLFRIEND JUST BE-CAUSE I SLEPT WITH YOU ONCE?!
OH, I GET IT! YOU WANT MONEY!
AM I SUPPOSED TO HEIST IT FROM THE COUNCIL'S TREASURY?!
HOW MEAN!
WAP
KOKI ...

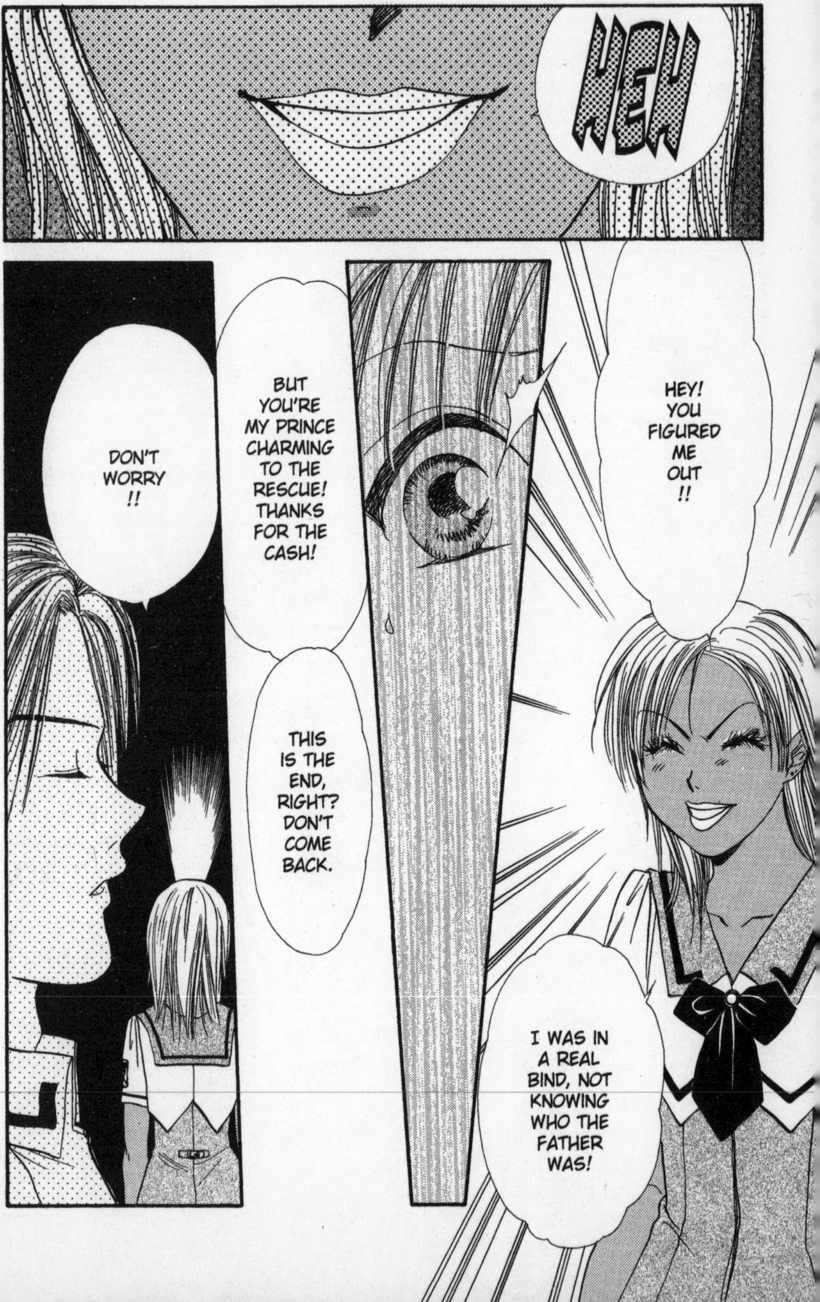
HEH
HEY! YOU FIGURED ME OUT !!
I WAS IN A REAL BIND, NOT KNOWING WHO THE FATHER WAS!
BUT YOU'RE MY PRINCE CHARMING TO THE RESCUE! THANKS FOR THE CASH!
THIS IS THE END, RIGHT? DON'T COME BACK.
DON'T WORRY !!

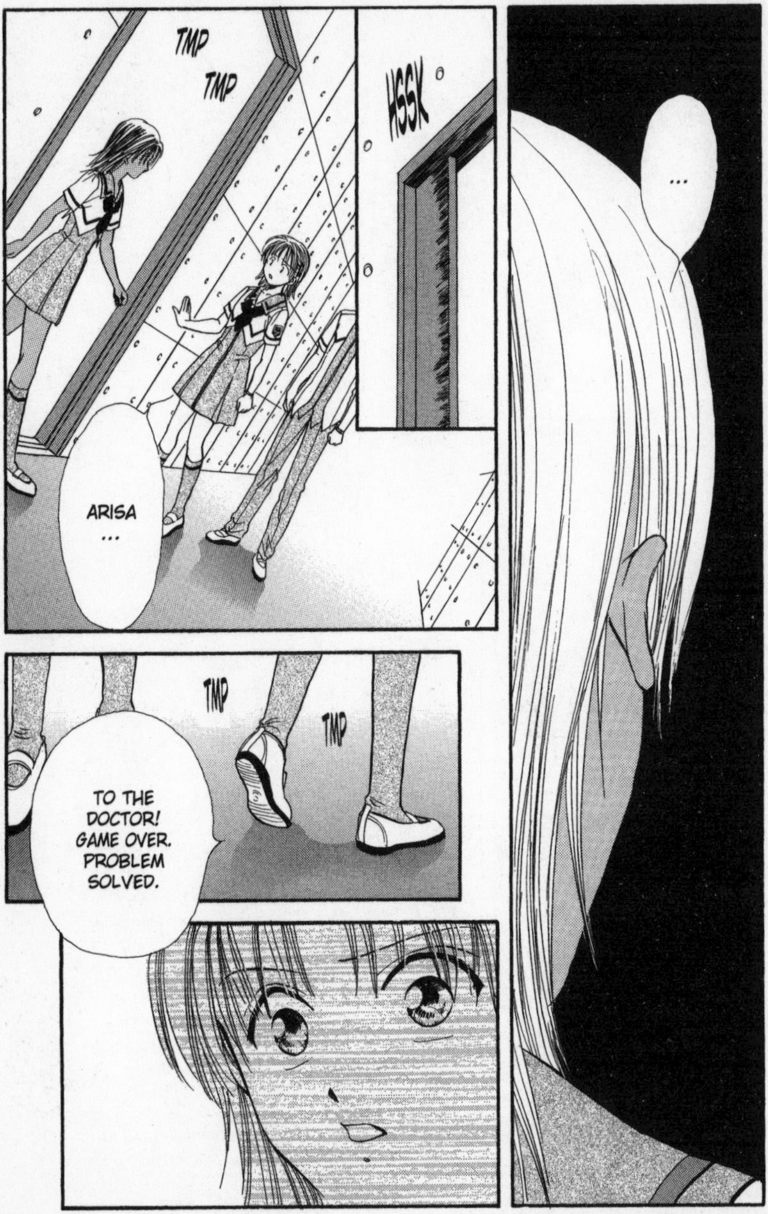
...
HSSK
TMP
TMP
ARISA ...
TMP
TMP
TO THE DOCTOR! GAME OVER. PROBLEM SOLVED.

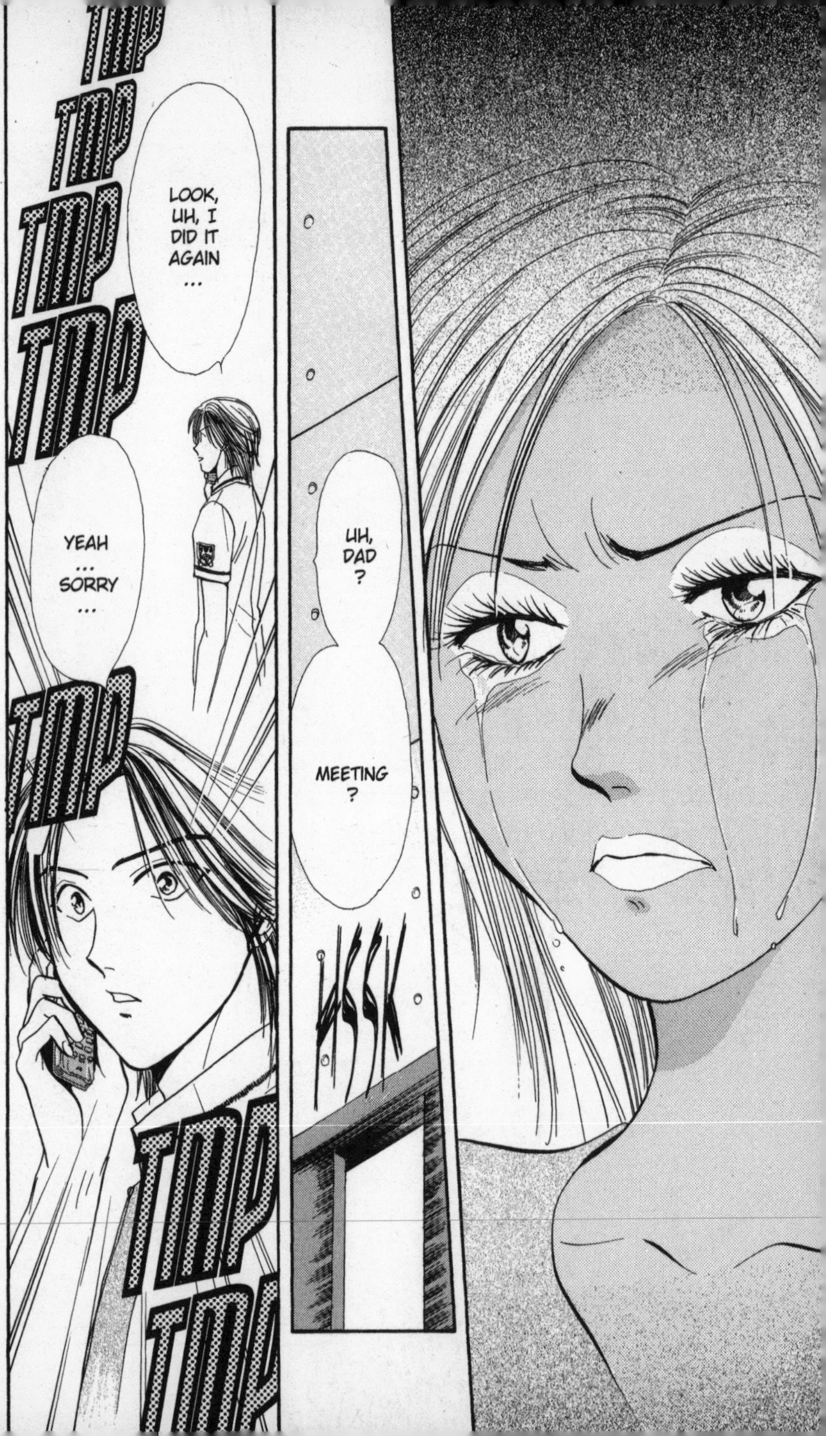
UH, DAD?
MEETING?
HSSK
LOOK, UH, I DID IT AGAIN ...
TMP TMP TMP TMP TMP
YEAH ... SORRY ...
TMP TMP TMP

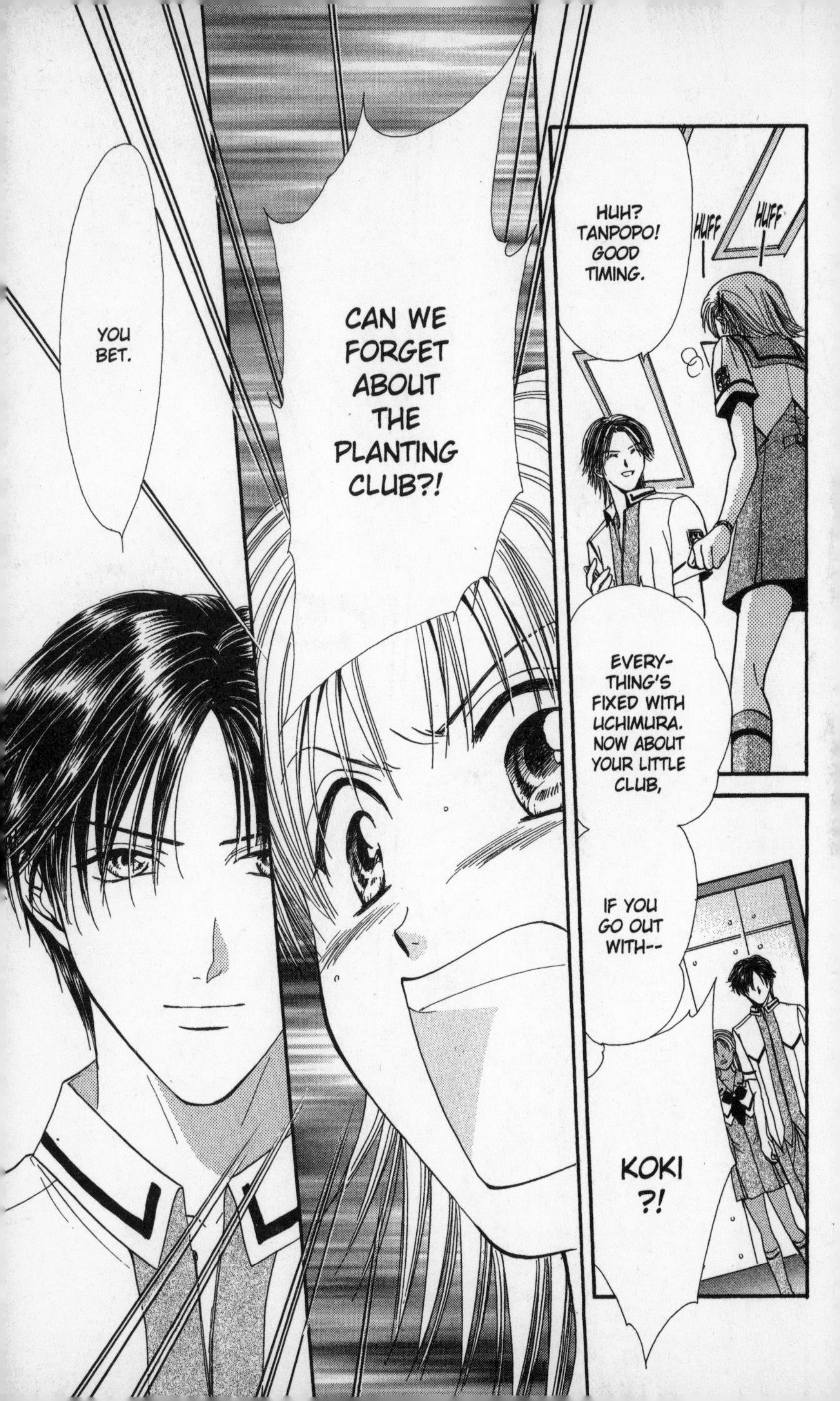
HUFF HUFF
HUH? TANPOPO! GOOD TIMING.
EVERY-THING'S FIXED WITH UCHIMURA. NOW ABOUT YOUR LITTLE CLUB,
IF YOU GO OUT WITH--
KOKI ?!
CAN WE FORGET ABOUT THE PLANTING CLUB?!
YOU BET.

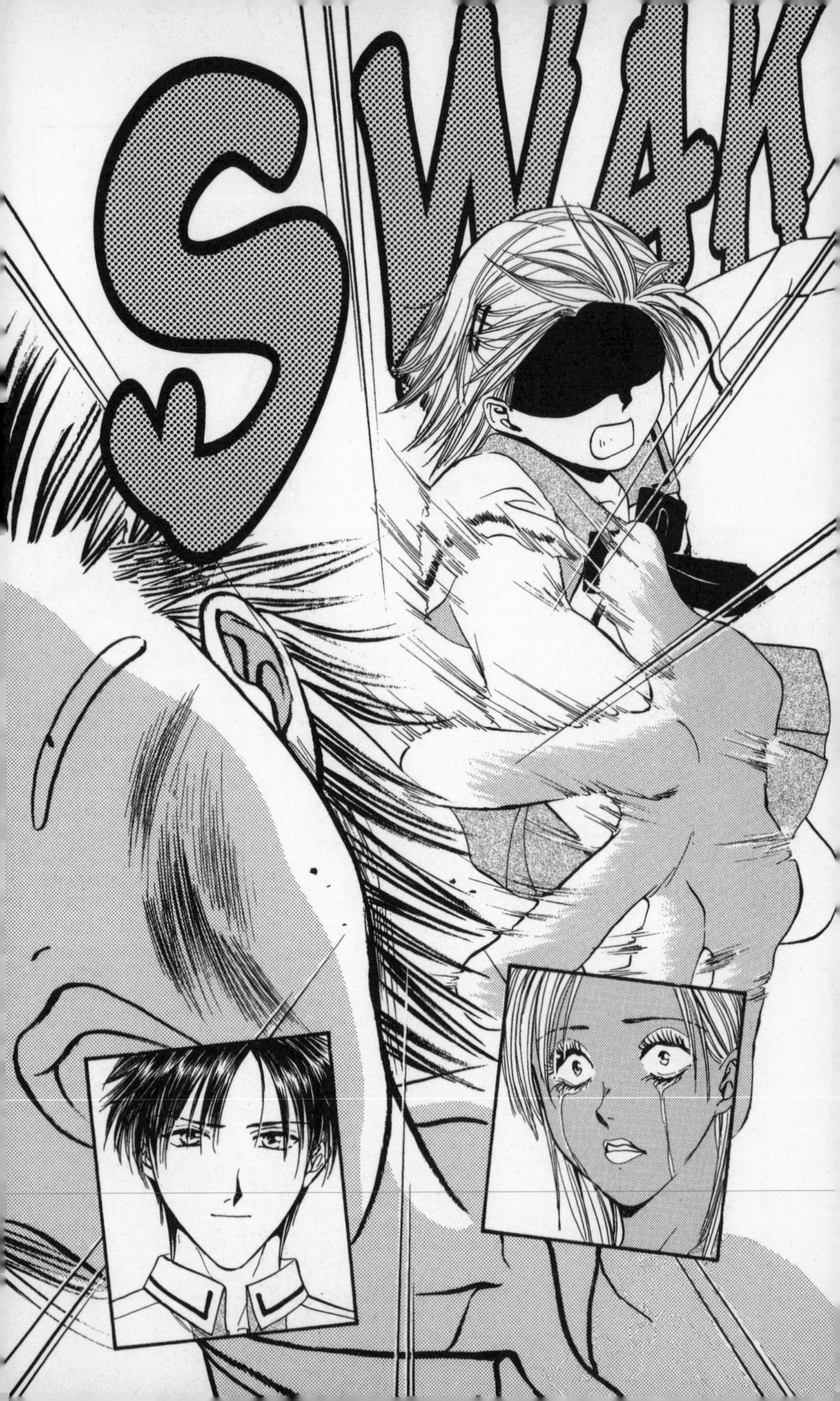
SWAK

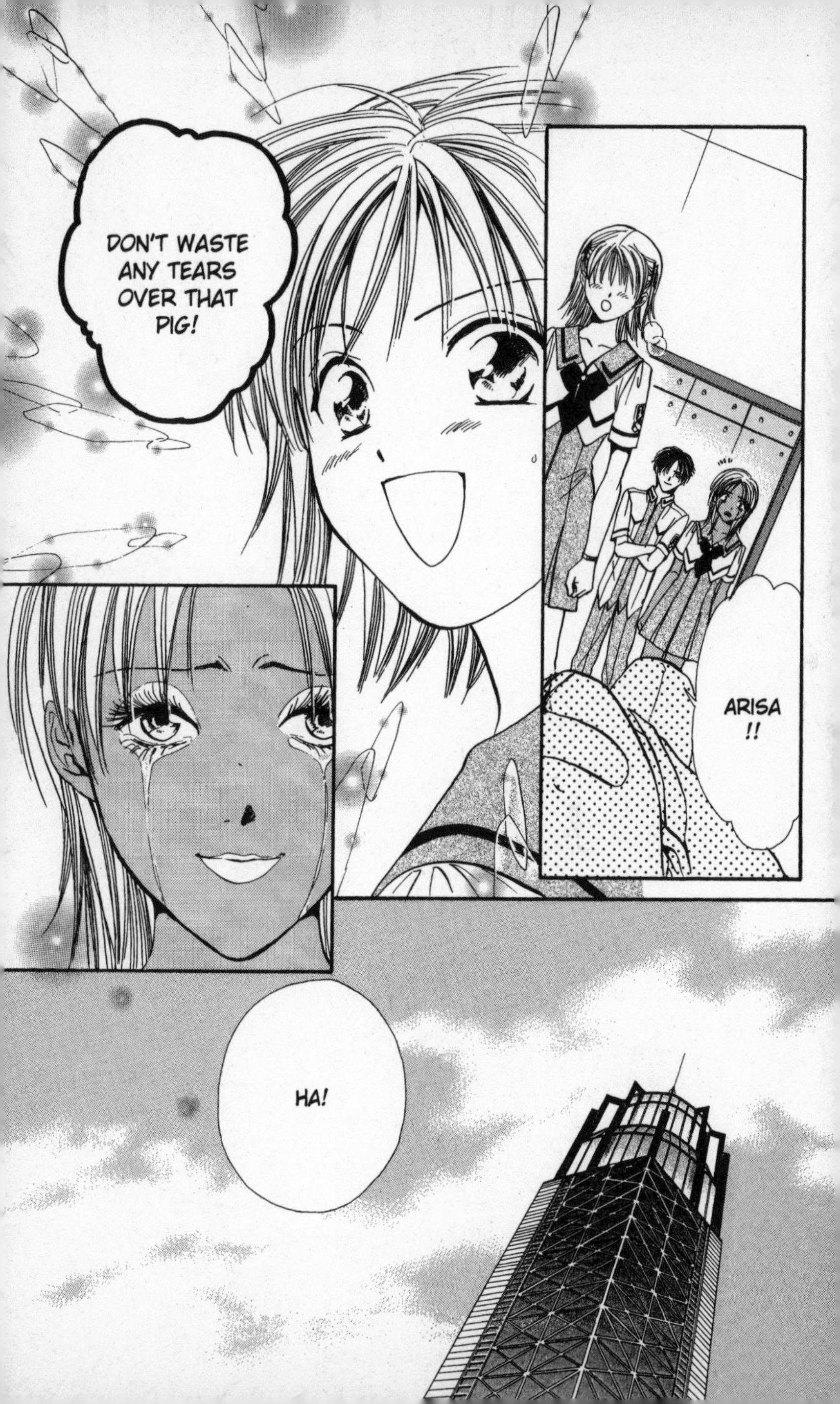
ARISA !!
DON'T WASTE ANY TEARS OVER THAT PIG!
HA!

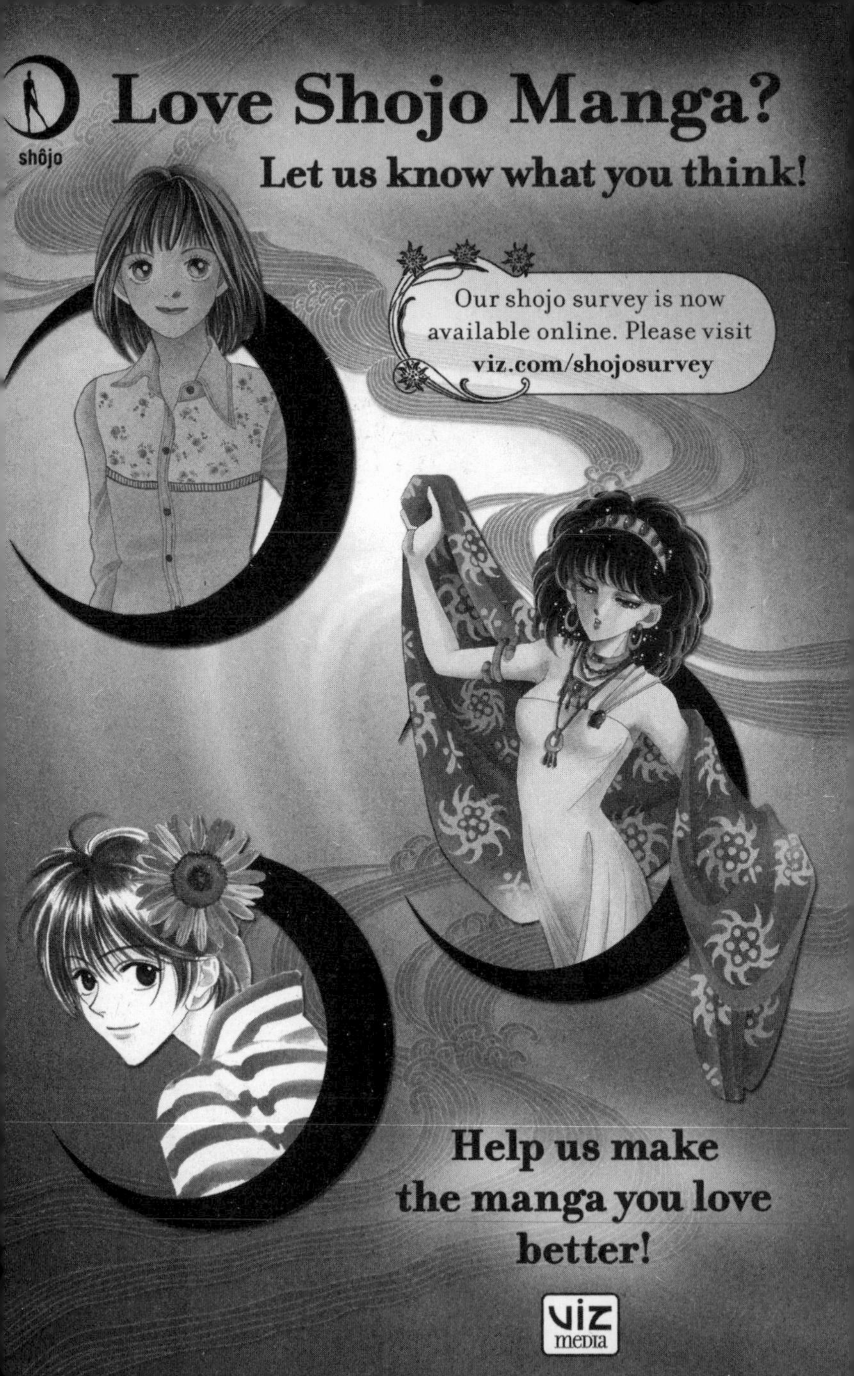
shôjo
Love Shojo Manga?
Let us know what you think!
Our shojo survey is now available online. Please visit viz.com/shojosurvey
Help us make the manga you love better!
viz media